ECONOMIST IN
AN UNCERTAIN WORLD

✦

Columbia Studies in Contemporary American History

WILLIAM E LEUCHTENBURG, GENERAL EDITOR

ECONOMIST IN
AN UNCERTAIN WORLD

◆

Arthur F. Burns and the
Federal Reserve, 1970–78

Wyatt C. Wells

Columbia University Press   New York

Columbia University Press
New York   Chichester, West Sussex
Copyright (c) 1994 Columbia University Press
All rights reserved

Library of Congress Cataloging-in-Publication Data

Wells, Wyatt C.

Economist in an uncertain world : Arthur F. Burns and
the Federal Reserve, 1970–78 / Wyatt C. Wells.
  p.   cm.—(Columbia studies in contemporary American history)
Includes bibliographical references and index.
ISBN 0-231-08496-X
1. Board of Governors of the Feederal Reserve System (U.S.)—history.
2. Burns, Arthur F. (Arthur Frank), 1904–1987.
3. Economists—United States—Biography.
4. Monetary policy—United States—History.
I. Title.   II. Series.
HG2563.W363   1994
332.1'1'092—dc20
[B]   94-8905
CIP

Casebound editions of Columbia University Press books
are printed on permanent and durable acid-free paper.

Printed in the United States of America

c 10 9 8 7 6 5 4 3 2 1

Contents

Preface

✦

Everyone had an opinion about Arthur F. Burns. Labor leader George Meany called him a "national disaster." Economist Herbert Kaufman considered him "the symbol of economic integrity and stability." Senator Hubert Humphrey described him as a "Simon Legree." German Chancellor Helmut Schmidt characterized Burns as "the Pope of Economics." President Gerald Ford thought of him as "a great economist, but more, . . . a great educator."[1]

When Arthur Burns became chairman of the Federal Reserve in 1970, Americans were confident about the economic future. In the quarter-century since the end of World War II, strong economic growth had provided for smart advances in living standards even while financing the Cold War and easing social change. American companies were the most productive and innovative in the world. The dollar dominated international trade and finance. Economists assured the public that Washington could, by manipulating taxes, spending, and interest rates, adjust the demand for goods and services as needed to maintain high employment and stable prices. Indeed, the nation was so prosperous that many intellectuals had concluded that the United States should stop worrying about economic growth and instead concentrate on spiritual and aesthetic concerns—an attitude that only the wealthy can afford.

The events of the 1970s changed everything. Trouble first appeared in 1970 in the form of "stagflation," a debilitating combination of inflation and recession that defied conventional economic thinking. Economists had long assumed that inflation and recession were opposites, with the former reflecting demand in excess of production and the latter the result of demand below available output. Stagflation did not fit this model, leaving economists and government officials at a loss for remedies. Nor was stagflation the only difficulty. In 1971 the Bretton Woods system, which had governed international finance since 1945, collapsed, throwing the world's currencies into confusion. The United States had not really come to grips with either of these problems when, in 1973 and 1974, the nation had to confront a series of even more damaging crises. The most traumatic of these was the Arab oil embargo, which created a severe shortage of the world's most precious commodity—petroleum. The United States also suffered from the highest inflation in the nation's peacetime history and the deepest economic downturn in a generation. Efforts to restore order to international exchange failed, and financial crises shook the banking system. Worst of all, the steady growth in productivity, which had characterized the American economy for decades, ceased, and with it the regular advance in living standards.

These events changed the whole complexion of American politics and society. Since 1945, the nation had been extraordinarily prosperous, and the large majority of its people had enjoyed the benefits of this abundance. Indeed, those under thirty—the numerous "baby boom" generation—knew only good times. Now the people of the United States suddenly found themselves in an unforgiving economic atmosphere. The regular increase in real (inflation-adjusted) wages stopped, and many once secure jobs vanished, particularly in old-line industries like steel and automobiles, which had been the core of the American economy. Politicians, who had become accustomed to the higher revenues generated by economic growth, found themselves unable to pay for the new initiatives that constituents had come to expect. Instead, the cost of programs already begun escalated, squeezing budgets.

Americans had trouble adjusting to these changes. They had become accustomed to prosperity, and hard times entailed changes for which people were not ready. Moreover, many Americans believed that the nation's problems were the result of one-time events like the Arab oil embargo, and they assumed that, given time, things would return to normal. Others sought villains on whom to blame their suffering, latching onto a host of alleged culprits—the international oil companies being perennial favorites. Prosperity would return once these malefactors were brought to heel.

Nor was the nation well equipped intellectually to deal with the crisis. The ideas of John Maynard Keynes, first elucidated in the 1930s, dominated economic thinking, but these dealt primarily with the demand for goods and services, not with output. This latter question had received attention from economists, but the high productivity of the American economy during the postwar years had kept the subject from the center of professional discourse. In addition, government officials and interested members of the public, who rarely had the time or inclination to absorb the nuances of economic thinking, accorded the matter a marginal place in public debate of economic issues. Yet it is clear in retrospect that the economy's problems during the 1970s sprang primarily from slower growth in productivity and output, not from insufficient demand. People did not, however, quickly discard ideas absorbed over decades, and economists and government officials often used Keynesian techniques, however inappropriate, to analyze and respond to the problems they faced. Lord Keynes's famous dictum, "Practical men . . . are usually the slave to some defunct economist," applied to himself as well as others.[2]

Arthur Burns had to deal with these problems. Between 1970 and 1978, he was chairman of the Federal Reserve Board—the central bank—probably the nation's most powerful economic institution. It managed interest rates and the supply of money, regulated banks and bank holding companies, and conducted Washington's international financial transactions. In one way or another, its activities bore on every aspect of the economic crisis. But despite its power—or perhaps because of it—the Fed had to be careful. The wrong decision might exacerbate problems—indeed, the central bank had badly botched its responsibilities in the 1930s, intensifying and lengthening the Great Depression. In the 1970s the Fed's leaders were determined to do better. But the crises they faced not only inflicted great hardship but also disrupted accepted economic verities. Beyond simply maintaining a measure of order and stability, the "correct" course of action was rarely obvious.

Arthur Burns therefore faced a problem of intellectual reconstruction as well as one of economic management. Of course, a lot of the time he made things up as he went along, responding to crises that arose suddenly as best he could, hoping that instinct and good luck would carry him through. But Burns was also a respected academic economist determined to explain what was going on and to devise coherent, lasting solutions. The Fed chairman's background gave him a special advantage in this task. Because he had received his training as an economist in the 1920s, before the Keynesian revolution, Keynes's thinking did not bind him to the degree that it did many of his colleagues. By the mid-1970s, Burns had concluded that economic policy had to shift its focus from demand to output, and he had developed a controversial plan to encourage investment and enterprise by reducing taxes and government spending and regulation and by tightly restricting monetary growth.

The public temper and political atmosphere made it particularly difficult to sell these ideas. Into the late 1970s, many assumed that the nation's economic problems were a passing (if unpleasant) phase, and such people naturally viewed drastic reform skeptically. Moreover, Keynesian thinking still dominated economic discourse, and it was difficult to get people to grasp ideas that were not framed in its terms, even if these, which were developed to explain the mass unemployment and deflation of the 1930s, did not explain the inflation and shortages of the 1970s very well. Therefore, Burns not only had to come up with a new perspective on economics but also had to shake people out of unproductive habits of thought.

Burns's special importance lay in his dual role. Many officials wrestled with the economic crisis, and many economists tried to explain what was going on. Burns was a formidable presence in each camp, but he was not unique. He did, however, link these two worlds in a way that none of his contemporaries managed, combining great official responsibilities with considerable intellectual prestige. Moreover, these two aspects of his position reinforced each other. As chairman of the Fed, he could actually implement some of his ideas, and his office gave him a high pulpit from which to expound his thinking. For eight years, this marriage of political and intellectual authority made Burns the country's most powerful economist. Though Arthur Burns did not resolve the many economic problems that confronted the United States in the 1970s, his actions and thinking during this era, in which fear about the economic future was pervasive, played a vital role in shaping the American response to the crisis.

Acknowledgments

✦

Without the help of many friends and colleagues, I would never have been able to complete this book.

My adviser at the University of North Carolina at Chapel Hill, William E. Leuchtenburg, provided encouragement and wise counsel at every turn. David Wightman first suggested that I investigate Arthur Burns's career. Dewey Daane and Otis Graham both played important parts in helping me launch this project. Tom Baker, Peter Coclanis, Sam Crewse, Richard Froyen, Robert Gallman, Dewey Grantham, Tom Havrilesky, William Keech, George Tindall, and Arne Westad all read and provided valuable comments on my manuscript at different times.

The able staffs of the Jimmy Carter Presidential Library, the Gerald R. Ford Presidential Library, and the Richard M. Nixon Papers Project all assisted my research immensely, as did those at the Bentley Historical Library, the Dwight D. Eisenhower Presidential Library, the Fromkin Collection, and the Lyndon B. Johnson Presidential

Library. Dewey Daane kindly let me use his papers. Many people generously allowed me to interview them, and Jean Balestrieri, Dewey Daane, Alexander Heard, and Philip Jackson all helped me arrange interviews.

The Gerald R. Ford Foundation, the University of North Carolina at Chapel Hill, and the Department of History at the University of North Carolina at Chapel Hill all provided funding for my research.

Finally, I would like to thank my family and friends, particularly my parents, Charles and Ann Wells, for their constant encouragement and support, without which I would have accomplished nothing.

ECONOMIST IN
AN UNCERTAIN WORLD

1

The Chairman

I

Arthur Burns represents a classic American type—the immigrant who made good. Born Arthur Burnseig in Austrian Galicia in 1904,[1] he came to the United States with his family in 1914, settling in Bayonne, New Jersey, just across the Hudson River from Manhattan. A school teacher soon shortened the name to Burns. Burns's father made a living as a house painter, and Arthur helped him, first by soliciting work door-to-door and then, as he got older, by wielding a brush himself. The family was poor, but as many Jewish families in the New York area at this time found, education offered opportunity for the talented. Although the young Arthur spoke no English when he arrived in the United States, he excelled in his studies and as a high school debater and, in 1921, earned a scholarship to Columbia University. From the start Arthur Burns displayed an unshakable sense of his own importance. Before deciding to attend Columbia, he interviewed its president to make sure that it was the place for him.[2] Burns worked at a variety of odd jobs, ranging from stock clerk to seaman, to support himself as an undergraduate, but he nevertheless managed to graduate from Columbia a member of Phi Beta Kappa.[3]

Although he considered many careers while at Columbia, Arthur Burns decided on economics after taking a class from Wesley Clair Mitchell, perhaps the most renowned American economist of the time. Mitchell's thinking fell squarely within the tradition of Progressive thought. As a student at the University of Chicago, he had absorbed the ideas of philosopher John Dewey, who considered experience, examined through the lens of "scientific" method, the basis of all reliable knowledge, and of economist Thorstein Veblen, who rejected the tenets of classical economics and argued that organization and culture affected economic life at least as much as the abstract forces of supply and demand. Mitchell refused to accept on faith that the "invisible hand" of the market governed the economy. He thought the task of economics was not to make deductions based on untested assumptions but to investigate the economy systematically, with statistical techniques, and to use this information to construct verifiable theories about economic operations. Mitchell's interests, however, went beyond his own discipline. He was an enthusiastic supporter of social causes such as women's suffrage and adult education, and he helped organize the New School for Social Research in New York, whose task was, as two historians of the school put it, "to generate a body of critical social science that would contribute to the 'reconstruction' of western society along more egalitarian and scientific lines."[4]

Mitchell's greatest contribution, however, was his study of the business cycle, the pattern of expansion and contraction that characterizes capitalist economies. He hoped that, if he could construct a scientific explanation for this phenomenon, governments and private groups, such as large corporations and trade associations, could implement reforms that would eliminate it or at least mitigate its consequences. In 1913, Mitchell published *Business Cycles*, an initial examination of the subject.[5] Soon, however, he realized that a thorough investigation of the business cycle was beyond the capability of any individual and began to explore the possibility of a larger study. During World War I, Mitchell played a leading role in a government effort, inspired by the needs of military mobilization, to systematically measure economic activity. With peace, Washington discontinued the program, but Mitchell was convinced that the project had value beyond organizing for war. In 1920 he helped put together the National Bureau of Economic Research (NBER) at Columbia University, which would carry on and expand Mitchell's war work. Mitchell led the bureau. Encouraged by Commerce Secretary Herbert Hoover and financed by private foundations, the NBER would try both to develop reliable statistical measures for the economy, which did not exist in 1920, and to construct a comprehensive picture of the business cycle.

For Mitchell, these tasks were inseparable. He thought that the business cycle occurred because firms, imperfectly informed about events around them, got caught up in speculative booms that inevitably led to collapse. "If we could foresee the business cycle," he said, "there would be none."[6] Moreover, for Mitchell, accurate data was necessary for any serious study of economics. Theoretical speculation was interesting, but unless backed by reliable information, it had limited use.

The NBER provided a vital support for Herbert Hoover's "New Era," the commerce secretary's plan to reorganize the American economy along more rational lines. In Hoover's vision, trade associations, with the encouragement and guidance of the Commerce Department, would coordinate activity within their own industries, but to do this properly they needed accurate information. The National Bureau would provide this. Indeed, the NBER, a quasi-public institution dominated by technical experts, accorded particularly well with the secretary's ideas of economic management. By the late 1920s, the Bureau enjoyed immense prestige and a reputation for influence in the government.

The Great Depression, which discredited Hoover and his plans, also damaged the bureau, which had been so closely associated with both. But Franklin Roosevelt's New Deal reforms needed the sort of data only the NBER was equipped to provide, and the National Bureau survived and prospered in the 1930s—though Mitchell was careful never again to let it become too closely identified with any one politician. Though the NBER enjoyed less political clout during the New Deal era, its subsequent high reputation among economists rests largely on its output during the 1930s, when several projects initiated in the previous decade bore fruit. The most important of these was the national income accounting program, which formed the basis for subsequent calculations of economic growth and production.

Burns started as Mitchell's student and became, in time, his collaborator and eventually his successor. It is no surprise that Burns found the National Bureau attractive. The NBER's efforts had important implications for economic thought and policy, and association with it naturally appealed to an ambitious man like Burns. Its careful statistical work also appealed to Burns's disciplined mind. Besides, the bureau was an exciting place to be—Mitchell had assembled many of the best economists of the time and proved adept at getting good work out of them. Burns and Mitchell complemented each other especially well. Burns, who had tremendous stamina and an ability to absorb and organize huge amounts of information, was just the sort of person Mitchell needed to oversee the bureau's statistical research. Mitchell, in turn, gave Burns an intellectual framework in which to operate. Burns's mind was powerful but not particularly original. He needed some sort of fulcrum to bring his talents to bear, and Mitchell's ideas about building a scientific base for economics on statistical research provided just that.

Mitchell's ideas dominated Burns's thinking for the rest of Burns's life. Like his mentor, Burns preferred empirical research to abstract theory. As one of his students wrote, "Repeatedly he advised us that in our intellectual journeyings (as in his) connections between trains of abstract thought were, at best, tenuous and, when made, were often painfully difficult. He always counseled patience—more examination of more data could possibly bring along another (and better) thought: better to miss the available intellectual 'trolley' than get on one with either an uncertain destination or a convoluted route."[7] Moreover, though Burns did important research on his own, the outcome of his work usually confirmed and built on Mitchell's thinking. For instance, in the late 1960s Burns wrote a long, widely read essay on the business cycle—a subject on which he was the acknowledged expert—describing the phenomenon largely in terms that Mitchell had first used fifty-five years earlier.[8]

From the first, Burns did well professionally. He received his B.A. and A.M. from Columbia in 1925, and in 1927 he got a teaching job at Rutgers. In 1930 he joined the National Bureau as a researcher, and at about the same time he began to write articles for the business section of the *New York Herald-Tribune*, a sideline that he continued for several years.[9] Also in 1930 he married Helen Bernstein, a sprightly woman always more interested in poetry than economics. She reflected a side of the man not often visible to the public—a gregarious person with an interest in art and painting. The young couple lived in Greenwich Village, from which Arthur Burns commuted to New Jersey on Tuesdays and Thursdays to teach. He devoted the rest of the week to the National Bureau, but managed to do much of his work for it at home, thereby reconciling a very heavy professional schedule with a normal family life. Burns needed little sleep and would stay up writing until early in the morning—sometimes he would rouse his wife at one or two in the morning and take her out for a milkshake because he was too excited by his work to sleep.[10]

In 1934 Burns completed his Ph.D., which he soon published as *Production Trends in the United States since 1870*.[11] This book looked at patterns of expansion within different industries and discovered a universal tendency toward slower growth. An industry grew rapidly at first, but the rate of growth soon slackened, and eventually *every* industry's relative position in the economy declined as newer industries took the lead. Economic expansion, it concluded, depended on the continual development of new industries. This book also revealed that the performance of different industries depended at least as much on their nature as on overall economic conditions, convincing Burns that, as one of his students wrote, "it was essential to look beneath the surface of the aggregates, such as the national production, total employment, the general price level, in order to discover how the economy really worked."[12]

Burns's career advanced rapidly after he completed his dissertation. Mitchell put him in charge of the bureau's business-cycle project, where he oversaw the work of other researchers in this field and set about organizing the vast amount of information they produced into a consistent whole. By the late 1930s, Burns was Mitchell's chief lieutenant and was handling much of the day-to-day management of the National Bureau for him. In 1941 Burns received a temporary appointment at Columbia, which became permanent in 1944. The next year he succeeded the retiring Mitchell as research director of the NBER.

Burns had a reputation as an excellent, though intimidating, teacher. As one of his students said, "Arthur Burns was a good destructive teacher and everyone should have a good *destructive* teacher at least once," by which he meant that Burns criticized his students' work from every side and demanded that they know their subject completely.[13] Burns developed this way in part because of his exceptional critical abilities, which were perhaps his most impressive intellectual quality, and in part because of the way he worked with Mitchell. At the bureau, Burns would, as he said, "pick up someone's report, take it apart sentence by sentence and phrase by phrase, and leave it in a battered mass expiring on the floor," at which point Mitchell would step in to extract some value from the work in question, resurrecting (one hopes) the author's ego.[14] Having settled into this way of dealing with students, Burns adhered to it even after Mitchell had retired and was no longer around to clean up after him. Nevertheless, most of those who endured developed great respect for their teacher. Burns was not capricious—his demands reflected high professional standards, and he recognized and praised good work. Moreover, as students got to know him, they discovered a warm personal nature somewhat at odds with his forbidding professional demeanor. Burns's students at Rutgers included such prominent economists as Milton Friedman, Geoffrey Moore, and Julius Shiskin, and at Columbia Alan Greenspan. Many of these people became close friends—Milton Friedman, for instance, stated, "Save for my parents and my wife, no one has influenced my life more than Arthur."[15]

Burns's standard of living increased with his prestige. In 1936, with the birth of the first of their two sons, he and his wife moved to a Central Park West address. Eventually, they bought a farm in Vermont, where the family would spend its summers as part of a group of economists that already included Mitchell and would later count Friedman and Moore. At his farm, Burns constructed an office separate from the farmhouse, where he kept up with his work. But he took time out to listen to baseball games with his sons—Burns was an avid fan of the New York Yankees—and to paint. The economist produced bright, geometric abstract canvases that he refused to sign, on the grounds that he was merely an amateur.

By the time he took over at the NBER, Burns had taken on the appearance and manner that would characterize him for the rest of his life. He dressed conservatively, parted his unruly hair down the middle, sported rimless, wire-framed glasses, and was never without a pipe, which he used to great effect as a prop while speaking. He would clean, fill, light, relight, empty, and refill his pipe several times during a conversation, emphasizing his deliberate nature and controlling the pace of discussion. His speech was considered and forceful, and although he occasionally seemed ponderous—the uncharitable likened his nasal accent to that of comedian W. C. Fields—he invariably conveyed a great sense of confidence and authority. As one observer later put it, "Where Arthur sits, there is the head of the table."[16]

During the years he worked for Mitchell, Burns thought of himself as a scholar, not a policymaker. In this he followed the lead of his mentor, whose reputation had been damaged by his close association with Hoover and who was now inclined to keep his distance from politicians. Naturally, Burns realized that his research had implications for government policy, but he imagined himself a technician whom officials would consult much as they might an engineer. Burns was not oblivious to politics. He was a registered Democrat who voted for Franklin D. Roosevelt and generally approved of the New Deal, especially its financial reforms and extensive relief programs to help the unemployed. Burns did object to Roosevelt's rhetorical blasts against business and measures such as the wealth tax that punished the rich because he thought that these increased uncertainty and so retarded recovery. But Burns was not a political activist—he sought to wield influence through his professional accomplishments.

Burns did assist the government in matters requiring his technical expertise. In 1938 he helped the Commerce Department draw up the index of leading economic indicators, a still widely consulted measure whose decline usually precedes recession. In 1941 he served as chief statistician for the Railway Emergency Board, which the president set up to resolve labor disputes involving the railroads. But Burns always subordinated government work to the study of the business cycle.

This effort culminated in 1946 when Burns and Mitchell published *Measuring Business Cycles*—Burns's greatest scholarly contribution.[17] This book, Mitchell wrote, "is mainly his [Burns's] work."[18] It examined hundreds of economic factors across time to form a comprehensive picture of the swings in economic activity. But although it was, and remains today, an invaluable source of information on what happens during the business cycle, it did not, as one reviewer noted, "reveal at all . . . what explanations of cyclical fluctuations, if any, they [the authors] believe to constitute plausible models or hypotheses" for this phenomenon.[19] Mitchell had hoped to use the information in *Measuring Business Cycles* to construct just such a theory, but he failed to do so before he died in 1948, and his successor fared no better. Eventually, Burns concluded that no comprehensive explanation existed, arguing that "history discloses . . . a succession of business cycles that differ considerably in length, in the intensity of their phases, in the industrial and financial developments that gain prominence during their course, and in their geographic course."[20]

Although he had no general theory of the business cycle, Burns did isolate consistent patterns within it. An expansion, he found, usually began with an increase in investment—perhaps housing construction or new plants for manufacturing. This reemployed idle workers who, in spending their paychecks, stimulated further economic activity. Manufacturers, who generally had substantial idle capacity, rapidly increased productivity as they used their facilities more fully. Larger profits encouraged investment in new equipment and plants, further speeding expansion. But faster growth eventually led to deterioration. As production approached capacity, shortages and bottlenecks reduced or even reversed productivity growth; lower unemployment pushed up wages; and heavy investment increased the demand for loans, driving up interest rates. By pushing up costs, these all reduced profits and therefore investment, the drop in which signaled the end of expansion. As investment fell, workers making capital goods—machinery, houses, and the like—lost their jobs, and as they cut back their spending, economic activity fell further. Retailers, who had planned for brisk sales during the boom, found themselves with large inventories that they could not sell and so had to cut purchases.[21]

As Burns saw it, contraction worked much like expansion—although initially self-reinforcing, it eventually gave birth to corrective forces.[22] For a while, the economy declined unchecked, but, in time, it began to right itself. Once retailers sold their excess inventories, they bought more goods. Businesses, beset by falling demand and tougher competition, cut costs to restore profit margins. The end of bottlenecks and drops in the prices of basic materials further expanded profits. Interest rates fell as lower investment reduced the demand for loans, and often new technologies opened up promising avenues for investment. These factors encouraged a resurgence of capital spending and of the economy in general.

Burns did not think depression natural to this process.[23] Depression resulted only when a recession, for one reason or another, touched off a financial crisis severe enough to paralyze the banking system. In that case, recovery required an extensive financial reorganization that usually took years. Burns, however, believed that a well-run central bank, such as the Federal Reserve, could prevent depression by expanding credit in times of financial stress.

With the publication of *Measuring Business Cycles*, business-cycle research had reached a dead end. The NBER had produced much useful information on the cycle of boom and recession but could not explain the phenomenon. The ideas of John Maynard Keynes, however, offered just such an explanation, and they commanded an ever-larger following among American economists after the Second World War, gradually pushing business-cycle research to the side.

Keynes, an Englishman who wrote in the 1930s to explain the Great Depression, argued that capitalist economies tend to stagnate. Traditionally, economists had thought that in producing something, business created the income to buy it. They reasoned that the money spent to make goods went into people's pockets as wages, dividends, and other forms of income.[24] Keynes, however, believed that people did not necessarily spend all of the income the economy generated. Put simply, he argued that spending had two components, consumption and investment. People spent part of their income and saved the rest, and business borrowed from this pool of savings to make investments. But, Keynes thought, the amount of investment depended not on the level of savings but on expectations of future profits. If the future looked bright, business invested heavily, using all savings, and production expanded. But if prospects seemed poor—say, the stock market had collapsed—companies cut capital spending and savings remained unused. In this case, the demand for goods and services fell short of the supply. Companies, unable to sell all they produced, cut output and laid off workers. The newly unemployed spent less, further reducing demand and economic activity. As income fell, so did savings, which eventually dropped to the level of investment. At this point, production stabilized because, once again, output (savings plus consumption) equaled demand (investment plus consumption). The economy, however, had unused capacity, idle workers, and little prospect for improvement since these conditions discouraged the capital spending needed to get production going again.

Keynes thought that only vigorous state action could extract a nation from this trap. The government must run a deficit, borrowing and spending those savings that business did not use. He believed that even limited deficit spending could have a big impact on the economy because of the "multiplier." The beneficiaries of government expenditures saved a certain portion of the money they received and spent the rest, just like everyone else. Those who benefited from their spending did the same, and so on. Through this process, money worked its way through the economy, multiplying the impact of government spending. Since Keynes assumed that the ratio of savings to total income was stable, the central authorities could estimate with a good deal of confidence how much a deficit would stimulate the economy.[25] Armed with this knowledge and statistics on the level of investment and economic potential, a government could hope to keep its economy operating at close to capacity.[26]

The central bank had an uncertain role in Keynes's system. Those who popularized his ideas in the 1940s (often simplifying them in the process) described trying to stimulate economic activity by expanding credit as "pushing on a string." They reasoned that while a central bank could make credit available, it could not force anyone to borrow, and in a depressed economy profit was scarce and few would take out loans to make investments. In the late 1940s, though, other scholars, led by James Tobin, disputed this view. They argued that interest rates represented, in a sense, the cost of investment and that, as such, rates could influence the willingness of business to make such commitments. This latter view, which experience after 1945 supported, prevailed, and by the late 1950s Keynesians had come to assign the Fed an important role in managing the American economy.

Keynes's ideas revolutionized economic thinking. They not only seemed to explain the Great Depression of the 1930s but also outlined a program to prevent such disasters in the future—two matters that, for good reason, deeply concerned postwar economists. Even those such as Burns who rejected much of Keynes's system accepted that government could influence demand by manipulating spending and interest rates. In a recession, Washington could run a deficit and cut interest rates to spur demand and encourage greater production. If inflation posed a threat, the government could cut spending and raise interest rates to reduce demand, slowing purchases of goods and services and forcing companies to cut prices. Indeed, so powerful were these ideas that many came to think that government decisions about deficits and interest rates *were* economic policy.

Throughout his career, however, Burns displayed what one colleague described as a "skepticism about the usefulness of *any* highly simplified theoretical structure that purported to capture the enormous complexity of our economy."[27] Burns conceded that Keynes's theoretical apparatus, his "analytical filing case for handling problems of aggregate income and employment," promised to help in "analyzing certain broad problems of economic organization and evolution."[28] But Burns did not think that Keynes adequately explained the business cycle and, drawing on his own extensive knowledge of economic history, raised several serious objections to Keynesian theory. He argued that the ratio of savings to income did not remain stable over time, casting doubt on the ability of scholars to estimate the link between, on one hand, the amount of investment or the size of a government deficit, and, on the other, the level of economic activity. He also considered Keynes's understanding of investment far too simplistic. Burns thought that capital spending was the balance wheel of the economy, not an exogenous variable that delivered random shocks to it. In a recession, when Keynesians assumed that excess capacity would discourage investment, Burns thought that certain forces encouraged capital spending and, therefore, recovery. Most recessions in American history, he argued, had ended after twelve or eighteen months with higher capital investment leading the way. Companies would modernize plants regardless of whether they were operating below capacity to gain competitive advantage, and even in a depressed economy some firms, particularly those in newer industries, would be running their facilities at full tilt and so would consider capital outlays.

Of course, the Great Depression did not follow this pattern. The economy operated well below its full capacity for years, and only government spending during World War II revived it. Many Keynesians argued that the depression ushered in a new era in which the "mature"

American economy offered fewer opportunities for profitable investment. Burns, however, attributed the length and depth of the depression to the speculative frenzy that had gripped this country in the late 1920s, weakening the financial system to the point where it collapsed at the first blow. Furthermore, he thought that "government policies in the United States after 1929, which brought on tax increases and— worse still—tolerated the destruction of a third of the nation's money supply, cannot escape a very large part of the responsibility for the Great Depression."[29]

These arguments, set forth in various publications, established Burns as one of the most formidable of Keynes's critics. But while he could raise doubts about Keynesian theory, he had no alternative to offer. His talents were those of an economic historian and a critic, not of an original theorist. Other scholars might refine their ideas in response to Burns's objections, but they also wanted an intellectual framework in which to operate. Keynes provided this while business-cycle research, the tradition that Burns championed, did not.

II

Arthur Burns's life changed in important ways after he took the helm of the National Bureau. He continued to be a prominent economist. Under Burns's direction the NBER, though it no longer dominated economic research as it had in the interwar years, remained central to such work, producing such important studies as Milton Friedman and Anna Schwartz's *A Monetary History of the United States, 1867–1960*.[30] Burns himself retained a high reputation in the field and eventually served as president of the American Economics Association in 1959. But his role had changed. As research director of the National Bureau, Burns devoted more and more of his time to administrative duties. He had extensive dealings with the businessmen and lawyers who headed the foundations that backed the NBER, and he found that he got along very well with these people. Despite his serious and often intimidating professional demeanor, Burns was, as one friend put it, a "social creature."[31] His manners were courtly and his nature warm—for instance, he never failed to hold the elevator for others or to inquire after a sick child or spouse—and he was especially popular among women, who appreciated his gallant attitude toward them. Burns and his wife soon became popular figures in New York society.

Burns's political orientation changed as well. Mitchell had always strongly identified with social and economic reform, and one might have expected his chief disciple to do the same. Burns, however, apparently lacked much of his mentor's optimism in humanity's ability to shape its environment. Whereas Mitchell came of age as a thinker during the heady 1900s, Burns was, as one of his students described him, "a creature of the Great Depression. . . . He saw the whole economic system disintegrating before him. The lesson he learned was that the avoidance of catastrophic change is the first objective of economic policy."[32] The outcome of the National Bureau's business cycle project may also have had something to do with Burns's attitude. A quarter-century of work by the profession's ablest minds had failed to explain this phenomenon—an outcome that inevitably raised doubts about humanity's ability to fully understand and master the world around it. Burns did not conclude that people were helpless against events, but he approached change cautiously and incrementally. He thought that the government should aim, first, to preserve stability and, second, to ensure a rising living standard. To advance these ends, the economist believed that Washington had to make sure that business, which was central to the economy, prospered. Reform, however desirable, had to be subordinate to these concerns.

In and of themselves, these attitudes probably would have pushed Burns toward the Republican Party, but other factors, less philosophical in nature, also led him in that direction. Most of his friends in the New York business and financial community were Republicans, and they must have influenced him. Moreover, the ascendency of Keynes among intellectuals in the Democratic Party naturally inclined Burns, a leading anti-Keynesian, toward the GOP. In 1952, Burns voted for General Dwight D. Eisenhower for president and belonged to "Democrats for Eisenhower," and he joined the Republican Party fairly soon thereafter.

In the late 1940s and early 1950s Arthur Burns was restless. He did lead a very pleasant existence. He was prosperous, enjoyed a happy family life, had a distinguished career, and moved in important circles. But business-cycle research no longer held out, as it once had, the promise of reshaping economic thought and policy, and Burns had tremendous ambition. He wanted to be a great man, not just a distinguished scholar. When offered a chance to strike out in a new direction, he took it.

In 1953 the newly elected president, Dwight Eisenhower, appointed Burns chairman of the Council of Economic Advisers (CEA). Burns owed his appointment to Gabriel Hauge, an economist who had taught at Harvard and Princeton and had advised the general during the presidential campaign. Hauge was at the forefront of Eisenhower's "New Republicanism," which sought to defend the leading role of private enterprise in American society while reserving an important place for government in dealing with social and economic problems. Burns's reputation as a student of the business cycle and as a critic of Keynes made him an obvious choice for the CEA.[33] He had not expected the post but accepted it eagerly, though he was careful before assenting to make sure that he would have the authority to do the job properly.[34] Some had doubts whether an academic like Burns would survive in an administration dominated by businessmen. Sherman Adams, Eisenhower's chief of staff, remembered, "When I took my first look at Burns, . . . I had a sinking sensation. If someone had asked me to describe the mental image I had of the type of New Deal official we were in the process of moving out of Washington, this was it—the glassy stare through thick lenses, peering out from under a canopy of unruly hair parted in the middle, a large pipe with a curved stem: the very incarnation of all the externals that were such anathema to Republican businessmen and politicians."[35]

Burns inherited a difficult situation. Congress had created the CEA in 1946 to provide the government with professional advice on economic policy. But Burns's predecessor at the council, Leon Keyserling—an eclectic economist who saw growth as the solution to most problems—had aroused opposition from representatives and senators of both the right and left. The council itself had a history of internal squabbling that raised further doubts about its utility. Its stock had fallen so low that Congress had given it only enough money to operate for nine months in fiscal 1953,[36] and the new administration was inclined to abandon it altogether, settling instead for a single economic adviser—a position it expected Burns to fill. Burns, however, persuaded Eisenhower to keep the council and to allow him to reorganize it. The new chairman centralized the CEA around himself, asserting his authority over the staff and other members of the council—a task no doubt facilitated by Burns's own forceful personality. He controlled contacts between his people and other agencies and made all decisions about policy recommendations himself. Burns believed that the council should concentrate on providing the president with expert information and advice on policy. Accordingly, he eschewed publicity, even avoiding congressional testimony when possible, while forging a good working relationship with Eisenhower. Soon Burns had the rare privilege of a regular weekly meeting with the chief executive, which often developed into a seminar on various economic topics.[37] The professor had learned quickly how to operate in Washington.

Burns played an important role in committing the administration to a cautious policy of economic stabilization. In September 1953 he warned the president that a recession was under way. He did not think the situation critical but believed that the government needed to act. Eisenhower directed him to report regularly to the cabinet on the course of events and what the administration could do about them. Burns pushed for measures to stimulate the economy. Although the president badly wanted to balance the federal budget, the CEA chairman, in concert with like-minded officials such as Hauge, persuaded him to accept cuts in income, corporate, and excise taxes passed by Congress and due to go into effect between January and April 1954. Burns, again with others in the administration, also encouraged the Federal Reserve to ease credit more rapidly. As the economy deteriorated over the winter, the president adopted Burns's suggestion that the administration expedite the spending of money already appropriated, and Eisenhower directed Burns to plan a large-scale public works program in case the economy failed to turn around of its own accord. By July, however, the situation was clearly improving, and so this last contingency was not implemented.[38] As the recession drew to an end, Eisenhower told Burns, "Arthur, you'd have made a fine chief of staff during the war"[39]—a compliment Burns treasured for the rest of his life.

Burns's responsibilities, however, went well beyond dealing with recession. In 1953, he helped shape the administration's proposals to reduce taxes on business, make more credit available to the housing industry, and extend unemployment insurance. In subsequent years, he led the Cabinet Committee on Small Business, worked to increase federal highway construction, pushed to improve the quality of Washington's economic statistics, and devised measures to help chronically depressed areas, such as New England textile mill towns. The last were not enacted into law but did become a basis for the 1961 Area Redevelopment Agency.[40]

Within the administration, Burns's willingness to expand the role of government earned him the reputation of a "liberal" and sometimes brought him into conflict with the businessmen who dominated the cabinet, especially George Humphrey, the powerful and volatile treasury secretary. In later years Burns enjoyed telling stories about his conflicts with and victories over Humphrey. For instance, in 1955 the two clashed over tax policy—the treasury secretary, eyeing a federal surplus, wanted reductions, while Burns, seeing signs of worsening inflation, preferred to stand pat. Humphrey insisted that the CEA, by tendering advice to the president in this area, was trespassing on the treasury's responsibilities and told Burns, "The President will have to choose between you and me." The two arranged a meeting with Eisenhower to settle their differences. As they walked into the Oval Office, the president said, "Just the two men I wanted to see. I just had a damn fool businessman in here saying that we ought to lower taxes now, this at a time when inflation is beginning to heat up—to lower taxes! Can you imagine any idiocy like that?"[41] That put an end to talk of tax cuts.

Stories like this should not obscure Burns's real position on the political spectrum or in the White House. His opinions were far closer to Secretary Humphrey's than to those of prominent Democratic liberals in the Senate such as Hubert Humphrey of Minnesota and Paul Douglas of Illinois, who were frequent critics of administration policy. Nor was Burns the president's chief economic adviser—the treasury secretary played that role. Certainly, the CEA chairman had Eisenhower's respect and strongly influenced his decisions, but the broad outlines of policy reflected Humphrey's concern with balancing the budget at least as much as Burns's desire to flatten out the business cycle.

Burns left Washington in late 1956 because he was not ready to give up academic life for a career in Washington. Although he had originally promised Columbia that he would be absent only two years, he had been on leave for four, and Burns knew that he had to return to the university if he wanted to retain his position there.

Burns's tour at the CEA had been quite successful. He had contributed in a meaningful way to policy and had earned the reputation of a man to be reckoned with. Sherman Adams, who had initially been skeptical, noted, "Arthur Burns turned out to be a pleasant surprise. . . . Far from being the abstract and impractical professor, Burns had his feet planted solidly on the ground and had no difficulty in more than holding his own in arguments at the cabinet table."[42] But Burns took perhaps the greatest pride in having revived the Council of Economic Advisers. Finding the institution on the verge of extinction, he had remodeled it and demonstrated its utility, setting the standard for all CEA chairmen.

Burns returned to the National Bureau as its president, but he still felt the pull of government service very strongly and would spend a great deal of time away from the NBER. His advice commanded respect within the administration, and he served on a number of commissions set up by it to examine specific questions, such as the financing of the Social Security system. Burns became especially close to Vice-President Richard M. Nixon. He had recognized Nixon's intelligence after seeing him perform in cabinet meetings, where the vice-president had demonstrated great skill at synthesizing all the arguments and presenting them fairly. "It's extraordinary," Burns said of Nixon, "that he's been so unpopular over the years with intellectuals. He's really one of us."[43] Burns would play an important role in the "Scholars for Nixon and Lodge" organization during the 1960 presidential campaign.[44] The corporate world, too, claimed much of Burns's time. He became a director of the Nationwide Securities Company, Dividend Shares, Inc., and the Mutual Life Insurance Company of New York,[45] and he worked as an economic consultant for Morgan Guarantee Trust.[46] The economist also served as a trustee for the Twentieth Century Fund and somehow found time to travel extensively with his wife, visiting Western Europe, Israel, and Japan several times, as well as making trips to other countries in the Far East, India, the Soviet Union, and Eastern Europe. The Burnses developed a custom of buying a painting in each country they visited to remind them of their travels there.[47]

Public policy became Burns's chief intellectual interest. He devoted a great deal of attention to the problem of inflation, warning that while "we command new tools for curbing recession, [and] we are willing to use them with promptness and vigor, in dealing with inflation, we have been less imaginative and less enterprising."[48] Burns noted that though the usual government responses to recession—tax cuts, spending increases, and the like—were generally popular in and of themselves, the same was not true for measures designed to curb inflation—higher interest rates, spending cuts, and tax increases. In addition, he argued that Washington continually faced "political pressures for higher minimum wages, larger trade union immunities, higher farm price supports, higher import duties, more import quotas, larger stockpiling programs, and other protective measures that serve either to raise prices or to prevent them from falling."[49] The government, he said, had to learn to ignore such pressures and to act aggressively to restrain demand when prices began to rise.

Burns feared inflation not only because it hurt those on fixed incomes and the poor, who he thought "rarely know how to protect themselves against inflation,"[50] but also because he saw it as a prelude to recession. Inflation usually reflected shortages of materials, bottlenecks in production, and wages that rose faster than productivity. It also led to higher interest rates, since lenders wanted compensation for the depreciation of their dollars over time. Burns's research told him that these factors all reduced profit margins and, as a result, investment, which was the key to prosperity.

Therefore, although Burns devoted more words to inflation than to recession, the latter was never far from his mind. During the severe 1957–58 downturn he urged Eisenhower to cut taxes by about $5 billion, but the president followed other advice and took no big steps to resuscitate the economy.[51] Recovery did begin in 1958, but it did not last very long. In early 1960 Burns warned Nixon that a recession was developing and that the government needed to reduce taxes and interest rates to counteract it. The vice-president, although convinced himself, failed to persuade Eisenhower to act. As Burns had predicted, the recession started in the fall just before the presidential election, which Nixon lost by an extremely thin margin to Senator John F. Kennedy. The defeated candidate would not forget the recession, which he blamed for his defeat, nor would he forget Burns.[52] The two never became close personal friends, but Burns became one of Nixon's most trusted advisers.[53]

III

The 1960 election put Burns back where he had been in 1952. He remained a distinguished voice in Washington but retained little if any real influence over policy. He would testify before Congress, and the Kennedy administration would appoint him to commissions that it thought needed a Republican economist, but that was all. Within the academic community his position also eroded. The 1960s were the golden age of Keynesian economics, and students of the business cycle, such as Burns, seemed out of date. When Burns retired as head of the NBER toward the end of the decade, its trustees brought in an outsider to replace him because they believed that the bureau needed to strike out in new directions.[54]

The triumph of Keynes owed much to President Kennedy. He entered the White House without strong ideas on economic policy, but he had campaigned for office criticizing the sluggishness of the American economy in the late 1950s and was willing to consider new approaches to, as he said, "get the country moving again." The president appointed prominent Keynesians such as Walter Heller and James Tobin to his Council of Economic Advisers, and they eventually won him over to their ideas.

These men practiced an updated Keynesianism. It relied on complex mathematical models with hundreds of variables, rather than on calculations of multipliers, to predict economic activity and the effects of government action on production and prices. It also emphasized rapid economic growth as an object of policy along with high employment. Nevertheless, Kennedy's CEA operated more or less within the framework laid down by Keynes. Its members thought that, left to itself, the economy would not generally use available resources fully— the sluggishness of the late 1950s showed that. Policy should, therefore, aim to ensure that the economy operated at its full potential. With a wide range of government tools to manage demand and powerful models to predict the results of policy, Kennedy's advisers believed that Washington could maintain prosperity indefinitely, effectively abolishing the business cycle. As Paul Samuelson, a supporter of the president and perhaps the most prominent Keynesian economist of the time, argued, "With proper fiscal and monetary policies, our economy can have full employment and whatever rate of . . . growth it wants."[55]

Kennedy's CEA thought of inflation and recession as opposites. The former was the result of too much demand, the latter of too little. In theory, inflation would not exist as long as the economy operated at or below its full potential because, at these levels, none of the shortages and bottlenecks associated with it existed. Keynesians, however, conceded that "friction" within the economy—the result of government policies such as minimum wages and tariffs that drove up costs and of the "market power" exercised by large unions and corporations over wages and prices—could create inflation even if production was below capacity. They postulated that a tradeoff existed between inflation and unemployment, and forced to make such a decision, Keynesians had no doubt where they stood.[56] As James Tobin put it, "Inflation is greatly exaggerated as a social evil. Even when prices are rising year after year, the economy is producing more and more of the goods, services, and jobs that meet people's needs. That . . . is its real purpose."[57] After considering the options, Kennedy's CEA decided that "an unemployment rate of 4.0 percent is taken as a reasonable target for full utilization of resources consistent with reasonable price stability."[58]

The president only gradually adopted the ideas of his advisers. Although unemployment stood at 6.7 percent when he took office, Kennedy was at first reluctant to act. He had not yet accepted Keynesianism and was not ready to dispense with balanced budgets. The recovery that started a few months after his inauguration reduced the incentive to stimulate the economy. But unemployment remained stubbornly high throughout Kennedy's tenure while investment expanded more slowly than most had hoped. As a result, the president became increasingly receptive to Keynesian thinking. The first step came in 1961, after the construction of the Berlin Wall, when the administration increased military outlays without any offsetting tax increases or spending cuts. The first purely economic measure came in 1962, when at the president's request the Congress enacted an investment tax credit, which allowed companies to deduct a certain percentage of capital spending from their tax bill—effectively subsidizing investment. Finally, in late 1962, Kennedy proposed a massive cut in income and corporate taxes, which Congress enacted in early 1964, soon after his death. To minimize inflation while all of this was going on, the CEA laid down wage-price guidelines in early 1962, encouraging business to stabilize prices and labor to limit wage hikes to the increase in productivity. President Kennedy soon made it clear that these guidelines were more than suggestions when he forced the steel industry to rescind a price increase that violated them. These policies paid off. Between 1961 and 1965 the economy grew rapidly, at more than 4 percent a year; the inflation rate averaged 1.5 percent annually; and unemployment dropped from 6.7 percent in 1961 to 4.5 percent in 1965.[59]

Burns agreed with the basic thrust of policy but seriously doubted the intellectual foundation on which it rested. He agreed that the economy needed stimulus in the early 1960s—he had suggested just that to Nixon before the 1960 election. But Burns distrusted the whole idea that government should keep the economy operating at its full potential, preferring instead a policy attuned to the business cycle. He believed that this cycle was basic to the capitalist system, and that while wise policy might flatten it out, nothing could eliminate it completely. Promises of eternal prosperity, he thought, smacked of hubris—a point that many who made such claims would later concede. He also doubted that the economy had an inherent tendency to operate below its full potential. "There is no chronic slack in our economy," he said in 1961. "The problem of recovery that we face is not very different from that which we faced in 1949 or in 1954 or in 1958 [after recessions]." The evidence for economic stagnation, he argued, "turns out to rest fundamentally on one fact, namely, that the business-cycle expansion of 1958–1960 was exceptionally short and incomplete"—an outcome that the economist blamed on too-restrictive government policy.[60] In any event, Burns doubted that anyone really knew what the economy's potential was or could keep track of it as it changed, and he feared that political pressures would lead the government to set too ambitious a target for production. If Washington did this, it would overheat the economy and unleash a serious inflation that would inevitably lead to recession. Burns wanted a more cautious, flexible approach in which the government would stimulate the economy while watching cyclical indicators that had historically warned of inflation. He believed that Washington should keep an eye on the prices of certain raw materials that responded quickly to any shortage and on delays in the delivery of merchandise that would determine if companies were having trouble supplying the demand for goods.[61] Keynesians believed that their opponents exaggerated the dangers of inflation and that their economic models would warn if it threatened, but Burns declared, "These models are bankrupt."[62] He thought that they relied too heavily on abstract calculations, used aggregate statistics that grossly oversimplified economic conditions, and often made the mistake of averaging together data from very different historical periods. Burns had no use at all for the wage-price guidelines. He feared that arbitrary rules would distort the price structure and thus the allocation of goods and services throughout the economy. He also suspected that the guidelines would give Washington an excuse to avoid the difficult tasks of cutting its own budget and raising interest rates when inflation threatened.[63]

Nor did Burns think that administration economists fully understood their successes. The economy had responded so well to stimulus in the early 1960s, he thought, because the Eisenhower administration had reduced inflation to practically nothing, creating an atmosphere in which business responded to higher demand by increasing output, not prices. Kennedy's advisers, however, considered Eisenhower's fear of inflation obsessive and unwarranted and blamed it for two recessions. Burns also viewed the tax cuts somewhat differently from the administration. In addition to spurring demand, Burns believed that they encouraged enterprise. With lower taxes, he argued, "Individuals and businessmen will begin to think very differently about the future. They will be in a position not merely to use the larger cash income which is at their disposal, but they may well be in a mood also to dip into their accumulated assets and to use their credit." They would "use their brains, their energy, their disposable income, and also their assets and even their borrowing power in the interest of enlarging their economic activities and through that the nation's economy."[64] Kennedy's CEA certainly took such factors into account, but it did not put as much emphasis on them as Burns did.

Whereas prosperity in the early 1960s had discredited critics of administration policy like Burns, economic problems in the second half of the decade seemed to bear them out. During 1965, when Burns warned that the economy showed signs of strain, President Lyndon B. Johnson pursued an increasingly stimulative policy, cutting excise taxes, proposing expensive Great Society programs, and as the year went on, shouldering the cost of waging an ever-expanding war in Vietnam. Despite the advice of most of his economists, the president refused to raise taxes to pay for the war, fearing that such action would undermine political support for the conflict. Inflation accelerated throughout 1965 and on into early 1966, when the Federal Reserve stepped in and forced interest rates to postwar highs. This halted the growth of money and credit, slowing inflation but also bringing economic growth to a halt. Shaken by this close brush with recession, the Fed backed off and cut interest rates, and the economy surged forward in 1967, as did inflation. When President Johnson finally acted, persuading Congress in 1968 to impose a 10 percent surcharge on income taxes, the measure proved too little too late.[65] By that time, the inflation rate had risen to 4.2 percent, the highest level since the Korean War. After Johnson left office in early 1969, inflation continued unabated. Keynesians blamed the situation on bad management—the government should have raised taxes when they told it to in 1966. Burns, however, thought the problem went deeper. He believed that Keynesianism, by ignoring the business cycle, led policymakers to concentrate on the wrong signals, making the sort of policy mistakes that Johnson committed inevitable.

The events of the late 1960s brought a new school of economic thought to the forefront: monetarism. Monetarists based their thinking on a simple identity—the level of economic activity, in dollar terms, equaled the amount of money available multiplied by how often that money changed hands. They believed that the speed at which people spent money (velocity) held fairly stable over time, and therefore that changes in the money supply roughly mirrored changes in economic activity. If monetary growth matched the growth in production, all was well. But if it rose slower than output, people could not buy all the goods available and the economy shrank. On the other hand, if the money supply increased more rapidly than output, people had more money than goods, and prices went up. From these calculations, monetarists deduced that the Federal Reserve should expand the money supply steadily at a rate equal to the speed with which the nation could, over time, increase the production of goods and services without strain. Such a policy would keep the economy on an even keel, stimulating demand if growth lagged and restraining it if prices increased.

These ideas seriously threatened Keynesian theory. The latter postulated that capitalist economies were inherently unstable and needed government intervention to impose order. Monetarists reversed the formula. They were strong supporters of free markets and deeply suspicious of government interference with the economic decisions of individuals. To them, the private economy was basically stable and could take care of itself, provided that the central authorities expanded the money supply at a regular rate. Keynesians responded to monetarism by arguing that velocity was not stable. Just because money was available, they said, did not mean that people would borrow and spend it at some constant rate. Although this objection may seem technical, it is extremely important. If the pace at which people spend money is unstable, a regular expansion of the money supply will not keep the economy on an even keel. Keynesians also considered the level of interest rates a better index of monetary policy than the money supply. In the late 1960s, however, changes in the money supply correlated fairly closely with economic performance, apparently supporting the monetarists.[66]

Burns, always suspicious of all-embracing economic theories, had strong disagreements with monetarism. But he was also a close friend of the most prominent monetarist, Milton Friedman, whom he had taught as an undergraduate at Rutgers and had sponsored at the NBER. Their friendship led some observers to believe that Burns was more sympathetic to Friedman's ideas than he actually was. Burns's imposing manner convinced many that he was an intellectual autocrat, whereas in fact he counted among his friends many with whom he disagreed on important issues—Friedman among them. Burns did feel somewhat more comfortable with monetarism than with Keynesianism because the former emphasized the durability of the capitalist economy. He also accepted that changes in the money supply greatly influenced production and prices. But Burns refused to accept any economic theory that placed so much emphasis on one factor—his study of economic history indicated that a variety of interlocking factors governed economic performance. Just as important, he agreed with

Keynesians that the velocity of money was not stable over time but varied with the business cycle. Burns also dismissed the possibility that constant policies could keep the economy on an even keel—"neutrality," he said, "is a myth."[67] The federal government was simply too big and too deeply involved in the economy to opt out through some monetary sleight of hand. Burns summed up his attitude toward the economic debates of the late 1960s when he wrote, "I wish the world were as simple as the Friedmanites and Keynesians wish to make it, but it never has been and, I dare say, it never will be."[68]

IV

In 1968 Arthur Burns seemed in many ways a figure of the past. Certainly, with his white hair parted down the middle, rimless wire-framed glasses, and ever-present pipe, he looked old-fashioned—one reporter described his appearance as that of "a small-town druggist, circa 1940."[69] His approach to economics, with its emphasis on the business cycle, also seemed passé. In addition, Burns was sixty-four, an age at which men usually think more of retirement than of new projects.

Nevertheless, Arthur Burns remained hungry for achievement. Although a success by any reasonable standard, he had not, except during his four years as chairman of the Council of Economic Advisers, really met the high goals that he had set for himself. Religious conviction reinforced his ambition. Burns, who read from the Bible every night and attended synagogue on high holy days, believed that he had an obligation to use his God-given talents to serve others.

Burns remained as formidable as ever. He still had a capacity for work that very few men half his age could match and a sense of authority that invariably commanded respect. He possessed a knowledge of the history and workings of the economy second to none and great political skills. Perhaps most important, Burns had absolute confidence in himself—he knew he could do great things. After Richard Nixon won the presidency in 1968, Arthur Burns would get the opportunity to prove that.

2

White House Prelude

I

Arthur Burns belonged to Richard Nixon's inner circle. The two had been close during the mid-1960s, when Nixon's career seemed dead, and remained so as the former vice-president's fortunes revived. During the 1968 presidential campaign, Burns led the staff that examined issues and wrote position papers for the candidate. After Nixon won, the economist oversaw the work of more than a dozen task forces that examined fields such as transportation, welfare policy, and government organization and suggested federal initiatives in these areas. Burns put these recommendations, along with his own suggestions and critiques, in a report that would serve as a blueprint for many of the new administration's domestic reforms.[1] Burns also helped the president-elect find qualified people to fill government posts. Largely on his recommendation, Nixon appointed George Shultz secretary of labor and Paul McCracken chairman of the Council of Economic Advisers.[2]

Burns, however, did not join the new administration himself. Nixon had asked him to coordinate domestic policy from a position on the White House staff, but he refused the offer. Burns had already served on Eisenhower's staff and, twelve years later, had no desire to repeat himself. Besides, a more attractive prospect presented itself. The chairman of the Federal Reserve Board, William McChesney Martin, had to retire in January 1970, and Nixon told Burns that he could have the job when it became available.[3] The post would put Burns in charge of perhaps the country's most powerful economic institution and give him the opportunity to put his extensive knowledge of the business cycle to use, and he let Nixon know that he would consider such an offer very seriously indeed. To occupy himself in the meanwhile, Burns agreed to become a fellow of the Hoover Institute at Stanford University.[4]

Nixon still wanted Burns to join his staff and tried hard to change the economist's mind. For instance, soon after the inauguration, when Burns visited the Oval Office to present Nixon with the report on domestic policy, the president took the economist into the cabinet room and showed him which chair would be his.[5] Under such pressure, Burns gave in, and not altogether grudgingly. He had long felt the conflicting pulls of scholarship and public office, and the president's flattering attention persuaded him to surrender to the latter. Nixon appointed Burns counselor to the president—a new title—and gave him the responsibility for coordinating domestic policy as well as membership in the cabinet, the latter a privilege no other staff member enjoyed. The counselor would help the new administration get off to a good start and then move over to the Fed.

Arthur Burns's sudden elevation raised concerns among much of the rest of the White House staff. No one doubted that, with his powerful position and long association with the president, Burns would, as the *New York Times* put it, "emerge as a superpower in the government's vast array of social and economic programs."[6] But Nixon had already hired Daniel Patrick Moynihan, a Harvard sociologist who had worked in the Labor Department during the Kennedy and Johnson administrations, to head the Urban Affairs Council, which was supposed to develop measures to deal with poverty and the problems of cities. Naturally, Moynihan worried that Burns, whose responsibilities overlapped his own, might overshadow him. Members of the CEA feared that, as one of them said, "this fellow [Burns] who was close to Nixon and a well-established economist . . . was going to intervene with the functioning of the Council."[7] Chief of Staff H. R. Haldeman and his lieutenant, John D. Ehrlichman, who between them managed the day-to-day operations of the White House, were no doubt taken aback when Burns, acting on his own authority, scheduled a daily staff meeting at which everyone was supposed to report to him on their activities.[8] It was inevitable that Burns would encounter resistance from those whose plans his unexpected rise to power had disrupted.

The opposition to Burns, however, stemmed as much from questions of substance as from those of power. In domestic policy, President Nixon had to decide, first and foremost, what to do about the dozens of social programs inherited from his predecessor, Lyndon Johnson. Collectively known as the Great Society, these included the much-discussed War on Poverty as well as measures to improve education, the environment, and health care, to encourage scientific research and the fine arts, and many more. These efforts had increased both the scope of government and expectations about what it could accomplish. Some around the president, such as Secretary of Health, Education, and Welfare Robert Finch, had absorbed Great Society attitudes toward reform, while others, taking their cue from the student protests and ghetto riots of the 1960s, thought that failure to push ahead could spark further social unrest.

Burns, however, had doubts about the Great Society. He believed that the government had enacted much of it in haste without proper planning, and he thought that, with inflation a serious problem, Washington needed to cut spending. His objections were philosophical as well as practical. A self-made man, Burns had worked hard for everything he had and thought others should do the same. Indeed, he doubted that people could fully appreciate anything for which they had not labored. "The amount of money being spent on the poor," Burns said, "simply astounds me."[9] "What is urgently needed," he told the president, "is a thorough reexamination of existing welfare programs and policies with a view to their simplification, to the elimination of abuses, and—most important of all—to the creation of opportunity and incentives for moving poor people off welfare rolls and onto private payrolls."[10] Burns suggested that Washington work to improve vocational training and worker skills generally, set up computerized "job banks" to make more information available on employment, offer tax credits to companies that invested in depressed urban areas or trained the poor for employment, and start voluntary partnerships with business to rehabilitate metropolitan slums. At the same time, the government should reduce direct handouts, such as welfare payments.[11] These measures would both give the poor the incentive and opportunity to help themselves and enlist groups outside the federal government in the fight against poverty. Burns also believed that Great Society programs too often neglected the problems of the middle class. In a discussion of urban problems he noted, "We should not forget . . . that of the 128 million people who live in metropolitan areas, almost 90 percent have incomes above the officially designated poverty line. These, too, suffer from many problems associated with city living, and in a sense are the forgotten city dwellers."[12]

Burns's ability to turn these ideas into policy, however, depended on his relationship with the chief executive, which deteriorated rapidly. When he and the president had first become acquainted, Burns had been the senior partner: he was older than Nixon and enjoyed more influence with Eisenhower and his lieutenants than did the vice-president. Burns thought of Nixon as a protégé and treated him with what one friend described as "slight condescension."[13] After Nixon became president, Burns had trouble adjusting to a subordinate position. Whereas others flattered the chief executive and played to his prejudices, Burns had, as one White House staffer put it, "an avuncular style that drove Nixon bats."[14] He lectured Nixon on whatever issue was at hand, usually at great length and in considerable detail. Burns would also bluntly contradict the president or anyone else in the administration with whom he disagreed, even though the chief executive hated confrontation. Soon, Nixon began to dread his encounters with the man one journalist described as "the ultimate pedagogue."[15]

Some in the White House did their best to encourage these feelings. Chief of Staff Haldeman considered it his job to protect the chief executive from those who would waste the president's time, and he thought that Burns often did just that. Nor were he and Ehrlichman blind to the likelihood that a reduction in Burns's authority would increase their own. These two and their aides derided Burns to the president as a blowhard unable to separate vital information from trivia, and wicked impressions of the counselor became a staple of their humor. Burns returned their hostility. He thought of Haldeman and Ehrlichman as clerks promoted far above their natural talents and referred to them as "the boys in the basement." Burns, however, had made a crucial mistake when he had passed up a cramped office in the West Wing of the White House near the president for more spacious quarters across the street in the Executive Office Building. All the White House staff's authority flows from the chief executive, and because of his physical distance from Nixon, Burns was often out of touch with the source of power. In contrast, Haldeman and his lieutenants were firmly ensconced in the West Wing and saw the president constantly. They also had another advantage that they used to the utmost—they controlled access to the president. By April, Haldeman had, with the president's acquiescence, limited Burns to one half-hour meeting with the chief executive a week—less time than Burns had had with Eisenhower. By summer, the counselor was reporting to the president through Ehrlichman. For some reason, Burns never responded by forcing his way into the Oval Office, even though as a member of the cabinet he outranked those who stood in his path.[16]

Burns's decline gave those in the White House with different ideas on policy, especially Daniel Patrick Moynihan, an opportunity. One of the architects of the War on Poverty, Moynihan had nevertheless developed doubts about many of the measures designed during the Johnson administration to help the poor. He feared that they encouraged dependence on the government and weakened family ties. He sought to solve these problems, however, not by cutting programs but by expanding them in such a way as to reinforce the family and to encourage beneficiaries to get jobs. Moynihan proved adept at navigating the White House bureaucracy. He got along fairly well with Haldeman and Ehrlichman and, in part because his office was in the West Wing, saw a good deal of the president. He put a lot of effort into cultivating Nixon and proved quite good at it—Moynihan had a sharp wit and was one of the few people in Washington who could actually get the chief executive to laugh.[17] But Moynihan's ideas appealed to Nixon as much as his manner. The president yearned for dramatic action that would both leave his mark on history and knock his opponents off balance. Burns's counsel of retrenchment and cooperative efforts did not satisfy this desire, whereas Moynihan's plans did. "Four minutes with Pat," Nixon reportedly said, "is worth four hours of Arthur Burns."[18]

Largely at Moynihan's instigation, President Nixon proposed the most ambitious reform of the welfare system since the Social Security Act: the Family Assistance Plan. This grew out of Moynihan's suggestion that Washington guarantee every family a minimum income. All agreed that, as it then stood, the welfare system was a mess. Its centerpiece, Aid to Families with Dependent Children (AFDC), only helped unemployed women with children. Couples could not receive help, and if a woman on AFDC got a job, she lost all of her benefits. These provisions encouraged men to abandon their families and women to avoid work. The administration of the program caused further problems. States determined the level of benefits, which varied greatly from jurisdiction to jurisdiction. Inevitably, the poor gravitated toward more generous states, such as New York, to take advantage of the higher benefits and looser rules for eligibility. Moynihan proposed that the federal government junk the whole system and instead guarantee everyone an income that would total approximately $1,200 for a family of four. If a parent took a job, he or she would lose only fifty cents of benefits for each dollar earned. This new system would help keep families together and at least reduce the incentive for idleness while imposing uniform rules on the confusing patchwork of welfare programs. It represented the sort of political masterstroke that Nixon loved. The higher and more widely available benefits would please liberals while provisions to strengthen family ties and work incentives would appeal to conservatives.

Moynihan's proposal horrified Burns. He already considered Moynihan a sort of liberal "mole" within the administration and summed up his opinion of the man in one word: "spender."[19] The guaranteed income proposal confirmed Burns's doubts. "I'm afraid," he said, "of what it would do to our society to distribute government checks to people whether or not they're willing to work. . . . Advocates of guaranteed income . . . have not thought through all the social and moral implications of this approach. Aside from the effect it would have in encouraging dependency, any such program would cause great bitterness among people who do work for a living."[20] He realized, however, that welfare reform appealed strongly to the president and so developed a plan of his own. He revived a proposal that had been around Washington for years—revenue sharing—under which the federal government would give to states and localities large sums of money to spend more or less as they wished. Burns added one condition to these funds, however—states would have to change their welfare systems. They would have to bring benefits up to certain minimum levels and make entire families as well as single mothers eligible for AFDC. Local authorities would also have to attach a "work requirement" to benefits. Welfare recipients who were physically able would have to accept either employment or job training if they wanted to continue getting government checks. Burns's approach would remedy the worst abuses of the welfare system, cost less than Moynihan's proposal, and encourage people to get jobs.[21]

The plan that emerged from the White House, entitled the Family Assistance Plan, followed Moynihan's ideas, with one important exception. It guaranteed every family a minimum income but attached to this a work requirement like that in Burns's proposal. The president also sent to Congress a bill for revenue sharing, similar to Burns's except that it was not linked to welfare reform. Even this, however, represented only a limited victory for the counselor. He thought that the federal government could not really afford revenue sharing at the moment and had suggested it only to derail the even more expensive guaranteed income proposal.[22]

Burns's defeat over welfare reform was but one of many. The counselor had wanted the president to eliminate subsidies for the supersonic transport airplane (SST), but Transportation Secretary John A. Volpe persuaded Nixon to keep the project alive. Burns hoped to do away with the $750 million Model Cities program, which was supposed to finance "model" programs to combat urban blight, but Moynihan and Housing and Urban Development Secretary George Romney persuaded the chief executive to continue the effort. Burns opposed the repeal of President Kennedy's investment tax credit, which was part of a tax reform measure devised by the treasury, but Nixon decided to send the package to Congress anyway. In each of these cases, Burns's advice was good. The SST was a white elephant, Model Cities never amounted to much, and the administration had to reintroduce the investment tax credit in 1971. Nevertheless, in each instance other government officials outmaneuvered the counselor.[23]

Why did Burns, whom Henry Kissinger described as "one of the canniest bureaucratic infighters in Washington," stumble so badly as counselor to the president?[24] First, he overextended himself. Burns was not an expert on domestic policy and underestimated the task at hand. John Ehrlichman, who headed Nixon's Domestic Council after 1969, later remarked, "The domestic issues that poured into the White House came in a vast tide which never ebbed,"[25] and he maintained a staff of over thirty to deal with them. In contrast, Burns's aides numbered less than a dozen—too few to keep up. Second, Burns misjudged his relationship with the president. During the 1960s Burns had been one of a loyal few who had stayed with Nixon through difficult times. Naturally, these people enjoyed considerable influence with him during these years, and Burns assumed that this authority would persist after Nixon became chief executive. A new president, however, never wants for advisers, and Nixon did not automatically defer to his veteran supporters but listened attentively to the new people around him. Accordingly, a newcomer who cultivated the president assiduously could outmaneuver an old loyalist who took his position for granted. Henry Kissinger did this to Secretary of State William Rogers, and Moynihan did it to Burns. Third, Burns's portfolio as counselor was extremely vague. Nixon created the post at the last moment, and so it had no clear place in the White House organization and no distinct responsibilities. Whatever Burns did inevitably trespassed on others' bailiwicks, which naturally caused resentment and encouraged resistance. Fourth, Burns was out of step ideologically with the new administration. He still thought in terms of Eisenhower's "New Republicianism," which emphasized that the government had a useful role to play but gave the private sector priority. In 1969, at least, Richard Nixon was inclined to be more aggressive. Finally, and perhaps most important, Burns just did not seem to have his heart in the fight. He had been reluctant to join the White House staff and knew that he would be moving to the Federal Reserve at the end of 1969. In such circumstances he may not have been willing to engage in a bruising contest to impose his will.

II

In early 1969 Arthur Burns paid little attention to economic policy, his specialty. In part, other matters took his time, but he also did not want to encroach on the territory of CEA Chairman Paul McCracken, whom he had recommended for the post. Furthermore, a broad consensus existed within the new administration about the proper course of action—an outlook that Burns shared.

When Richard Nixon took office, almost everyone, including Burns, believed inflation to be the nation's most serious economic problem. Though unemployment was at the lowest level in fifteen years and production was expanding, consumer prices were going up at more than 5 percent a year. Most attributed price increases to government policy, which had countenanced large deficits and an expansive monetary policy even though, after 1965, the economy was operating at close to its full potential. In and of themselves, these mistakes were easily corrected. But the President's Task Force on Inflation—one of those organized by Burns—noted that, because price increases had been accelerating for four years, "anticipations of still further inflation were . . . already incorporated into a wide range of economic decisions and arrangements."[26] To restore price stability, the administration had to change these expectations. It could use shock therapy, adopting fiscal and monetary policies so tight that the economy simply could not accommodate higher prices. Unfortunately, this solution would almost certainly cause a recession, and Nixon's advisers thought such action unnecessary and destructive. Instead, the task force recommended, "National policy be directed towards moderating inflation in a gradual and systematic manner rather than stopping inflation abruptly."[27]

This approach suited President Nixon. He remembered how, in the late 1950s, the Eisenhower administration had fought inflation with frugal budgets and tight money. Though it had successfully reduced price increases to a very low level, this policy had also contributed to two recessions that had hurt the Republican Party badly and had quite likely cost Nixon the 1960 presidential election. He was determined to avoid a repetition of the experience. "We'll take inflation if necessary," the president said, "but we can't take unemployment."[28]

The administration's economic "game plan," laid out by McCracken, called for it to slow the economy, but not enough to create recession. Using the figure favored by the Kennedy administration, the CEA decided that a 4 percent unemployment rate represented full employment and reasoned that, if the government pushed joblessness up to a still-low 4.5 percent, inflation would gradually decline. Business, unable to sell all it could produce, would limit price increases, while workers, less sure of their jobs, would accept more moderate wage hikes.

To accomplish its objectives, the administration imposed an austerity program. The president persuaded Congress to cut outlays by about $4 billion and to extend Johnson's income tax surcharge and excise taxes on telephone service and automobiles, all of which were due to expire.[29] Together, these measures yielded a federal surplus of $3.2 billion for fiscal 1969. The CEA, however, thought that the Federal Reserve would have to bear the brunt of the battle against inflation. The council's members had absorbed many of Milton Friedman's ideas and considered changes in the supply of money and credit the most important factor in determining economic performance over the short term. The Fed's chairman, William McChesney Martin, did not concede these arguments. He believed that decisions about government spending were as important to the economy as monetary policy and that the level of interest rates had more influence over prices and production than did the rate of growth in the money supply. Nevertheless, he agreed that the economy was overheated and raised interest rates. The prime rate, which banks charge their best customers, went from 6.75 percent at the end of 1968 to a post-1945 record of 8.5 percent in June 1969, with other rates up accordingly. This policy yielded the results the administration desired. Growth in the money supply slowed from a 7.9 percent annual rate in the second half of 1968 to a little less than 5 percent in the middle of 1969.[30]

The new administration ignored, quite consciously, one device that might have reduced inflation: direct controls on wages and prices. All of the president's economic advisers, including Burns, opposed government intervention in free markets. Nixon himself, during the Second World War, had worked for several unhappy months in the Office of Price Administration and had developed a visceral antipathy toward such measures. Burns, long a critic of President Kennedy's wage-price guidelines, spoke for everyone in the White House when he warned Congress that controls would create a huge, stifling bureaucracy and encourage black markets.[31] The new president quickly abandoned Kennedy's wage-price guideposts, which had fallen into disuse, and pledged to fight inflation "by relying upon free markets and strengthening them, not by suppressing them."[32]

Generally, the administration's policy met with approval. At the time, the economy was not a great political issue—attention focused on the Vietnam War and on domestic issues such as civil rights and crime. The economics profession still enjoyed a high degree of consensus, and the White House's plans went in the direction favored by the discipline's mainstream. Arthur Okun, who had chaired President Johnson's CEA, declared himself in "full agreement" with Nixon's program and said, "I would think . . . that it wouldn't take that much of a change in economic environment to put discipline back into wage and price setting."[33] This accorded with Paul McCracken's estimate that the administration's policy would significantly reduce inflation after about a year.[34] The only important point of contention was the president's decision to do away with the wage-price guidelines. Okun stated, "I do believe that the Nixon administration made a mistake in scrapping the guideposts as blatantly and clearly as they did. . . . The guideposts are not a substitute for good fiscal and monetary policy but . . . we need everything we can have."[35]

Burns had a different objection to administration policy. Though approving of its substance, he thought its rhetoric inappropriate. He doubted that businessmen and workers would refrain from increasing prices and wages unless they feared that hikes would risk sales and employment. But the president, by constantly stressing that he would not tolerate recession and that his policy would slow inflation "gradually," dispelled such concerns. Burns thought Nixon ought to take a tougher line in public. "I think," the counselor said, "we have to create a little more uncertainty."[36]

III

Although Arthur Burns kept his distance from domestic economic policy for much of 1969, he did intervene in international finance, a subject with which he had little experience. The web of trade and investment that linked the industrial democracies seemed in danger of coming apart, and Burns viewed this prospect with alarm. He remembered how, in the 1930s, competitive currency devaluation, national default, and rising protectionism had sharply reduced international transactions and had contributed mightily to the depression. The administration, Burns thought, needed to act.

After 1945, the industrial democracies had constructed a monetary system based on the dollar. The United States valued gold at $35 an ounce and agreed to redeem with the precious metal, on demand, any of its currency held by other governments. Other countries "pegged" their currencies to the dollar, buying and selling the greenback in markets to stabilize the value of their own money. Central banks also kept their reserves in dollars, and the greenback dominated trade in certain commodities, such as petroleum. Hence, everything rested on the American currency, and if events called its value into question, confidence in the whole edifice could fail.[37]

By the time Richard Nixon took office, this prospect seemed a real possibility. Throughout the 1960s, the United States had run balance-of-payments deficits despite a trade surplus because it spent more for troops stationed abroad and for foreign aid and investment than it earned.[38] This situation became worse after 1965, as inflation made American exports more expensive and reduced the relative price of imports, wiping out most of the trade surplus. The central banks of other countries began to acquire large claims on the U.S., far more than Washington could redeem in gold. In 1968 the price of gold on the open market went above $35 an ounce, despite sales by the United States and the other industrial democracies.[39] The gap between the official and market prices for the precious metal opened up the prospect of a run on American gold stocks. The dollar was no longer "as good as gold," and other countries might decide to convert their greenbacks into the precious metal while they still could. The Johnson administration overcame the immediate problem by persuading the other industrial democracies not to demand gold for the dollars they held, except in limited amounts to pay international obligations that required it.[40] To improve the balance of payments, the American government imposed controls on the export of capital, limiting borrowing by foreigners in domestic markets and foreign investment by U.S. citizens.

After Nixon took office, Burns proposed to end the balance-of-payments problem by increasing the official price of gold. This would effectively devalue the dollar, making American exports cheaper and imports more expensive, thus improving the trade balance.[41] Moreover, he said, "When the dollar is devalued with respect to gold, the existing system of foreign exchange rates can—and as a matter of probability will—continue. The dollar value of our gold resources would be much higher after the price of gold is raised; hence, direct controls over investment, travel, etc. can be kept to a minimum, and business can go on pretty much as it is."[42] In late 1968 Burns went to Europe at Nixon's behest, and rumor had it that while there he quizzed European politicians and business leaders about their reactions to a change in the official price of gold—though this story was never confirmed.[43]

An interagency group led by Treasury Undersecretary Paul Volcker, which the president set up to examine international finance, had a different recommendation. It doubted that any devaluation of the dollar would improve the trade balance. Other countries had payment surpluses, it concluded, because they engineered them by subsidizing exports, restricting imports, and keeping currencies undervalued. They would match any American devaluation with their own. The Volcker group also feared that an increase in the price of gold would reduce the role of the dollar in international finance. As it stood, the privileged position of U.S. currency gave American economic policy a degree of freedom no other country enjoyed. If it suffered from a balance-of-payments deficit, the U.S. could simply allow dollars to accumulate overseas—essentially printing up money—rather than borrowing from the International Monetary Fund (IMF) or raising interest rates to attract foreign capital to finance the shortfall.[44] But once it became clear that the dollar's value was not immutable, other countries would resist accepting greenbacks and instead demand something else—quite likely gold. The Volcker group recommended that Washington stand firm and rely on the anti-inflation program to reduce the trade deficit while trying to persuade other countries with large surpluses, such as West Germany and Japan, to increase the value of their currencies.[45]

These arguments did not impress Burns. He was confident that other nations would take an enlightened view of their own self-interest and not cut the price of their currencies in response to an American devaluation. They benefited from existing financial arrangements and, he thought, would accept measures to ensure that the system continued to work smoothly.[46] The possibility that an increase in the price of gold might lead to a greater role for it in international finance at the expense of the dollar did not seem to worry Burns. His attitude toward the precious metal would change with greater exposure to international issues, but at this time Burns apparently believed that the link to gold helped guarantee stable exchange rates, which he valued highly.[47]

The president decided against his counselor. Nixon had almost no interest in international finance and was unwilling to take the initiative if he could avoid it. He also thought that an increase in the price of gold, which would require congressional approval, would involve considerable political risks. Questions involving gold have always carried great symbolic weight in American politics, and a measure such as Burns proposed, which would at once reduce the gold content of the dollar while possibly increasing its role in the international economy, would anger both enthusiasts and foes of the precious metal. Finally, Nixon tended to agree with the Volcker group that other countries would act to neutralize the effects of any devaluation. He was, as one member of the CEA put it, "very nationalistic [and] rather inclined to believe that others were out to exploit us economically."[48]

In practice, Nixon decided to "muddle through."[49] In the first eighteen months of his administration, the president made only one public statement on international finance, announcing the relaxation of capital controls and declaring that the balance of payments could be repaired best by "restoring stable and noninflationary growth to the U.S. economy."[50]

As it turned out, events delayed the final reckoning for two years. In 1969 high interest rates attracted money to this country and gave the United States a balance-of-payments surplus. In 1970 recession cut demand for imports and so improved the American trade balance. But once these special factors disappeared, the payments deficit reemerged on an even larger scale.

IV

Starting in the middle of 1969, Arthur Burns turned his attention to the domestic economy. It was clear by this time that production was slowing, but the rate of inflation was running near 6 percent. This development did not panic Burns or anyone else in the White House because they all anticipated that it would take time for the downturn to affect prices. Nevertheless, Burns thought that the momentum of inflation justified his fears that, by emphasizing "gradualism," President Nixon had reduced pressures on labor and business to restrain wages and prices.

To counteract this impression, Burns attempted to get the president to administer a shock to the construction industry. Its unions were pushing up wages at about 15 percent a year, which not only increased the cost of building substantially but also threatened to encourage workers in other sectors of the economy to press for similar increases. In September, at his counselor's urging, the president announced that he would cut federal construction spending by 75 percent in an attempt to contain building costs. This action was not as drastic as it sounded. Nixon did not reduce federal grants to the states for construction, which accounted for far more building than Washington undertook itself. He did ask the states to cut spending on their own, but he did not press them very hard, and few responded. Nixon ignored the sheaf of proposals Burns gave him to reduce the cost of construction labor. The president hoped to win the political support of "hardhats" in the building trades, most of whom were Democrats, and so was reluctant to attack their interests directly.[51] Consequently, construction wages continued their rapid climb.[52]

In late September Nixon tried again. He sent a memo to business and labor leaders telling them that "because the government's house is now in order, we can turn to business and labor to remind them that fighting inflation is everybody's problem and fighting inflation is everyone's business."[53] In other words, he expected them to limit price and wage increases. Burns, who supported this statement, denied that it represented any sort of move toward direct government intervention in the marketplace. "The President," he said, "is essentially conducting an educational function. He's told the country he has taken steps, rather vigorous steps, to bring inflation under control. He's told, therefore, businessmen that if they're counting on a continuation of inflation at something like the pace that we have experienced . . . they're going to be making a serious mistake."[54] Privately, though, Burns mused that the government might have to impose controls to contain price increases.[55]

Democrats were beginning to say the same thing publicly. The persistence of inflation in a slowing economy worried them, and many concluded that Washington had to reinforce its austerity program with direct intervention in wage- and price-setting. In November Walter Heller, who had chaired President Kennedy's CEA, declared that the administration had underestimated the strength of inflation and urged Nixon to convene a conference of labor and business leaders to work out "ground rules" for wages and prices. Arthur Okun endorsed this suggestion, as did the *New York Times*.[56] In early 1970 Representative Henry Reuss, a prominent Democrat, argued, "What the President should do immediately is to impose an across-the-board price freeze for at least six months, so that sound fiscal, monetary, incomes, and supply policies could take hold."[57]

Inflation concerned the Fed too, though its solution differed from that favored by most Democrats. The central bank had never been comfortable with the gradual approach to reducing inflation, and the failure of price increases to slow over the summer confirmed its doubts. President Nixon may have shied away from administering a shock to the economy, but the men at the Fed did not. They kept interest rates at the record high levels of June throughout the rest of 1969, drastically slowing growth in the money supply for the second half of the year. This policy was not popular. Burns objected, "We are pursuing a very highly restrictive monetary policy and one that which, if continued long, will prove very dangerous to our nation."[58] Milton Friedman, George Shultz, and Paul McCracken all issued comparable warnings, as did Keynesian economists. In a letter to the *New York Times*, Paul Samuelson, James Tobin, and two others argued, "We think the time has come for monetary policy to move towards less tightness."[59] Representative Wright Patman, the chairman of the House Banking Committee, raged, "The nation is being crushed under record-high interest rates."[60] Needless to say, all this alarmed the chief executive, who had never been a great supporter of the central bank. Nixon blamed it, in large part, for the 1960 recession that had cost him the presidential election that year, and he would not allow it to hurt him again.[61] He said, we "*must* loosen—must risk inflation," and he ordered his advisers to lobby the Federal Reserve for a more liberal policy.[62]

V

In October, the president took a step that would, he thought, eliminate disagreements with the Fed. He appointed Arthur Burns to succeed William McChesney Martin as chairman of the Federal Reserve when Martin retired in January. The announcement surprised many because Burns was not a financial economist—the operation of the Fed and banks had not been a subject of his research. But the choice was an obvious one for Nixon. He did not trust the central bank and wanted one of his own people in charge of it, and though Burns's stock had fallen over the year, the president retained confidence in his economic judgment. Although it caught some off balance, the appointment went over well. A respected student of the business cycle with considerable government experience, Burns had no trouble obtaining Senate confirmation—even Senator William Proxmire, who would become his most formidable congressional critic, greeted his appointment "with enthusiasm."[63] Burns himself was pleased to get the job. Working at the White House had been one frustration after another, and he was no doubt happy to get out.

Nixon made his expectations of Burns brutally clear: the economist was to reduce interest rates and avoid recession. When the new chairman took the oath of office in January 1970, the president remarked, "I have some very strong views on some of these economic matters and I can assure you that I will convey them privately and strongly to Dr. Burns. . . . I respect his independence. However, I hope that independently he will conclude that my views are the ones that should be followed." When Burns received a standing ovation, Nixon interjected, "You see, Dr. Burns, that is a standing vote of appreciation in advance for lower interest rates and more money."[64] In private the president was, if possible, blunter. He told Burns, "You see to it: no recession."[65]

3

Managing the System

✦

I

Like all effective Fed chairmen, Arthur Burns led by persuasion. The
Federal Reserve system is a vast, decentralized entity run by committees. It consists of twelve autonomous regional banks, each with its
own president and board of directors, as well as the seven-member
board of governors located in Washington, D.C.[1] In the mid-1970s
these together employed over twenty-five thousand people and had an
annual budget of more than $250 million. The Fed managed the sup-
ply of money and credit; regulated banks, bank holding companies,
and consumer credit;[2] handled the federal government's international
transactions; printed and destroyed currency; collected and published
a wide variety of economic statistics; provided financial services to
member banks;[3] and more. The regional banks actually carried out
policy, but the board of governors, which Burns chaired, set most of
the rules, such as guidelines for bank examinations. Monetary policy,

however, fell to the Open Market Committee (OMC), which met once a month to consider the economic outlook and to issue a directive that outlined the Fed's objectives and guided its actions over the next month. The seven governors and twelve bank presidents made up the OMC, although only five of the presidents could vote on decisions.[4] On both the board and the OMC, the chairman was but one of many and enjoyed only as much authority as the others allowed him.

Burns's accession changed the tone of the Fed. His predecessor, William McChesney Martin, who had led the central bank for nineteen years, was a master of building consensus. At OMC meetings under Martin, discussion went around the table in a formal pattern, with each member giving his assessment of the situation. The chairman always spoke last, and he usually managed to put together a directive for monetary policy on which all could agree. Burns was quite different. He abolished the formal "go-round," instead calling on members who wished to speak in the order in which they raised their hands. When he felt strongly about an issue, Burns would speak first so that he could shape discussion. Confident of his own judgment, he put a higher priority on getting the "right" policy—his own—than on achieving unanimity. He would occasionally have to make concessions to win a majority of the OMC or board of governors, but the chairman would surrender nothing to placate a minority. As a result, official dissent from the OMC's monthly decisions, rare under Martin, became common under his successor. Many disliked the change, believing that the chairman should defer more to the other governors and fearing that discord at the Fed could weaken its authority, but Burns made no apologies. "What is the Chairman supposed to be," he asked, "a purely passive regulator, a policeman who keeps order? Or a leader?"[5]

The new chairman dominated the Federal Reserve through talent and force of personality. As always, Burns worked very hard—twenty-hour days were not unknown—and this effort, coupled with his exceptional intelligence and encyclopedic knowledge of economic history, gave him an extremely good grasp of the issues. Nor was it easy to disagree with Burns. His confidence and sense of authority made him an intimidating figure—if he disagreed with someone, he would bluntly contradict them, saying "that's wrong," and giving his reasons.[6] But Burns could be subtle, too. As one governor said, "He's an extraordinary politician who knows how to get people to do things his way. He'll take the time. He'll work a guy over in his office. Then he'll drop in on the guy on Saturday, put his feet up on his desk and start talking about what the economy did in 1907 or 1917. He'll work and work at it. He's a very persuasive fellow."[7] This combination of intellectual toughness and persuasion, coupled with the deference that many governors automatically accorded the chairman, allowed Burns to dominate policy throughout his tenure at the Fed, but it inevitably created some resentment. "He was such a strong individual," one staff member noted, "that sometimes board members felt they were being overshadowed."[8]

Nevertheless, the OMC and the board of governors remained collegial bodies. Burns thought of himself as a professor leading a seminar, not as a general giving orders to the troops. As one associate noted, "Burns was not a man who thought he knew it all. He thought he knew most of it, but he would listen to a well-reasoned argument."[9] Thoughtful dissent earned the chairman's respect, even if he did not agree. In 1974, for example, Burns persuaded President Gerald R. Ford to promote Philip Coldwell to the Federal Reserve board, even though, as president of the Dallas Reserve Bank, Coldwell had often opposed the chairman's monetary policies. On the other hand, Burns had no tolerance for sloth or sloppy thinking and often dealt with them brutally. As one staff member put it, "When Burns didn't have respect for a person's mind, they had trouble."[10] For instance, he regularly humiliated one governor who failed to go through briefing materials. Burns would, at the beginning of a meeting, ask this man about some item on the agenda, and he, trying to conceal his ignorance, would inevitably say that he agreed with the staff's recommendation. The chairman would then begin to elaborate on the issue while asking for clarifications from his victim, who hemmed and hawed at every question. By the time Burns finished, the staff was choking down laughter and the poor man looked a complete fool.

The chairman also acted the demanding professor toward the Fed's staff. The people working for the board of governors at the highest levels were, for the most part, economists who provided information on the economy and how the central bank's policies might affect it. A prominent economist himself, Burns often understood their jobs as well as they did. Staff members making presentations to the board faced, as one said, "a particularly trying experience," because the chairman questioned them very closely.[11] Careless work earned an immediate reprimand. One governor recalled how, after a low-level staffer had finished a presentation, Burns asked him the source of his information. When he responded that he had spoken with a couple of officers in New York banks, lightning struck. "Young man," the chairman said, "the Board of Governors . . . does not operate on information based on the personal opinions of some junior officers of crack-brained New York banks, and don't you ever come back in here if that is the only basis of [the] information you have given us."[12]

Nevertheless, the staff generally appreciated Burns's interest in their work. As one said, "Burns was a good thing for me—he made me use what I had. . . . He was very constructive and helped me think more precisely and express myself more precisely."[13] The chairman generally worked through a few top members of the staff, and he often conducted floating seminars with them, calling them into his office to discuss matters or dropping in on them to ask questions.[14] Not all Fed chairmen have taken such an interest in the staff's work. Many people at the Fed also came to value Burns for his warm personality, discovering, as had his students at Rutgers and Columbia, the gracious qualities behind his intimidating professional manner. For instance, one high-ranking staffer recalls that the chairman never asked him to stay late to work after learning that he had young children who expected him home in the evenings.[15] Burns's gruff manner put off some members of the staff, but the large majority respected him, and quite a few counted him as a friend. For his part, Arthur Burns respected the Fed's economists. He listened attentively to their opinions and—the ultimate compliment—arranged for the appointment of two of them to the board of governors.[16]

Burns worked closely with the staff to improve the process of monetary policy, which had received much criticism in the late 1960s. Though he had some training in the subject, Chairman Martin was not an economist, and he was suspicious of the discipline because he thought it emphasized abstract calculation at the expense of practical experience. Accordingly, he conducted policy according to the "feel and tone" of financial markets, "leaning against the wind" to even out the swings in economic activity. The weakness of this approach began to tell in the late 1960s, when the Fed seemed to overreact to every development—squeezing hard in 1966, overstimulating the economy in 1967 and 1968, and then tightening up again in 1969. As *Business Week* noted in 1969, "Through most of the last few years, credit has been either too loose or too tight."[17]

New approaches to policy, however, required more sophisticated statistical tools. For instance, though few at the central bank accepted Milton Friedman's prescription for monetary policy, they increasingly agreed that the Fed should pay close attention to the money supply. Yet as Burns said, "We get into the habit of talking about the money supply as if all of us knew precisely what we are talking about. That isn't so."[18] Money had to be defined and measured—no easy task. Likewise, although by buying and selling government securities the Fed exercises considerable control over the supply and cost of credit in short-term money markets, the effect of conditions there upon the economy as a whole depends on a wide variety of factors such as business confidence, the prospects for prices, and the supply of key commodities. Without such information, policy could not move beyond the "feel and tone" of markets and "leaning against the wind."

Burns worked hard to improve the information available to the Fed. Martin had already started this process, but the new chairman was particularly well-equipped to carry through on it. Burns was, as one staff member said, a "bear for numbers" who could not imagine making policy without an extensive array of economic data.[19] He had made his reputation as a statistician, and few knew the subject better. The chairman not only encouraged the staff to refine its measures but also reviewed its work and suggested changes. He "pushed the staff to greater limits," one Fed economist said, encouraging them to develop ever-more sophisticated models and to constantly upgrade the information available to the board and the OMC.[20] He got Fed economists to replace anecdotal or impressionistic information with more objective yardsticks and persuaded the regional banks to put together monthly, comprehensive surveys of business conditions in their districts, replacing oral summaries given by bank presidents at OMC meetings—a change that not only improved available information but also shortened the meetings. Perhaps the most important effort came in the realm of statistical modeling. Despite some statements to the contrary, Burns considered economic models, which were used to project the future, a helpful if imperfect aid for policy, and in the 1970s, under his direction, the Fed's staff improved their model until most considered it the best available within the federal government. All these efforts created a basis for decisions that was, as a staff member said, "more systematically and objectively rooted."[21] The chairman, of course, made his own estimates about the economy, and these sometimes ran counter to those of the Fed's staff. But though he did not always follow the advice of the central bank's economists, he invariably took their opinions quite seriously. Paul Volcker thought it one of Burns's greatest accomplishments that "he developed and defended a professional staff that he saw, correctly, as second to none in Washington."[22]

Nevertheless, monetary policy remained an uncertain business. During most of Burns's tenure, the OMC oriented policy toward money supply growth. It would review the economic situation, go through the projections of its staff, and decide on a target or set of targets for monetary expansion that seemed best to promote its goals. But the central bank had no direct control over the money supply. Rather, it influenced the cost and availability of credit in short-term money markets by buying and selling treasury obligations, exercising the greatest control over the Fed funds rate, which banks charged each other for funds lodged with the Fed. Since banks had to keep a certain portion of their deposits with the central bank, this rate in a sense constituted the price of extending credit. But the link between the funds rate and changes in the money supply was quite uncertain, and the Fed usually just nudged rates up when expansion seemed above its target and reduced them when money growth fell short. Moreover, rapid changes in the financial system during the 1970s—the development of interest-bearing checking and money market accounts, among others—rendered the links between traditional measures of the money supply and economic activity ever more tenuous. The Fed had to work hard just to avoid falling behind.

As chairman, Burns also tried to rationalize the central bank's administration. Believing it unwieldy and time-consuming to refer questions of day-to-day operations to the board of governors, as had been the case under Martin, Burns persuaded the board to delegate power over most of these matters to him.[23] He also encouraged the Fed to rely more heavily on committees of two or three governors, which might review the budgets of the regional banks or oversee consumer credit regulations. Burns did not invent these bodies, but under him they took on greater responsibility. He liked them because they relieved him of duties he found uninteresting and made full use of the specialized talents of other governors, which the central bank might not otherwise tap.[24] For instance, Philip Coldwell, a former president of one of the Fed's regional banks, led the committee that reviewed those institutions' budgets. Philip Jackson, a mortgage banker, helped manage the central bank's regulation of consumer credit. These committees also made it easier for the Federal Reserve to deal with the heavy administrative burdens imposed on it in the late 1960s, when Congress gave it responsibility for regulating consumer credit and for new laws on bank holding companies.[25]

Burns attempted to control information coming out of the central bank. When the new chairman took over, he insisted that the Fed was "speaking with too many voices" and ordered governors to clear all speeches with him before delivering them.[26] When one governor, Andrew Brimmer, refused to mute his disagreement with the rest of the board over a bill before Congress, Burns, as Brimmer put it, "hit the ceiling."[27] He was so angry that he tried to persuade President Nixon to make Brimmer an ambassador just to get rid of him.[28] The chairman also mercilessly hunted down and plugged press leaks. When one staff member gave an internal report on consumer credit to a magazine, Burns called in the Federal Bureau of Investigation to track down the culprit and then forced him to resign.[29]

The chairman made one change at the Federal Reserve with which no one quarreled—he created a fine arts program, the only one at any central bank in the world. In 1970 the walls of the Fed's impressive granite headquarters on Constitution Avenue lacked even pictures. This condition horrified the new chairman, who had an interest in the arts, and he put together a committee to borrow paintings and sculpture for display at the central bank. Subsequent chairmen expanded the program to purchasing art. Mrs. Burns also contributed to the central bank's cultural activities by organizing poetry readings, which became a fixture in Washington circles.

II

Whereas Burns owed much of his authority within the central bank to his forceful personality and intellectual talents, his prestige outside of it depended more on his social and political dexterity. American politicians, who are constantly dealing with constituents and raising money, are almost inevitably gregarious creatures, and in Washington personal contacts count for a great deal. Arthur Burns flourished in this milieu—he knew and got along with almost everyone. He and Mrs. Burns, both of whom possessed considerable charm and stamina, went out several nights a week, often to more than one party a night. A Fed governor a quarter-century Burns's junior recalls how one evening, around eleven, as a party wound down, Arthur and Helen Burns asked him and his wife to join them and go to a ball in progress. The younger governor and his spouse were far too tired to attend, but the chairman and his wife went and danced until well into the morning.[30] Burns also joined a predominately gentile prayer group that consisted mainly of representatives and senators. As befits a central banker, he kept in close touch with commercial bankers, speaking, for instance, with John Meyer, the chairman of the Morgan Guarantee Trust, every Sunday on the telephone.[31] Burns was on good terms with almost all the finance ministers and central bankers of the other industrial democracies, and he even had close ties with the president of the Soviet central bank, whose wife he supplied with medicine unavailable in Moscow.[32] These contacts were not just a matter of political calculation—Burns valued them in and of themselves and kept them up until the end of his life. For their part, his many friends liked and respected the Fed chairman. "He had an enormous capacity for relationships," one associate noted, "and that's what made Burns powerful."[33]

One constant principle guided Burns's dealings with other members of the federal government: protect the central bank's autonomy. Though theoretically dependent on the Congress and the president, the Fed, as a practical matter, ran itself. Governors, once appointed to their fourteen-year terms, answered to no one but themselves, and the presidents of the regional banks owed allegiance to their own boards of directors. The central bank even set its own budget. Having over the years accumulated a huge portfolio of government securities purchased with funds that it, in effect, printed up, the Fed earned giant profits out of which it paid its own bills before turning over the rest to the treasury. Burns and most other members of the financial community thought this independence a virtue since it insulated monetary policy from the vagaries of politics, and they often likened the position of the Fed to that of the Supreme Court—an institution given special privileges to carry out an important but not always popular task that, in the Fed's case, consisted of defending the dollar's value. Many outside the financial realm, however, demanded greater accountability.

The chairman fiercely resisted anything that might reduce the Fed's independence. The central bank was his bureaucratic base, and anything that weakened it weakened him. Moreover, Burns's position within the Fed rested, in part, on his unconditional defense of the institution. As one associate noted, even though other members of the board occasionally resented his overbearing manner, "The saving grace was that everyone really felt that . . . Arthur Burns had the best interest of the institution at heart."[34] The chairman dared not risk the support of those whose help he needed to run the central bank by giving ground on an issue as basic as the Fed's independence. Finally, Burns accepted the basic justification for the central bank's autonomy. He suspected that most elected officials had little interest in the long-term economic consequences of their actions, being guided instead by immediate political considerations, and he thought it best to protect monetary policy from their influence.

Burns had the greatest difficulty dealing with Congress. Since the Constitution gives Congress the power to coin money, it has final authority over the central bank. But the two institutions often disagree. The Fed, dominated by bankers and economists, views its chief responsibility as the defense of the financial system and the value of the dollar, whereas the Congress, generally mindful of the next election and often influenced by populist thinking, usually wants rapid economic growth and low interest rates. This divergence creates tensions in the best of times, but in a turbulent period such as the 1970s, denunciations of the Fed become a staple of congressional rhetoric. The chairman did not always help matters. "Burns . . . thought he was entirely capable of deciding all by himself what the appropriate course of monetary policy was," one Fed staffer noted. "He didn't have much respect for the people in Congress, but he recognized that ultimately they had oversight responsibilities."[35]

On the one hand, Burns carefully cultivated representatives and senators, especially members of the banking committees. He invited new members of these two committees over to the Fed for breakfast individually and met with the senior members socially.[36] Nor was Burns above flattering legislators, provided that doing so cost him nothing. As Representative Henry Reuss (D-Wis.), long a critic of Burns, noted, "Even a preposterous statement by a Congressman wouldn't be the subject of his denouncing the statement. He would simply say . . . 'Congressman, you may well be proved right.' "[37] The chairman even managed to stay on good terms, personally if not politically, with Wright Patman (D-Tex.), the chairman of the House Banking Committee, whose hostility to the Fed was legendary.[38] This stance reflected a considerable change from Martin's tenure. Though many within the central bank considered Martin a more genial man than Burns, the former had few personal contacts with lawmakers, many of whom considered him something of a loner.[39] Burns, however, took great pains to create and maintain friendships with legislators. These contacts, along with the well-organized and carefully managed lobbying efforts of the Fed's staff, gave Burns and the central bank a strong base of support in the legislative branch.

On the other hand, the chairman aggressively defended the Fed in his frequent testimony before Congress. Burns put a tremendous amount of effort into these appearances, digesting huge amounts of briefing material and having his staff put together dozens of likely questions, for which he would prepare answers. By the time he went over to Capitol Hill, the chairman would be ready for confrontation—one person who saw him going into a hearing noticed that he was bouncing on the balls of his feet, "like a prizefighter going into the ring."[40] To these preparations and this energy one must add Burns's presence. When asked a question, one observer noted, "He would light about ten matches to light his pipe, and he would puff and puff and think and think, and give you the impression that this answer was coming out the depths of his soul"—even if what he said was fairly routine. At other times, Burns seemed to "speak in the voice of Old Testament Prophets."[41] "Testimony under Arthur Burns," one Fed staffer said, "was high drama."[42]

Despite these curmudgeonly displays of independence, however, Burns was always conscious of the political context in which he operated. He knew that Congress could, if it so desired, restrict or even eliminate the Fed's independence. Accordingly, the central bank could only go so far against prevailing political opinion without risking its valued autonomy. Though economic calculations always provided the starting point for policy, Burns sometimes modified his course for fear of the political consequences—though he never conceded as much until after he had left the Fed.[43]

To eliminate the need for such trimming, Burns sought to educate the public. The chairman was a natural pedagogue who, in his congressional testimony and numerous speeches, tried to explain and win over to his ideas not just bankers and economists but the whole class of educated people. He believed that a sound public understanding of economic realities was the best foundation for wise policy and did his best to construct such a foundation.

4

Stagflation

I

Arthur Burns went to the Fed in early 1970 with a mission. Economic indicators suggested to him that a recession was likely, in large part because the central bank's tight monetary policy had halted growth in the money supply and had kept interest rates at record highs throughout much of 1969. Production had contracted slightly over the previous months while unemployment had edged above 4 percent, and though these developments were not alarming in and of themselves, since they involved little hardship and promised to lower inflation, a continuation of this trend could do much damage. Because it would take time for any change in the central bank's posture to affect the economy, the new chairman thought that the Fed had to act immediately and reverse course.

The Federal Reserve had already started to move in Burns's direction. At its January meeting, the OMC had decided to aim for "modest growth in money and credit" and to reduce interest rates if necessary to achieve this goal.[1] Burns, however, considered this step insufficient, and his determination to ease policy further made his first OMC meeting, in February, one of the most raucous in the institution's history. Many members denied that a recession was in the offing and, pointing to continued inflation, opposed any easing of policy beyond that agreed to a month earlier. Burns met their objections head-on, telling one detractor that his arguments denying an impending downturn could have been made "in September 1929."[2] Although four members dissented, Burns got what he wanted. The OMC decided to aim to expand the money supply at a 5 percent rate over 1970, which would almost certainly push interest rates down. As a result of this policy the prime rate, which banks charged their best customers, declined from 8.5 percent in late 1969 to 5.25 percent in early 1971, while the money supply increased more than 6 percent over 1970.

This development delighted the administration. The president and his advisers feared that recession was likely and desired a looser monetary policy to prevent it. In April, Peter Flanigan, a member of the White House staff, noted approvingly, "Dr. Burns has created a monetary policy appropriate to the Administration's game plan."[3] Nevertheless, the president remained deeply suspicious of the Federal Reserve as an institution. At a meeting in March, Nixon declared, "Responsibility for a recession is now on the Fed," and he warned that he might "take the Fed on publicly" if it did not do enough to expand the money supply.[4]

The Fed's new policy won approval from the opposition, too. Democratic legislators, as well as many Republicans, had been denouncing high interest rates for months, and they considered the central bank's moves long overdue. The Democratic Policy Council, a group of economists associated with the Democratic Party, announced, "The time for an economic policy of severe restraint has long since passed."[5] This group drew on a consensus among Keynesian economists who agreed that, for the moment, recession was a greater danger than inflation. Gardner Ackley, leader of the Democratic Policy Council and CEA chairman under President Johnson, thought that because of the economic downturn, "the advance of prices will surely slow down."[6]

Unfortunately, inflation did not slow down. In 1970 consumer prices increased 5.7 percent, nearly as much as in 1969. Normally the central bank would have responded by raising interest rates, but economic weakness rendered such a course untenable. The economy was anemic throughout 1970, and in the fourth quarter, propelled downward by a long strike at General Motors, it contracted at a 4.1 percent annual rate. At the same time, unemployment increased to around 6 percent, the highest level in nine years.

Burns soon concluded that the nation faced an entirely new problem: stagflation, or simultaneous inflation and recession. At first, he thought it a transitory phenomenon caused by the slow adjustment of business and labor to the economic downturn. But as time passed without relief, he lost his confidence that conditions would improve of their own accord. The Fed chairman blamed the situation primarily on organized labor. Inflation in the late 1960s had cancelled out most of the wage gains achieved by workers, and they quite naturally wanted to make up the loss and hedge against future price hikes. Moreover, during the same years, construction and public service unions had won spectacular wage increases, setting a high standard to which others aspired. Changes in labor law in the late 1950s, which had made unions more responsive to their rank and file, left leaders far less able to moderate the demands of members, even if they so desired. The success of the government in preventing or moderating economic downturns also had made workers less willing to temper their demands in the face of a slowdown. Why, most reasoned, give up long-term benefits for fear of a recession that government would prevent? Finally, organized labor was generally strong enough to get what it wanted. In 1970, although profit margins would drop to the lowest level since 1945 and productivity would grow anemically, the Fed's staff estimated that labor unions would negotiate agreements calling for 9 to 10 percent annual wage hikes over the life of contracts. Under these conditions, higher labor costs would inevitably translate into higher prices, propelling a wage-price spiral in which rising wages pushed up prices, and price increases, in turn, led workers to push for higher wages. "At best, it will take an extended period of slack," one Fed staff assessment concluded, "to overcome underlying inflationary pressures."[7]

The Fed chairman was not alone in his reasoning about the problem. George Shultz and others in the administration agreed that excessive wage increases were the chief cause of stagflation.[8] Even James Tobin, who had belonged to Kennedy's CEA, admitted, "One of the sources of inflationary bias is the insensitivity of wage settlements in many labor markets to unemployment," and he concluded that, under certain conditions, "perhaps privileges granted unions under national legislation should be revokable."[9]

This wage-price spiral created special problems for the Fed. Most students of the subject agree that, over the long run, inflation is a monetary phenomenon—that is, prices cannot go up year after year unless the central bank creates the money to finance the increases.[10] But often the central bank believes that it has little alternative but to permit inflation. For instance, if it fails to expand the money supply to accommodate rising labor costs, then firms forced by higher wage bills to increase prices will lose sales and have to lay off workers. Of course, companies could accept lower profits instead of raising prices, but in the United States in 1970 profit margins were already quite thin, and so this was not a realistic option for most companies. In these circumstances, the Fed had to choose between allowing higher prices and creating more unemployment—an unattractive pair of options, to say the least.

To avoid this trap, Burns decided that Washington should adopt an "incomes policy," intervening directly in wage- and price-setting to keep the increase in labor costs in bounds. Such measures had apparently helped contain wages and prices during the Kennedy administration, and though Burns disliked them, he did not know what else to do. In May, the Fed chairman declared, "There may be a useful, albeit very modest, role for an incomes policy to play in shortening the period between suppression of excess demand and restoration of price stability."[11] Exactly what this step would entail he did not say, largely because he himself was not sure.

This announcement shocked many. Burns was, after all, a rock of economic orthodoxy who had strongly opposed Kennedy's wage-price guidelines, but this statement put him in the same camp as the Democratic Policy Council, which had called for "voluntary restraints on prices and wages."[12] Milton Friedman wrote Burns that his call for an incomes policy had "saddened, dismayed, and depressed me. I can only convey my emotional state by saying that . . . the word that keeps coming to mind is 'betrayed.' "[13] The administration, though less hysterical, interpreted Burns's statement as criticism of its consistent rejection of wage-price guidelines. Realizing this, the chairman did his best to reassure the president and those around him. The minutes of one meeting record, "Arthur fervently denied any such suggestion [criticism of administration policy], claiming the press misrepresented his statement. What he was referring to was merely a desire for you [Nixon] to make a general statement regarding the need for responsible action by both labor and management."[14]

The administration did make some gestures in Burns's direction. The president authorized a National Committee on Productivity, made up of representatives from business, organized labor, and the public sector, to meet and see how the country could, as Nixon put it, "achieve a balance between costs and productivity that will lead to more stable prices." He may have hoped that this body would hammer out an agreement on wage increases, but it never did so. The president also announced that the Council of Economic Advisers would issue "inflation alerts" to spotlight and put pressure on companies or unions whose actions seemed likely to make inflation worse. Finally, Nixon established a Regulations and Purchasing Review Board to change government policies, such as tariffs, that drove up prices.[15] Burns praised these actions, but they amounted to little.[16] Neither the National Committee on Productivity nor the Regulations and Purchasing Review Board did much, and companies and labor unions ignored the inflation alerts, which lacked sanctions. Indeed, Herbert Stein of the CEA has said that Nixon took these measures mainly to defuse calls for an incomes policy.[17]

II

Financial crisis monopolized Burns's attention during the late spring and early summer of 1970. Wall Street was in the midst of a terrible shakeout. The stock market dropped precipitously during the year as the speculative bubble built up in the late 1960s burst, wiping out approximately $100 billion of wealth. The crash threatened dozens of brokerage firms whose existence had already been rendered precarious by the giant administrative problems created in the previous decade by the explosion of business.[18] The board of governors played a limited role in this ongoing crisis, which the New York Stock Exchange, the New York Federal Reserve Bank, and the brokerage firms themselves resolved by merging troubled companies with healthy ones. But Burns knew what was going on and realized how fragile the financial system was at the moment.[19]

Events in May forced the board of governors itself to intervene in money markets. A large issue of bonds by the treasury coincided with the invasion of Cambodia by South Vietnamese and American forces. The latter event led to student protests across the country and created fears that the Vietnamese war was not winding down, as President Nixon had promised, but heating up. Frightened investors refused to absorb the government issue, and the Fed had to pump money into markets to save it and prevent a sudden run-up of interest rates.[20]

In June the nation faced its greatest financial shock in decades when the Penn Central Railroad collapsed. This event completely disrupted the commercial paper market and threatened many sound corporations with insolvency. Commercial paper consists of short-term, unsecured corporate IOUs, and the Penn Central defaulted on tens of millions of dollars worth of it. This failure destroyed confidence in all such notes, and investors refused to renew them as they matured. But many otherwise sound companies did not have the cash on hand to redeem their paper and faced bankruptcy if they could not obtain new loans. Fortunately, the Fed had had several days advance warning of the Penn Central debacle, and it had devised a plan. The central bank suspended interest rate ceilings on certificates of deposit (CDs) over $100,000, permitting banks to offer rates comparable to other investments and so allowing them to attract the funds removed from the commercial paper market. The banks then turned around and lent this money to corporations paying off commercial paper.[21] To tide the system over until this rechanneling was complete, the Federal Reserve informed member banks that they could borrow from its discount window, no questions asked, to finance customers paying off maturing commercial paper. In the week after the Penn Central collapse, $3 billion made its way into high denomination CDs, and banks borrowed $1 billion more than usual from the Federal Reserve.[22] Markets stabilized, but, as one Fed governor said, "It's not extreme to say we avoided another 1933."[23] The central bank had done its job and preserved financial stability. At the same time, though, financial crisis made fighting inflation with tight money an even less attractive option.

III

During the subsequent fall and winter, relations between Burns and the White House fell into an uncomfortable pattern. The chairman pressed the president for an incomes policy, and the administration pushed the Fed for a more liberal monetary policy. Each thoroughly annoyed the other while making limited gains.

It became clear during the fall that the economy was in recession, and this downturn coincided with off-year elections that disappointed the White House. The Republican Party failed to gain control of the Senate and lost a net of eleven governorships, and the president became convinced that he had to restore prosperity if for no other reason than to win reelection in 1972.

Nixon's opponents were zeroing in on economic weakness. In September, a group of Democratic economists charged that output was $40 billion below the economy's "potential" and demanded more government spending to close the "gap."[24] Gardner Ackley, who had chaired President Johnson's CEA, argued in the summer of 1970, "Voluntary methods—'guideposts,' 'incomes policies,' whatever you wish to call them—can confidentially be used to fight against inflation. . . . The rejection of these methods by the administration up to this point has cost us appreciably."[25] At roughly the same time, congressional Democrats attached to a defense bill a provision allowing the president to impose a ninety-day wage-price freeze. They assumed that Nixon would never actually use this power and that its existence would embarrass him.

In the administration's eyes, Burns was not helping matters. Monetary growth appeared sluggish at only a 3.8 percent annual rate over the first ten months of 1970, and Nixon's advisers believed that this was not enough to finance recovery.[26] Paul McCracken argued that the economy needed a big, one-time increase in money and credit. He thought that prosperity required average monetary growth of 5 percent a year over the long run, and since the increase had been very low in 1969, the CEA chairman thought that the Fed should aim for a 9 percent jump during 1970 to make up for the deficiency.[27]

Burns refused to give the White House what it wanted. Always ready to tell others what to do, the Fed chairman resented any incursion into his bailiwick, monetary policy. Nor did he think McCracken's 9 percent target prudent. The central bank had to steer a course between the twin dangers of inflation and recession, providing enough money to finance recovery but not enough to push prices up even faster. Though Burns clearly thought 3.8 percent growth insufficient, and argued in the OMC for more expansion, he aimed for a 6 rather than a 9 percent target because he considered the latter inflationary. Revisions of the money figures for the first ten months of the year, from 3.8 to 5.5 percent, strengthened Burns's position for the moment.[28] But because of weak demand for credit, the money supply expanded only slowly in the fourth quarter despite lower interest rates, disappointing the administration.

The Fed chairman's call for an incomes policy further alienated the White House. To Burns, the case seemed clear. Inflation remained high and, despite recession and very weak profits, labor unions were negotiating contracts that called for, on the average, 10.9 percent annual pay increases.[29] Burns reasoned that escalating wages had to be behind inflation and that Washington needed to slow their advance. Monetary policy could not do the job without making the recession worse and perhaps creating another financial crisis, whereas an incomes policy promised a relatively painless way to deal with the problem. The administration, however, viewed the situation in political rather than economic terms. Nixon remained opposed to government intervention in free markets; Democrats in Congress were attacking his reluctance to move on this front; and the chairman's talk of an incomes policy only added credibility to their line of attack. The belief that Burns had no concrete plan but had, as McCracken said, "proposed [an incomes policy] without anything in mind but the phrase," irritated the administration further.[30]

By November, Nixon was furious with the Fed chairman. He feared that Burns would end up playing the role that Treasury Secretary Robert Anderson and Fed Chairman Martin had played in 1960, when their restrictive policies had caused the recession that had cost him the presidency.[31] "He'll get it right in the chops," Nixon warned.

"Should I give the Fed a good kick now?" he asked one of his aides.[32] As always, the president was more restrained when dealing with Burns in person, but his displeasure was still evident.

In December the administration tried to break through this political and economic impasse. President Nixon delivered a speech before the National Association of Manufacturers (NAM) containing several new initiatives to restore prosperity and restrain prices. He would roll back recent hikes in oil prices by permitting more Canadian petroleum into the country and by allowing more offshore drilling.[33] Washington would combat exorbitant construction wages by trying to centralize the industry's bargaining process. Under arrangements then in force, union locals negotiated independently with contractors, and since the former were usually much stronger than the latter, they generally got what they wanted. By concentrating bargaining for the entire nation into one set of talks, the government would redress the balance of power and moderate pay increases. At the same time, the president proposed to increase government spending. He adopted the idea, suggested to him by George Shultz but long accepted among economists, of a budget balanced at full employment. The federal government would spend as much as it would collect in taxes if the economy was operating at its full potential. Since the country was in a recession, this meant that Washington would run a substantial deficit, but presumably not one that would make inflation worse. Finally, Nixon implied that, as a quid pro quo for his actions on the price front, the Fed would expand the money supply more rapidly. "I have been assured by Dr. Burns," he said, "that the independent Federal Reserve System will provide fully for the increasing monetary needs of the economy."[34]

Burns soon made it clear that no such deal existed. On December 7, just three days after Nixon's speech, he delivered a speech of his own at Pepperdine College in which he barely mentioned monetary policy but did give a specific outline of an incomes policy that went far beyond what the president had promised. The Fed chairman wanted Washington to 1) liberalize import restrictions on petroleum and raw materials; 2) enforce antitrust laws more vigorously; 3) expand training programs to increase the number of skilled workers; 4) set up a national system of local productivity councils to deal with problems such as union work rules that impaired efficiency; 5) organize computerized job banks to help the unemployed find jobs; 6) encourage investment by allowing firms larger tax deductions for the depreciation of equipment; 7) suspend the Davis-Bacon Act, which bound the government to pay the "prevailing" wage—the highest union rates—to workers on federal construction projects and so helped prop up the cost of construction labor; 8) modify the minimum wage so that companies could hire teenagers at a sub-minimum rate; 9) enact a national building code to supersede local codes that often precluded innovative, more efficient construction techniques; 10) require compulsory arbitration of labor disputes, "in industries that vitally involve public interest;" and 11) create a wage-price review board that, Burns said, "while lacking enforcement power, would have broad authority to investigate, advise, and recommend on price and wages changes."[35]

In early 1971 the Fed chairman refined his ideas for an incomes policy, promoting the wage-price review board to first place among them. He realized that his other proposals would take considerable time to affect price levels and that many attacked powerful interest groups, especially organized labor, on whom the Democratic majority in Congress depended heavily. The wage-price review board, however, promised to show results fairly quickly and seemed to gibe with the desires of congressional Democrats. As Burns described it in early 1971, "the review board would not have enforcement powers, but it could initiate inquiries into specific wage adjustments or into specific price adjustments. It could hold hearings on such developments at the request of the President or the Council of Economic Advisers. . . . I would expect that after several months such a wage and price review board would evolve, through a process akin to case law, guidelines for prices and wages."[36] He was sure that, if Nixon backed it up, labor unions and companies would abide by the board's decisions because of the "great moral authority of the President."[37] The Fed chairman did not believe that mandatory controls were either desirable or necessary but conceded, "There are times when in the dead hours of night, I find myself even thinking about a price and wage freeze. But when I rise and have a cup of coffee, I still don't want one."[38]

Congressional Democrats ate up this sort of talk. Along with President Nixon's inability to end the Vietnam War, they made economic weakness their main line of attack against the chief executive. They urged greater economic stimulus and an incomes policy, calculating that they could always outpromise Nixon on the first and that he would never agree to the second. Burns's call for direct government action to contain wages and prices lent credence to their position. Senator Hubert H. Humphrey (D-Minn.) told Burns, "I wish to join in expressing a very active interest in the administration establishing an incomes policy along the lines you have outlined."[39] Senator Proxmire declared, "The [Joint Economic] Committee has recommended the administration adopt a voluntary system of wage-price guideposts," and he added, "Such a program of voluntary wage-price guideposts was also recommended by Arthur Burns."[40] Obviously, this situation did not endear the Fed chairman to the president.

Nevertheless, as in 1970, President Nixon made gestures in Burns's direction despite his irritation with the chairman. In January he publicly denounced a 12 percent increase in steel prices and, in response, the steel companies limited the hike to 6 percent.[41] On February 23 he suspended the Davis-Bacon Act on the grounds that it was pushing up wages and prices in the construction industry. Within the next month the administration organized the Construction Industry Stabilization Committee, which consisted of representatives from contractors, organized labor, and the government and would set wages for all the building trades. Union leaders acquiesced to this move because it increased their hold on locals, which had strayed beyond their grasp in recent years.[42]

While making concessions to Burns on incomes policies, the administration tried, once again, to get the Fed to adjust monetary policy. Despite their new "full employment" budget rule, which allowed deficits in a slow economy, the president's advisers still considered the supply of money and credit the most important factor determining economic performance. In its annual report for 1971, the CEA projected that the output of goods and services in the United States over the next year would reach $1065 billion, an ambitious target most economists viewed skeptically—Paul Samuelson, for one, denounced the estimate as "poppycock."[43] Even the White House agreed that the country would only achieve its goal if the Federal Reserve expanded the money supply quite rapidly. Estimates within the administration of the rate of monetary growth necessary for success differed, but the lowest was 6 percent, and Nixon believed, "to get 6 percent the Fed has to aim at 8 percent."[44] Soon the White House was pressing the central bank very hard. One Fed staffer noted, "Wittingly or not, Administration witnesses before the Joint Economic Committee are leaving the impression that the Federal Reserve will bear a very large part of the responsibility for what happens to the economy in 1971."[45] White House economists bombarded the central bank with memos arguing for more rapid monetary growth, which the Fed strongly rebutted.[46] The administration also used press leaks about policy disagreements to put pressure on the Fed—a tactic that greatly annoyed Burns. "Resort to the press for purposes of prodding the Fed," he said, "strikes me as mischievous; it cannot possibly do any good. As one wise commentator recently put it, 'Business and consumer confidence are key needs for a recovery. They won't be built up by seeming policy inconsistencies at the top.' "[47] When Peter Flanigan and George Shultz went to speak to the Fed chairman about monetary policy, Burns let them know that he was not interested. "I'm going to tell the President," he said, "that if he ever again sends one of his assistants to talk to me on this question [monetary policy], I'll throw him out bodily."[48] Instead of worrying about the money supply, the chairman urged the administration to do more on the fiscal side, perhaps restoring the investment tax credit.

Despite his apparent intransigence, Burns encouraged the OMC to adopt a more liberal monetary policy, just as he had done in the fall of 1970. He told the Open Market Committee, "The shortfalls from the Committee's targets for the monetary aggregates that had occurred had caused difficulties for the system, and further shortfalls would cause continued difficulties."[49] He himself continued to think it wise to expand the money supply at about a 6 percent rate. In the first three months of 1971, the Fed forced interest rates down further, and the money supply expanded at an 8.3 percent annual rate. This rapid growth would, the central bank hoped, counterbalance the slow expansion in the fourth quarter of 1970, and once this "catch-up" was complete, monetary expansion would presumably slow to a pace more acceptable over the long term.

IV

While devising means to deal with stagflation, the central bank and its chairman also had to respond to the worst international economic crisis since World War II. The drop of interest rates during 1970 and early 1971 in the United States, coupled with increases in the cost of money abroad, led to a tremendous outflow of capital as investors sought higher yields. During the first nine months of 1970 alone, $5 billion left the country.[50] This movement was ominous. First, it meant that other governments were again acquiring dollars in large amounts and might, at some point, demand that the American government redeem them in gold—something the U.S. did not have the resources to do. Second, it demonstrated that, in the more than two years since the 1968 crisis, the United States had made little if any progress in resolving its balance-of-payments deficit.

The Federal Reserve proposed two measures that, it believed, would help stabilize the dollar. First, it wanted "a strong incomes policy that is designed to decelerate the wage-price spiral as quickly as possible."[51] This would reduce inflation, presumably making American exports more competitive and improving the trade balance. Such a program would also have beneficial psychological effects on currency markets. Second, the Fed took steps to prevent commercial banks from sending dollars abroad. When interest rates in the United States had skyrocketed in 1969, American banks had borrowed in foreign markets where money was cheaper.[52] This action effectively reduced dollar holdings overseas and improved the balance of payments. As rates in the U.S. declined, however, these banks had an incentive to borrow from American sources and to use that money to repay credits obtained in other countries, which were now more expensive. This reshuffling of debt could create a capital outflow of as much as $3 billion, and the Fed took measures to make sure it did not happen. It changed the rules on the reserves that banks had to hold against foreign balances, making such borrowing more attractive, and it encouraged the treasury and the Export-Import Bank to sell notes in London to retrieve some of the money flowing abroad.[53]

Nevertheless, Burns feared that these measures would not suffice. Continued deficits were sapping confidence in the greenback, and only drastic actions, such as much higher interest rates and extreme fiscal austerity, could be certain of restoring its status. But President Nixon refused to "let concern for the balance of payments wreck our domestic economy."[54] Somewhat reluctantly, Burns and most others at the Fed agreed. Though they valued a stable dollar, they did not think its preservation worth putting the economy through the wringer, and they knew that such action would not receive public support. In December 1970, the chairman told President Nixon that he might well have to sever the link between the dollar and gold, but that the time to act was not yet.[55]

The crisis gathered steam throughout the spring as more and more people traded dollars for Swiss francs, Dutch guilders, Austrian schillings, and especially West German deutschmarks. In early April the Fed increased interest rates slightly to stem the outflow of money—something it almost never does.[56] This action was not enough. In April the Germans had to purchase $3 billion to keep the deutschmark stable, and on May 4 they had to buy another $1 billion. Finally, in the first hour of trading on May 5, they had to purchase yet another $1 billion. Unwilling to accept any more greenbacks, the Germans and Dutch stopped intervening in currency markets, instead "floating" their currencies, or allowing them to find their own value in the marketplace. At the same time, the Swiss and Austrians revalued their currencies by 7.1 and 5 percent, respectively.[57] These events unsettled financial centers around the globe, and the Fed had to inject $1.3 billion into American money markets to restore calm.[58]

People in the American government reacted very differently to these events. CEA Chairman McCracken told the president that the crisis proved "a system that combines rigidly fixed exchange rates with free trade and capital movements appears to be unworkable. . . . There seem to be two alternatives—either more extensive use of direct [capital] controls to support a system of fixed exchange rates or an internationally agreed upon system of great flexibility." Believing that strict capital controls "would be highly burdensome to our trade and investment interests," he urged Nixon to open negotiations for international reforms that would provide for more flexible exchange rates.[59] Herbert Stein, a member of the council, took another view. "The changes in European currencies this weekend," he said, "represent a major success for our international economic policy."[60] Washington had wanted other countries to revalue their currencies, and they had. This view found support in the Congress. Most legislators who paid attention to such issues—a relatively small club dominated by Representative Henry Reuss and Senator Jacob Javits (R-N.Y.)—thought the dollar overvalued and welcomed any change that remedied the problem. They agreed with economist Paul Samuelson when he called Germany's decision to float the deutschmark "a step in the right direction."[61] In contrast, the president of the New York Fed, Alfred Hayes, considered the situation disastrous. He declared, "No financial surgery in the form of a devaluation of the dollar, bloc revaluations of foreign currencies, or a U.S. gold embargo could be performed without shattering effects on U.S. business activity, employment, foreign trade, and the functioning of the entire international financial system," and he spoke of the "appalling risks" associated with change.[62] Hayes wanted Washington to fight to the last to defend the greenback.

Burns had a more balanced view. He thought that the U.S. might very well have to sever the link between the dollar and gold but was in no rush to do so. As he told the president in May, "If things come to the pass of a U.S. suspension of gold sales and purchases, we should do all we can—both substantively and cosmetically—to make it appear that other governments have forced the action on us. . . . The opposite tack—initiating suspension without being forced to it by the actions of others—would probably leave us in a much weaker bargaining position for post-suspension negotiations. . . . It is therefore desirable to pay out gold and other reserves in substantial amounts— perhaps two billion dollars—*before* a suspension."[63] After all, a decision to end the link between the dollar and gold, however momentous in and of itself, would also put into motion talks to establish a new monetary regime, and the government had to plan for these.

V

During the summer of 1971, on top of international difficulties, inflation, and disagreements with the administration over monetary policy, Burns faced the possibility of yet another domestic financial crisis. He feared that the Lockheed Aircraft Company would fail—the second major corporation to go under in two years. Lockheed had invested heavily to develop a commercial jetliner, the Tristar L-1011, but in February 1971 Rolls-Royce PLC of Great Britain, which had agreed to build engines for the airplane, declared bankruptcy. The British government came to Rolls-Royce's aid, but because cost overruns associated with the L-1011 project had forced the company under in the first place, Whitehall refused to advance money to finish the engine unless Lockheed agreed to share the cost, which it could not afford to do. The American firm, however, had already sunk so much money into the Tristar that, if it could not produce and sell the plane, it, too, would go out of business. Lockheed went to Washington, hat in hand, to ask for loan guarantees from the federal government to save itself.[64]

Burns supported the Lockheed bailout. The chairman believed that the failure of the aerospace firm might contribute to the bankruptcy of Trans World Airways and Eastern Airlines, which had both made substantial deposits for the delivery of L-1011s, as well as Avco, a major subcontractor for the project. His staff estimated that the cancellation of the Tristar would cost sixty thousand jobs.[65] Nor could anyone guess what such a corporate bankruptcy would to do to financial markets already shaken by international crisis. But the Fed chairman's thinking went beyond the immediate problem. For him, the first object of economic policy was to preserve stability, and as he noted— the Penn Central debacle no doubt in mind—"We have nothing that can prevent a national emergency, a serious injury to the national economy, from a failure of a well-established, credit-worthy firm."[66] Burns proposed a permanent $2 billion bailout fund, to be administered by the Federal Reserve chairman, treasury secretary, and commerce secretary, that could issue loan guarantees of up to $250 million to companies in trouble, provided that they had realistic plans to save themselves. The Fed Chairman had conceived this idea in the months following the Penn Central crisis, but the Lockheed episode gave him a chance to turn it into law.[67] He persuaded Democratic Senator John Sparkman of Alabama, a good friend and chairman of the Senate Banking Committee, to introduce the measure.[68]

The Lockheed bailout generated fierce contention. Many Democrats opposed giving money to a large corporation, particularly one like Lockheed that was a huge defense contractor closely linked to the military, but others feared the loss of jobs its bankruptcy would entail. Likewise, many Republicans opposed such direct government intervention in the economy, while others feared that the collapse of Lockheed would impair the nation's defense capability. The administration supported the rescue plan, fearing damage to both the economy and the military from the failure of Lockheed, but though its stance won over some Republicans, it reinforced the doubts of many Democrats. Finally, the presence of Lockheed plants in lawmakers' districts had an important influence on many votes.[69]

After long debate and a series of very close votes, Congress enacted, in August, a $250 million loan guarantee for Lockheed.[70] Burns's more ambitious proposal had been too sweeping for the legislative branch, and though the company survived, the nation still lacked a mechanism to protect itself from the side effects of the bankruptcy of a large corporation caught in financial straits.

The aftermath of the Lockheed bailout gave Burns second thoughts about the principle that he had advanced. The Fed chairman, along with the treasury and commerce secretaries, oversaw the loan guarantees, and he became unhappy with Lockheed, which missed its timetable, fell short of performance goals, and became involved in a scandal that, among other things, brought down the Japanese government.[71] Burns would be less enthusiastic about such rescue operations in the future.

VI

As Arthur Burns surveyed the economic scene in the summer of 1971, he saw little encouraging. Recovery from the recession had been slow. The economy had expanded quite rapidly in the first quarter, but in the second quarter it had grown at a sluggish 2.9 percent, with no improvement in sight. Unemployment was stuck at around 6 percent. Inflation seemed lower, with consumer prices up at only a 3.8 percent annual rate between December 1970 and August 1971, but this progress was illusory. Wholesale prices had increased at a 5.2 percent rate over the same period, and this jump would inevitably feed back into the prices consumers paid. In any event, much of the improvement in consumer prices reflected a drop in home mortgage rates, a one-time gain that would not continue.[72] Most important, wages continued their inexorable climb. In the first half of 1971, telephone workers won a 33 percent raise over three years and a cost of living adjustment; postal workers between 7 and 9 percent annual increases; copper workers a 31 percent raise over three years and a cost of living adjustment; one railroad union a 42 percent increase over 42 months; and steelworkers a 31 percent raise over three years and a cost of living adjustment.[73] With profit margins very narrow and productivity gains weak, these increases would inevitably translate into higher prices. The international scene looked no more hopeful. In June, a subcommittee of Congress's Joint Economic Committee issued a report declaring that the link between the dollar and gold was no longer realistic and that Washington should refuse to redeem greenbacks with the precious metal. Though an accurate analysis, it further weakened confidence in the American currency. Throughout the summer, the United States ran a substantial trade deficit for the first time in decades, further undermining the dollar. Negotiations to revamp the world's financial system produced no tangible results. In August, CEA Chairman McCracken warned the president that other central banks had taken in $21 billion over the previous months and that "holdings of dollars abroad are growing at an unsustainable rate."[74]

Nor did monetary policy offer Burns much room to maneuver. After a rapid 8.3 percent annual rate increase in the money supply during the first quarter, the Fed had expected growth to slow. Instead, money expanded at a 10.6 percent rate in the second quarter—much faster than anyone at the central bank, including Burns, considered prudent. With a sluggish economy and in the midst of an international crisis that had shaken markets, the Fed was loathe to push up interest rates. Nevertheless, it decided that it had to slow monetary growth, and it took steps that drove the prime rate from 5.25 percent in March to 6 percent in July. Still, to achieve an acceptable rate of money growth for all of 1971, the central bank would have to keep expansion at a very low level for the rest of the year—no mean feat, either economically or politically.

Burns considered a strong incomes policy the only solution to the nation's economic problems. The continued advance of wages was pushing up prices while, at the same time, cutting profit margins to the bone. Weak profits, the chairman thought, discouraged investment, a prerequisite for vigorous recovery. Uncertainty about prices also discouraged consumers, who could not know if the next paycheck would suffice to cover necessities. In response, Burns believed, they saved a higher percentage of their income to build up a cushion against adversity, reducing the demand for goods and services.[75]

Though the chairman's call for an incomes policy seemed to put him in the same camp as Keynesian economists, his thinking actually challenged one of their basic assumptions. Keynesians believed that a tradeoff existed between inflation and unemployment—that is, reducing one required accepting an increase in the other. They supported an incomes policy because it offered to improve that tradeoff, containing prices while the government stimulated production. Burns, however, used a completely different formula. To his mind, inflation caused unemployment, at least in the long run, and an incomes policy would not only keep prices down but, in doing so, spur recovery. Though no one remarked on it at the time, in later years this distinction would take on great importance.

Burns expressed his concerns about the economy bluntly. In July he told a congressional committee, "The rules of economics are not working the way they used to. Despite extensive unemployment in our country, wage rate increases have not moderated. Despite much idle industrial capacity, commodity prices continue to rise rapidly." Burns saw "little evidence as yet of any material strengthening in consumer or business confidence. . . . Greater success in the battle against inflation is probably the most important single prerequisite of more rapid and enduring economic expansion." "I wish," he said, "I could report that we are making substantial progress in dampening the inflationary spiral. I cannot do so."[76]

As had been the case all year, the administration's Democratic opponents used Burns's arguments to their advantage. For instance, Senator Proxmire declared, "The administration's do-nothing attitude with respect to incomes policy is a costly mistake. . . . Dr. Burns's testimony . . . makes the administration's position on incomes policy inexcusable." Editorial pages across the country echoed these calls. The *Des Moines Register* said that Burns "has again recommended that stronger action is needed to stop inflation, and he favors a wage-price review board to establish an 'incomes policy.' " It then noted Nixon's opposition to such a move and continued, "It is hard to see how the Administration can reduce unemployment without spurring inflation to a new high rate, unless it is willing to use its power in some way to check soaring wage rates."[77] Even a solidly Republican paper like the *Baltimore Sun*, though unwilling to endorse an incomes policy as such, urged the president to do something about spiraling wages.[78] The Congress seemed poised to demand action. Both Senator Proxmire and Senator Edward Brooke, a Republican (from Massachusetts), had introduced bills requiring the president to take direct action to contain wages and prices, and sentiment was such that these measures had a good chance of passage.[79]

The situation infuriated the president, and he focused his anger on the Fed chairman. The failure of the economy to improve frustrated him, and he did not think Burns was helping. "A major reason for this lack of [business] confidence," one of his aides wrote, "is the undermining of present policies by authoritative voices which have, for six months, contended that the Administration's program is not working."[80] Nor did Nixon appreciate it when wits, inspired by the Fed chairman's wide-ranging prescriptions for policy, quipped, "Nixon fiddles while Burns roams."[81] Perhaps worst of all, the president, who was a suspicious man, thought Burns was helping his enemies. After all, an incomes policy was the rallying point for Democrats attacking the administration's economic program. Moreover, the Fed's monetary policies, of which the White House disapproved, had found defenders among the likes of Walter Heller, President Kennedy's CEA chairman, who said that the central bank had "brought water to the horse [by expanding the money supply]. Now it is up to Mr. Nixon to make him drink."[82]

Nixon unleashed one of his cronies, Charles Colson, against Burns. Colson spread rumors that Burns had asked for a 50 percent raise even while complaining about the wage hikes won by labor unions. This story was false. The Office of Management and Budget (OMB) had recommended a $20,000 pay hike for the Fed chairman, to $62,000 from $42,000, to bring his income into line with that of other central bank presidents, but Burns had rejected it. The Fed chairman thought it inappropriate to accept a raise when calling for wage restraint. The president's role in this attack is unclear. Some, such as Nixon's speechwriter William Safire, thought Colson acted without instructions, but this explanation seems unlikely. As John Ehrlichman said, "Colson did what he was told—that was the problem."[83] It may be that the president concocted this scheme as a way to blow off steam, not thinking that his aide would actually carry through on it.

This slander infuriated Burns, and the refusal of White House spokesman Ronald Ziegler to comment on it made him angrier still.

He was sensitive about anything that reflected on his integrity and indicated to Safire, who took it upon himself to negotiate a settlement, that "he will have to live with that smear, and he is personally deeply offended." "I hope Colson can sleep at nights," the chairman said.[84]

The administration soon found that it had stirred up more trouble than it could handle. Burns enjoyed a good reputation among journalists, who accepted his denials and attributed the rumors to White House malice. The prospect of a split between the administration and the Fed alarmed Wall Street bankers, most of whom supported Nixon, and they let the administration know that they blamed it for the rift. Finally, Burns seems to have persuaded Senator Sparkman to hold hearings on his competence as a central banker, hearings that would almost certainly have led to a resounding vote of confidence.[85]

Faced with such opposition, the president backed down. Nixon declared at a press conference, "Arthur Burns . . . has taken a very unfair shot," and he declared that he and the Fed chief more or less agreed on the proper course for economic policy. Burns was delighted. "It warmed my heart," he said of the announcement. "I haven't been so deeply moved in years. . . . This just proves what a decent and warm man the President is."[86]

Despite this ugly altercation, the administration was moving toward the sort of program Burns desired. Ideas for an incomes policy had been bouncing around the White House for several months. In February, Paul McCracken had suggested that the president create a special trade court that would enforce rules against price or wage increases "excessive in relation to market or economic conditions."[87] Herbert Stein urged Nixon to adopt either McCracken's idea or Burns's wage-price review board.[88] Treasury Secretary John Connally, a former Democratic governor of Texas appointed by Nixon in early 1971, finally forced the issue. Throughout the spring and summer, he seemed to hang tough on economic policy. In June, for example, he propounded the "four nos": no wage-price freeze, no wage-price review board, no tax cuts, and no new spending. His thoughts, however, did not accord with his words. He became convinced that the administration had to do something about inflation or Congress would take matters into its own hands, and by early August Connally had persuaded the president to impose a wage-price freeze. "I'm not sure this program will work," he said, "but I *am* sure than anything less will not work." The secretary, Nixon, and OMB director George Shultz decided to impose the freeze in early 1972, fearing that if they did so earlier the frictions inevitably generated by controls would make themselves felt before the presidential election.[89]

The British government, however, accelerated the timetable. On August 12, London asked the United States to "cover," or guarantee the value of, $750 million that it held.[90] The message was garbled, however, and the treasury believed that the British wanted Washington to cover all $3 billion in the Bank of England. If the U.S. acquiesced, it would likely have touched off a scramble by other countries to get the American government either to guarantee their dollar holdings or to convert them into gold. At best, this would saddle the treasury with huge losses should the United States decide to devalue the greenback. At worst, it would wipe out Washington's gold stock.

President Nixon called all of his top economic advisers to Camp David, the presidential retreat in the Maryland mountains, to hammer out a response. Present were John Connally, Paul Volcker, George Shultz, Paul McCracken, Herbert Stein, Peter G. Peterson (Nixon's personal assistant on international economic affairs), H. R. Haldeman, John Ehrlichman, William Safire, and Arthur Burns. As always, Nixon, with an eye toward the "big play," wanted not merely to overcome the immediate hurdle but to put together a new program that would conquer stagflation. Over the weekend at Camp David, the president decided to impose a ninety-day wage-price freeze "to break the vicious circle of spiraling prices and costs."[91] He also agreed to ask Congress to reinstitute the investment tax credit, repeal the excise tax on automobiles, and expand the personal income tax deduction, all of which would stimulate the economy. At the same time, Nixon took steps to reduce spending so that these cuts would not make the federal deficit any worse. Everyone at Camp David supported these decisions, believing they would go a long way toward curing the nation's economic ills.

Unanimity did not exist, however, on the international front, the ostensible reason for the meeting. All agreed that the United States should impose a 10 percent tax on imports to improve its trade balance and, more important, to provide a bargaining chip in future currency negotiations. Most in attendance also wanted to "close the gold window"—that is, to refuse to redeem dollars in gold and to float the greenback in the marketplace. Paul Volcker said, "I hate to do this, to close the window. All my life I have defended [fixed] exchange rates, but I think it's needed." Burns, however, dissented. He told Nixon, "You will be doing something dramatic—a wage and price policy, a border tax. You will order a cutback in government spending. These major actions will electrify the world. The gold outflow will cease. If I'm wrong, you can close the window later." He warned that, by ending gold convertibility, "we are releasing forces that we need not release." Instead of doing this, Burns thought, "Paul Volcker should go ahead and start negotiations with other countries on a realignment of currencies." By delaying suspension as long as possible, the Fed chairman hoped to gain international good will—a commodity he valued more than gold and without which the construction of a new world financial order would be very difficult. Connally, for one, was skeptical. "We'll go broke getting their [European and Japanese] good will," he warned. But Burns saw no alternative to cooperation. "They're powerful," he said. "They're proud, just as we are."[92]

The president decided against Burns. Paul Volcker convinced him that suspension was inevitable and that delay would only create financial chaos. Perhaps more important, Nixon realized that if he announced the move as part of a new economic package, he would appear to be acting decisively to take charge of the crisis, making, as Volcker put it, "the devaluation of the dollar into a political triumph, which was no mean feat."[93] If Nixon took the same action in isolation, in response to a run on the dollar, he would seem a slave to events.[94]

Burns and Nixon staged a reconciliation at Camp David. Once the president had made up his mind on gold suspension, Burns "told the President he would have my wholehearted support."[95] Nixon, for his part, did his best to win over the Fed chairman. During a telephone conversation with speechwriter Safire, he said, "You're sitting next to Arthur? You know, Arthur is a fine man. Really, a fine man. Tell him I said that."[96]

On the whole, the weekend at Camp David was a triumph for Burns. Although defeated on international matters, he conceded that on these "I didn't feel so cocky—nobody can be sure."[97] On the domestic side, Burns got everything he wanted—an incomes policy and tax cuts to stimulate the economy. Almost as important, the Fed chairman had reestablished himself as a member of the president's inner circle, at least on economic policy. Throughout his presidency, Nixon's feelings toward Burns gravitated between respect and frustration, but for the moment, respect predominated.

How much credit (or blame) does Burns deserve for Nixon's new policy, especially the decision to impose a wage-price freeze? Certainly, he helped create an atmosphere in which it was difficult for the president to resist such measures. As Herbert Stein said, "Everybody else, every editorial writer in the country, could say, 'Even conservative Arthur Burns, friend of the President, is in favor of an incomes policy, so how can the President say that it's not a good thing to do?' "[98] But the Fed chairman's prescription was compelling largely because it seemed to describe accurately the problems at hand. The nation was caught in a wage-price spiral that was fueling inflation and retarding recovery, and an incomes policy seemed the easiest solution. Burns's was hardly a voice in the wilderness—the New York Chamber of Commerce, David Rockefeller (president of the Chase Manhattan Bank and brother of New York's Republican Governor Nelson Rockefeller), and William McChesney Martin were all saying the same thing.[99] The surprise, one might argue, is not that Nixon imposed a wage-price freeze but that he held out against it as long as he did. As Burns himself said, "It was the logic of events that decided."[100]

5

New Arrangements

I

President Nixon's new economic policy transformed the political land-scape. Arthur Burns, recently an administration pariah, became one of the White House's chief allies, throwing his considerable weight behind its program. Charles Colson, who had been busy slandering the chair-man just a few weeks earlier, told Nixon, "Arthur Burns is a major asset."[1] For his part, the Fed chairman was eager to be at the center of action. He did turn down Nixon's offer of membership in the Cost of Living Council (COLC), a group of department heads and White House staffers that oversaw the freeze, because he thought it inappropriate for the chief of the independent central bank to serve on such a body. But Burns agreed to become an "adviser" to the council, and as a practical matter he took part in all major decisions.[2] The Fed chairman also attended meetings between Nixon and business and labor leaders that the White House convened to secure support for the new policy.[3]

Nixon's program also threw his Democatic opponents into confusion. They had planned to make the economy's poor performance their chief issue in the upcoming presidential campaign, but now the chief executive had appropriated most of their ideas. Herbert Stein, who succeeded McCracken as CEA chairman at year-end, exaggerated only slightly when he said, "There is no serious, coherent policy that is an alternative to the one the administration has initiated."[4] The Democrats might have done things a little differently, perhaps aiming tax cuts more at individuals rather than at business, but the administration's plan met most of their demands. Senate majority leader Mike Mansfield (D-Mont.) said, "I'm delighted," by the president's new policy. Arthur Okun called it "a leap forward into reality." Paul Samuelson and Senator Proxmire also expressed support for most of the program's provisions.[5] Should the economy falter again, the Democrats would no doubt return to the offensive, but for the moment Nixon had neutralized them.

The White House had little choice about its course of action when the freeze expired. Most people in the administration had been inclined to replace it with something like Burns's wage-price review board, but the ceiling on wages and prices had proved both successful in slowing inflation and very popular. During the ninety days it lasted, consumer prices had increased at a mere 1.6 percent annual rate and wages at 0.6 percent, while wholesale prices had actually declined a bit.[6] The administration could hardly abandon a program with such a record and concluded that it had to continue some sort of mandatory controls.

Herbert Stein drew up the plans. A seven-member Price Commission, appointed by the president, would regulate what companies could charge for goods and services. Restrictions on pay, however, posed a special problem. Union officials believed—not without reason—that Nixon had imposed controls mainly to contain wages, and they demanded a say in decisions about compensation. Drawing on a precedent set during the Second World War, Stein put together a "tripartite" Pay Board (Burns suggested the name), consisting of five representatives from labor, five from business, and five from the public, all fifteen of whom the president would appoint. This body would set rules for wages and review union contracts. The COLC stood over both the Price Commission and Pay Board, but it would avoid interfering in their day-to-day operations.

Arthur Burns led a third arm of the structure, the Committee on Interest and Dividends (CID). In addition to Burns, this body included the secretaries of the departments of the Treasury, Commerce, and Housing and Urban Development, as well as the chairmen of the Federal Home Loan Bank Board and the Federal Deposit Insurance Corporation.[7] The central bank's staff, however, handled the CID's paperwork, and Burns thoroughly dominated the committee.[8] After the first few months, the other members started sending deputies to the meetings in their steads.

Burns did not want to control interest rates. As the minutes of one early CID meeting record, "Chairman Burns explained that interest rates are fundamentally different from wages or commodity prices. . . . Ceilings were necessary for wages and prices because competition was working poorly—in some cases, not at all. By contrast, the money markets are highly competitive. . . . It is the Committee's function to improve the economy; any attempt to interfere with the workings of the money and capital markets would in all likelihood have the exact opposite effect and lead to nothing but trouble."[9] But many in Congress saw things differently, reasoning that interest rates should face the same restrictions as wages and prices. Representative Wright Patman, chairman of the House Banking Committee, argued, "If controls are needed on the wages of workers and the prices of businessmen, then surely the prices—interest rates—charged by banks also need to be controlled."[10] Burns hoped that by its existence the CID would "stave off attempts to establish such controls."[11]

The committee avoided setting hard and fast rules for interest rates. Burns argued before Congress that such edicts would be harmful and that, as inflation declined, so too would long-term rates. The gradual drop in the cost of money over the six months following the freeze strengthened his hand. The Fed chairman did, however, promise that the CID would keep a close eye on "administered" rates—those set by banks and other financial institutions—to make sure that they reflected money market conditions. He further assured lawmakers that he would pay especially close attention to "those interest rates that most directly affect the American family," such as the cost of home mortgages and consumer credit.[12]

Many at the Fed thought that Burns should never have become involved with the CID. They feared that sooner or later he would find himself whipsawed between the exigencies of monetary policy, which might dictate higher interest rates, and the logic of the controls program, which demanded stability.[13] Burns apparently shared these concerns, but he worried that if he did not take the job, the CID would fall into the hands of someone like John Connally, who might use it to interfere with monetary policy.[14] Besides, if monetary policy and controls did find themselves working at cross-purposes, it was best to have one person with responsibility to resolve the conflict.

Though it steered clear of interest rates, the CID did impose strict limits on dividends. It declared that a company could not increase its payout more than 4 percent over the next year, with either 1969, 1970, or 1971 as the base—whichever was highest. Alternatively, a firm could give to shareholders one quarter of its earnings for 1971. Technically, the committee had no way to enforce its rules, but few companies violated them, and Burns bullied most of these back into line.

The CID imposed these guidelines for dividends, Burns said, to "set an example for the Pay Board."[15] The Fed chairman estimated that, to reduce inflation to the administration's goal of 2 to 3 percent for 1972, the government would have to limit pay increases to 3.5 to 4.5 percent.[16] By getting in the first blow and imposing a 4 percent standard on dividends, the Fed chairman hoped to influence the Pay Board's deliberations about wages.[17] The major labor unions, however, refused to heed Burns's precedent. "Just say an AFL-CIO official laughed," one of that body's spokesmen said.[18]

Burns viewed the Pay Board and the Price Commission quite differently. He believed the object of controls was to slow wage increases, which he blamed for the stubborn wage-price spiral, and he supported restrictions on prices mainly to reconcile workers to limits on pay. Indeed, Burns believed that for the moment prices needed to go up faster than labor costs. He thought of profits as the engine driving investment and innovation, and after 1969 rapid wage increases had cut earnings to the bone.[19] "There is a great need in our country," Burns said, "to improve the profitability of industry. Profits have sunk to a dangerously low level in our economy. If we are going to have a growing number of jobs, particularly good jobs, business must be profitable."[20] The Fed chairman often met with the Price Commission to encourage it to be as liberal as possible with companies, while he urged the Pay Board to take a hard line.[21]

The Pay Board, however, seemed to have different ideas. In November 1971 it voted to limit wage hikes over the next year to 5.5 percent and benefit increases to 0.7 percent of total compensation, for a total of 6.2 percent. Burns thought this rule, if anything, on the generous side, but the labor members dissented from it, preferring an even higher standard. The board also decided not to apply its yardstick to contracts already under negotiation when the president had imposed the wage-price freeze, examining them on a case-by-case basis, and the union representatives were determined to be very liberal with these pacts. When the first such agreement, which granted coal miners a 13.4 percent wage hike in the first year, came up for consideration, the labor and business members of the Pay Board approved it over the objections of the public members. Labor and management had negotiated this contract only after a long strike during which consumers had drawn down coal stocks, and the business contingent feared that altering it would set off a new walkout that would seriously hurt the economy. Roughly similar considerations spurred business representatives to support labor members and approve a contract giving railway signalmen a 37 percent pay increase over 43 months.[22]

These developments alarmed Burns. He warned Congress in very blunt terms that the gains made against inflation would not last unless wage increases slowed. "It is of great importance," he said, "that the Pay Board resist pressures to reach compromises in specific cases that threaten to undermine its overall objective."[23] Two journalists reported that, in early 1972, Burns actually called the business members of the Pay Board over to the Fed, both individually and as a group, to lecture them about the need for a tougher line.[24]

The Fed chairman's stance pleased neither organized labor nor the administration. Like most other economic actors, unions are inclined to take what they can, and they naturally resent government-imposed limits on their gains. But Burns did more than that—he challenged labor's vision of itself. He refused to concede any moral superiority to organized labor and argued strenuously and in a sophisticated fashion that unions were working against the best interest of the nation—not an uncommon thought, but one rarely expressed so bluntly outside the halls of the National Association of Manufacturers. Burns had never been a favorite of George Meany, the head of the powerful AFL-CIO and a firm believer that what was good for his organization was good for the country, and these events confirmed the economist as one of Meany's foremost bêtes noires. In subsequent years, the labor leader would see Burns's hand behind almost every economic malady that afflicted the country and would demand his resignation with monotonous regularity. For its part, the administration had had enough criticism from the Fed chairman in the months before it had imposed the wage-price freeze. The president had his agents tell Burns that since the Fed chairman owed his job to the chief executive, he had an obligation to support administration policy—especially a policy that he had urged on the White House in the first place.[25]

Burns and the White House also disagreed over monetary policy. From the imposition of the freeze to the end of 1971, the money supply expanded at less than a 2 percent annual rate, even though interest rates fell. The prime rate went from 6 percent in August 1971 to 4.75 percent the following January—its lowest level during Burns's tenure at the central bank. Yet monetary expansion was quite modest, in good part because the freeze had reduced expectations of inflation. With the value of money less likely to depreciate, interest rates suddenly seemed higher. Moreover, uncertainty about international finance encouraged caution among firms that did business abroad. Finally, the rapid increase in the money supply during the first half of the year had already created enough credit to satisfy demand.

Monetary stagnation did not bother the Fed—at least not at first. Indeed, it desired lower growth to balance out the rapid expansion earlier in 1971. As Burns said, "To help create confidence in the new economic policy, and to create confidence that inflation was going to be brought under control, instead of opening up the money spigot we clamped down for a little while. Enough money was already there to do its work. There was no shortage of money or bank credit. In fact, bankers were looking for customers."[26] Moreover, Burns hesitated to push rates down because he knew that the central bank would probably have to raise them again as the economy picked up. Calculating that any such increase would generate congressional opposition, and perhaps weaken the credibility of the controls program, he preferred not to move rates at all.[27]

The administration took a less relaxed view. In October McCracken warned the president that the economy might be sluggish in 1972 and commented, "The recent tendency of the money stock to decline must be watched," although he added, "it is not yet cause for alarm."[28] By December, the White House had become alarmed. Herbert Stein told Nixon, "My great concern is that the economy is not going to rise fast enough in 1972 to cut the rate of unemployment very much," and he suggested, "We should be looking for ways to pump up the economy more rapidly."[29] But instead of stimulating economic activity, the Fed seemed to be restricting it. George Shultz feared that, because of central bank policy "it may be . . . that the current expansion is already destined to falter in mid-1972."[30] Milton Friedman summed up these doubts when he asked Burns, "What in God's name is happening?"[31]

Concern about the economic future was widespread. The Conference Board Economic Forum, a group of business-oriented economists, warned in early 1972 that the economic outlook was still uncertain and that output might stagnate yet again.[32] Representative Henry Reuss noted at about the same time, "The national unemployment rate has been at or near 6 percent for about a year and a half—since November 1970. More than five million people across this country are out of work and looking for a job." Despairing of a solution from the administration or the central bank, Reuss, backed by twenty Democratic senators and sixty-three Democratic congressmen, introduced a bill to create half a million public service jobs.[33]

By late 1971, Burns too had concluded that the Fed needed to expand the money supply more rapidly. His defense of the Fed's performance, confident in October, had by December become uncertain.[34] In the OMC, he argued for lower interest rates and a more aggressive policy to expand money and credit. As was the case in 1971, Burns aimed for monetary growth of about 6 percent for 1972. The Fed chairman also pushed the administration to use fiscal measures to stimulate the economy. Although the deficit for fiscal 1972 was supposed to total $40 billion, he thought that the nature of many appropriations was such that the money might not actually get spent for quite a while.[35] For instance, state and local governments were receiving revenue sharing funds for the first time and would probably need time to figure out what to do with the cash. Accordingly, the Fed chairman urged the president to order cabinet members to spend their appropriations as fast as possible. This Nixon did, though only the Defense Department managed a substantial burst of purchases.[36] The administration also tried, with some success, to target spending to areas with above-average unemployment, especially in Texas and California, which were also important states in the upcoming election.[37]

Over the winter and spring of 1972, the president hit upon a subtle way to make Burns feel his displeasure about their disagreements over controls and monetary policy. Nixon had the opportunity to appoint two new governors to the Federal Reserve Board, and in both cases he completely ignored Burns's recommendations and instead appointed his own men, John E. Sheehan and Jeffrey M. Bucher.[38] This action did not weaken the chairman's authority at the central bank, but it did remind him that Nixon could make his life difficult.

II

At Camp David, Arthur Burns had opposed floating the dollar, and he believed that subsequent events bore him out. Throughout the fall of 1971, most countries tried, with varying degrees of success, to prevent their currencies from appreciating against the greenback. The Bank of Japan, for instance, sold huge amounts of yen to keep it stable, while the French imposed strict controls on the movement of funds into and out of their country to prevent speculators from buying francs. Concerns about exchange rates and payments imbalances also encouraged protectionism. The United States had already imposed a 10 percent import surcharge, and many other nations were exploring retaliation. Looking back on the period, Burns declared, "Restrictive measures were developing all over the world. . . . Subsidies for foreign trade were being instituted. The broad effect was a growth of protectionism and restrictionism around the world."[39] "Businessmen both here and abroad," he continued, "faced acute uncertainty regarding exchange rates and governmental restrictions under which trade would be carried on in the future. This uncertainty aggravated recessionary forces already evident in Europe and Japan. It also adversely affected the profit expectations of American companies engaged in foreign operations or foreign trade, thereby inhibiting investment expenditures and economic expansion in the United States."[40] The Fed chairman believed that Washington had to end this anarchy and negotiate a new set of currency parities with the other industrial democracies. But

Burns had to proceed cautiously because, in international finance, the Fed is subordinate to the Treasury Department. The chairman could not simply act but had to persuade the administration that his policy was the wisest course.

The administration did not share Burns's concerns. George Shultz preferred floating to fixed rates. The latter, he thought, "makes domestic policy a function of [the] balance of payments," forcing countries to take steps that they would not otherwise consider to defend their currencies.[41] Instead, he thought that the market should determine exchange rates. That way, a nation with a payments deficit would find its currency in surplus on financial markets, which would reduce the value of its money relative to that of other countries, cutting the costs of its exports and increasing the prices of imports and so improving the trade balance. Countries with surpluses would face the reverse.[42] John Connally had no strong predispositions but simply wanted to make as good a deal for the United States as possible, and he was willing to live with floating rates as long as it took to get an acceptable agreement. Neither he nor Shultz thought that uncertainty about exchange rates was seriously hurting business.[43] Paul Volcker agreed with Burns that the U.S. should try to fix new parities, but most other figures in the administration, such as McCracken and Stein, were not sure what to do, and matters such as wage-price controls monopolized their time.

The debate within the government reflected disagreements among economists over the relative merits of floating and fixed exchange rates. Partisans of the latter, such as Burns and Volcker, argued that stable currencies encouraged international trade and investment by eliminating the important element of uncertainty entailed in currency fluctuations. Trade between the United States and Japan, for instance, becomes much easier if everyone knows what the relative value of the dollar and yen will be from day to day. But critics of such systems, including Shultz and Milton Friedman, pointed out that the defense of fixed exchange rates often required domestic policies that were otherwise inappropriate. For instance, if a country went into recession, its imports would decline with the general level of economic activity. This country's trading partners would then find themselves in deficit, which would tend to weaken their currencies and might well force them to raise interest rates and cut government spending to defend the value of their money—essentially importing recession. Better to let rates float in the market, allowing currencies to adjust automatically to changing conditions. But partisans of stable rates argued that speculators, interested chiefly in short-term gains, dominated currency markets, and that the outcome of their trading would not necessarily reflect underlying economic conditions. Floating exchange rates could well turn international finance into a giant game of chance. Both sides cited evidence to back up their opinions of currency markets, and subsequent events showed both that traders sometimes understood payments conditions better than did government officials and that speculative booms and panics affected currency markets just like every other financial exchange.

Of course, this disagreement, like so many others on issues of public policy, hinged not on what was "right" but on the relative costs of different actions. Stable exchange rates offered considerable advantages but entailed substantial costs, whereas floating rates avoided both. But as is often the case, partisans of different views, including Burns, spoke only of the beneficial effects of their plans and ignored or seriously understated the risks—sometimes even to themselves.

The differences within the American government and between it and the other industrial democracies quickly became evident during the fall of 1971. At the annual IMF meeting in September, Secretary Connally outlined an ambitious program. He wanted to improve the American balance of payments by $13 billion by revaluing other currencies against the dollar, reducing trade restrictions against American exports, and "burden sharing," or getting other countries to cover the costs of American troops stationed on their soil. In exchange, the United States would drop its import surcharge. The Europeans and Japanese wanted a quick settlement that centered around a devaluation of the dollar against gold and, by implication, their own currencies. Washington strongly opposed any change in the official price of the precious metal, fearing that if its value seemed more reliable than that of the greenback, gold might find a larger role in international finance at the dollar's expense. Domestic pressures, however, prevented many European governments from simply revaluing their currencies. In parts of the continent, such as France, many people kept their savings in gold, and an increase of, say, the franc against the dollar, without any corresponding change in the relationship between the greenback and gold, would reduce the value, in francs, of gold held by savers. The other industrial democracies also considered the American demand for a $13 billion improvement in its balance of payments excessive. Burns apparently considered Connally's demands unrealistic and tried to bridge the differences between the U.S. and its allies by asking Jelle Zijlstra, the respected head of the Netherlands Bank, to act as an "honest broker" and sound out possibilities for a settlement. Connally did not forbid this move, but he did not like such an obvious crack in the American negotiating front.[44]

Though initially resolved to stick to its tough line, Washington weakened during the autumn. Some currencies, such as the deutschmark and the yen, did appreciate considerably against the dollar, but others, such as the French franc, moved little at all. A negotiated settlement seemed likely to provide a more substantial devaluation than floating had achieved. Nor did the United States seem to have much to gain by delay. As Burns warned Nixon in October, "Many Europeans have stressed that Europe is on the edge of a distinct slowdown in economic activity, if not a recession. . . . As time goes on, it will become increasing difficult for European governments to agree on a significant upvaluation of their currencies in relation to the dollar, since such a change in exchange rates will aggravate recessionary conditions. The same is true of the Japanese."[45] By November, McCracken had added his voice to Burns's and was recommending a settlement. "The international part of the new economic program will have been massively successful," the CEA chairman said, "if we now cash in. We can get a major exchange rate adjustment."[46] Henry Kissinger, the president's National Security Adviser, weighed in for an agreement, arguing that continued friction over currencies could permanently damage the Western alliance.[47] Nor were many outside the government supportive of delay. The issues that divided the administration seemed arcane, even to most economists—for instance, Milton Friedman and Paul Samuelson both argued that the price of gold was a minor issue, not worth holding up negotiations.[48] For his part, Nixon was tiring of the whole subject and wanted to clear it out of the way.

In a series of meetings in November and December between the wealthiest industrial democracies—the Group of Ten—Burns, Connally, and Volcker negotiated a new set of currency parities.[49] At the last of these conferences, held at the Smithsonian Institution in Washington, the United States agreed to increase the official price of gold from $35 an ounce to $38, or 8.57 percent.[50] The other countries then increased or decreased their official "pegs" from this new mark. In the end, the Japanese yen appreciated 16.9 percent against the dollar, the Swiss franc 13.9 percent, the deutschmark 13.6 percent, the Dutch and Belgian currencies 11.6 percent, the franc and pound sterling 8.57 percent, and the Swedish and Italian currencies 7.5 percent.[51] The Canadians decided not to set a new value for their currency but continued to float.[52] The United States agreed to end the 10 percent surcharge. Everyone also promised to work to reform the international monetary system to prevent the reoccurrence of the sort of crisis that had forced the U.S. to float the dollar in the first place. The Smithsonian agreement contained one very important concession to the United States: it did not require the U.S. to resume converting dollars into gold or anything else. As one observer put it, "The other Group of Ten countries were so eager to get the United States to fix a new parity that they said to us, 'You don't have to convert the dollar. We will support the dollar by buying all the dollars necessary to maintain the new par value.' "[53] At the end of the conference, President Nixon hailed the Smithsonian accord as "the most significant monetary agreement in the history of the world."[54]

The settlement pleased Burns. It was exactly the sort of thing he had pushed for since the president had floated the dollar and, indeed, since 1969. The Fed's staff estimated that it would improve the American trade balance by between $7.75 and $8.75 billion—not as much as Connally had initially demanded, but enough to restore the country's international payments to health.[55]

III

In early 1972, relations between Burns and the White House seemed likely to continue in the same uncomfortable pattern as the previous eighteen months. The Fed chairman was nagging the administration about its incomes policy, warning that wages were rising too fast. The president was worried about slow monetary growth and sought to put pressure on Burns.

Surprisingly, though, economic policy came together. First, the money supply started to increase rapidly, growing at a 7.4 percent rate in the first quarter of 1972 and even faster in the second. Soon, the Fed was nudging up interest rates to slow expansion. The economy, stimulated by plentiful credit as well as government spending and tax cuts and encouraged by the apparent success of controls and international negotiations, expanded an impressive 7 percent over 1972. By midyear, unemployment had declined from 6 percent, where it had remained throughout 1971, to 5.5 percent, even though the labor force increased rapidly as the children born during the post-1945 baby boom began to come of age.

At the same time, the Pay Board delivered on wage restraint. Early in 1972, it reviewed two more contracts that had been in negotiation when Nixon imposed the wage-price freeze. In January, the board's business and public members joined to cut raises for aerospace workers from 11.4 percent to 9.5 percent, and in March, they did the same for west coast dockworkers, reducing a 25.9 percent pay hike to 14.9 percent.[56] Though these decisions still left unions with large wage increases, they established the Pay Board's authority. The second case led to a walkout by four of the five board members representing organized labor, who claimed that the entire controls program was tilted against unions and workers. But the president quickly reconstituted the Pay Board as a seven-member group similar to the Price Commission, and it continued to operate successfully.[57] Labor walked out mainly to embarrass Nixon before the presidential election, not to wreck controls. It realized that these were popular and that damaging them would be politically dangerous, both hurting the candidates that labor supported and encouraging anti-union legislation. Contracts negotiated in 1972 averaged 6.4 percent annual wage increases over the life of the agreement, compared with 8.4 percent for 1971 contracts.[58] Rapid productivity increases, which accrued as economic expansion allowed companies to use their facilities more fully, complemented wage restraint. In 1972, consumer prices went up only 3.4 percent, while profits increased substantially— 15.5 percent in the year after Nixon imposed the freeze.[59] At the same time, though, higher per capita output allowed workers to enjoy a substantial increase in real (inflation-adjusted) wages.

Why this sudden success? After all, the White House had started 1972 worried lest slow money growth choke off recovery, while Burns had been concerned that the Pay Board would not effectively contain wages. In retrospect, it seems that each side misinterpreted the other's intentions.

The Fed chairman and the administration were not that far apart on monetary policy. Burns aimed for 6 percent growth in the money supply for both 1971 and 1972, a figure most around the president considered appropriate—and indeed, currency and demand deposits expanded more rapidly than that in both years. The Fed chairman, however, attached far less importance to month-to-month changes than did the White House. As long as the money supply expanded at the desired rate on a year-to-year basis, a few months of sluggish growth did not worry him. But short-term figures mesmerized the administration and often led it to misjudge the Fed chairman's objectives. For his part, Burns confused the Pay Board's stance toward the small number of union contracts already in negotiation when President Nixon imposed the wage-price freeze with its attitude toward pay hikes in general. The Board considered the former special cases, and once it had cleared them out of the way, it applied its rules fairly consistently. Of at least equal importance, the American economy was poised for expansion as 1972 began. It had a good deal of slack, which meant that companies could easily increase both production and productivity by using facilities more intensively. Uncertainty about inflation and, to a lesser extent, international arrangements had held back the economy in 1971, but by taking strong steps to deal with these problems, Washington had cleared away doubts and set the stage for a boom.

Arthur Burns saw the relative stability and prosperity of 1972 as an opportunity to put the American economy on a sounder footing. "Some trade unions have been abusing their power by acting monopolistically," Burns argued.[60] "The time is ripe for a reexamination of the special immunities that our trade unions have accumulated over the past thirty or forty years." Among beneficial changes he included "compulsory arbitration of labor disputes in industries that vitally involve the public interest."[61] The Fed chairman also desired stricter enforcement of antitrust laws. "Once our labor and product markets become more competitive," he said, "there will be little or no need in the future for direct wage and price controls."[62] On another front, he wanted the government to get a firmer grip on fiscal policy. He argued for a ceiling on total federal spending that would require the president to cut outlays should they go above a certain figure. As it was, Washington had no mechanism to control its overall spending—Congress appropriated money without having to relate different outlays to each other. Burns also wanted to allow the chief executive to vary the investment tax credit between zero and fifteen percent, which would give the president considerable influence over investment, the most unstable component of the total demand for goods and services.[63] Finally, he thought environmentalists were "losing [their] sense of proportion" and argued that Washington should stretch out the time-table for compliance with new regulations, thereby reducing their cost to business.[64] Little came of these proposals. The 1972 election discouraged dramatic action. Besides, Burns wanted to go after some very powerful interests—big business, organized labor, and Congress itself, which did not look kindly on any diminution of its authority over taxing and spending. Of his suggestions, only the spending ceiling, which had long enjoyed support from lawmakers such as Senators Proxmire and William Roth (R-Del.), received serious attention, and it did not become law.

Even failing extensive reform, though, Burns hoped that a period of stability would improve economic performance and social harmony in general. Pointing to the Vietnam War, urban riots, student protests, and accelerating inflation, he contended that Americans "are not reacting to classical [economic] remedies the way they did because they are living in a disturbed world and are themselves disturbed and, to a large degree, confused." "If only life would quiet down for a while," he lamented, "if only both the administration and Congress would become just a little less active in pushing new reform for a while, if only some of my academic colleagues would keep quiet for a while, then I think the country might absorb a little better all these tumultuous changes around us and we might find that old-fashioned economic policies are working better."[65] This desire might seem to contradict his arguments for reform, but Burns thought that the restoration of national calm required "strong and decisive leadership, so that God's children on earth, many of whom are now unhappy and afraid, can continue to feel—or perhaps feel for the first time—that their government is headed by a strong man who will even risk personal failure in behalf of their welfare."[66]

IV

During most of 1972, friction between Burns and the White House centered on foreign issues. Few in the administration were in a hurry to move forward with international reform because the Smithsonian accord had given the United States a substantial devaluation without imposing on it any real obligations. Nor were the president and his advisers sure how reform should work or how to negotiate it. The administration knew that it did not want to make the dollar convertible into gold or to continue talks within the Group of Ten, where it thought the other members tended to gang up on the United States, but it had yet to develop a program of its own. Although the Fed chairman shared some of these uncertainties, he believed that the United States had to take the lead and push reform. The 1971 crisis had severely weakened confidence in the world financial system, and unless something reinforced that confidence, the Smithsonian parities would not hold. Burns also feared that if the United States fashioned international policy without reference to the well-being of the system as a whole, emphasizing instead only its own interests, it would erode the basis of cooperation on which world finance rested.

The Smithsonian agreement gained acceptance only after several months. Many around the world doubted that the new parities would last, and declining interest rates in the U.S. further stoked uncertainty. Central banks had to intervene heavily in currency markets to defend the greenback. President Zijlstra of the Netherlands Bank stated that his institution had taken in $300 million on one day and "didn't hesitate for a second."[67] The Fed, however, did not participate in these efforts. It could not act without approval from the Treasury, which saw no cause for intervention since the Smithsonian accord required none. Why, the Treasury reasoned, risk money when other countries would do the work? This attitude annoyed the other industrial democracies, which believed that the United States had shifted all of the burden for defending the system onto their shoulders. Although Burns vigorously defended American policy at international conferences, privately he seems to have thought that our allies had a point. He believed that the United States had a moral responsibility to defend its own currency and thought it unwise to take advantage of the other industrial democracies, even if the Smithsonian accord permitted it, because the U.S. would need their cooperation in the future.

Fortunately, the situation stabilized by March. Interest rates in the United States began to rise while those abroad declined, making the dollar more attractive. Congress officially raised the price of gold, formalizing the new parities. Finally, the regular intervention of central banks in currency markets had bolstered confidence.[68] Circumstances, however, remained far from ideal. American officials had expected that those who had sold dollars in 1971 because they anticipated devaluation would now buy greenbacks again since one had been implemented. But this "reflow," as it was called, did not materialize, indicating continuing doubts about the Smithsonian agreement. The large U.S. trade deficit during 1972 reinforced uncertainty. It takes time for a devaluation to improve the trade balance: to take advantage of a cheaper currency companies must find foreign buyers, gear up production, and develop new products, all of which take time. In the short run, though, a drop in a currency's value raises the prices of imports and cuts those of exports, intensifying any payments imbalance. Such was the case for the United States in 1972, when the trade deficit jumped to over $3.1 billion from a little under $2.7 billion the previous year.[69]

Burns believed that Washington had to resolve these continuing doubts and decided to take matters into his own hands. In May, in a speech in Montreal, he noted that the Smithsonian agreement "did not attempt to deal with the structural weaknesses in the old international monetary system," and argued that these "must eventually be remedied if we are to build a new and stronger international economic order." He then laid out ten "elements that one might reasonably expect to find in a reformed monetary system": 1) better procedures for international cooperation; 2) "responsible domestic policies in all major industrial countries"; 3) enough autonomy within the system so that nations would not have to abandon price stability or full employment to achieve international objectives; 4) "more prompt adjustments of payments imbalances" with "definite guidelines" about how to do so; 5) an equal division of responsibility between surplus and deficit countries to rectify imbalances; 6) "systematic long-range plans for the evolution of world reserves"; 7) a reduced role for gold as a reserve asset and a larger place for Special Drawing Rights (SDRs), a type of fiat currency created by the IMF;[70] 8) a reworking of the status of "reserve currencies" such as the dollar; 9) the reestablishment of a convertible dollar; and 10) a reduction of trade barriers.[71] Burns floated these proposals because he sensed that "a certain hopelessness and despair had settled on international financial markets," and he believed he had made "the first outgoing, constructive statement by a senior U.S. official indicating a willingness on this country's part to help in reestablishing monetary order."[72]

Generally, this speech went over well. The *New York Times* and the *Wall Street Journal* reacted positively, as did Senator Jacob Javits, one of the few legislators who followed such issues. "Dr. Burns is clearly not setting up a straw man here," the senator said. "Negotiations regarding the reform of the international monetary system are increasingly urgent. . . . Dr. Burns's speech has moved negotiations a step forward."[73]

The administration, however, kept its distance from Burns's proposals. Paul Volcker said of the chairman's concerns, "Certainly, I would share some of them," but continued, "you don't solve these problems overnight."[74] The White House did not oppose Burns's reform agenda, save for making the dollar convertible, but neither did it think that international negotiations deserved the priority that the Fed chairman attached to them. It was content to leave matters to the Treasury, where a special interagency committee was making slow progress on the subject.

Another financial crisis in June and July made reform seem more urgent. The pound sterling came under heavy pressure because prices and wages in Britain were increasing very quickly, and London eventually decided to quit defending its currency and to allow it to float down in the market. This event called all the Smithsonian parities into doubt, and many who held dollars began unloading them. European countries and Japan had to buy $6 billion to support the greenback.[75]

To defend the dollar, the Federal Reserve intervened in currency markets. It persuaded George Shultz, who had replaced Connally as treasury secretary in the spring, to allow the Fed to reactivate its swap, or credit, lines with other central banks. It then used these to borrow foreign currency, which it sold for dollars. In July, the Fed bought $30 million. Although small in proportion to the amount of money that changed hands each day in international markets, this action electrified the financial world. One ecstatic banker declared that the Fed's interventions had brought the United States "back into the human race."[76] Germany's decision to impose restrictions on funds coming into the country and a better report on the American trade deficit further reinforced confidence. The dollar stabilized.

In September, negotiations for international reform finally got under way. At its annual meeting the IMF set up the Committee of Twenty, which consisted of the Group of Ten as well as ten developing countries, to serve as a forum for reform talks. Though Burns preferred that the industrial democracies—the world's chief trading nations—work things out on their own, the administration strongly supported the formation of this new body because it thought such a forum would be more receptive to American arguments than one including only the members of the Group of Ten. At the same meeting, George Shultz gave a speech outlining the American reform proposal, which Paul Volcker had devised. Volcker reasoned that a country with a payments surplus could only keep its currency stable by selling it consistently in money markets and thereby accumulating foreign currency—namely, reserves. The reverse would apply to countries with deficits. The United States proposed to set rules for changes in reserves, requiring countries to take action to cut their surpluses (or deficits) if reserves increased (or decreased) beyond a certain point. Such a system would make currency parities responsive to market conditions and would not require the United States to convert dollars into gold or anything else.[77] The Treasury ran its proposal by Burns before making it, and he and the Fed's staff suggested some technical changes that were adopted, though no alterations in the basic idea.[78] The Fed chairman had no plan of his own for international reform—his speech in Montreal was more of an agenda for discussion than a program of action. His object had been to get talks started.

After the Committee of Twenty convened, Burns played a limited role in its activities. The chairman was not a regular member of the Committee of Twenty. He attended several meetings but did not participate in the regular work of the committee's staff. Moreover, Burns's talents were not really appropriate to the task of the committee. It was taking an intellectual step in the dark, devising something completely new to supplant the international system organized after World War II. Burns was not very good at this sort of thing—he was an able economic historian and a formidable critic, but his mind was not especially original. Finally, starting in 1973, Burns had to deal with one international crisis after another and had little time to devote to the more abstract questions of how the system ought to work. The Fed chairman did make significant contributions. He helped devise the formula of "stable but adjustable par values"—fixed currencies that nations might change under certain conditions—that the committee took as its ideal, and he also took part in the debate over whether to link monetary reform with aid for developing countries, opposing such a move.[79] Nevertheless, he was not one of the chief figures in the talks.

V

In mid-1972, the direction of economic policy shifted. The administration began to fear that the economy might be expanding too fast and could overheat. Not only was production in the United States growing very rapidly, but so too, despite earlier fears of a slowdown, was that in Europe and Japan. Already, food prices were going up quickly because of bad harvests in the United States, the Soviet Union, China, and India. Over 1972, wholesale prices increased 6.5 percent, largely because of jumps in the cost of agricultural products. The danger did not appear immediate, but since it would take time for any change in policy to affect the economy, preemptive action seemed in order. The president, with strong support from Burns, asked the Congress to impose a $250 billion ceiling on spending for fiscal 1973, and although the legislative branch refused to do this, the administration nevertheless managed to keep outlays under this level and to cut the deficit to $14.3 billion, nearly $10 billion less than the previous year.

Again with Burns's encouragement, President Nixon tightened price controls. In a letter to the president in June, the Fed chairman noted that consumer prices were still advancing at about 3.5 percent a year and that to slow them further the government would have to reduce wage increases even more than it had already. He observed that prices for meat, which were exempt from controls, had increased at a 17 percent annual rate from December through April, and he warned, "If the average housewife cannot perceive that pressures on the family budget are lessening, there is little hope that we will be able to get the moderation in wage demands—with or without controls—that is essential to a reduction of inflationary pressures." He suggested that Nixon abolish import quotas on meat and impose a ceiling on its price. He also thought that the administration should take the opportunity to limit profit margins. Although favorably inclined toward business, Burns was not mindless on the subject. Rapid growth in corporate earnings had resolved his earlier concerns about inadequate profits, and he argued that the Price Commission should clamp down and limit price increases to jumps in corporate costs.[80] President Nixon suspended import quotas for meat and imposed controls over raw agricultural products like beef and pork, but he did not take up the Fed chief's other recommendations.[81]

At the same time, Burns tried to persuade the Pay Board to tighten its rules. He had the Committee on Interest and Dividends extend for another year its 4 percent limit on dividend increases, hoping that its example would encourage the Pay Board to roll back its wage standard to 4 or 4.5 percent.[82] The Pay Board retained its 5.5 percent rule but did restrict exceptions to it. It suspended "catch-up" raises for workers earning less than $3 an hour and brought merit pay increases under the 5.5 percent limit. Previously, the Pay Board had allowed people qualifying under these two categories raises 1.5 percent above the guideline, or 7 percent overall.[83]

In contrast to fiscal policy and the controls program, monetary policy remained very accommodating throughout the second half of 1972, with the money supply increasing at more than an 8.5 percent annual rate. The Fed allowed this increase, in part, because its preliminary figures suggested that money growth was a more modest 6.5 percent.[84] Even this rate of expansion, however, was quite high for a booming economy, but the central bank took no decisive steps to contain it. The Fed did tighten somewhat, forcing up interest rates—the prime rate went from 4.75 percent in March 1972 to 6 percent in December, and the return on three-month treasury bills went from 3.44 percent in the first quarter of 1972 to 4.86 percent in the final quarter. But the demand for credit was so stong that these rate hikes could not slow monetary expansion much—and most people at the central bank, including Burns, knew it.

The Fed pursued this course because the chairman backed it with all his authority. Many members of the Open Market Committee and Fed's staff thought rapid monetary growth risked reigniting inflation, but Burns stood his ground and had his way. He had become convinced that expectations of ever-higher prices perpetuated inflation. "Many businessmen," he said, "have come to believe in recent years that the trend of production costs will be inevitably upward, and their resistance to higher prices—whether for labor, materials, or equipment—has therefore diminished. Labor leaders and workers now tend to reason that in order to achieve gains in real income, they must bargain for wage increases that allow for advances in the price level as well as for the expected improvement in productivity."[85] Because of these perceptions, "wage rates and prices no longer respond as they once did to market forces."[86] Burns believed that only a firm incomes policy could remedy the situation, and he often spoke, both in public and in private, of "the important contribution that relatively stable interest rates can make, and must continue to make, to the success of the government's stabilization plan."[87] Burns thought it safe to reinforce controls by keeping interest rates down because he estimated that the economy still had considerable slack, and he lectured OMC members who believed otherwise saying, "An unemployment rate in excess of 5 percent, we're in a recession. . . . I'm not afraid of prosperity. I can't stand recession."[88] Nor did the Fed chairman think monetary policy particularly loose. Noting that growth of the money supply had been "far below the increase in the current dollar value of output," he argued that the Fed's policy had favored only "moderate economic expansion."[89]

Burns also used the CID to keep interest rates in line. Although the committee had no formal authority over banks, few were willing to risk the wrath of the Fed's chairman by ignoring its instructions. He argued that financial institutions should keep "administered" rates, like those for home mortgages, below market rates, reasoning that banks raised a good deal of money through checking accounts and the like on which they paid no interest. In October, Burns stated publicly that an increase in the prime rate from 5.5 to 5.75 percent concerned him and implied that he would not tolerate a further jump.[90]

The chairman was pursuing a dangerous course. If he was wrong and the economy did not have much room to expand, then the Fed's accommodative monetary policy would cause demand to outrun supply and create shortages, which would, in turn, undermine controls. Indeed, restrictions on wages and prices made such miscalculation more likely. Since they prohibited companies from raising prices in response to shortage, they made it more difficult to detect if the economy was under strain. For instance, in 1972 the world prices of fertilizer and plastic increased substantially, indicating that companies were having trouble supplying these products, but controls in the United States hid this development from both consumers and policymakers.[91] Burns had fallen into the trap against which he had warned in the 1960s. He had his eye on the unemployment rate and was not paying attention to the constraints imposed on output by plant capacity and the supply of raw materials—a serious error at any time, but especially so in a period like the early 1970s when the labor force was growing very fast.

Subsequently, some observers accused Burns of pursuing a liberal monetary policy mainly to keep the economy humming during President Nixon's reelection campaign. In a famous article in *Fortune*, journalist Stanford Rose went so far as to accuse Burns of disappearing in the midst of an OMC meeting at which the tide seemed to be running against him and of returning an hour later to announce, "I have just talked to the White House." Reportedly, the rest of the OMC quickly gave in.[92] In fact, the story of Burns's manipulating monetary policy to the benefit of the man who appointed him, Richard Nixon, has found a permanent place in Washington folklore.

The evidence does not support these charges. Burns himself claimed that there was "not one grain of truth" in Rose's article. Fed Governor Andrew Brimmer, who did not get along well with Burns and who dissented from monetary policy during much of 1972, stated, "These assertions are false—both in general and particular."[93] Burns's record shows that he was not reluctant to stand up to the chief executive when he thought the president was wrong. In 1970 and 1971, his enthusiasm for an incomes policy had infuriated the administration, but Burns had persisted until the White House adopted the idea. When Nixon's frustration with the chairman had boiled over in 1971, leading to Colson's slander of Burns, the chairman had secured a public apology from the president. Even in 1972, Burns had disagreed publicly and privately with the administration on international finance and had helped push it into reform negotiations. The chairman was clearly no pliant tool of the chief executive but rather did whatever he thought was best.

Why then did Burns allow rapid monetary growth in 1972? The best explanation is the one he gave at the time: he believed that stable interest rates reinforced the controls program. He thought that inflation persisted because it was ingrained in the attitudes of businessmen, workers, and consumers, and that an effective incomes policy offered the best way to change these attitudes. Many people, however, were suspicious of wage-price controls, particularly organized labor, and they focused closely on interest rates. If the cost of money increased, these people might well conclude that controls were a sham benefiting business and the wealthy. To assuage these concerns, Burns tried to keep interest rates stable not only in the months leading up to the presidential election but also well into 1973, months after Nixon's landslide reelection.

The Fed chairman followed this course because he honestly believed in 1972 that the economy could continue to expand rapidly without strain for quite a while—an opinion shared by many policymakers in the executive and legislative branch. As Herbert Stein put it, "We all thought, 'We're a long way from full employment, we still have a lot of room for expanding the economy, and the inflation rate is low.' We misinterpreted."[94] Indeed, even the modest attempts at economic restraint late in the year, such as spending limits or slightly higher interest rates, generated sharp criticism. Economist Walter Heller argued in a memo to Representative Reuss that he did not think that the economy would begin to fully exploit its industrial capacity until mid-1974 and that the administration was tightening prematurely. Heller warned the White House and the Fed, "Don't tighten money and don't clamp down on a $250 billion budget ceiling in the face of 5.5 percent unemployment and a $50 billion gap [shortfall] in gross national product."[95] Senator Proxmire concurred, "You don't get demand-pull [shortage-induced] inflation, before you get to 4.5 or 4 percent unemployment."[96] At the time, the Fed's decision to keep interest rates down generated little public criticism.

Burns did not ignore presidential politics. He wanted Nixon to win and offered advice to the chief executive on how to strengthen his position—urging, for instance, that the executive branch spend appropriations as fast as it could in early 1972. But no evidence suggests that these concerns affected monetary policy. Had there been no election, the Fed would probably have acted in more or less the same way.

As 1972 drew to an end, the administration sensed difficulty and looked forward to 1973 with some trepidation. George Shultz warned the president in mid-1972 that the country was "in the eye of the storm."[97] The White House worried that, as the economy used its resources more fully, greater inflationary pressure would develop, while controls, which prevented prices from going up in response to shortage, would be more likely to create distortions. At the same time, though, it thought growth was likely to slow, retarding progress against unemployment.[98] The administration estimated that these problems would become acute in mid-1973 and concluded that it would be fortunate to hold on to the gains it had made in the eighteen months after Camp David. Comparable warnings came from sympathetic economists outside the government. Even before the election, Milton Friedman had decided that monetary policy would have to tighten soon if the country was to avoid a resurgence of inflation.[99] Burns saw the same dangers but believed that the country could make progress—indeed, that it had to. "A further reduction during 1973 in the rate of increase in wages and prices is essential if the inflationary trend that has so long plagued our economy is to be brought to a halt," he warned.[100]

6

The Great Crash

I

By the end of 1972, Arthur Burns had decided that wage-price controls offered diminishing returns. He still believed the country needed a strong incomes policy to contain inflation, but he also thought that competition worked well in many sectors of the economy and that these did not need government regulation. Indeed controls, if continued long, risked distorting the price structure. When George Shultz asked the Fed chairman for recommendations about the future of the wage-price program, Burns suggested that: 1) Congress extend legal authority for controls;[1] 2) the program remain comprehensive in theory but concentrate on wages in the construction industry and state and local government and on prices for food and medical care; 3) Washington end rent controls; 4) the COLC get more authority over the day-to-day management of the program; 5) the government somehow get organized labor involved in controls again; and 6) the administration set a goal of 2 percent inflation for 1973.[2]

The Nixon administration accepted most of these ideas. It had never liked regulating wages and prices and feared that, if it did not end the practice soon, controls would become permanent. But the White House also worried that the sudden lifting of restrictions might create a burst of inflation and so trigger an irresistible public clamor for their reimposition. Gradual decontrol was the logical solution, and Burns's support was vital to it. As an early booster of incomes policies, his approval would go a long way toward rebutting critics who might charge that, by weakening controls, the administration was abandoning the fight against rising prices.

In early 1973 George Shultz announced a new wage-price program, which the press soon dubbed "Phase III."[3] Though controls would remain comprehensive in theory, enforcement would cease except in the food, medical care, and construction industries. Rent controls would end. Burns's CID would continue to function, but the Pay Board and Price Commission would close up and the COLC would take over their responsibilities. Finally, the COLC would create a special committee including prominent labor leaders to advise it about wages and benefits.[4]

This new policy got mixed reviews, largely because people were unsure about their own thinking. The Democratic-controlled Joint Economic Committee had released a report in late 1972 stating, "The present temporary controls are a temporary expedient and should be removed as soon as this is feasible," though it further stated, "Some form of incomes policy must be continued."[5] Yet Phase III, which seemed to fit this prescription, encountered strong criticism from many Democratic lawmakers. Representative Reuss called the action "incomprehensible." "Just when indications are strong that inflation is heating up once again," he said, "price controls are removed." Senator Proxmire urged the administration to tighten rather than loosen restraints.[6] Controls might be an expedient, but they were an expedient with which many were unwilling to part at the moment. But economists Ackley, Heller, and Okun, who between them had chaired the CEA during the Kennedy and Johnson administrations, were generally supportive. They agreed with the White House that strict controls could not last indefinitely without distorting the price structure and thought some relaxation in order.[7] Republicans were also generally favorable toward Phase III, as were business and labor leaders, who wanted Washington out of their affairs.

To strengthen confidence in its new program, the administration talked tough about going after those who might abuse the latitude Phase III gave them. President Nixon told Burns, "You should be reassured that the administration meant what it said when we stressed that the Cost of Living Council stood ready to move against any wage or price decision that threatened national economic stability."[8] George Shultz spoke of the "club in the closet" and warned business executives, "If any of you want to offer yourselves up as that juicy target, we'll be delighted to clobber you."[9] These statements convinced Burns, at least, that Phase III would contain inflation.[10]

The administration reinforced its wage-price program with sweeping budget cuts. After his landslide reelection victory over Senator George McGovern (D-S.D.) in November 1972, President Nixon took steps to impose his authority in many areas of the federal government. Among other things, he impounded, or refused to spend, billions of dollars appropriated by Congress. This action would, he hoped, both strengthen the White House vis-à-vis the legislative branch and head off any resurgence of inflation.

Impoundment created a furor on which Burns did his best to capitalize. Earlier presidents had impounded funds, but none had done so on such a scale, and Democrats in Congress, as well as many Republicans, thought the president's action an unconstitutional impingement on the legislature's power over appropriations. Burns avoided this particular debate. He did approve of the methods used to decide on cuts, which involved a careful examination of existing programs to determine how effective they were and whether they addressed what the administration considered pressing needs. But on the tactic of impoundment itself, he kept quiet. He may simply have wanted to avoid a fight in which he had no stake, or he may have disapproved of Nixon's maneuver—though he favored a strong presidency, Burns had occasionally voiced concerns about possible abuses of executive authority. In any event, the Fed chairman saw the controversy as an opportunity to encourage budget reform. As it was, the Congress had no overall budget and passed appropriations measures without relating them to each other, and it was this confused state that, Nixon claimed, justified impoundments. Legislators realized that they would strengthen their hand against the president if they could impose financial order on themselves. Burns supported the effort wholeheartedly, testifying at every hearing on the subject to urge a spending ceiling, which would require the president to cut outlays should they exceed a certain level. This exertion bore little fruit. The measure finally enacted in 1974 provided for a budget resolution to determine the size of each major appropriation bill, but it lacked sanctions and rarely enforced restraint. The measure did, however, ban impoundment.

II

In early 1973, a series of crises threw Burns and the administration on the defensive on economic policy. Disaster struck first on the international front. As the year started, the Fed chairman was worried about the stability of the dollar. He sensed unease in exchange markets, and the Fed's staff was warning him that the American balance of payments might not improve without a further devaluation.[11] Most European central bankers, however, remained confident, believing that capital controls would keep the flow of money between countries at a manageable level.[12]

Events proved Burns right. To currency traders, the dollar seemed an ever-less certain investment. Phase III apparently portended higher inflation in the United States, while recent trade figures showed no decline in the large American trade deficit. In money markets, psychology is everything—at least in the short run—and in the atmosphere of early 1973, people would seize on any excuse to dump the greenback. The spark came from southern Europe. In late January, uncertainty about the Italian currency led people to move huge amounts of lira to Switzerland, and the Swiss, overwhelmed by the inflow, floated the franc. Of course, this action made the franc more valuable against the dollar as well as the lira, and traders took it as a signal that the greenback was headed down. Soon, they were dumping huge amounts of the American currency. The Germans alone had to take in $5 billion over the week of February 5, while every other central bank, including the Fed, bought dollars.[13]

On February 6, President Nixon met with Burns and Shultz to decide what to do. They agreed to dispatch Paul Volcker to Europe and Japan to negotiate a second devaluation. In six days, Volcker covered thirty-one thousand miles and persuaded the other industrial democracies to accept a 10 percent devaluation of the dollar, to be effected by raising the official price of gold to $42.22 an ounce. The Japanese, however, decided to float the yen, which left four members of the Group of Ten (Japan, Canada, Britain, and Switzerland) without official "pegs" for their currencies.[14]

In the United States, this action won general acclaim. Representative Reuss said that the admininstration had done "an excellent job." Walter Heller declared, "I am really pleased that at last we are getting some common sense about currency parities, and are willing to devalue them when we really need to."[15] At this time, most officials and economists saw flexible rates as a way to insulate the American economy from those of other countries, allowing the United States to pursue policies attuned to domestic conditions. As a memo written a couple of years earlier for the Joint Economic Committee's Subcommittee on International Finance noted, "The external and internal economic policy goals of the United States should be synonymous—the maintenance of full employment and price stability. . . . The chief technique in avoiding excessive payments surpluses will probably be exchange rate adjustments."[16] That the world had not ended when the dollar was initially floated in 1971—an outcome often prophesied—had helped remove the uncertainty that had inclined many against flexible exchange rates. The possibility that changes in the terms of trade wrought by devaluation might have a significant impact on the American economy seemed remote.

Arthur Burns considered the devaluation unavoidable but he did not like it. "I cannot emphasize too much or too often," he said, "that as far as I am concerned this is the last devaluation. . . . If we travel the devaluation route, what little discipline exists in the world with regard to currency parities will leave us."[17] He did not consider floating the dollar in the marketplace a realistic alternative. "As far as the exchange market goes," he argued, "it moves up and down because of the whims of man as well as because of the knowledge of man. I would not accept the exchange rates that emerge in a free market as giving you anything like an infallible indication of what is fundamental equilibrium."[18]

Exchange markets, however, proved stronger than Arthur Burns. Constant devaluations had demolished confidence in the very idea of fixed parities. Inflation in the United States was accelerating, raising new doubts about the dollar. In late February, the price of gold went through the roof, hitting $89 an ounce, and soon traders were once again selling dollars in huge quantities. On March 1 alone, European central banks bought $3.6 billion. President Zijlstra of the Netherlands Bank spoke of a "catastrophic situation" and said to one Fed governor, "We wonder where all these dollars are coming from."[19] On March 2, governments around the world closed exchange markets.[20]

Over the next two weeks, Burns, Shultz, and Volcker attended two major summits in Europe convened to resolve this latest crisis. No one thought another devaluation appropriate. All calculations showed that the 10 percent drop in the greenback would, in time, give the United States a trade surplus, and besides, there was no reason to expect a second devaluation to succeed where the first had failed. But no one expected the Europeans to absorb dollars indefinitely either, and they refused to continue doing so unless Washington raised interest rates, imposed stricter controls on capital leaving the United States, tapped its credit lines with the IMF and other central banks to the utmost to support the greenback in exchange markets, and promised in the event of another devaluation to redeem the dollars that they held at the old parity. George Shultz rejected these conditions and proposed instead that currency values be left to float in the marketplace. The other members of the Group of Ten accepted this, and after a hiatus of seventeen days, exchange markets reopened.[21] Burns opposed this decision until the last minute, and even then may have hoped to hammer out some sort of modus vivendi with the Europeans to maintain fixed parities. He strongly disliked the uncertainties inherent in floating rates and accepted them only as a last resort.[22]

The collapse of the Smithsonian agreement represented a major defeat for Burns. He had championed the accord within the administration, had helped negotiate it, and had tried to defend it in financial markets, but the last had proved too much for him. Of course, the accord was not a total failure. The Committee of Twenty, operating under a mandate set forth in the agreement, was still hard at work on financial reform, and Burns hoped that its efforts might yet yield fruit.

Moreover, the Smithsonian accord had delayed floating exchange rates until they seemed inevitable, and so their advent stirred little bitterness. Had the United States forced a float on the world in 1971, opinion might have been different. Nevertheless, unless reform negotiations succeeded, Arthur Burns had earned a meager return on his considerable investment of time and energy.

These events also demonstrated a grave weakness in Burns's approach to international finance. As Paul Volcker put it, "Burns . . . was extremely sensitive to charges that international considerations were influencing domestic interest rates. Hence, despite his enthusiastic support of fixed exchange rates, he seemed . . . to have a kind of blind spot when it came to supporting them with concrete policies."[23] Though the Fed chairman would intervene in currency markets to defend the dollar, he would not raise interest rates to the same end, even though this was the most effective way for a country to make its currency more attractive to traders and investors. Indeed, experience suggests that, although market intervention is helpful, it is nearly impossible to maintain fixed exchange rates without the support of monetary policy. But during the international crises of 1973, Burns was actually struggling—without success—to hold American interest rates down. Of course, raising the cost of money to protect the dollar's international value would almost certainly have been extremely unpopular, and the political dangers may have prompted the chairman to avoid this course. But usually, when Burns was convinced that an otherwise beneficial policy was politically impossible, he would try to educate elected officials and the public about the advantages of this path and so change the political realities. The Fed chairman, however, never spoke of the need to take international factors into account when making monetary policy—indeed, quite the opposite. In early 1973, after a conference in Paris, a reporter asked Burns if he had agreed to raise interest rates to defend the dollar. The chairman responded, "American monetary policy is not made in Paris; it is made in Washington."[24] In the international arena, Arthur Burns refused to utilize the most powerful tool available to him to achieve his goal of financial stability.

Surprisingly, the dollar did not depreciate any further in the spring of 1973. While markets had been closed, interest rates in the United States had risen, making the dollar more attractive. Moreover, the latest trade figures showed a smart advance in American exports. Financial markets are mercurial institutions, and this good news about the dollar had considerable effect. The crisis, especially its second phase, had been as much one of the system of fixed parities as of the greenback, and with currencies floating, the dollar stabilized—at least for the moment.

Nevertheless, the Fed chairman remained wary. That summer, under his direction, the Fed negotiated to increase its swap, or credit, lines with other central banks by approximately 50 percent, from $11.75 billion to $18 billion, giving the Federal Reserve greater resources with which to defend the greenback if it came under pressure.[25]

III

As the currency crisis peaked in March, Americans found themselves caught up in a new, more severe wave of inflation. Starting in January, prices leapt forward. Agricultural prices led the way, thanks to bad harvests around the world in 1972, which had curtailed supply, and huge Soviet grain purchases in the United States, which had stoked demand. Consumer food prices jumped 14.5 percent in 1973, and wholesale prices 41 percent.[26] The cost of basic industrial materials, such as steel, aluminum, petroleum, and chemicals, were close behind, increasing 18 percent in the year after August 1972.[27] Together, these factors pushed wholesale prices up at a whopping 21.1 percent annual rate during the first quarter of 1973 and even faster during the second. Consumer prices jumped less, at an 8 percent rate, but this still represented the fastest rise since the Korean War.

The severity of the crisis caught everyone by surprise. Most economists recognized that food supplies would be tight, but they underestimated the scale of the problem, and the sudden jump in the cost of industrial commodities came as a shock. Even the most pessimistic calculations had indicated that problems were unlikely in this area until midyear. The Fed's staff developed three explanations for the situation, all of which probably had some validity. First, declining profit margins in the United States during the late 1960s and early 1970s had discouraged investment in industries such as cement and steel, limiting output. Second, the entire world was booming in late 1972 and early 1973, with production up at a 7 percent annual rate in the United States, at between 7 and 9 percent in western Europe, and at an incredible 19 percent in Japan. To achieve such rapid growth, companies had to strain their plants to the utmost. Bottlenecks developed, and the heavy demands placed on facilities often pushed up costs per unit of output. Finally, the devaluation of the dollar intensified demand for the limited supply of American products because it made them that much cheaper for foreigners, who rushed in to buy.[28]

An inflationary boom engulfed the United States. Exports surged, giving the U.S. a $1.4 billion trade surplus for 1973. Business invested heavily in new capacity, and unemployment fell below 5 percent. But prosperity was uneasy. Inflation was out of control and shortages of various goods—especially petroleum—threatened further growth. On the price front, wages offered the only bright spot. Union contracts negotiated during 1973 provided for raises somewhat smaller than those agreed to in 1972, but few believed that this restraint would continue indefinitely in the face of skyrocketing prices.[29] Besides, in sharp contrast to 1972, productivity improved little if any during 1973. Many companies were running their facilities flat out and could only increase output with disproportionate effort.

These developments put Burns and his Committee on Interest and Dividends in a terrible bind. The Fed chairman believed that "fundamentally, it is the expansion of the money supply over the long run that will be the basic cause of inflation."[30] The money supply, however, was growing at a very fast 8.2 percent annual rate during the first quarter of 1973, and to slow it, the Fed would have to raise interest rates. But as Burns put it, "In the United States, there is an acute political problem regarding interest rates. Congress and the unions have become quite concerned about interest rates. Congress could unwisely legislate statutory limits on interest rates, or fail to act promptly to approve an extension of the Economic Stabilization Act [controls]."[31] The Fed chairman, though, feared more than a political backlash against higher rates. In the short run, he considered psychology key to inflation—if people believed prices would go up, they would raise prices and wages in anticipation, creating the inflation they dreaded. Controls could check this perception, but if people saw the price of capital (interest rates) rising, they might well conclude that restraints were a sham for the benefit of the wealthy. With galloping prices already weakening faith in the program, Burns feared that a large jump in the cost of money would deal controls an irreparable blow. He was in the position against which others in the Fed had warned him when he had first agreed to lead the CID in 1971, under simultaneous pressures to raise and stabilize interest rates.

This contradiction was a variation of that which had led Burns to advocate an incomes policy in the first place. In 1970 rising wages forced the Fed to choose between accommodating the increase and permitting inflation or restricting the money supply and throwing people out of work. In 1973 the central bank faced an equally unappealing choice. It could accommodate controls by keeping interest rates low, which would pump money into the financial system and exacerbate already severe inflationary pressures, or the Fed could raise interest rates and restrict monetary growth, which might well finish controls and touch off a scramble to increase wages and prices.

Burns tried to finesse this conflict. Under his leadership, the Federal Reserve's Open Market Committee acted firmly to slow monetary growth. It drove the Fed funds rate, which banks charge each other for money on deposit with the central bank, from 5.14 percent in the last quarter of 1972 to 10.56 percent in the third quarter of 1973.[32] The yield on three-month Treasury bills went from 4.86 percent to 8.32 percent over the same period. Burns, however, undermined this policy through the Committee on Interest and Dividends. As CID chairman, he had been working since late 1972 to keep interest rates in line. In November, the CID had allowed banks to raise the prime rate, which they charged their most reliable customers, to 6 percent, but as market rates increased in early 1973, financial institutions began to consider further hikes. In early February, four large New York banks, led by First National Citibank, raised their prime rates to 6.25 percent. Burns immediately went to New York to confer with the head officers of the banks in question, and under his prodding they rescinded the increase.[33] Although the CID had no way to enforce its wishes, few bankers were willing to risk the wrath of the Federal Reserve's chairman. As Burns told a congressional committee, "At the present time, the only penalty [for violating the CID's guidelines] is a frown from the Chairman of the Committee, . . . but that frown has been rather powerful and sufficient."[34]

In late February, the CID issued rules governing how and when banks could raise lending rates. Institutions could only increase their charges in line with the cost of funds in money markets, and even then, their rates ought not go up as steeply because they took in deposits on which they paid no interest—through checking accounts, for instance. The cost of consumer, small business, and farm loans was supposed to increase slowly if at all. When the CID issued these regulations, however, Burns let bankers raise their prime rates to 6.25 percent.[35]

As market rates continued to climb, another increase became necessary. In late March, several banks, led by Chemical Bank and Manufacturers Hanover, raised their prime rates from 6.25 percent to 6.75 percent. Burns made his displeasure clear, and these institutions rolled the hike back to 6.5 percent—which may have been their goal in the first place. At the time, most economists estimated that, taking into account the demand for funds and rates in money markets, the prime rate should have stood at between 7 and 7.5 percent. Low bank rates encouraged companies to borrow liberally to finance expansion, and some who tapped cheap credit from banks turned around and placed that cash in lucrative money markets. Business loans increased at a breathtaking 30.7 percent annual rate in the first half of 1973, and Burns was reduced to making ineffective calls on banks to restrain lending.[36]

Arthur Burns realized that he had boxed himself into a bad corner. Low interest rates were helping fuel an inflationary boom, and as he succinctly put it, "The effects were not wholesome."[37] But opposition to higher rates had, if anything, become stronger. Representative Wright Patman, chairman of the House Banking Committee, was urging a freeze on interest rates. He insisted, "The latest game-playing over the prime rate is designed to forestall Congressional action and public pressure for mandatory controls over interest rates."[38] In April, an unprecedented measure introduced in the Senate to roll back the cost of money failed by only four votes, forty-five to forty-one—a close call that rattled the Fed. Burns found the attention focused on the prime rate by Congress and the press especially galling, since it only applied to large businesses—not the consumers and small businessmen about whom all expressed paramount concern. "To a large degree, we are chasing shadows here," he said.[39] Richard Nixon summed up the situation well when he told Burns, "What an ugly tree has grown from your seeds."[40]

In mid-April, Burns hit upon a device that promised to solve his problem: the dual prime rate. Under rules quickly promulgated by the CID, banks were required to charge farmers and small businessmen with assets of less than $1 million below the going prime rate for loans of less than $350,000. Having acted to protect these favored groups, Burns let the prime rate go up, although he made it clear that the CID's rules governing the cost of money still applied. This action coincided with a vote by Congress to extend controls for yet another year without any special provisions concerning interest rates. By September, the prime rate had increased to 10 percent, a record, and growth of the money supply had slowed to under a 6 percent rate.

Having implemented the dual prime rate, Burns told the president he wanted to quit the CID. He was in an impossible position that, quite likely, hurt the standing of the Federal Reserve. Nixon and Shultz, however, dissuaded him, arguing that no one else had the prestige to keep bankers in line and that, if Burns left the CID, it would appear that the administration had given up on containing interest rates. The Fed chairman agreed to stay, but his concerns about the central bank's reputation were well founded. In September 1973, a poll of economists employed by banks reported that only 1.4 percent thought that the Federal Reserve was doing an excellent job, while 41.2 percent rated its performance poor.[41]

During this difficult episode, and indeed the rest of Nixon's presidency, Burns enjoyed strong support from the White House. The president and his advisers agreed with Burns that the Fed had to slow monetary growth. Perhaps more important, as the Watergate scandal loomed larger, Nixon simply could not afford the time and energy for quarrels with the central bank. The relationship was hardly frictionless, but it remained solid despite difficult economic circumstances. In March, for instance, George Shultz defended higher interest rates to unhappy representatives, writing, "These increases . . . are a direct outgrowth of the vigorous expansion in business activity that is taking place. Such increases cannot be avoided if we, the Administration and the Federal Reserve System, are to honor our responsibility to maintain a sound economic policy. . . . I am determined to prevent the economic expansion from running away with itself and creating much more serious inflationary pressures, much higher interest rates, and a subsequent recession."[42] In contrast to 1972, Nixon followed Burns's recommendations for new Federal Reserve Board governors, appointing Robert Holland, a senior staff member at the central bank, in the spring of 1973, and Henry Wallich, a Yale economist, in early 1974.

IV

Cooperation between Burns and the administration extended to Phase III, which suffered even more because of the price explosion than did the CID. Doubts about the wisdom of the program swelled with inflation. Senator Proxmire declared, "Phase III is a very, very ineffective operation. . . . Anyone who thinks Phase III is working must be in a cocoon completely insulating himself from what is going on in the world."[43] Most people seemed to think that the relaxation of wage and price controls was a terrible mistake, culpable for the rapid inflation. This perception was not quite fair, since shortages of agricultural and industrial commodities accounted for most of the increase, and attempts to contain prices in the face of shortages would probably have created more problems than it would have solved. As economist Arthur Okun said, looking back on events, "I don't think any reasonable set of controls would have changed the story much."[44] Nevertheless, popular belief that controls were key to checking inflation soon forced the administration to bring "the club out of the closet" and impose regulations on petroleum and put ceilings on beef, pork, and lamb prices.[45] Others, such as Senator Proxmire, urged further steps—in the senator's case, another wage-price freeze.[46]

Burns also thought Washington had to do more. Concerned as always about the psychological atmosphere, he warned the president, "Most people—Americans and foreigners, businessmen and consumers, investors and working men—have no use for Phase III. They seem to regard it as a mistake, and some regard it as a downright disaster. . . . This country is now in danger of being buffeted by a crisis of confidence. This sort of problem clearly requires a political approach. It requires strong leadership on your part. It requires visible proof to the American people that you care about their concerns, that you are doing something real in their interests, that you intend to continue to do more as needed."[47] In April, Burns advised Nixon to strengthen controls by requiring large companies to inform the Cost of Living Council before raising prices and by giving the COLC authority to prohibit such increases if it considered them unwarranted.[48] This the president did early in May.[49] In June, Burns put forward a new set of suggestions: a further tightening of controls, sales out of American stockpiles of strategic minerals to force prices down, repeal of the tax on ground grain, further cuts in federal spending, a compulsory savings plan for individuals and corporations to reduce demand, and a horsepower tax on new cars and trucks to encourage the production of more fuel-efficient machines.[50]

Richard Nixon, however, wanted quick results. Politically, he was growing weaker as more and more aspects of the Watergate scandal were coming to light. Already, the president had had to dismiss two of his top aides, Chief of Staff H. R. Haldeman and the head of the Domestic Council, John Ehrlichman. The continued advance of prices further sapped his support. Democrats in Congress branded his policies "an unmitigated failure," and Senator Proxmire spoke of the administration's "paralysis."[51] Nixon remembered how the first wage-price freeze had both stabilized the economy and allowed him to seize the political initiative, and he began to think that another might do the same.

All of the president's economic advisers, including Burns, strongly opposed any such move. They argued that, in 1971, inflation was the result not of shortages but of a wage-price spiral in which escalating labor costs forced up costs. The freeze represented a logical response to this situation. In 1973, however, the United States just did not have enough goods to go around at current prices, and a price freeze would merely substitute shortage for inflation. Herbert Stein, citing the Greek thinker Heraclitus, warned Nixon, "You can't step in the same river twice." This aphorism did not sway the president. "You could," he responded, "if it was frozen."[52] On June 13, he issued an edict banning price increases for sixty days.[53]

The freeze worked poorly, just as Nixon's advisers had warned. Higher costs had been working their way through the economy, and many companies found their prices frozen below their cost of production. Farmers proved especially uncooperative. Some withheld produce from market and engaged in dramatic protests, such as drowning chicks, to show that they would not allow Washington to cut into their profits. Shortages of some goods developed, which media attention magnified. Public opinion turned strongly against controls.[54]

The administration imposed yet another program—Phase IV—even before the freeze expired. These controls resembled those that had been in place in 1972 and had worked effectively, but enthusiasm was lacking. As the *Wall Street Journal* put it, "The stage is set for an unhappy production of a rewritten play opening before a weary audience, authored by White House scriptwriters who don't like the plot and backed by a producer who hopes it closes after a short run."[55]

The administration did not think Phase IV could actually prevent price increases but merely hoped that it would spread them out. The president's advisers believed that special factors, such as poor harvests and the devaluation of the dollar, had caused inflation in 1973, and they reasoned that once these had worked their way through the economy, price increases would subside. Herbert Stein, for one, predicted that inflation would slow to between a 3 and 5 percent rate in early 1974.[56] The administration, however, feared that if all the price increases it anticipated fed through the economy in just a month or two, the political repercussions would be disastrous. Controls were primarily a holding action against this eventuality.

Even Burns, who retained some enthusiasm for incomes policies, had given up on controls. Looking back on events, he said, "Last year [1973], I think that program did more harm than good."[57] In June, the CID eased its rule for dividends. It allowed companies to pay out to shareholders the same proportion of profits as they had in 1968–72. The Fed chairman conceded, "These new guidelines will make it possible for many corporations to increase their dividend payments significantly this year, and to a still greater degree next year," but claimed, "This should be of particular help to elderly individuals and widows dependent on dividend income."[58] More to the point, Burns saw no reason to subject shareholders to regulation when the whole controls program was on its last legs. The CID did not completely shut down—for instance, when banks raised the prime rate to 10 percent in September, it demanded that institutions prove that their costs justified the hike.[59] Nevertheless, it did not intervene then, or at any other time, to force changes in dividends or interest rates.

Fiscal and monetary restraint became, once again, the mainstays of the struggle against inflation. George Shultz called for "a return to the old-time religion—balance the budget."[60] Although the administration fell short of that goal for fiscal 1974, it did limit the deficit to $3.5

billion. Burns and the Fed played their part, keeping monetary expansion at a 5.2 percent annual rate in the third quarter of 1973 by driving interest rates to record highs.

These policies were not popular. High interest rates caused hardship, especially in homebuilding, where demand depends largely on the availability and cost of home mortgages. Housing starts fell 13.5 percent in 1973, or by three hundred thousand, idling thousands of construction workers.[61] Representative Patman raged, "We are in a recession right now. . . . The big banks and the Federal Reserve are making a depression right now." Economist Paul Samuelson worried that the administration and the Fed were being "stampeded by the food inflation into following drastically restrictive fiscal and monetary policies" that "could bring on a serious period of stagnation."[62] Even Ronald Reagan, the Republican governor of California, expressed concern. But the administration stood its ground and defended the central bank. George Shultz cited "the exceedingly pressing need to restrain overall growth of credit. Inflation is our most important domestic problem, and this administration firmly believes that the nation is best served in the longer term by a vigorous effort now to curb inflation."[63]

Arthur Burns argued that the administration ought to do more with fiscal policy. He doubted that price increases would subside in 1974 as Stein and others in the administration hoped because the events of 1973 had greatly increased expectations of inflation. To dispel these, the government had to give things a strong push. In all likelihood, Burns also thought that his own agency was bearing a disproportionate burden in the fight against rising prices and thereby attracting more than its fair share of the political flak. In any event, the Fed chairman urged dramatic fiscal action to curb spiraling prices. He proposed that Washington impose a surcharge on income taxes that it would refund at some future date when the economy was less buoyant, as well as enact an adjustable investment tax credit that would allow the president to reduce tax breaks for investment while leaving open the possibility of reinstating them at a later date if the economy faltered.

Burns's suggestions led to an embarrassing mix-up with the White House. Upon taking office for the second time in 1973, President Nixon had promised not to raise taxes. He dismissed the Fed chairman's refundable surcharge out of hand and derided the variable tax credit as a "gimmick." But Melvin R. Laird, a former congressman and the defense secretary during Nixon's first term whom the president had brought onto his staff to "open up" the administration and dispel some of the onus of Watergate, thought that the chief executive had been too curt. Soon after Nixon had rejected Burns's suggestions, Laird announced that the president had an open mind on tax increases and apparently encouraged Nixon to give Burns what the chairman later described as a "sympathetic" hearing. At this point, George Shultz returned from a trip to the Far East, furious about what had been going on in his absence. As with all Nixon loyalists, the strain of Watergate and economic instability was taking a toll. Though normally the epitome of calm, Shultz said, "I think the President's adviser on domestic affairs [Laird] can keep his cotton-picking hands off economic policy. . . . Laird always sounds off about economic policy when I'm away." Turning to Burns's idea for a refundable surcharge, Shultz declared, "It doesn't sound to me like an idea whose time has come. . . . It is important to have an economic policy, to do the best you can and then stick with it, not keep sharpshooting it week after week."[64] This statement put an end to Burns's proposals. Tax increases are never popular, and even with the support of the administration, which was now politically weak, the passage of one through Congress was uncertain. Without the president leading the way, the cause was hopeless.

George Shultz had a better grasp of the limitations of the American government than did Arthur Burns. In Washington, power is dispersed and wheels turn very slowly. Even had the administration and Congress agreed on a tax increase, enacting and implementing one would have consumed months, by which time conditions might have changed a lot. Burns often produced ideas that assumed a political nimbleness that just did not exist and so set himself up for inevitable disappointment. But at the same time, institutional rigidity actually enhanced the power of the Fed chairman. The central bank could adjust monetary policy quickly in response to changing conditions, whereas fiscal policy moved very slowly if at all, since the president and a majority in both houses of Congress had to agree on any new policy. As politically sacrosanct and administratively inflexible middle-class benefit programs, such as Social Security and Medicare, took up more and more of the budget, the importance of the Federal Reserve would only increase.

Although the evidence was far from conclusive, it seemed in the early autumn that the administration's economic policy might work. Growth in output had slowed to less than a 3 percent rate, which experts believed the economy could sustain without strain. Though consumer prices were going up at a 10.3 percent annual rate in the third quarter, wholesale prices were up only 13.2 percent, little more than half the pace of the previous six months. Since wage increases remained moderate, there was good reason to think inflation would slow in early 1974, though perhaps not to the 3 to 5 percent for which Herbert Stein hoped.

V

In the summer of 1973, the United States faced yet another international crisis. After Washington floated the dollar in March, the currency held stable in exchange markets for several months. But escalating inflation in the United States and the mounting political uncertainties flowing from the Watergate scandal undermined confidence in the greenback, which began to drop in June. Soon it was off by more than 10 percent against the currencies of America's main trading partners.[65]

This development greatly worried Burns. The February devaluation had contributed heavily to the explosion of prices, and he feared that another would make inflation worse. Besides, he thought that stable exchange rates helped keep the entire international financial system on an even keel. Nor were America's allies happy about the prospect of further devaluation, which would hurt their trade balances. By July, Burns and others at the Fed had persuaded a somewhat reluctant Treasury to let it act. George Shultz had a strong ideological commitment to floating exchange rates, but he recognized that the situation in currency markets was dangerous. He let the central bank activate its swap network, borrowing European currency with which to buy dollars.

Starting on July 10, 1973, the Fed bought $512 million—a considerable sum for it. Several factors abetted the central bank's action.

Interest rates were increasing in the United States, which made the dollar more attractive, and the American trade balance was improving and would show a narrow surplus in the second quarter and a large one—over $700 million—in the third. Together, these pushed up the greenback's value, and the Fed was able to purchase enough foreign exchange to repay its swap borrowing by the end of July. Soon the dollar was back to where it had been in March.[66]

Though hardly earthshaking, these events set precedents that would apply to subsequent international crises. A currency would begin to appreciate or depreciate in a way that officials around the world considered unhealthy, and together they would intervene in currency markets. Such action followed no hard and fast rules but rather proceeded on an ad hoc basis, requiring constant consultation and considerable trust among the governments involved. There was no guarantee that even sizable, well-organized intervention in currency markets would achieve the results desired. These measures usually floundered when they ran contrary to factors like the differences in interest rates between countries and the state of the balance of payments, and succeeded, as in 1973, when they moved in tandem with them.

VI

In November 1973, the economic crisis went from bad to worse. In October, the armies of Egypt and Syria attacked Israel, starting the Yom Kippur War. After several weeks of fierce fighting, the Israelis repulsed the assault, thanks in part to military equipment sent by the United States. In retaliation, the Arab oil-producing countries embargoed petroleum shipments to the U.S., which already had an oil shortage. Soon thereafter, the Organization of Petroleum Exporting Countries, the OPEC cartel, quadrupled the price of crude oil for all buyers.

These events dealt the American economy a terrible blow. Energy is basic to any industrial society, and in the United States it became both scarce and much more expensive, forcing prices up and production down. Wholesale prices in the first quarter of 1974 increased at a staggering 24.5 percent annual rate, while consumer prices jumped at a 14.2 percent rate, the most rapid increase in the nation's peacetime history. Starting in November 1973, the American economy began contracting at a 3 to 4 percent rate, a pace that would continue for about ten months. Americans everywhere found themselves waiting in long lines at gas stations to buy fuel at prices beyond anything they had ever imagined. People had to turn down thermostats in offices and homes, and the oil shortage threatened to close down many factories. Consumers of petroleum scrambled to find supplies, and as one buyer for a refinery described it, "We were bidding for our life."[67] For a people accustomed to think of cheap energy as their birthright, it was an awful shock.

Though the embargo created tremendous uncertainty, the Nixon administration did not change course. Herbert Stein told the president, "The economic prospect at this time is as complicated and uncertain as at any time in the past five years. . . . The range of possibilities for next year is exceptionally wide, and includes a very bad combination of unemployment and inflation." Still, he concluded that the administration should concentrate on prices. Stein argued that the economy had slowed because the energy shortage had cut production as well as the purchase of goods like automobiles that used petroleum, and in the short run, economic policy could do little about the oil embargo.[68]

Arthur Burns certainly saw no reason for the Federal Reserve to relax monetary restraint. As he said, "Rapid growth of money and credit is hardly an effective remedy for a shortage of oil."[69] The Fed did allow interest rates to fall. According to initial figures, the money supply grew at a fairly low 3.9 percent annual rate in the last quarter of 1973. With monetary expansion under control and the economic slowdown likely to further dampen the demand for credit, the central bank believed it could allow the cost of money to decline without compromising its goals for monetary growth.[70] The rate for three-month Treasury bills fell from 8.3 percent in the third quarter of 1973 to around 7.6 percent at the new year, while the prime rate went from 10 percent in September 1973 to 8.75 percent in February 1974.

For the time being, the international aspects of the energy crisis commanded more of Burns's attention than the domestic ones. The sudden increase in oil prices threw every industrial country into deficit except the United States, which, because of the embargo, found itself importing much less petroleum. Financing these deficits would be difficult, especially for countries like Italy and Britain, which were in trouble before the oil shock. Uncertainty created the danger of an international free-for-all in which countries, desperate for cash to buy petroleum, devalued their currencies and erected trade barriers in a frantic attempt to earn surpluses.

The end of reform negotiations further muddied the waters. The members of the Committee of Twenty decided that, with almost every industrial nation in deficit, oil producers accumulating huge financial reserves that they could not soon use, and inflation out of control in most countries, they simply could not devise a realistic blueprint for reform.

Surprisingly, this decision did not seem to upset Arthur Burns, who had worked so hard to start these negotiations. During 1973, he had become increasingly discouraged about the talks. Participants failed to agree on how to resolve payments deficits, the most important issue before them. Perhaps more important, discussions within the Committee of Twenty bore little relationship to the problems with which Burns had to deal. Negotiators assumed that currencies would have fixed parities but did not address the huge capital flows that had wrecked these during 1973. Burns clearly regretted the failure of reform and the passing of fixed exchange rates, but he thought the uncertainties flowing from the energy crisis made both inevitable.

Burns could take this setback with equanimity in part because the oil shock actually strengthened the dollar. Alone among the industrial democracies, the United States had substantial oil reserves, which seemed likely to partially insulate its economy from the effects of the OPEC price hike.[71] More important, though, the greenback dominated the petroleum trade, where transactions were conducted with and prices quoted in dollars. In a sense, OPEC had made the dollar convertible once again, this time into black gold. For years, the billions of dollars held outside the United States, called the "overhang," had depressed the greenback's value and worried policymakers because Washington had no way to redeem them. But as one Fed staff assessment noted, "Past concern about a dollar overhang has largely evaporated in the wake of the petroleum crisis. Most dollar-holding countries are not presently reluctant dollar holders, and some countries even want to exchange gold for dollars."[72] The greenback appreciated in world markets until it stood about where it had under the Smithsonian agreement.

With the American currency safe—at least for the moment—Burns worked to help other countries finance their oil imports. Gold was first on the agenda. During the 1968 crisis, when the market price of gold first went above its "official" price, the United States, the United Kingdom, West Germany, Switzerland, Italy, Belgium, and the Netherlands had agreed not to buy or sell the precious metal on the open market, exchanging it only among themselves at the official price of $35 an ounce. After 1971, when Nixon had cut the dollar loose from gold, even these transactions had ceased. Gold reserves were, for the moment, useless, which made governments uneasy—what if they suddenly needed these immobile resources? The energy crisis forced the matter, driving the market price of gold to over $100 an ounce while leaving many countries with substantial gold reserves desperate for cash. In November 1973, Burns negotiated with other central bankers an end to the 1968 agreement on the precious metal. At the subsequent press conference, he announced that, with the termination of this accord, the IMF's rules concerning gold were again in force. Under these, a country could only sell gold above the official price—$42.22 an ounce—and only buy below that mark. This maneuver not only allowed countries to turn their gold stocks into badly needed dollars but also promised to deplete these stocks over time, since gold's market price seemed unlikely to drop below the official price. Smaller reserves of the precious metal would probably reduce its role in international finance—long a goal of Washington's.[73] Burns had been one of the few defenders of the precious metal in the American government, but the recent instability of gold prices seemed to have changed his mind about the precious's metal's ability to contribute to financial stability.

Soon the international community took more comprehensive steps to stabilize the world financial system. The IMF formally asked its members to avoid using competitive devaluations and protectionist measures to earn foreign exchange to pay for oil. Twelve of the thirteen countries that attended the February 1974 Washington Energy Conference, in which Burns participated, agreed to this prohibition. Only the French abstained, largely because they disliked following the lead of the United States.[74] Of course, this agreement would stick only if the international community developed mechanisms to help nations pay for petroleum imports. This the IMF did, organizing a facility to lend money to countries in difficulties, and in 1974 and 1975 it provided approximately $3 billion in badly needed credit.[75] The Federal Reserve, following Germany's lead, also came to the aid of Italy, whose chronic political instability prevented rapid response to the energy crisis.[76] The central bank expanded its swap line with the Bank of Italy from $2 billion to $3 billion to help that country finance imports in the short run.[77] Of course, these measures treated the symptoms of the energy crisis, not its cause, but as Burns had said, financial policy could do little to relieve an oil shortage. The Federal Reserve could only stave off collapse, and acting in tandem with the Treasury, the IMF, and officials in other countries, it did so.

In the spring, the crisis eased somewhat. The embargo against the United States ended, and oil prices stabilized, albeit at a very high level. At least, though, countries knew what they were dealing with and could plan accordingly.

In the late winter of 1974, the dollar started on yet another cycle of decline and eventual recovery. Washington had taken the opportunity provided by the strong greenback and by 1973's $1.4 billion trade surplus to end restrictions on the export of capital, on which the Nixon administration had never been keen.[78] The world, however, needed dollars to buy oil, and American bankers eagerly supplied loans. As a result, greenbacks began to flow out of the U.S. The end of the oil embargo in the spring also created a large trade deficit, which further undermined the dollar. By May, the dollar had dropped nearly 9 percent against the currencies of the United States' chief trading partners. The Fed resisted this depreciation by purchasing $377 million with deutschmarks borrowed from the German central bank, the Bundesbank. This intervention, coupled with that of Germany and Switzerland as well as firm statements by all parties about the greenback's strength, turned the tide in May. Higher interest rates in the United States and a perception among traders that the dollar had fallen too far further reinforced the greenback, which in September peaked at approximately the level of March 1973.[79]

By the spring of 1974, Arthur Burns realized that he lived in a new world in which markets determined exchange rates. That summer, the IMF, bowing to the inevitable, set aside its long opposition to floating rates and laid down rules to govern them. These allowed central banks to intervene in markets to counteract "instability" but forbade them to aim at any fixed target for a currency without first seeking the fund's approval.[80] Burns did not particularly like the new system. He feared currency instability would retard trade and thought floating rates made managing economic policy, especially fighting inflation, more difficult. "With exchange rates floating," he argued, "faster inflation in the United States than abroad would tend to induce a depreciation of the dollar in exchange markets, which in turn would exacerbate our inflation problem."[81] Still, the Fed chairman saw no ready alternative. An uncertain world required flexible exchange rates, and he could only hope that a more stable system would develop over time. "International monetary reform," he said, "is bound to be an evolutionary process and to reflect unfolding experience."[82] In the meanwhile, Burns worked closely with other central bankers to keep the swings of currencies to a minimum. He operated by two simple rules of thumb: "In my judgment, the dollar is basically a very strong currency,"[83] and, "We in the U.S. certainly can't accept with equanimity exchange-rate movements that undervalue the dollar."[84]

VII

During the winter and spring of 1974, on top of inflation, recession, and the energy crisis, Burns fought congressional attacks on the Federal Reserve. For decades, Representative Wright Patman, the chairman of the House Banking Committee, had been a thorn in the central bank's side. A populist, Patman favored low interest rates in all circumstances, once claiming, "Inflation has been due solely to the rise in interest rates. Every time you increase the interest rate, prices would go up. Even the goods on the shelves would go up and then wages would have to go up to compensate for the increase in the cost of groceries and everything else. Then prices go up again."[85] He thoroughly distrusted the Fed and once actually told Burns, "Many of your answers are obviously designed to cloud the issue and mislead the public."[86] The congressman attributed the central bank's power to the sinister influence of financiers, arguing, "The banks have built-in intimidation against every member of Congress and against every member of the legislatures of the fifty states."[87] Fortunately for the central bank, Patman's intemperance repelled many others in Congress. For example, during one hearing, Representative William B. Widnall (R-N.J.), the ranking minority member of the Banking Committee, said he was "sick and tired" of Patman's "unwholesome and completely unfair" characterizations of witnesses. Representative Edward I. Koch (D-N.Y.), later mayor of New York City, agreed with Widnall, saying that the committee chairman "cannot tarnish the reputation of those who come before us."[88]

Events in 1973, however, tipped the balance of power more in Patman's favor. Record-high interest rates in the summer and fall created much hardship, especially in the housing industry, and this put pressure on representatives and senators to do something. As one of Patman's aides said, because of higher interest rates, "all the traditional housing groups will be in here raising holy hell."[89] Revelations about abuses of power by the Nixon White House also generated demands for openness in government and more legislative oversight of executive bureaus, and no agency in Washington, outside the national security establishment, operated more independently or more secretly than the Federal Reserve. Though few besides Patman expected to unearth any great abuses of power at the central bank, many thought it inappropriate that so powerful a government organization operated behind closed doors. The atmosphere was such that even the *New York Times* supported change.[90]

Patman dusted off a proposal that he had long supported, an audit of the central bank by the General Accounting Office (GAO). He noted that the Fed was the largest agency exempt from such audits and claimed that lawmakers needed to make sure that the central bank spent money carefully. The Federal Reserve would have none of this. It pointed out that Patman's bill directed the GAO to examine not only administrative expenses but also the vast number of financial transactions that constituted monetary policy. By digging into these the GAO could, the central bank feared, disrupt delicate arrangements with securities dealers, with whom the Fed often conducted several transactions a week, or compromise relations with other governments, for whom the central bank carried out operations in American money markets. It also worried that a GAO audit would give hostile congressmen the opportunity to conduct "fishing expeditions" for evidence to discredit it. This second concern, at least, was justified. Every few months, Wright Patman denounced some new budgetary outrage by the Fed that, upon investigation, usually involved oversights such as paying $9.67 for score sheets for an employee bowling team.[91] Burns certainly did not want to give more opportunity for such harassment. "I wish you [Patman] would ask me sometime," he said, "how much time is devoted by my staff in answering your questions. . . . I would furnish you with the answer promptly."[92]

Opposition within the central bank to the GAO audit, however, had deeper roots. The Fed was probably the most important government bureau created during the Progressive era, and its people clung to the Progressive ideal of government by "experts." They simply did not trust the legislative branch, which they saw as a political weather vane, to support responsible monetary policies. Fed loyalists thought that representatives and senators, their eyes firmly focused on the next election, would inevitably push for low interest rates and monetary expansion whether or not it was appropriate. The Fed saw the audit as a "foot in the door" that would lay the groundwork for further congressional meddling. The argument that, in a democratic society, elected officials should oversee government policy, especially in an area that has as great an influence on people's lives as monetary policy, simply did not resonate at the central bank. The people at the Fed concentrated on economic outcomes, not on political processes, and they firmly believed that greater legislative oversight would compromise the quality of economic policy. Arthur Burns summed up this line of thinking when he stated, "The Federal Reserve was endowed by legislative mandate with a substantial degree of independence within government. Freedom from the daily pressures of the political process has given the Federal Reserve the opportunity to make the hard choices that continually confront those who are responsible for economic and financial policies."[93]

The fears of the Fed for its independence had a strong basis. Though Patman insisted that a GAO audit "is plain and simple—a protection for taxpayers," everything about his record indicated otherwise. One Banking Committee memo, reflecting Patman's influence, noted, "Monetary policy has been mismanaged almost without letup since 1929"; it went on to state, "The chief reason for this lack of hope [for better policies] . . . rests on the clearly outmoded and discredited concept that the Federal Reserve should have an independent status from executive economic, policymaking branch of government and be permitted to ignore the economic policies advocated by Congress and the administration." This document then listed several steps necessary to rectify the problem, among them regular audits of the central bank.[94]

As chairman, Burns acted as both point man and chief strategist in the struggle against the GAO audit. As always, he cut quite a figure when testifying before Congress. As one journalist said, Burns "in the witness chair is intimidating. The white hair, the old-fashioned suit with the pants held up by suspenders, the waving of extinguished matches around. Dr. Burns had presence."[95] As usual, he treated representatives and senators like students who had not fully thought through what they were saying. "Directing the Comptroller General," he said, "to enlist the services of unnamed individuals—with or without the necessary background but clearly without responsibility for making decisions—about policies that the responsible system officials have spent sleepless nights considering would, in my judgment, be bad government. . . . I believe that direct communication between the [banking] committee and the Federal Reserve, which is itself an arm of the Congress, is the most effective and efficient method for Congress to discharge its oversight responsibilities."[96] Sometimes he simply scolded legislators. "We're a highly efficient system," he told senators. "This isn't your problem. This isn't your purpose introducing this legislation. The purpose is to gain greater control over monetary policy and that, of course, is the prerogative of Congress. But I say to you, if that is what you want to do, you're taking on more of a job than you realize and you'd better think twice."[97]

The Federal Reserve launched an intense lobbying campaign to defeat the audit. The Fed's staff planted "horror stories" in newspapers and periodicals such as the *Wall Street Journal*, the *New York Times*, the *Washington Post*, and *Business Week* about what a GAO audit might entail.[98] The central bank tapped into its powerful grassroots organization. Its twelve regional banks had on their boards of directors and various advisory committees many prominent businessmen and professionals from each district. The Federal Reserve mobilized these people, informing presidents of the regional banks, "The Board was thinking in terms of contacts with Representatives by individuals such as Reserve Bank directors and ex-directors, F[ederal] A[dvisory] C[ommittee] members and alumni, bankers, and knowl-

edgeable businessmen."[99] Soon members of the Congress were getting
letters and telephone calls from many of their most influential constituents urging votes against the GAO audit or at least amendments
to exempt monetary policy from scrutiny. The central bank also persuaded former commerce and treasury secretaries and CEA chairmen
to argue its case. Burns not only organized lobbying but participated
in it, speaking with twenty-five congressmen himself.[100] He made a
critical alliance in Nairobi, Kenya, where, during an IMF conference,
he persuaded Ohio Representatives J. William Stanton and Thomas
Ashley, a Republican and Democrat, respectively, to back an amendment that strictly limited the scope of any GAO audit to purely administrative expenses. Between them, these two congressmen, in alliance
with Represenative Garry Brown of Michigan, another Republican
legislator, could often command a majority on the House Banking
Committee, and they would constitute a vital bulwark for the Fed not
only in this conflict but in many future ones.[101] Against this onslaught,
supporters of the audit warned that concerns that a GAO examination
would disrupt monetary policy were a "red herring" and that the Congress needed to make sure that the Fed was not making "sweetheart"
transactions with securities dealers.[102] But this last point won over
few lawmakers, because barely any believed that corruption was a
problem at the central bank.

The Fed's effort proved successful. The House voted for Ashley
and Stanton's amendment to restrict the audit to administrative matters and so remove monetary policy from GAO scrutiny. Thus weakened, the bill passed to the Senate, where it died in committee, thanks
largely to the efforts of Senator John Sparkman, chairman of the
Banking Committee and a good friend of Burns and the Federal
Reserve.

The Fed had won the battle but not the war. Patman and other supporters of the audit were furious at the Fed's lobbying, which they
considered improper. They concluded that the central bank was not
only undemocratic itself but actually a threat to other, democratic
institutions, and within a year they would redouble their efforts to rein
in the Fed. Burns, of course, denied that the Fed had acted wrongly
and stood ready to launch other lobbying efforts if necessary. "My
impression," he later said, "is that members of Congress want to hear
from their constituents."[103]

VIII

By early 1974, many of Burns's economic policies lay in ruins. The Smithsonian accord was dead. Wage-price controls were self-destructing. Though imposed mainly to hold wages in line, they had encouraged the Fed to keep interest rates down in 1972 and 1973, leading to rapid monetary growth that had fueled an inflationary boom. This, in turn, had led to price increases that had discredited controls. The Fed's monetary policy had also fallen into disrepute. Milton Friedman, the leading monetarist economist, pointed out in late 1973 that "monetary growth has been both higher and more variable in the past three and a half years than in any other postwar period of equal length," and he blamed this situation for rising prices.[104] Many found this argument convincing, including people like Senator Proxmire, who was not usually an admirer of Friedman's. "The Federal Reserve Board deserves central responsibility for the serious inflation that has become the nation's number one problem," the senator said. "The mammoth increase in the money supply created by the Federal Reserve in 1972 contributed seriously to the present inflation. About all that can be said of the policy is that it served a useful political role. . . . The 1972 monetary policy gilded the economic expansion and helped assure the Nixon landslide."[105]

Nor did the economy in early 1974 offer much hope of improvement. Wholesale prices were going up at a 27.1 percent annual rate, and consumer prices at 13.3 percent. Businesses, spooked by these increases, were buying raw materials as fast as they could to protect themselves from further price hikes, and companies that produced industrial commodities were building new capacity as quickly as possible to satisfy this demand. Financing this investment in inventories and plants was what Burns described as a "veritable explosion" in business lending, which grew at a 22 percent annual rate in the first quarter and even faster in the second.[106] The money supply was also growing fast, at more than a 7 percent rate in the first quarter of 1974—far too fast for an economy with runaway inflation. Moreover, revised figures for the last quarter of 1973 suggested that monetary expansion over that period had not been at a modest 3.9 percent annual rate, as first thought, but rather at a high 7 percent.[107] The American economy had all the symptoms of a speculative boom that, unless checked, would end in grief. At the same time, though, total output continued to shrink. Even after oil started flowing again in May, higher petroleum prices disrupted production. Consumers also bought less, largely because inflation had eroded their purchasing power and had encouraged them to cut spending to a minimum, since no one could be sure that in the future, as prices shot up, paychecks would cover even necessities.

Economists did not know what to do. For years, they had emphasized how government policy could maintain stability by manipulating demand. But now the nation suffered from shortages of oil and other materials, for which demand management offered no solution. At the very end of 1973, Walter Heller said in his presidential address to the American Economics Association that economists "were caught with their parameters down" and "had to go back to the drawing board."[108] But though "back to the drawing board" might have been an appropriate slogan for academics, it offered little to those like Burns who had to make policy.

On top of these problems and uncertainties, Burns had to take more responsibility than ever for economic policy. As the Watergate scandal approached its climax, President Nixon had little time for anything other than political survival. His chief public statement on the economy in early 1974 centered around a promise that there would be no recession—an assertion soon labeled the "King Knute doctrine," after the medieval English king who supposedly forbade the tide to come in. Nixon reappointed Burns to another four-year term as chairman of the Federal Reserve and kept abreast of events but could do little more. During the first four months of 1974, Burns did not even meet officially with the president.[109] George Shultz remained a formidable presence at the Treasury, but after he returned to private life in the spring, the executive branch had no strong man to coordinate policy. The Congress, only marginally less obsessed with Watergate than the administration, produced much talk but little action that bore on the economic crisis.

Burns had to try to salvage something from the wreckage, defend his reputation, and devise a new economic policy. With respect to wage-price controls, he concluded that "in the current economic environment, direct controls cannot be of much benefit in curbing inflation. In fact, comprehensive and relatively inflexible controls over wages and prices would probably do more harm than good, because they would prolong the distortions in production and distribution that have become a major problem during the last year."[110] Nevertheless, Burns still thought that an incomes policy could be of use. "I would like to see us work toward a system where prices and wages in key industries will be subject to a review by a government board, but where the price system at large would be characterized by considerable freedom."[111] The Fed chairman recommended that, when authority for controls expired in April 1974, the Congress allow the Cost of Living Council to continue as a sort of wage-price review board such as he had first suggested in 1970.

The Nixon administration seemed to go along with Burns's idea. During the winter of 1973–74, the COLC had ended controls in many sectors, including furniture, rubber, and aerospace. In April, the administration planned to get rid of all restrictions on wages and prices except those in the petroleum, health-care, and construction industries, where it believed competition worked poorly. The president also asked the Congress to retain the COLC. George Shultz insisted that it would not become a wage-price review board, but its very existence made such an outcome likely.[112] Nixon's support, however, did little good. Business and organized labor both lobbied hard against controls, which they saw as limiting profits and compensation, and after the failures of 1973, the population as a whole had become disillusioned with incomes policies. Congress allowed the COLC and all regulations on prices, except petroleum, to lapse.

Throughout late 1973 and early 1974, Burns also responded aggressively to those such as Milton Friedman who blamed Fed policy for the nation's many economic ills. The chairman claimed, "Our inflationary problem this year [1973] has arisen in substantial measure from sources well beyond the influence of domestic monetary and fiscal policy. A worldwide boom has been underway, the dollar has been devalued, and both agricultural products and basic industrial materials have been in short supply. Violent price increases that stem from such sources cannot be readily handled with customary weapons of economic stabilization policy." Increases in the prices of food and oil, he noted, made up 60 percent of the jump in consumer prices in 1973. "The most important underlying cause" of inflation, he continued, "has been the looseness of our Federal fiscal policies," not expansive monetary policies.[113] Burns conceded, "If I could relive history, I think I would try to achieve a somewhat slower rate of monetary growth [in 1972]. But it is my considered judgment that the difference that would make would be quite small."[114] He asked critical lawmakers, "What would you have wanted the Federal Reserve to do in a year like 1972, when the year started out with an unemployment rate of 6 percent?" knowing full well that some of those who were now denouncing the Fed's policy in 1972 as too loose, such as William Proxmire, had at the time opposed it as too tight.[115]

The Fed's policies in 1972 and early 1973 remain controversial. Many, such as Friedman and Proxmire, have blamed the central bank's loose monetary program for the inflation in 1973 and 1974 and for the subsequent recession, which owed much of its severity to the speculative excesses of those years. Some, such as journalist Stanford Rose, have gone so far as to contend that Burns kept interest rates down in 1972 chiefly to bolster Nixon's reelection, thereby blaming the economic crisis of the mid-1970s on a Nixon-inspired conspiracy. In this extreme form, these arguments are untenable. Burns held interest rates down in 1972 because he believed such a policy would strengthen the controls program, and his calculations, and those of most other economists, showed (incorrectly) that the economy had a good deal of slack. Certainly the Fed chairman was not ignorant of the political context, but had there been no election he probably would have acted in more or less the same way. Nor could wiser monetary policy have prevented the economic crisis that started in 1973. The events of that year affected all the industrial democracies, not just the United States, and marked the beginning of a long-term decline in the growth of production and productivity around the globe.[116]

At the same time, however, the central bank made matters worse by pursuing a policy that reinforced underlying inflationary trends rather than resisted them. One economist has calculated that had the Fed followed a more cautious monetary policy in 1972 and early 1973, inflation would have been 1.3 percentage points less over 1973, while unemployment during the 1974–75 recession would have peaked 1.5 percentage points lower than it actually did.[117] Such estimates are, of course, uncertain at best, yet it seems clear that monetary policy in 1972 was badly misguided and that Burns, who pushed that policy over the objections of many within the central bank, deserves much of the blame. Despite his forceful defense of his actions, the Fed chairman himself apparently realized this—his subsequent course suggests that he feared repeating the mistakes of 1972 and 1973.

Clearly, the speed with which prices were increasing in early 1974 frightened Burns. "If long continued," he said, "inflation at anything like the present rate would threaten the very foundations of our society."[118] "Inflation has been having debilitating effects on the purchasing power of consumers, on the efficiency of business enterprises, and on the conditions of financial markets," he warned, and it would lead to recession if not checked. The dangers, however, were more than economic. "Once inflation takes root in a country and if the government does not deal properly with it, the road is wide open for demagogues to explain the sense of frustration, the sense of misery, that is felt by many."[119] Burns took this danger very seriously—he had been born in one of the Jewish ghettos in Eastern Europe destroyed by the Nazis, who had come to power in part because of the social disruption caused by the German hyperinflation of the 1920s.

These worries changed Burns's view of economic policy. Whereas prior to 1974 he had thought that government had to remain equally vigilant against recession and inflation, he now gave priority to the latter. "No country that I know of," Burns said, "has been able to maintain widespread economic prosperity once inflation got out of hand."[120] Though at first glance, price increases seemed the result of a series of special, one-time phenomena—the Vietnam War, the scramble of powerful labor unions for higher wages in 1970 and 1971, the mismanagement of policy in 1972, and the oil embargo—Burns had become convinced that deeper social maladjustments accounted for continuing inflation. "We are a nation in a hurry for more and more of what we consider the good things in life. Of late, individuals have come to depend less and less on their own initiative, and more on government to achieve their objectives. The public nowadays expects the government to maintain prosperous economic conditions, to limit such declines in employment as may occasionally occur, to ease the burden of job loss or illness or retirement, to sustain the incomes of farmers, homebuilders, and so on. These are laudable objectives, and we and other nations have moved a considerable distance toward their realization. Unfortunately, in the process of doing so, government budgets have gotten out of control, wages and prices have become less responsive to the discipline of market forces, and inflation has emerged as the most dangerous economic ailment of our time."[121] Put simply, people wanted more than the economy could provide, and politicians, who often shared their constitutents' unrealistic expectations and were certainly loathe to disappoint the voters, did their best to provide for the collective wants of society. President Johnson had insisted on fighting the war in Vietnam even while expanding Great Society programs. In 1970 and 1971, labor unions had pushed wages up without reference to productivity. In 1972, legislators had demanded both stable prices and low interest rates—demands to which Burns had acquiesced.

By 1974, however, the chairman was convinced that the Fed needed to strike a blow against rising prices. The scale of inflation made both action imperative and people more willing to tolerate drastic measures. A restrictive monetary policy would do much to rein in demand and slow price increases. Moreover, by espousing a hard line and sticking to it, the central bank could help convince people that prices would indeed stabilize. Burns considered psychology important in determining inflation and believed that someone in the government had to take a firm stand. With most of the rest of Washington obsessed with Watergate, the task fell to him. As Robert Holland, a governor of the Federal Reserve, said, the central bank bore "a heavy share of the burden of fighting inflation, for the very practical reason that no other public policy tool seems capable now of doing more of the job."[122]

Soon Arthur Burns had laid out a tough new policy. The country, he said, had "to face up squarely to the gravity of the inflation problem."[123] The Federal Reserve, he insisted, was not "going to sit back and prepare a monetary path to a continuation of rapid inflation. . . . On the contrary, we hope to do our part in subduing it. . . . Let there be no mistaking our determination in this."[124] He conceded that this policy would be painful but argued this was necessary. "The government should not," he said, "try to compensate fully for all the inconveniences or actual hardship that may ensue from its struggle against inflation. Public policy must not negate with one hand what it was doing with the other."[125] For a time, the Open Market Committee matched these words with action. The demand for loans during the spring and summer of 1974 was extremely heavy as companies borrowed to expand capacity and build up inventories, and to contain monetary growth, the Fed pushed interest rates to record highs. In July, the prime rate peaked at 12 percent, with the cost of money in the open market even higher. The demand for credit, however, was so strong that the monetary aggregates nevertheless grew quite fast, and the Fed, uncertain what such sky-high rates would do to the economy, dared not go any further. Burns could reasonably claim in mid-1974, "Although money was commonly described as tight the rate of monetary expansion had in fact been quite ample so far this year and . . . interest rates were high because the demand for credit was high, particularly in view of inflationary expectations."[126]

Nevertheless, the image of Burns as the relentless inflation-fighter took hold. A story in the *Washington Post* described him as the only person in the government effectively resisting higher prices. Wall Street reportedly considered him "the devil and savior rolled into one," lauding his war against inflation but fearing where it might lead. *Business Week* gushed, "Inflation threatens to tear apart not only the economy but American society, and only Burns and his Fed seem to be doing anything about it. Burns stands as a titanic figure at a time when official Washington is woefully short of such figures." Economist Walter Heller spoke of "Arthur Burns and the Fed man[ning] their lonely ramparts in the battle against inflation," and worried that they would overdo it.[127] Some, seeing interest rates at record highs, thought the central bank had already gone too far. George Meany of the AFL-CIO angrily declared, "The advisers that made these policies and followed them to their disastrous results must be replaced. . . . If unemployment must rise, then let Dr. Burns be the first to volunteer."[128] Senator Russell B. Long, Democrat of Louisiana—who was hardly a radical—spoke of Burns's "Herbert Hoover type of economics" and warned that his approach would "break this country and put it on its knees just as it did back in 1928 and 1929."[129] The surprise, however, is that even more did not oppose the Fed's new policy. It seems that many agreed with Senator Proxmire when he said in April that inflation was the "prime, central, and certain economic threat."[130] Most people were frightened and grateful for any action to contain prices. Editorial pages around the country gave evidence of this sentiment. The *Los Angeles Times* had reservations about some aspects of the Fed chairman's plans but agreed, "Burns is on the right track." "What isn't needed," it continued, "is election-year pretense by Mr. Nixon that the situation is less serious than it really is, or by Democrats that there is some magical solution that the Republican administration is unwilling to embrace."[131] The *Des Moines Register* went further. "If inflation goes on the way it is going," it argued, "the philosophy that a recession must be avoided at all cost may need revision. The goal of full employment may have to be set aside . . . if roaring inflation is not to destroy the whole system."[132]

Arthur Burns had turned an important corner. In December 1972 he had stated, "We can no longer cope with inflation by letting recessions run their course; or by accepting a higher average level of unemployment; or by neglecting programs whose aim it is to halt the decay of our central cities, or to provide better medical care for the aged, or to create larger opportunities for the poor."[133] But in 1975 he would thunder, "The recession [the worst by far since the Depression]. . . . must not, however, be viewed as being a merely pathological phenomenon. Since we permitted inflation to get out of control, the recession is now performing a painful—but also unavoidable function. . . . The recession is wringing inflation out of the economic system."[134] This new thinking reflected the changing fortunes of the American economy. The United States had entered a new economic world, less certain and less forgiving than the old one. After 1973 the regular increase in per capita income that during the postwar era had improved living standards and eased social change ceased. Jobs considered permanent vanished, and institutions thought eternal crumbled. Of course, in 1974 Burns could not have known what the future held. But he did sense dangerous weaknesses in the economic structure to which he attributed inflation, and he was convinced that prosperity would return only after the nation had corrected these. At a time when most officials and economists thought that the country's difficulties, however unpleasant, were a passing phase, Arthur Burns had at least begun to grasp the new reality and address it.

7

Under Siege

✦

During the summer of 1974, a series of financial crises threatened to overwhelm the American banking system. Although the economy had been slowing for over a year, inflation had encouraged investment in real estate, commodities, and anything else that promised to benefit from rising prices. Borrowing financed much of this activity. As with other speculative booms, everyone assumed that prices would go up indefinitely, and when the climb halted, many found themselves in deep trouble. These people turned for salvation to the lender of last resort, the Federal Reserve.

Real estate suffered the heaviest blow. In contrast to homebuilding, commercial construction had been brisk for several years and remained so even as inflation accelerated because land and buildings seemed a good hedge against higher prices. But in late 1973, the Fed staff noted that builders "were incurring substantial cost over-runs owing to inflated materials and labor prices, delays in completion due to materials shortages, increased costs of construction credit, and slow final sales reflecting in part uncertainties about energy."[1] It soon became evident that most cities had more buildings than they could use, and in the summer of 1974 a spectacular crash sent real estate values tumbling from London to Tokyo.

This debacle hit every sort of financial institution hard, but real estate investment trusts (REITs) suffered most. REITs were financial intermediaries that borrowed money by selling short-term IOUs (commercial paper) in money markets and then invested the proceeds in mortgage and construction loans. By the spring of 1974, their liabilities totaled $21 billion. As real estate markets collapsed, REITs found themselves unable to float the new paper they needed to refinance maturing debts, and they had to turn to commercial banks for credit. But these banks were naturally reluctant to loan to institutions with uncertain futures. Desperate, REITs began quietly to ask the central bank for help.

The situation thoroughly alarmed the people at the Fed. Without credit, REITs would fail, sending shockwaves through the financial system and cutting off an important source of loans for construction. Burns met with officers of the REIT trade association, and though he refused direct aid, the central bank did contact critical lenders to encourage them to make credit available.[2] Though such action may seem modest, it carried great weight because the Fed almost never makes such requests. The largest New York and Chicago banks, which shared the Fed's concern that defaults might set off a general panic, extended sufficient loans to prevent bankruptcies.[3] Many REITs, however, remained unsteady. Banks, prodded by regulators such as the Fed, kept a close eye on them to make sure that they resolved their problems.[4]

Financial troubles, however, were not confined to real estate but also affected such diverse industries as cattle feedlots, airlines, and electric utilities. Most feedlot operators had bought livestock at high prices in early 1974, intending to fatten them up and sell them at even higher prices a few months later. But the price of meat dropped in the interim, saddling operators with severe losses. As a result, frightened bankers threatened to cut off financing, which would doom most feedlots. If this happened, many rural banks would face substantial—

and in some cases fatal—losses, and an important part of American agriculture would be crippled.⁵ Airlines had suffered from the massive jump in oil prices because jet fuel was a major part of their expenses, and it seemed possible that Pan American, the weakest of these companies, would fail. It owed creditors $900 million, and the collapse of such a venerable firm would almost certainly deal a serious blow to business confidence.⁶ Electric utilities had similar difficulties—the energy crisis had pushed up the price of the fossil fuels that they used to generate power. But state regulatory commissions, deferring to popular pressures, refused for the most part to countenance higher electric rates. The problem was particularly acute because utilities were in the midst of building much new capacity, which consumed money but had yet to produce revenue. The combined debts of electric utilities were huge, and substantial defaults would severely hurt financial stability as well as the credit of a vital industry.⁷

In all three cases, Burns worked to retrieve the situation. With respect to feedlots, he sent a letter to rural bankers telling them, "Taking due account of the relative credit risks . . . the first obligation of bankers is to the credit requirements of their service areas."⁸ This was a none-too-subtle hint that these institutions should provide needed loans to feedlot operators. Soon the Congress stepped in, issuing federal guarantees for these credits. Fortunately, the vast majority of feedlots remained solvent despite heavy losses and continued to operate. Burns also served on an interagency task force that struggled to solve Pan Am's problems, though it was the Iranian government that finally rescued the company with an investment of $300 million.⁹ Burns did his best for electric utilities too, meeting with state regulatory commissioners to persuade them to permit higher rates. The industry saved itself, however, by cutting capital spending by about $22 billion, allowing the utilities to balance their books.¹⁰

While Burns and others worked to resolve the problems of various industries, another crisis struck at the very heart of the financial system. The Franklin National Bank, which had $5 billion in assets and was the twentieth largest bank in the United States, became insolvent—the largest such failure thus far in American history. Franklin had obtained about $2 billion by contracting short-term debts in various money markets, and it had invested these funds in long-term loans. But the run-up of short-term interest rates in 1974 had squeezed the bank badly since its income from long-term investments had remained static while short-term costs had skyrocketed, and it had to come up with a lot of money fast to refinance its rapidly maturing debts—a tall order even for a healthy institution.[11] On top of this mess, Franklin employees had been able, without the approval of management, to lose tens of millions of dollars in foreign exchange transactions, enough to deplete the bank's capital. Depositors were withdrawing their money, and unless Franklin got credit somewhere it would have to close its doors.

This prospect horrified Burns, who later stated that if the bank had gone under "it would have sent shock waves, not only throughout our financial system, but across the entire world."[12] Though heretofore uninvolved in the crisis, the central bank intervened to keep Franklin afloat, extending $1.75 billion in loans through its discount window and taking over the management of Franklin's confused foreign exchange portfolio, which the New York Federal Reserve bank eventually managed to straighten out.[13] After five months, the Federal Deposit Insurance Corporation, which had seized Franklin, merged it with the European American Bank and Trust Company. It had been a close call. To lend a bank money, the Fed must have security in the form of high-quality assets, and Franklin had had enough of these to cover its borrowing—barely. But as Burns said, "While I think we did our jobs well and skillfully, we were basically lucky. . . . If deposits had fallen more rapidly than they did, the chances are we would have to close the bank."[14]

Many banks encountered difficulties in the summer and fall of 1974. They had been caught up in the speculative boom, making risky loans in real estate and other areas that, in many cases, went bad. Burns thought that the long prosperity of the previous thirteen years had eroded financial caution and allowed sloppy practices to flourish. "You have," he said, "a new generation of bankers that has been taught by economists that the business cycle is dead and we will no longer have depressions in our country. . . . They came to believe all this [predictions of eternal prosperity]. They are not highly educated men; history is not one of the favorite subjects in our universities."[15] In the summer of 1974, the Fed's staff warned that some bank holding companies were having trouble obtaining credit, and as the economy weakened in the fall and winter, these difficulties increased.[16]

Though no major institution failed, many had deep-seated problems that required them to work out bad loans and strengthen their capital bases, and the Fed and other regulatory agencies kept a close watch on troubled banks to make sure that they did so. The Federal Reserve, for instance, might deny an institution the right to open new branches or undertake new business until it had made provisions against uncertain loans.[17] The process demanded none of the heroics of the Franklin case but much hard, unglamorous work. As late as 1976, twelve of the nation's fifty largest bank holding companies were on the Fed's "problem" list, indicating that the central bank considered their condition below par.[18]

Throughout this difficult period, Burns was determined to prevent anything that might further weaken financial institutions. For instance, in late 1974 the Securities and Exchange Commission (SEC) proposed that banks value their portfolios at market rather than book prices. This would have forced institutions to write off many assets that, though not performing at the moment, still had promise of rehabilitation, and would also have required them to reduce the price of bonds whose market value was down but which they intended to hold to maturity and so redeem at face value. Moreover, this change would have forced weak but salvageable banks to immediately reveal all their problems, making resuscitation more difficult. Burns called the SEC's chief accountant, whom he had taught at Columbia, to a meeting in which he told the official to "advise the [SEC] commissioners that they were taking a grave risk with the economic future of the U.S. in the interest of a somewhat dubious accounting principle." The next day, the SEC abandoned its proposal.[19]

Though little remarked outside financial circles, these events, taken together, constituted an important accomplishment. Conditions in 1974 had the potential for a general financial crisis. The speculative boom had left many banks overextended, and it is quite possible that a large default, say by Franklin National or Pan Am or a series of rural banks hurt by feedlot bankruptcies, might have sparked a panic. Such a crisis has preceded every one of the nation's depressions, and another in 1974 might have turned the severe 1974–75 recession into an even deeper and more prolonged downturn. Fortunately, Burns and the others responsible for managing the financial system prevented any such disaster. For the moment, difficulties forced lenders to pull back and so put a crimp in the economy, but when the recovery began, credit would be available to finance it.

II

Burns steered clear of the crisis that monopolized public attention during the summer of 1974—Watergate. He believed that the central bank "must stay out of impeachment politics."[20] This stance not only accorded with propriety and prudence but also reflected the chairman's own ambivalence. Despite their long association, he had never figured out the president. Speaking of Nixon's foreign policy, Burns once said to spechwriter William Safire, "Who can say what his motive is?" though he quickly added, "It's moving him in the right direction."[21] Burns owed a lot to the president, who had appointed him to the Fed, and despite their disagreements, he genuinely admired Nixon's talents and would continue to do so. But the Watergate revelations apparently shocked the Fed chairman, raising doubts in his mind about the president. Though no stranger to political hardball, Burns was neither petty nor vindictive—two adjectives that describe all too well the underside of the Nixon administration.

Although he avoided anything that smacked of Watergate, Burns continued to work with the administration on economic policy. President Nixon supported the Fed's tight money program and did his best to back it with fiscal restraint. To those who argued that interest rates were too high, the chief executive responded, "Holding down money and credit in the face of rapid inflation causes high interest rates, which nobody likes. But allowing more rapid monetary expansion would soon cause even more rapid inflation and even higher interest rates."[22] For his part, Burns joined in White House budget deliberations. Washington was slated to spend $305 billion in fiscal 1975, but the administration wanted to reduce this figure. Most preferred a $5 billion cut, but Burns and the new treasury secretary, William E. Simon, pushed for $10 billion. As Herbert Stein later pointed out, the $5 billion difference was insignificant considering the size of the American economy.[23] Burns, however, stressed psychological factors. "As far as the average American citizen is concerned," the chairman argued, "he doesn't understand monetary policy. It is too complicated. It is too technical. . . . But there is one thing that the average citizen can understand, and understand very clearly, and that is that when the Federal government reduces the level of its spending, then the pressure of demand for goods and services is smaller. Upward pressures on prices are reduced."[24] The president nevertheless decided to opt for a $5 billion cut, and the Congress failed to enact even that.

Arthur Burns performed one last service for President Nixon by persuading Alan Greenspan to become CEA chairman. Herbert Stein had already postponed leaving the administration several times and was unwilling to stay longer, having agreed to teach at the University of Virginia in the fall. But finding a replacement proved difficult—no one wanted to join a dying administration. The White House wanted Alan Greenspan, who ran a profitable economic consulting firm in New York. He had studied under Burns at Columbia and had worked in Nixon's 1968 presidential campaign, and he enjoyed a strong reputation as an economic forecaster among both business leaders and academics. But Greenspan refused the job. He was not at all sure he would enjoy working for Nixon, about whom he had developed doubts even in 1968, and he did not want to leave his company. In desperation, the administration asked Burns to go to work on his former student. The Fed chairman told Greenspan that the country needed him and that, if he had done his job properly, his consulting firm would function without him at the helm. These arguments prevailed. "Burns was unquestionably the key factor in my accepting the position," Greenspan later said. "Had I not had that conversation with him, I would definitely have said no."[25]

After President Nixon's resignation in August 1974, Burns lost no time ingratiating himself with Gerald R. Ford's new administration. He would not repeat the mistakes of 1969 and take his relationship with the chief executive for granted. During the first few weeks of the Ford administration, one staffer said that "you can't have a White House meeting without Arthur walking in."[26] This effort paid large dividends. In contrast with Nixon, Ford had considerable respect for the central bank as an institution and a genuine interest in economics. Since Burns was touchy about the Fed's autonomy and tended to go on at great length when discussing economic policy, these qualities made their relationship much smoother. Politically, the two men faced a common problem—namely, a Congress controlled by their opponents and determined to increase its authority at their expense. Finally, they agreed on the proper course of economic policy. Ford's claim that "the fight against inflation provided the basic theme of my administration"[27] could have applied just as well to Burns's second four-year term as Fed chairman.

Burns worked with the administration to create what one student of the central bank has called "the closest relationship between a president and a Fed chairman in history."[28] The White House coordinated economic policy through meetings of the aptly named Economic Policy Board, to which Burns had a standing invitation that he often exercised. If something important was on the agenda, Greenspan would inform the Fed chairman, who would then show up.[29] Burns also met with Ford alone sixty-nine times during the latter's presidency, or about once every other week—a degree of access that many cabinet members must have envied.[30] It helped immensely that the president and his advisers never discussed monetary policy with the chairman. They thought it improper to do so and apparently reasoned that, if they could get Burns to agree with them on the general direction of economic policy, he would supply the proper monetary component of his own accord—which he usually did. Summing up relations between the Fed chairman and the White House, Alan Greenspan said, "I could scarcely conceive of more discussion, more integration of policy, overall, than existed with Arthur. We . . . considered Arthur an integral part of the whole policymaking apparatus."[31] For his part, Burns later described the president's dealings with the central bank as "truly angelic."[32]

The administration and Burns exchanged many minor and not-so-minor tokens of respect. The board of governors invited Ford to visit its headquarters for the swearing in of a new governor, making him the first president to put in an appearance there since Franklin D. Roosevelt.[33] William Simon presented Burns with the Treasury's Alexander Hamilton Award, an annual honor that the department had previously bestowed only on its own employees.[34] Most important, Ford had the opportunity to appoint five Fed governors, and in each case he followed Burns's suggestion.[35] By the end of 1976, every governor owed his job to Burns's recommendation. These men were strong personalities with ideas of their own but they shared the chairman's basic outlook.

III

When Gerald Ford took office, inflation remained Arthur Burns's chief concern. Though ominous, the various financial crises seemed under control. Production had been shrinking for ten months, but Burns and most other economists attributed this to shortages of energy and other materials, which had limited output. Moreover, unemployment remained under 6 percent and the rate of economic decline seemed to be slowing. Consumer prices, however, were going up at more than 14 percent a year.

In September, a meeting of prominent economists convened by President Ford at the behest of Congress produced a roughly similar consensus. Almost all wanted tax increases and spending reductions to cut the federal deficit, and the belief that monetary growth was slowing inclined a large majority toward lower interest rates. Though most thought recession possible, few expected it to be severe—unemployment, most concurred, would not top 6.5 percent—and they agreed that inflation still merited priority. The chief point of contention was whether or not Washington should impose an incomes policy.[36] George Shultz said after the meeting that a hat could have covered all the different economic projections.[37]

The administration and the Fed more or less went along with this diagnosis. In early October, the president outlined a program that called for $5 billion in budget cuts, a 5 percent income tax surcharge, and various measures such as public service jobs to assist those hurt by the economic slowdown. Ford also launched his "Whip Inflation Now" (WIN) campaign, a vague, voluntary effort to contain prices. For its part, the central bank let interest rates fall. In the second half of 1974, the money supply expanded at less than the Fed's 6 percent goal, allowing the central bank to loosen its grip. The prime rate dropped from a high of 12 percent in July to 10.5 percent in November, while money market rates, which started higher, went down further.

Developments soon made Ford's program irrelevant. Ever since 1973, consumers had been spending less because inflation had both eroded their purchasing power and encouraged caution, since rising prices thoroughly obscured the future. Only investment in inventories and new facilities had kept the economy afloat, and in the fall and winter of 1974, both of these collapsed. Companies building new plants had assumed that they could finance these with revenues generated by higher prices, forgetting in their boom-induced euphoria that costs were going up too. By the fall of 1974, business realized that it had overextended itself and began to cut back. The Fed noticed a drop in capital spending in August and September, and by December its data showed huge reductions.[38] Likewise, managers grasped that the inventories they had built up as a hedge against inflation were grossly out of proportion to sales. With far more goods on their hands than they needed, they began to cut purchases to reduce their excess stocks. These two developments reinforced each other. As capital spending fell, demand weakened and inventories seemed all the more excessive. Declining sales made new investment even less attractive. The results were devastating. Output fell at almost a 9 percent annual rate between October 1974 and March 1975—a pace not seen since the Great Depression. In a single month, the number of jobless swelled by one million. At the new year, unemployment passed 8 percent on its way up—the highest level in thirty-five years. To the hundreds of thousands of workers laid off at steel mills, auto plants, and other industrial facilities, it seemed as though they had been transported back to the Great Depression of the 1930s. Meanwhile, the threat of inflation receded. Consumer prices increased only at a 6.6 percent rate in the first quarter of 1975, and wholesale prices actually fell. The administration forgot its plans for a tax increase, and the WIN campaign, which even the White House seems not to have understood, became a joke.

The suddenness and depth of the downturn surprised and frightened everyone. In its severity, the drop was reminiscent of 1930—economist Paul Samuelson declared that the situation "smells of deep depression."[39] Even Alan Greenspan said that, between mid-December and mid-February, he was not sure whether the economy would turn around or plunge indefinitely.[40] The recession was all the more disturbing because it was a complete surprise. No one had predicted anything like it. To project the future, economists relied on models that applied statistical correlations drawn from past experience to present circumstances, but 1974 had witnessed an entirely new combination of declining production and inflationary boom. Not only was the country floundering, it was also in uncharted waters.

Arthur Burns remained calm. Looking at the unpredictable economy of 1974, he said, "Now I know something of business cycle history. . . . and I cannot give you another instance of this kind."[41] In these circumstances, Burns refused to be hasty. Inflation was still high, and he did not want to repeat the previous winter when the Fed had let interest rates fall only to have to jack them up again. The chairman told the Open Market Committee, "Confidence in the Federal Reserve System was one of the country's important assets, and the Committee should do nothing that would risk dissipating that confidence."[42] Despite this cautious stance, interest rates fell substantially over the terrible winter of 1974–75, largely because the demand for credit weakened as companies mothballed investment and cut inventories. By March 1975 the prime rate stood at 7.5 percent, 4.5 percentage points off the highs of 1974, and the Fed funds rate, which banks charge each other for funds deposited with the central bank, had fallen to about half its summer peak. But the money supply grew sluggishly, at 4.2 and 2.3 percent annual rates over the fourth quarter of 1974 and the first of 1975, respectively. By this measure, to which even Keynesians were beginning to give weight, monetary policy remained quite restrictive—indeed, more so than in the summer when interest rates had been so high.

The Fed's policy drew fierce criticism. To be sure, six months earlier the unprecedented cost of money had angered many, but the fear of inflation had tempered opposition. The recession, however, changed things. Many believed that unemployment deserved priority over rising prices. Moreover, the downturn restored the nerves of many economists rattled by the oil crisis—their theories had little to say about shortages, but recession they understood. Keynesians urged aggressive government action to counteract the downturn and warned that the economy would not revive unless the Fed acted. Monetarists pointed to the stagnant money supply and blamed that for the crisis. Once again, they said, the Fed had thrown the country into recession by failing to keep monetary growth steady, and some monetarists organized the "Shadow Open Market Committee" to provide regular criticism of and alternatives to Fed policy. Many business economists also thought the central bank was reacting too slowly, and apparently even a large part of the Fed's staff supported a more liberal policy.[43] Andrew Brimmer, a former Fed governor, lamented, "This recession is going to last all through 1975," and Herbert Stein spoke for many when he said that the Fed "is squeezing the economy to death."[44]

Burns, backed by a majority on the Fed's Open Market Committee, stood his ground. The recession, he argued, was the culmination of a long historical process. The period from 1965 through 1974 had experienced "a succession of interrelated, partly overlapping, speculative waves—first, in buying up existing businesses; then, in the stock market; next, in markets for real estate; and finally, in markets for industrial materials and other commodities. . . . These basic maladjustments are now being worked out of the economic system by recession."[45] Monetary policy was not to blame for the nation's problems. "The country has plenty of money," Burns declared. "In fact, the country is awash with liquidity. The difficulty is that . . . the willingness to use the existing stock of money just is not there."[46] Burns placed his faith in the self-correcting forces of the business cycle. "We often go on the assumption," he said, "that we get economic recovery just because of what the government does. Nowadays, we tend to ignore what actually happens within the private sector of our economy. Actually, when a recession develops such as we have now, corrective forces come into play . . . in behalf of economic recovery."[47] Interest rates were down, and once business had reduced inventories, worked out financial problems, and cut costs, the economy would rebound. Historically, only financial collapse had shortcircuited this process, and the Fed had staved off that danger over the summer. The best thing the central bank could do now was to remain on guard against inflation. "Inflation," Burns said, "had caused the decline in real GNP, in real income of the working man, and in purchases of big-ticket items; inflation had caused the erosion in profits, the rise in interest rates to extraordinarily high levels, the weakness in the bond markets, and the price declines in the stock exchanges."[48] If the central bank directed its policy solely toward economic recovery and rapidly expanded the money supply, it would stoke fears of a new round of price increases that would discourage consumer spending and push up long-term interest rates, aborting any rebound.[49]

The Fed's policy in 1974 remains controversial. Critics have argued that the central bank overreacted to inflation, pushing interest rates so high as to inadvertently trigger recession. Economist Paul Samuelson said, "If you turn the present recession upside down and read on the

bottom, it will say, 'Made in Washington.' . . . The weakness in production has been by design and not by accident. They [the administration and the Fed] all desired that the economy be cooled off. But it
got out of hand like an avalanche."[50] But almost no one saw the scale
of the coming downturn before it hit. Inflation was out of control in
1974, and without clear evidence to the contrary, the Fed's first
responsibility was to combat it. Moreover, Burns was correct when he
stated that the recession reflected, to a large degree, the unwinding of
the speculative boom of 1973–74. Lower interest rates might have
slowed the liquidation of inventories and cutbacks in capital spending,
but they probably would not have prevented them. Finally, Burns's
warning that aggressive monetary easing might reignite fears of inflation and so undo the recovery was plausible. In 1974, people had good
reason to fear price increases, and this fear had discouraged consumption and pushed up long-term interest rates. Had the Fed cut the
cost of credit fast enough to allow vigorous monetary growth, people
might well have concluded that it had given up on inflation. Of course,
to a degree the Fed's plight was of its own making. A more cautious
monetary policy in 1972 and early 1973 probably would have limited
the size of the ensuing speculative boom and the pain of the accom-
panying bust. But by late 1974, such points were irrelevant—the truth
was that the central bank had no good options. At the time, however,
the reality of hardship, the uncertainty about the future, and the belief
that the Fed was not doing enough generated strong pressures for
changes in monetary policy.

In early 1975, Congress was ready to challenge Burns's judgment.
Thanks to economic problems and Watergate, the Democrats had won
a smashing victory in the 1974 elections. They had huge majorities in
both legislative houses, and many of their new members were eager to
change traditional ways of doing things in Washington. This new
atmosphere affected the banking committees. In the Senate, John Sparkman, a loyal friend of the central bank, moved to chair the Foreign Relations Committee, and William Proxmire, a critic of Fed policies and procedures, took over from him at the Banking Committee. In the House,
members unseated the elderly and unpredictable Patman and replaced
him with Henry Reuss. Though a far more even personality than his predecessor, Reuss shared Patman's suspicion of the central bank and his
desire to bring it under closer congressional supervision.

Burns remained determined to keep the legislative branch out of monetary policy. He had little confidence in the economic judgment of the average representative or senator, thinking them too attuned to immediate political pressures for easy money and not sufficiently alive to the long-term danger of inflation. When Senator Proxmire asked him, "Are you suggesting Congress is less dedicated to fighting inflation compared to the members of the Federal Reserve Board," Burns replied, "I sometimes think so: yes."[51] Such attitudes were common at the central bank. One staffer asserted, "There really isn't anyone else in the federal structure who is interested in maintaining any degree of price stability."[52] The Fed chairman also doubted that the legislative branch could effectively administer the central bank. "The Congress has not found it easy to legislate fiscal policy," he said. "If the Congress now sought to legislate monetary policy as well, it would enter a vastly more intricate, highly sensitive, and rapidly changing field— with consequences that could prove very damaging to our nation's economy."[53]

Outside of Washington, this position enjoyed a surprising amount of support. Burns had earned a lot of respect by taking a tough line against inflation, which most people considered the nation's chief problem. As an editorial in the *Atlanta Constitution* put it, "Burns is one of the handful of high government officials who have any idea about what's really wrong with the American economy." His opponents did not always rate such trust. The *Constitution* noted, "There is surely room for improvement in the Federal Reserve, but taking money supply decisions away from professionals and subjecting them to the politicians and demagogues in Congress is certainly not the answer." "What a fertile area for scandal," the *Denver Post* lamented, "were the politicians to get a grip on the nation's money supply." These opinions did not reflect unconditional support for Fed policy, which received criticism. But fairly or not, many granted Burns, the stern defender of monetary rectitude, a moral authority that they denied his critics.[54]

The emerging debate revolved around two questions, logically separate but practically intertwined. First, should Fed policy concentrate solely on reviving the economy or should it be more cautious, with an eye toward inflation? Second, how much control should Congress exercise over the central bank? Few in the legislative branch had much interest in monetary policy—it was an arcane subject that rarely swayed voters. True, high interest rates and recession had compelled lawmakers to pay more heed to the matter, but in most cases this interest reflected concern about the economy rather than a determination, as a matter of principle, to bring the central bank under greater congressional control. If Burns could convince legislators that the Fed was on top of the economic situation, their interest in the central bank would probably ebb.

The conflict played out in a series of contentious, exhausting hearings. These often went on for hours, and at times Burns seemed intent on simply wearing down his critics—despite his seventy years, his stamina remained awesome. But moments of real drama did shine through the barrages of economic statistics and theory. The leading participants had considerable wit and verve, and they played to a larger audience. Burns always appeared alone, assuming the role of the man in the arena, facing down the legislative lions. Congressmen and senators often rehearsed in front of their staffs, practicing delivering tough questions and snappy comebacks. No one pulled punches. Wright Patman said sarcastically, "The good doctor [Burns] is here to tell us that despite the fact that our economy is teetering on the brink of depression . . . we live in the best of all possible worlds."[55] At one point, Senator Hubert Humphrey denounced the Fed chairman as "the high priest of finance."[56] Burns gave as good as he got, sometimes allowing his ingrained sense of superiority free rein. When asked at one point by Senator Proxmire if the Fed could not do more to make credit available, Burns replied, "Sure we could do more. We could do a lot more. We could even wreck this country, but we are not going to do it, Senator."[57]

Representative Reuss fired the first shot. In February, he introduced a bill ordering the central bank to "direct . . . [its] efforts in the first half of 1975 towards maintaining an increase in the money supply (demand deposits and currency outside banks) of no less than 6 percent at an annual rate," and requiring the Fed to organize a system of mandatory credit allocation, directing money away from "inflationary uses" and toward "national priority uses." The former were defined as "purely financial activities," "loans for speculative purposes," and "loans to foreigners," the latter as capital investment, companies' working capital, low- and middle-income housing, small business and agriculture, and state and local government.[58] These regulations would presumably cut the total demand for credit by ridding markets of speculators, thereby allowing interest rates to decline even while the Fed kept monetary growth in bounds.[59] Reuss crafted this measure to satisfy a motley alliance of populists, who wanted low interest rates, and monetarists, who wanted a constant rule for monetary growth.

Burns demolished Reuss's proposal in testimony before the House Banking Committee. As for the rule on monetary expansion, he argued that "the narrowly defined money supply, taken by itself is an inadequate—and at times misleading—indicator of what is happening to the stock of highly liquid assets available to American families and business firms." He pointed out that while the money supply grew at a 4.3 percent rate in the last quarter of 1974, certificates of deposit (CDs) increased at 9 percent, deposits at savings and loans at 7 percent, credit union shares at 9 percent, and large CDs (over $100,000) at 26 percent. Besides, he claimed, "the rate of turnover of money— that is, the rate at which the public is willing to use the existing stock of money—is typically much more important than the size of the stock over periods of six months." In other words, there was plenty of money if only people would borrow and spend it. As for credit allocation, he argued that the terms of the bill were quite vague and did not provide enough guidance for running such a program. "Tilting credit in favor of some borrowers implies denying credit to someone else," Burns noted. "Are we to favor the credit needs of 'small business and agriculture,' as the bill requires, even if that means that large corporations will be denied the credit needed to keep their employees working? . . . Would we have to deny credit to finance a merger of two firms, even though such a merger was expected to result in a strong enterprise that can better expand job opportunities in its area?. . . Would it really be wise in an interdependent world to discourage loans to foreigners? Such a policy would handicap our exporters and importers; it would lead to retaliation by other countries; it would cause goodwill towards our nation to vanish. . . . Decisions as to social priorities in the use of credit are inherently political in character. If such decisions are to be made at all, they should be made by Congress—not by an administrative and nonpolitical body such as the Federal Reserve. . . . Administration of the credit control program envisaged . . . would be enormously complex and costly. I doubt whether it is even feasible." To work, the Fed would have to regulate banks, thrifts, insurance companies, finance companies, financial markets, and the flow of money into and out of the country—a tall order. "There is no good substitute," Burns claimed, "for the decision-making process provided by our highly developed, sensitive, and intensely competitive financial system."[60] In a surprising decision, the Banking Committee soon thereafter rejected its chairman's bill by a vote of twenty to nineteen.[61]

Senator Proxmire tried his hand next, to greater effect. The board of governors had suggested a compromise with the Congress in the form of a resolution requiring the chairman to appear before the banking committees once each quarter (twice a year for each committee) to report on "general objectives and plans with respect to monetary and credit policy." Proxmire, however, argued that such hearings would be "meaningless exercises" because "we know what they [the goals] are . . . maximum employment, stable prices, and moderate long-term interest rates." Hearings should concentrate on "numerical target ranges with respect to rates of growth of monetary and credit aggregates," which would give the Congress a firm yardstick by which to judge policy.[62] Burns resisted this course, claiming that such targets would be "a straitjacket, and we could damage our country."[63] But Proxmire argued that the resolution allowed the central bank to reevaluate policy as circumstances changed, and Burns finally acquiesced. The measure easily passed both houses of Congress.[64]

Arthur Burns made sure that this resolution did not restrict the Fed's freedom of maneuver. With respect to the numerical target, he announced that since no single measure accurately encompassed "money," the central bank would pay attention to six different yardsticks: M1, the supply of currency and demand deposits (heretofore referred to as the "money supply"); M2, M1 plus certificates of deposit under $100,000; M3, M2 plus thrift deposits; M4, M2 plus CDs over $100,000; M5, M3 plus CDs over $100,000; and the bank credit proxy, the funds available for banks to lend. At the quarterly hearings before the banking committees, Burns would give targets for M1, M2, M3, and the bank credit proxy and would usually at least mention M4 and M5. This statistical multiplication was not merely an exercise in obfuscation—as Burns had long contended, money is hard to define, and over time economists have emphasized different measures.[65] Moreover, changes in the financial system during the 1970s brought traditional ways of calculating the money supply into question—for instance, money market funds were becoming popular but did not fit into any of the different estimates of "money." But the variety of measures also served a political purpose by confusing legislators and allowing the Fed to emphasize whatever figures seemed best to fit its arguments at the moment. The central bank also set wide margins for its monetary targets, usually two to two-and-a-half percentage points. The difference between, say, 5 and 7 percent growth in the money supply is considerable, but Burns argued—with justice—that the Fed simply could not hit a narrower target and that such goals would be unrealistic.[66]

Burns's third tactic was not so defensible. At each quarterly hearing, when he announced targets for monetary policy, Burns in effect started anew. If, for instance, monetary growth had been weaker than desired in one quarter, the Fed would not allow more rapid growth over the next three months to compensate. This approach effectively absolved the central bank of responsibility for hitting long-term money supply targets. It was not a particularly honest ploy for a man who had long argued that the rate of monetary expansion mattered only over periods of a year or more. Finally, the chairman refused to give Congress the Fed's projections about how monetary policy would affect the economy. He would make a "personal" estimate but said that members of the OMC often supported the same policy for very different reasons and claimed, "I have no way of knowing what the precise thinking is of the other members of the Federal Reserve family."[67] As for staff projections, he said these "are highly speculative; past experience has indicated that they are subject to huge margins of error. Since projections of that character could be easily misused or misinterpreted, it would be inappropriate to put them in the public domain."[68] Moreover, he warned that publicizing these figures "could have highly damaging effects on staff work— that is, on the willingness to 'call the shots' as they are perceived, and yet stand ready to revise their figures frequently and with complete objectivity."[69] Legislators did consider Burns's agreement to give "personal" estimates a minor victory, since they reasoned that these would be close to staff projections, though they probably underestimated the extent to which the chairman's projections occasionally differed from his staff's.[70]

Many in Congress deeply resented Burns's obfuscation, especially on the matter of projections. The staff of the House Banking Committee attacked the chairman for giving the impression "that the Federal Reserve is some mystical body which has policies that can never be explained."[71] Senator Proxmire told Burns, "We don't get any answer from you at all except a word description that could mean everything or nothing."[72] Representative Reuss said, "It seems inconceivable that the Fed should set such [monetary] targets without a concrete notion of the amounts of unemployment and inflation they may produce. . . . The Congress, which bears ultimate responsibility for our nation's economic health, should not be kept in the dark about the choices now being made by the Federal Reserve."[73] Senator Humphrey commented trenchantly, "I do not find it at all reassuring that monetary policy may be being made on the basis of projections which are so highly speculative that it would be dangerous to let Congress look at them."[74] But no one could force Burns to provide more precise information.

Though Burns contrived to shield the details of monetary policy from congressional scrutiny, Proxmire's resolution nevertheless represented an important innovation. For the first time, the Fed had to reveal at least the general thrust of policy before implementing it, opening itself up to criticism and to pressures to follow different courses.

In the winter and spring of 1975, a strong consensus existed among economists for a liberal monetary policy. The economic outlook seemed bleak. Production was shrinking fast and unemployment would top 9 percent in May. But despite lower interest rates, monetary growth was anemic. To get a strong recovery, most economists calculated that the central bank would have to expand the money supply (M1) at an 8-to-10 percent annual rate. Since prices were going up at about 7 percent, and the turnover of money had over time tended to increase at about 3 percent, this would allow the economy to grow at 6 percent—historically, the average rate of recovery. Inflation was worrisome, but the economy had a lot of slack, so stimulus would not make it any worse. Economists across the ideological spectrum, from Walter Heller to Herbert Stein, endorsed this view.

Burns would have none of it. His opponents did not know what they were talking about. "In ancient and medieval times," he said, "kings would have around them soothsayers, necromancers, and they would prophesize and they would sing. Now we have economists performing the same function for presidents and Congress, . . . and I think the efficacy of the one group is perhaps no larger that the efficacy of the other."[75] By April and May, he saw signs that the recovery would begin soon if it had not already done so. Most companies had drastically reduced their inventories and would have to increase purchases to meet demand.[76] Burns scoffed at calculations that only 8 to 10 percent monetary expansion would assure an adequate recovery. "Most economists who move from platform to platform these days, and from one hearing room to another," he declared, "pay very little attention to the business cycle. They have never studied it thoroughly, or, if they have, they have forgotten what they once knew. . . . If you examine the historical record, you will find that in the first year of recovery it is the rate of turnover of money that shoots up dramatically in contrast to the change in the existing stock."[77] This higher turnover would permit recovery without an expansive monetary policy. Of those who argued for rapid money-supply growth, Burns said, "First they fail to take account of the sensitivity to rising rates of inflation that people in our country have exhibited in recent years. In practically every industrial nation, more rapid inflation has led to larger precautionary savings and sluggish consumer buying. Second, they fail to look far enough into the future, for it may not be until two or three years down the road that the full inflationary impact of more stimulative policies would be felt."[78] Moreover, though the chairman did not say this, the minutes of OMC meetings make it clear that he and a majority of the committee preferred a gradual to a rapid recovery, believing that such a course would lower inflation. In May, Burns announced targets for monetary growth of 5 to 7.5 percent for M1, 8.5 to 10.5 percent for M2, and 10 to 12 percent for M3. He argued that these goals "err on the side of ease" and would have to come down as the economy recovered, but for the moment they were not "too high when idle resources are extensive and financial needs still reflect rising prices."[79]

Though the administration supported this policy, few others did.[80] Economist James Tobin said that Burns "appears to be determined to go down in history as the man who broke inflation in the United States, and if it takes years of unemployment and economic stagnation, he is willing to have us pay the price."[81] A committee of prominent Keynesians claimed, "Under present economic conditions, with ample excess capacity and high unemployment, a recovery of output involves minimal risks of increasing inflationary pressures, while permitting the economy to continue its slide involves, with certainty, huge social costs (presumably about $150 billion per annum)."[82] The monetary targets needed to be higher—maybe 10 percent for M1, with the others up accordingly.

Much to Burns's consternation, fiscal policy followed a more accommodating path. In January, when production was collapsing, President Ford proposed a one-time tax rebate of $16 billion to resuscitate the economy. Burns was initially skeptical. "When I first heard of this proposal," he said in a congressional hearing, extending his arms out to his sides like wings, "I had a vision of airplanes flying all over the country dropping checks down chimneys."[83] Nevertheless, he eventually supported the measure as a good way to give the economy a boost without increasing the federal deficit in the long run. The bill that passed Congress, however, differed considerably from the original. It provided for $23 billion in cuts and contained a whole slew of benefits to favored groups, such as tax credits for those who bought homes. Burns urged Ford to veto it. "Many provisions of the bill will become permanent," he said, because "it will be virtually impossible to eliminate such 'reforms' as the increase in the standard deduction," even though it was scheduled to expire at the end of 1975. "Our government, which has been operating, year in and year out, on borrowed money simply cannot afford further erosion of the tax base," he continued. Nor did he like the various tax breaks for special groups, which he feared would "distort the equity or thrust of overall tax policy." Finally, though he did not consider this "a fundamental difficulty," Burns thought a $23 billion cut too large. "The financing job that will have to be done to fund the deficit is already gigantic. It threatens to overburden our financial markets, and to crowd out the private sector demands for credit that will accompany economic recovery."[84] Treasury Secretary Simon supported Burns, but other advisers, led by Chairman Greenspan, persuaded Ford to sign the bill. They did not particularly like the measure but believed that the political atmosphere made a tax cut inevitable and considered the proposal at hand as good a bill as they were likely to get.

The tax reduction made fiscal policy over the next couple of years quite stimulative. The federal deficit for fiscal 1975 was over $43 billion, and for the following year it totaled more than $66 billion. President Ford tried to contain spending by vetoing appropriation bills that he thought excessive, but he and his aides simply could not find the sort of savings needed to substantially reduce the deficit, and Congress sometimes overrode his vetoes. Such heavy fiscal stimulus inclined Burns toward a cautious monetary policy.

The recovery began in May. Having cut their inventories to the bone, retailers increased purchases substantially. Rebates authorized by the tax cut went out, giving consumers more to spend and thus speeding the rebound. The economy expanded at a healthy 6.3 percent annual rate in the second quarter—the first growth in fifteen months—and unemployment began to inch down. Production recovered because of the "natural" forces that Burns emphasized, especially the end of the massive inventory reductions. But the improvement owed much of its punch to the tax rebates. According to one broadly consulted economic model, recovery would have proceeded regardless, but without fiscal stimulus unemployment would not have declined substantially until the end of the year.[85] Such calculations are uncertain, but they do suggest that Ford acted wisely when he ignored Burns's advice and signed the tax cut bill. The president's own more modest proposal might well have yielded similar results, but the balance of power in Congress made its passage unlikely.

In the summer the Fed pushed up interest rates. Preliminary figures showed that in May and June the money supply (M1) had increased at a 15-to-20 percent annual rate, a pace the central bank thought far too rapid. In response, it drove the prime rate from 7 percent in June to 8 percent in September, with market rates up accordingly.

This action met sharp resistance. The big increase in the money supply, many argued, reflected the deposit of tax rebates in banks rather than any jump in the demand for credit. It was a one-time phenomenon, and things would soon return to normal. *Business Week* noted, "The interest rate rise is virtually unprecedented at this stage of recovery. Commercial and industrial loan demand is still weak, and bankers do not expect much of an increase before 1976. But higher rates now could affect business plans and the whole shape of recovery"[86] Franco Modigliani, president-elect of the American Economics Association, said that "with the depression, unemployment at over 9 percent, and now the very sluggish recovery," higher interest rates were "crazy."[87] Walter Heller and Arthur Okun, CEA chairmen under Presidents Kennedy and Johnson, also criticized the move.[88] Even Helmut Schmidt, the German chancellor and himself an economist, described Fed policy as "too restrictive" and likely to hinder recovery in all the industrialized countries.[89] Moreover, critics argued that since the increase in the money supply flowed from the tax cut, the Fed was effectively sabotaging an act of Congress. Journalist Eric Severeid expressed a common sense of outrage when he said, "The Federal Reserve in this system of ours is virtually a fourth branch of government. It is not checked or balanced by any other branch of government. It has the power to negate any economic recovery program that you [President Ford] or the Congress . . . put forward. . . . It is a political weapon."[90] Support for the Fed did come from some important sources. The administration, as usual, backed Burns. Milton Friedman also applauded central bank policy, which he interpreted as an attempt to keep monetary expansion on an even keel.[91] But the negative reviews far outweighed the positive.

Having defied his enemies for months, Burns was not about to give in now. He scolded senators, "Did you at the time anticipate that the tax rebates . . . would increase the rate of growth of the money supply in the months of May and June to a 15 percent annual rate? Did you anticipate that the rate of growth in the money supply in the month of June would be higher than any recorded in our postwar national history? Did that enter your minds?"[92] He claimed that, if the central bank had permitted this expansion "without doing anything at all, . . . that would have been interpreted by the business and financial community as indicating that the Federal Reserve had thrown in the sponge" on inflation.[93]

In spite of dire warnings from many quarters, recovery continued as Burns had predicted. The economy expanded at almost a 7 percent rate in the second half of 1975, and by year-end unemployment had dropped below 8 percent. At the same time, inflation subsided. Consumer prices increased at about a 7.5 percent rate in the last quarter, while for all of 1975 wholesale prices jumped 4.4 percent, less than one-fourth the pace of the previous two years. Though no one can be certain, the Fed's policy of limiting monetary growth, even at the cost of higher interest rates, apparently reinforced this trend by providing some insurance against more inflation. The money supply (M1) grew at only a 4.4 percent annual rate in the second half, far below what Burns's critics had declared necessary for recovery, but at the same time, the cost of money fell too, with the prime rate down to 7 percent by early 1976. Franco Modigliani declared, "I find it hard to understand how GNP could grow as rapidly as it did in the third quarter and interest rates not rise sharply when the money supply was growing so weakly."[94] The answer was that, as Burns had predicted, the velocity, or turnover, of money had increased at an 11 percent annual rate in the third quarter and at 9 percent in the fourth.[95]

Economic success begat political power. Events had gone as the Fed chairman had said they would, and in 1976 Senator Proxmire admitted to Burns, "Your proposals of monetary strategy have been borne out on the basis of our recovery."[96] As a result, many legislators concluded that monetary policy was best left to the Federal Reserve. As one congressman said, "There was a strong, generally prevailing view [in Congress] that if it's not broke, don't fix it."[97] Burns had always enjoyed considerable prestige on Capitol Hill because of his obvious intelligence, strong personality, and careful cultivation of representatives and senators, but now his standing was even higher. At subsequent hearings before the banking committees, most members would turn out when Burns appeared, but few attended when others testified about monetary policy.[98] At one of these latter meetings, Senator Proxmire lamented, "Here we have two of the most distinguished economic spokesmen in the country before this committee today, and I'm the only Senator who showed up."[99]

Attacks upon the Federal Reserve did not, however, cease. Some, such as Henry Reuss, firmly believed that the Congress needed to exert firmer control over the central bank. One House Banking Committee memo summed up his thinking when it argued, "An independent Fed means freedom to carry on day-to-day monetary policy but does not mean that the Fed can be unresponsive to the American public or to the requirements of our Full Employment Act."[100] Political calculation drove others. One of Senator Humphrey's staffers told a Fed lobbyist, "Chairman Burns is highly visible and the Chairman of the Fed stands as a symbol of economic conservatism [giving inflation higher priority than unemployment]. . . . [Economic conservatism] will be an important political issue in the upcoming [Presidential campaign]. . . . Unemployment and fear of unemployment is the major concern of the principal constituency groups of the Democratic party."[101]

IV

By mid-1975, Arthur Burns had decided that the American economy needed thoroughgoing reform. Keynesian techniques, he thought, had reached a dead end. "Keynesian policies designed to counter high unemployment—policies such as tax reductions, larger governmental expenditures, easier credit—were . . . based on the premise of a declining or stable price level," he argued. "We have entered a different world, a world in which inflation is present and in fact proceeding at an accelerated pace in recent times, a world in which trade union leaders, workers, and businessmen are all influenced heavily by expectations of inflation."[102] If in such circumstances the government pumped money into the economy, it would just raise prices, which would in turn disrupt production. Burns believed, "Our long-run problem of inflation has its roots in the structure of our economic institutions and in the financial policies of our government."[103] To address these, Americans needed to move beyond Keynesianism. "It is important," Burns said, "that the economic mind of America be reopened. We need a renaissance of economic thinking in our country."[104]

The chairman argued that government policy had built perverse incentives into the economic system. "Taxes have progressively reduced the rewards for working, while government at the same time has increased the share of national output going to persons who are not productively employed." By his calculations, the average family of four had seen its federal tax burden multiply from 1 percent of earnings to 13 percent since 1950, while at the same time transfer payments (Social Security, food stamps, and the like) had grown twice as fast as income and now equaled 20 percent of total wages. "A society as affluent as ours can ill afford to neglect the poor, the elderly, the unemployed, or other disadvantaged persons, but neither can it afford to neglect the fundamental precept, that there must be adequate rewards to stimulate individual effort."[105] Nor was the problem confined to welfare programs. "Protection from economic hardship," Burns noted, "has been extended by our government to business firms as well. The rigors of competitive enterprise are nowadays eased by import quotas, tariffs, price maintenance laws, and other forms of governmental regulation. Farmers, homebuilders, small businesses, and other groups are provided special credit facilities and other assistance. And even large firms of national reputation look to the federal government for sustenance when they get into trouble."[106] Such policies had two results. First, they discouraged hard work. "Workers nowadays are well trained," the Fed chairman said, but "many of them work with less energy than they should, and absenteeism has become a serious problem."[107] The same might be said of protected businesses, which had less inducement to efficiency.[108] Second, Burns argued that welfare programs "have been pursued without adequate regard for their cost or method of financing. Governmental budgets— at the federal, state, and local levels—have mounted and at times . . . have literally gotten out of control." Invariably, this created sizable deficits, and "in financing these large and continuing deficits," the Fed chairman explained, "pressures have been placed on our credit mechanisms, and the supply of money has frequently grown at a rate inconsistent with general price stability."[109]

Burns contended that the resulting inflation discouraged investment, which was the key to improving productivity and living standards and expanding national wealth. In the United States, output per man-hour had increased at an average of 3 percent a year after 1945, but the gains had slowed to 2 percent after 1965 and to less than 1 percent after 1973. According to Burns, "The unsatisfactory record of productivity stems in large part from inadequate investment by business firms in new plant and equipment. Business profits have fallen increasingly short of the amounts needed to finance the growth and modernization of our nation's industrial plant."[110] At first glance, this assertion seems improbable, since profits in 1974 totaled $141 billion, 46 percent above the healthy levels of 1972. But the Fed chairman argued that these gains were illusions conjured up by inflation. As prices leapt upward in 1974, companies made money selling out of inventory products that they had bought earlier at low cost, but eventually they had to replace these goods, usually at even higher prices. Inflation also understated depreciation. Companies wrote off facilities on the basis of their original cost, which, as prices went up, no longer reflected their real value. Worst of all, business had to pay taxes on these phantasmal profits, which ate into companies' real gains. Taking these factors into consideration, Burns estimated that profits in 1974 totaled only $20 billion, less than the $35 billion earned in 1965 when the economy was smaller and the dollar worth more.[111]

Burns also contended that inflation reduced consumer spending. Rising prices created uncertainty about the future, which encouraged people to save more to hedge against the unexpected. The chairman argued that this phenomenon accounted for much of the weakness of consumer demand in 1973 and 1974.

The Fed chairman had turned one of the basic assumptions of Keynesians on its head. Keynes's disciples considered inflation and unemployment opposites. As Walter Heller lamented, "The economics profession thus far . . . is unable to propose reasonable formulas that would reconcile these two objectives [full employment and stable prices]. Up to now, we've had to accept the proposition that the two are inherently incompatible."[112] Indeed, many Keynesians actually considered a little inflation a good thing if it reflected strong demand. Burns, however, argued that rising prices actually caused unemployment by discouraging investment and consumer spending—an assumption with important policy implications. If the chairman was right, lasting economic recovery would occur only after inflation stabilized, while stimulative policies that pushed prices higher would actually retard expansion.

Burns's arguments had a strong moral undertone. He had worked very hard all his life and could claim—as much as anyone can—to have succeeded because of his own efforts and talents. He firmly believed in the virtues of labor and the possibilities of self-improvement. To Burns, inflation reflected a deterioration of the national character. People desired higher living standards, but instead of working to achieve them, they demanded that the government provide benefits. Washington's attempts to meet these demands fueled rising prices year after year. But Burns believed that inflation only made the situation worse, since rising prices actually slowed the growth of output and productivity, which limited opportunity and increased the gap between aspirations and resources. Price stability required not merely changes in policy but a general reappraisal of the relationship between the population and its government.

Accordingly, Burns did not simply advocate that Washington contain monetary growth, balance its budget, and wait for things to turn around. He urged the Congress to cut corporate taxes, giving business both greater resources and more incentive to invest and thereby spurring the economy and increasing productivity. Higher output per worker would not only improve living standards but also slow inflation by cutting labor costs. The Fed chairman also suggested the government stretch out the timetable for implementing environmental and worker safety regulations, or at least be more generous in allowing companies to deduct these costs from their corporate taxes. "Environment and safety regulations, while desirable in their own right, have often delayed fulfillment of capital spending plans and at times have forced adoption of less efficient methods of production."[113] The Fed chairman also argued that Washington needed to prune back regulations like those on transportation, which discouraged competition and pushed up prices, as well as adopt a "modest" incomes policy. The first would reinvigorate competition in important sectors of the economy and, presumably, reduce prices, whereas the second would at least help contain the demands of powerful labor unions and companies in industries dominated by a few large firms, such as automobiles.

To address the cost of the welfare state and what he saw as the perverse incentives it created, Burns advanced a plan for radical change. He argued that the federal government should offer "public employment—for example in hospitals, schools, public parks, and the like—to anyone willing to work," albeit at a rate slightly below the minimum wage.[114] At the same time it should sharply reduce "the scope of unemployment insurance and other governmental programs to alleviate income loss" that "may be blunting incentives to work."[115] Such measures "would enable an individual to get by in some fashion for a time, while giving him a strong incentive to find a regular job or create a new opportunity for himself."[116] Burns thought work relief would help recipients far more than any sort of dole. "People are lonely," he said. "We have an industrial society. Not many people have farms to go back to. Family ties are no longer as close as they once were. . . . This [program] would stir people to industry. It would ignite their imagination."[117]

The administration agreed with Burns's broad view of the economy, though it differed on important details. Like him, it thought that welfare-state programs had gotten out of hand, forcing government spending ever higher and leading to inflationary deficits and higher taxes, both of which discouraged work, investment, and innovation. The thrust of the Ford administration's domestic policy was to arrest the increase in social spending, balance the budget, and cut taxes—a line epitomized by the president's proposal in early 1976 to link $28 billion in tax cuts with equal spending reductions. The administration also expressed interest in the deregulation of industries like transportation, though it left office before it could act on the matter. But the White House took a dim view of incomes policies, not wanting to meddle in free markets and finding little encouragement in the experience of 1971–74. It also doubted that the government could effectively administer Burns's employment plan, and it knew that such a program could not pass the Democratic-controlled Congress. Still, White House officials operated in an intellectual framework similar to that of the Fed chairman, and they agreed wholeheartedly with his most important economic point, namely that inflation caused unemployment.

Of course, Democrats took a dimmer view of Burns's proposals, particularly of his plan to reduce unemployment insurance and offer instead public service jobs at a subminimum wage. George Meany warned that the program would reduce Americans to "coolie labor."[118] How, critics asked, could a laid-off steelworker, who had been earning two or three times the minimum wage and had a mortgage, subsist in one of Burns's subminimum wage jobs? The Fed chairman usually dodged this question by pointing out that a program that offered everyone employment at wages above the minimum would lead to "a shift of private employment into public employment" as people sought higher pay, pushing up labor costs throughout the economy and so making inflation worse—a perceptive observation, but not a response.[119]

Burns was banging his head against one of the basic dilemmas of social policy. If government helps those caught by economic misfortune, it effectively supports the price of labor. People with unemployment insurance, for instance, do not have to take the first job that comes along but can wait for a better opportunity. Of course, such policies alleviate suffering and allow workers to claim higher wages, but by doing so, they also increase prices and reduce the number of jobs available and may, over time, reduce the willingness to work—though this last matter is extremely complex and depends on a wide variety of social and cultural factors. Burns wanted to eliminate this tradeoff, but the very nature of his proposal suggests that it is inescapable. For most of the unemployed, a subminimum wage job would mean a huge drop in living standards. In other words, the Fed chairman had not evaded the tradeoff but had shifted it. The idea of replacing government handouts with employment programs has long appealed to people across the political spectrum, but no one has been able to develop a workable plan. Burns himself seems to have realized the inadequacy of his own thinking on this matter. "Kick it around from right and left," he said, "and let's improve on it."[120]

Keynesian economists were not inclined to concede Burns's broader points either. They saw no basic economic maladjustment, attributing inflation and unemployment to bad luck and mismanagement. A group of prominent Keynesian economists argued, "A very substantial part of the accelerated inflation since 1973 is due to dollar devaluation, grain shortages, rising commodity prices, and the OPEC cartel pricing of oil. Attempts to deal with this type of inflation solely by restriction of effective demand by monetary and fiscal policies resulted in the extraordinarily high interest rates of mid-1974, with a full-employment budget surplus presently of about $30 billion. Thus, restrictive monetary and fiscal policies were primarily responsible, among purely domestic factors, for the present recession."[121] Keynesian policies, applied properly, could still keep the economy on an even keel. Keynesians conceded that the nation's economic structure, especially rigidities in the labor market, guaranteed inflation of 5 or 6 percent. But they did not think this rate of increase particularly damaging, and they shied away from the disruptions that attempts to rectify it would entail. Provided that price increases stayed in this vicinity and unemployment remained high, as was the case in 1975, Keynesians argued that policy should concentrate on stimulating demand and not worry too much about inflation. Their minds were not closed to reform—for instance, many wanted to end government regulation of transportation, which they saw as a license for monopoly. But Burns's critics lacked the sense of urgency and the desire for a thoroughgoing, even radical, change in the approach to economic policy that the Fed chairman and the administration shared.

V

Despite terrible domestic problems, international finance still commanded a large share of Burns's attention in 1974–75. In contrast to monetary policy, however, the Fed chairman did not dominate the field but belonged to a group within the administration that made decisions. He had a hand in everything, but often stood in the background—an unaccustomed position.

During the recession and recovery, the dollar went through yet another cycle of decline and rebound. Though all the industrial democracies suffered from recession in 1974–75, it hit the United States first. As a result, American interest rates dropped before those in other countries, making the greenback less attractive relative to other currencies, especially the deutschmark and the Swiss franc. Between September and January, the dollar declined by 12 and 17 percent against the mark and the franc, respectively, and by an average of 6.66 percent against the currencies of all U.S. trading partners.[122]

Burns and the Federal Reserve resisted this trend, fearing that a weaker dollar would worsen inflation in the United States and disrupt international transactions. Starting in October, the Fed began selling foreign currency—primarily marks borrowed from the Bundesbank— to support the greenback. The Germans for their part bought dollars. The Fed purchased an average of $118 million a month, and the Bundesbank $212 million. But these actions did not halt the decline, and in January 1975, Burns flew to London to meet with the heads of the West German and Swiss central banks. After the conference, he announced that the "Federal Reserve, together with other central banks, is intervening—and will intervene as needed—to maintain orderly financial markets."[123] Soon, all three were buying dollars on an even larger scale, with Fed purchases averaging over $200 million a month. But though the greenback rallied for the moment, it eventually resumed its decline. The turning point came in March. As the recession hit Germany full force, interest rates there fell to levels comparable with those in the United States. At the same time, it had become clear that the United States was running a large trade surplus because the recession had severely cut the demand for imports. The dollar stabilized, and over the summer the jump in American interest rates sparked a rally. By December, the greenback stood slightly higher than it had after the second devaluation in March 1973, and the Fed was able to buy enough currency to repay the over $1 billion in foreign exchange it had borrowed from other central banks.

This episode ushered in a period of relative stability that lasted until mid-1977. The greenback depreciated somewhat against the deutschmark and Swiss franc but gained against the yen, lira, and pound sterling—on average remaining stable against the currencies of the other industrial democracies.[124] Many factors accounted for this happy condition, but Burns's stated determination to defend the dollar—backed with action—no doubt contributed.

Just as the ups and down of the dollar continued, so too did efforts to provide credit for countries with oil-induced payments deficits. In the winter and spring of 1975, the Ford administration negotiated an agreement with the other industrial democracies that created a $25 billion fund to help signatories buy oil and required them to avoid "beggar-thy-neighbor" policies.[125] That summer, members of the IMF agreed to increase the organization's financial quotas—its working capital—by one-third.[126] Burns participated in both sets of negotiations.

Attempts to bring the rules of the international monetary system into line with present realities proceeded as well, although these matters—especially the issue of gold—generated endless debate, much of it within the American government itself. Washington had long wanted to minimize gold's place in finance, fearing that it might someday replace the dollar as the medium of international exchange. But some European countries, especially France, favored a larger role for the precious metal with just that goal in mind. It was the sort of issue that most officials would have preferred to ignore, but because gold made up such a large part of international reserves, and because the rules governing it no longer accorded with reality, they could not sidestep the matter. Ever since its creation after World War II, the IMF had stipulated an "official price" for the precious metal and had banned countries from buying above that price or selling below it, with the idea of maintaining a fixed relationship between currencies and gold.[127] It had also required governments to pay certain IMF obligations, including a portion of their quotas, in the precious metal. Unfortunately, by 1975 the official price of gold was no longer even close to the market price.

In the summer of 1975, the American Treasury and the French government hammered out an agreement on the precious metal to which the other members of the Group of Ten wealthiest industrial democracies were willing to adhere. The IMF would abolish the official price of gold and no longer require any payments in it. Countries would be free to buy and sell gold in the open market, but they could not conduct such operations with an eye toward defending any specific price for the precious metal. Finally, the IMF would place a ceiling over the combined gold stocks of itself and its members.[128] The fund also planned to return one-sixth of its gold to the members that had contributed it and to sell another one-sixth in the open market, putting the proceeds into a special fund to supply loans to the poorest developing countries.[129]

Burns resisted this compromise. In late 1974 he had argued without success against a new law that would permit Americans, for the first time since the 1930s, to own gold, arguing that in the current disturbed economic condition, people might flee to the precious metal and so undermine financial stability.[130] The compromise with the French he considered more dangerous. First, by allowing countries to value their gold stocks at the market price rather than at the official one, it would greatly increase global liquidity and give countries more freedom to pursue inflationary policies. Second, by allowing free exchange of the precious metal between nations, it opened up the possibility of a return to the practice of settling international accounts in gold, replacing the dollar, which currently served in that capacity. Burns saw no reason to rush an agreement and urged the president to wait until a more advantageous moment.[131]

Treasury Secretary Simon rejected Burns's arguments. Pointing to the appreciation of gold prices, he concluded that countries would not willingly part with the precious metal unless they absolutely had to— the dollar would remain the preferred medium of exchange. Nor did he think it likely that a country would allow higher inflation simply because its reserves had grown.[132] Simon argued that the United States needed to get the issue out of the way. The French had threatened to link gold with a variety of international issues that Washington wanted resolved, such as the increase in IMF quotas. Besides, countries had considerable resources invested in the precious metal, and until the international community did something, gold would remain a constant irritant.

President Ford accepted Simon's arguments, and that summer the IMF incorporated into its rules the agreement worked out beween the Treasury and the French.[133] As it turned out, none of the dangers Burns envisaged materialized. Gold prices have been no more stable than those of the major currencies, and the latter have an advantage over the precious metal in that they earn interest and can be transferred anywhere in the world almost instantly. Gold's position in international finance has remained subordinate to that of the dollar.

Though currency management and reform talks were already under way when 1975 began, the year did see one important innovation in the international sphere. The recession hit every industrial democracy hard, and their leaders naturally concluded that common problems required united action. The uncertainties of the world economy—the energy crisis and floating currencies—also seemed to require regular consultation between nations. George Shultz had started to build the machinery of coordination in the spring of 1973 when he convened an informal and confidential meeting between himself and the German, British, and French finance ministers. In September, at an IMF conference in Nairobi, Kenya, the Japanese, miffed that they had been left out of the first discussion, asked its four principals to meet with them, inaugurating the Group of Five (G-5) finance ministers, which became an important, though little-remarked, fixture in international finance. It was at this gathering that Burns made his contribution to the process. He invited himself along with George Shultz, who was unwilling to turn away an old friend and benefactor. His presence set a precedent for inviting the leaders of the central banks to G-5 meetings—a reasonable step in the case of the U.S. and Germany, which had independent central banks, but less so for Britain, France, and Japan, where the finance ministries dominated monetary policy.[134] But though the G-5 was useful, many saw a need for more public meetings between the leaders of the industrial democracies. In

November 1975, the heads of the six largest industrial democracies met in Paris, the first of a series of economic summits that have convened every summer since then.[135]

American monetary policy was a major point of contention at this first meeting between the allies. The recession had dealt a terrible blow to European self-confidence, following as it did more than two decades of almost uninterrupted growth, and the recovery there came later than in the United States and was weaker.[136] Secretary of State Kissinger said, "All of the Western societies are under siege. In all European countries Marxist parties are gaining more power, and moderate governments are questioning whether they can govern their fates."[137] As the Europeans saw it, lack of confidence was the chief barrier to recovery. Germans, for instance, were saving an average of 17 percent of their incomes in 1975 to hedge against the unknown, thereby keeping demand weak.[138] For salvation, European leaders looked to the United States. As one White House memo noted, they "frequently stated that a strong U.S. recovery would help their recoveries by increasing demand for their exports and convincing their citizens that their countries too can overcome current economic problems. This would, as they see it, cause consumers to be less cautious and, therefore, to increase spending thus stimulating more rapid growth."[139] But fear existed, especially in the German and French governments, that the Fed's cautious monetary policy would slow or even abort recovery in the United States. Higher interest rates in the summer of 1975 led Chancellor Schmidt and French President Valéry Giscard d'Estaing to express concern "about the increase in the interest rate in the U.S. which they feel has handicapped their recovery." Pressure on the Fed to loosen continued up through the November summit.[140]

Burns and the administration did not concede these arguments. The Fed chairman said, "The E[uropean] C[ommunity] still believes in the myth that what happens in Europe depends entirely on what happens in the U.S. The U.S. sneezes and Europe catches pneumonia. This was only true in the 1930s. But now the economic conditions in Europe depend primarily on what happens in Europe."[141] In a meeting with Schmidt, Burns defended his policies in what one observer described as "an aggressive manner."[142] The administration backed Burns. "Additional domestic stimulus," one White House memo noted, "on top of the measures already taken, would probably do little to restore confidence and, in fact, might be counter-productive by re-igniting inflationary expectations."[143]

Neither Burns nor the administration changed their position at the economic summit. Over time, these meetings have been useful not so much for resolving disagreements as for coordinating action on which a consensus already exists. They cannot bind one nation to follow the will of the majority. The Fed and White House refused to change their stance, and so the summit ignored American monetary policy.

VI

In 1975 Arthur Burns had to deal with one last financial crisis—the bailout of New York City. New York had rarely balanced its budget in good times, and the recession had seriously cut into its revenues. The city already had a huge debt, and as its condition deteriorated, financial markets were reluctant to absorb more. New York was a difficult city to govern under the best conditions, and many feared that financial crisis would devastate already-strained municipal services. Default could also damage the banking system, since New York's debts totaled in the billions. Finally, city officials naturally wanted to minimize the painful tax increases and spending cuts that a balanced budget would entail. New York turned first to the state for assistance, and when it became clear that Albany could not provide enough money, to the federal government.

When first approached by New York officials in the summer of 1975, the Ford administration refused to countenance any bailout. The city had no long-run plan to balance its budget that the White House considered viable, and the administration trusted neither the New York city nor state governments. With respect to Democratic Governor Hugh Carey, one internal memo stated, "It has become clear that avoiding a default is less important to the Governor than his own political future. . . . He had proposed two sets of unworkable plans, both designed to shift the blame elsewhere."[144] Besides, the administration thought its tough line politically wise. To many Americans, New York summoned up a host of dark images, from pluto-cratic bankers to decadent artists to unstable radicals. Bankruptcy seemed a mild punishment for the city's many sins. Naturally, New Yorkers did not appreciate rejection. After Ford turned down the city's request for aid, the *Daily News* ran its now-famous headline, "Ford to City: Drop Dead."

Though long a citizen of New York, Arthur Burns agreed with Ford's decision. He had no more respect for the city's leaders than did the administration, declaring, "New York City has not been governed properly for many, many years now."[145] In private, he warned the president, "Don't let them [New York officials] sell you a bill of goods."[146] He feared that if the federal government bailed out the city, it would have to accept liability for all municipalities, weakening fiscal discipline at the local level. In the event Washington came to New York's rescue, he said, "I do think that self-reliance in our country, which has been diminishing, would be dealt a further blow."[147] The city would only change its ways, Burns believed, under duress. "One reason why New York has not done more to date," he said, "is that the governmental officials with the city and the state have been encouraged to think that, one way or another, the Federal government will come to the assistance of New York."[148] If the city did default, the chairman said, "the city could function, in my judgment. . . . You are dealing here with a very unhappy situation, no matter how you look at it, but there is too much scare talk."[149]

As the fall progressed, however, Burns began to change his views. The New York Federal Reserve bank, which managed the system's currency transaction, warned him that uncertainty stemming from New York's financial crisis was hurting the dollar.[150] The Fed also discovered that many commercial banks held New York municipal bonds and that default would seriously hurt them. Over 234 institutions had more than 50 percent of their capital invested in these obligations, and another 718 had more than 20 percent of their capital in them.[151] Finally, Helmut Schmidt warned both Burns and President Ford that New York's default would be a disaster for economic confidence, both in the United States and abroad.[152] Though Burns and the chancellor often disagreed, the chairman respected him and always gave his views serious consideration. It was possible, Burns conceded, that "if the [New York City] financial crisis is not resolved it could injure the recovery process that is now under way in our national economy."[153]

Soon, Burns's statements on a bailout began to reflect an uncharacteristic ambivalence. In October he declared, "I am more concerned about possible consequences of a New York City default now than I was previously," but "if I were a member of Congress today, I would not vote for financial assistance for New York City."[154] In November, he said that although he had not yet decided to support a bailout, "I am perhaps closer to such a conclusion than I have been in the past."[155] It may have been that he really was uncertain, but the Fed chairman was not given to doubt. It seems that Burns had accepted that a bailout was necessary to protect economic stability—always a vital consideration to him—but wanted to draw out the issue as long as possible to force New York to put its house in order. In November, the chairman noted, "New York State and New York City have by now gone a considerable distance in helping to solve their own problems. One reason they have done so is that the Federal Government did not move in at an early stage."[156]

The Ford administration had altered its position too. In December, the president announced a measure, in whose planning Burns had a part, to save the city.[157] Washington would loan several billion dollars to New York, money that the city would have to repay by 1978. Ford insisted that he had not changed his position. New York had saved itself by trimming its budget, he claimed, and the administration was merely tiding the city over a difficult patch. The president had never been quite as adamant on the issue as he seemed—chiefly, he wanted to postpone any aid until the New York city and state governments had done everything possible to resolve the crisis themselves. Ford's decision broke the legislative deadlock, ending months of debate between Democrats, who wanted to protect the city's extensive social services and its municipal unions, not to mention its strongly Democratic electorate, and Republicans, who did not think these things worth saving—though naturally New Yorkers of all stripes favored a bailout. Congress passed the president's measure, and New York avoided bankruptcy. Burns's, and the administration's, plan—if that is indeed what it was—had succeeded. Thanks to federal help, the city avoided default, but at the same time it put its affairs in order and managed, after a few years, to balance its budget.

In Burns's mind, New York was a microcosm of the nation's economic difficulties. America's chief problem, inflation, existed because the country as a whole insisted on living beyond its means. Governments ran deficits, unions demanded wages higher than productivity justified, business sought profits in speculation, and households borrowed to obtain luxuries. The United States suffered from what in earlier times might have been called a want of virtue. New York's profligate municipal government had had perhaps the most virulent form of this disease, but it had managed, under duress, to right itself. Perhaps, Burns mused, the rest of the country could do the same—if pressed.

8

Monetary Caesar

✦

I

By 1976, Arthur Burns enjoyed perhaps greater prestige and notoriety than any previous Federal Reserve chairman. The press seemed to consider him synonymous with the financial system: a coin decorated with Burns's profile graced the cover of *Forbes* magazine's annual issue on banking, and a *New York Times* caricature showed him wrapped in a toga that looked suspiciously like a dollar bill.[1] In a survey taken a year later, business leaders ranked Burns the most important man in the country after the president.[2] Though earlier chairmen such as Marriner Eccles and William McChesney Martin had commanded great respect, none had been so much in the public eye.

Burns owed his prominence to a combination of circumstance and personality. During the 1970s, political deadlock and the growth of politically sensitive middle-class entitlements, such as Social Security and Medicare, made fiscal policy ever less flexible. As a result, monetary policy had to take more responsibility for the economy, increasing the importance of both the Fed and its chairman. Burns did not, however, back into this role but sought prominence. He fired off jeremiads about inflation and touted his tough line against rising prices, and because of his reputation and charisma, people listened. To a degree, his rhetoric accorded with public opinion—polls showed that most people considered inflation the nation's chief problem.[3] More important, Fed policy yielded results. In 1975, despite warnings that the central bank's caution would forestall recovery, the economy had rebounded well from recession while inflation had declined significantly. As one prominent business columnist wrote, "It is hard to argue with him. Burns and the Fed were right, and almost everybody else was wrong."[4]

Success changed the nature of debate about the Federal Reserve's future. The interest of legislators in monetary policy, so high during the recession, declined considerably with recovery. Though politicians like Senators Hubert Humphrey and William Proxmire and economists such as James Tobin and Walter Heller criticized the central bank's policy as too restrictive and insufficiently attuned to the plight of the unemployed, they could not force the Fed to do anything. But the economic upturn had not diminished interest in making the government more "democratic." The Watergate scandal and its aftermath had made people suspicious of executive authority and government secrecy, and it had whetted the desire of congressmen and senators for greater power. Opponents of the Fed, especially Representative Henry Reuss, would try to use these attitudes to cut the central bank down to size.

Certainly, the Fed enjoyed great privileges. Its governors, once appointed, were responsible to no one but themselves. The presidents of the system's twelve regional banks, who helped decide monetary policy, owed their jobs—in theory at least—to the nine directors of their respective institutions, not to anyone in Washington. These directors were, in turn, either appointed by the board of governors or elected by bankers in their districts. The Fed also kept much of its business secret, a practice that made criticism of the central bank very difficult. Some saw these arrangements as a sign of conspiracy—one particularly hysterical article described the Fed as a "uniquely scandalous institution . . . controlled by bankers and many of their principal borrowers."[5] But even many who did not entertain such notions thought it inappropriate that, in a democracy, an institution like the Fed should wield such great power. They agreed with Senator Humphrey when he said, "I think it is time that the Federal Reserve was shaken up."[6] In this case, Burns's prominence may have made things worse. Because of him, many who had not previously paid much attention to the central bank took a close look at it, and at least some did not like what they found.

Burns considered the Fed's independence a major virtue. "We at the Federal Reserve," he said, "have . . . sought to model our conduct on that of the Supreme Court."[7] Just as the Court received privileges so that it could defend the rule of law from popular enthusiasm, so too was the central bank insulated from public pressure so that it could perform the necessary but not always popular task of defending the currency. Experience had borne out the practice. "Among the major industrial countries," the chairman argued, "West Germany and the United States appear to have achieved the greatest success—albeit woefully inadequate success—in resisting inflationary pressures since World War II. It is no accident that both countries have strong central banks. In some other countries, where monetary authority is dominated by the Executive or legislature, inflationary financial policies have brought economic chaos and even extinguished political freedom."[8] Burns would fiercely resist the slightest encroachment on the central bank's independence. "The shortcomings," he said, "of these individual proposals [to reform the Fed] matter less . . . than what appears to be their common objective, namely, to reduce the Federal Reserve's independence and to restrict its scope for discretionary action."[9]

The Fed and its chairman had considerable resources with which to defend themselves. Burns's close contacts with the White House ensured its support. The chairman and the Fed as an institution had also cultivated good relations with many representatives and senators, so that in numbers the central bank's reliable partisans probably equaled its consistent critics. Among the most important of these friendly lawmakers were Congressmen Thomas Ashley, Garry Brown, and William Stanton, who between them could often command a majority on the House Banking Committee. In addition, the Fed had an extensive network of supporters in the business and financial communities linked to it through the boards of its district banks and various advisory committees, and the central bank did not hesitate to call on these people to lobby on its behalf. Finally, Burns himself was a formidable debater, able to state his case as clearly and as forcefully as anyone in government.

Though more than a little self-serving, Burns's unconditional defense of the Fed's independence reflected a sincere desire to separate monetary policy from politics. In the 1950s and 1960s, Burns had expressed concern that elected officials would lack the will to take the tough steps necessary to contain rising prices, and naturally when prices exploded in the 1970s, he came to see the Fed's independence as a good thing. He believed that inflation reflected underlying social problems—the decline of self-reliance and of respect for work—that had infected the political system, and he thought that the Fed's independence provided at least a brake on these tendencies. Moreover, the chairman was a disciple of the great economist of the Progressive era, Wesley Clair Mitchell, and so it is no surprise that he should find the Progressive idea that "politicians" should defer to "experts" appealing. Burns had deeply resented Richard Nixon's attempts to meddle with the central bank, and the chairman got along so well with President Ford in part because Ford never asked him questions about monetary policy.

Realistically, however, Burns could not divorce "politics" from "policy." For instance, the Fed chairman consistently argued that the long-term benefits of lower inflation would outweigh the short-term costs entailed in achieving this goal. But though this is a plausible argument, the chairman could not prove in any scientific sense that he was right. His case rested on a moral calculus balancing long- and short-term costs as well as on estimates of the future that were, by definition, uncertain. Many asked why, considering this uncertainty, the Federal Reserve rather than elected officials should make such decisions, which affected the well-being of millions. Of course, Burns was not inclined to dwell on the possibility that he might be wrong. He genuinely believed that, with the information at hand, he would make the best decisions possible, and this attitude undergirded his devotion to the Fed's autonomy, which shielded experts like himself from the day-to-day pressures of the political process. Despite his pose of being the supreme technician, however, Arthur Burns was very much a politician. He knew that Congress and the president could restrict or terminate the Fed's independence if they wished and that he had to retain their confidence. To maintain his position and expand his room for maneuver, Burns carefully managed relations with the executive and the legislature and tried, with some success, to influence public opinion though his speeches and congressional testimony. Despite a tendency to frame the debate in terms of "democracy" versus "responsible policy," the Fed did not stand outside the political system but, like the courts and the military, occupied a position designed to balance—however imperfectly—the sometimes conflicting requirements of political accountability and technical expertise.

Critics of the central bank, both inside and outside of Congress, consistently attempted to strip away the veil of secrecy that surrounded it. For decades, the Fed had stymied critics simply by keeping its activities confidential, and it had been so successful that "Fed watching" had become something of a cottage industry. Hoping to change things, a Georgetown University law student, David R. Merrill, tried to pry open the meetings of the central bank's Open Market Committee, which decided monetary policy. The OMC had long published brief minutes of its monthly meetings, containing a rough outline of discussions and the directive governing monetary policy, after a three-month delay. Under pressure to release this information sooner, the OMC voted in 1975 to publish its minutes after only forty-five days. But at about the same time, Merrill filed suit under the Freedom of Information Act (FOIA), demanding that the Fed make its minutes public immediately after each OMC meeting.[10] He won the first round in the courts, and while awaiting appeal the OMC decided to publish the minutes of its deliberations right after the subsequent meeting, which in practice meant a delay of four to five weeks.[11]

Burns strongly objected to making the OMC's minutes available right away. "If FOMC plans were disclosed immediately," he warned, "market professionals would know at once the key determinates of our open-market operations over the next four or five weeks. Sophisticated and experienced market participants, equipped with financial resources to act quickly, would be far better situated to interpret and trade on this information than members of the general public. . . . Not only would the large speculators gain trading advantages, but—being armed with these new insights—they would be apt to engage in more aggressive market behavior. . . . The result could well be greater short-run volatility in interest rates."[12] Many economists, however, pointed out that speculation thrives on uncertainty and argued that by releasing its minutes right away, the OMC would clarify the future. But the central bank preferred to keep people guessing. This practice not only inspired caution in market participants but had the added advantage of keeping potential critics in the dark.

In the end, Merrill's suit actually reduced the amount of information the central bank made public. The appeals court allowed the Fed to hold off publishing the minutes of OMC deliberations until after the subsequent OMC meeting, permitting a four- to five-week delay. The whole episode, however, raised a frightening specter for the central bank. Since the 1920s, it had kept complete transcripts of OMC meetings—infinitely more detailed than its minutes—that the Fed made public after a five-year delay. Someone might, however, file suit demanding that the central bank release these transcripts immediately, which would effectively open up central-bank discussion to full public view. Reasoning that no one could force it to divulge what did not exist, the Fed announced that it had stopped keeping these transcripts. Defending this decision, Burns cited the expense of maintaining these records and claimed that no one had much interest in them, but this argument was a transparent excuse to keep the Fed's discussions confidential.[13] Indeed, known only to a handful of its top officials, the central bank continued to keep detailed records of OMC meetings—a fact that remained secret for eighteen years.

An idealistic attempt to make the federal government more responsive to the public posed an even greater threat to the central bank than Merrill's lawsuit. In 1975 Senator Lawton Chiles (D-Fla.) proposed to open up to the public discussions within government commissions, excepting only those that dealt with subjects like national security and criminal prosecution. He called his measure the Sunshine Act because it would shed light on the dark recesses of the bureaucracy. Though not aimed specifically at the Fed, it promised to strip away the cloak of secrecy that had so long shrouded the central bank.

Burns argued strongly that the central bank ought to conduct most of its business in private. He reiterated warnings that immediate disclosure of OMC decisions would encourage financial speculation and lead to wider swings in interest rates. Moreover, he said, "we often have before us detailed information about the financial and managerial condition of bank holding companies or about individual banks and their customers. Sometimes we must deal with crisis situations that may call for emergency action. It is unthinkable to me that the national interest would be served by discussion of these issues in public."[14] The Fed's relationships with other governments posed problems as well, since they usually dealt with the American central bank on the basis of strict confidentiality. "I have been told by high officials in other countries," Burns said, "that they would be very reluctant to deal with us as they have if what they tell us would be subject to risk of public disclosure."[15] "It would be just as logical," the Fed chairman told one senator, "to require open meetings of the President's cabinet, or meetings of the Secretary of State with top aides, or of the Secretary of the Treasury with foreign finance ministers," as to require the central bank to admit the public to its discussions.[16]

Aside from the wisdom of revealing certain specific information, Burns doubted the general principle that guided sunshine legislation. "Debate conducted on a stage," he said, "is different in tone and quality from debate conducted in private. . . . Debate carried on before a public audience tends to take on some characteristics of the theater, rather than serve as a search for truth and wisdom."[17] "It is naive," he claimed, "to believe agency officials will debate publicly with the same candor . . . [with] which they will debate in private."[18] Though conceding that openness might deter corruption, Burns argued, in a somewhat circular fashion, "The mere thought that an anti-corruption bill need apply to the Federal Reserve would cast doubt on the integrity of our Nation's central bank and would undermine confidence in the dollar and the future of our economy."[19] The Fed chairman dismissed the possibility that greater openness might help restore public confidence in government. He said, "We should recognize that such trust ultimately will depend not upon the public's observations of the process of government decision making, but upon their perception that their government is comprised of men and women of intelligence and integrity making reasonable decisions in the public interest."[20]

The Senate, which took up the measure first, agreed with Burns that the central bank needed to keep certain information confidential. The bill it passed allowed the Fed, on the vote of a majority of its governors, to close meetings that involved financial regulation or whose subject threatened to encourage speculation—and most Fed officials believed that speculators could benefit from information on almost any aspect of their business. The measure, however, required that the board keep verbatim transcripts of what transpired in these closed gatherings.

Burns considered these exemptions insufficient. First, they seemed to pose serious administrative difficulties. The Fed's staff estimated that the governors would have to take as many as twenty votes a week, announce the agendas of all meetings at least a week in advance, issue a written explanation to justify every closed meeting, and prepare transcripts of everything that transpired at these gatherings. "The Board," one memo noted, "would be bogged down in procedural requirements relating to its meetings."[21] Second, Burns contended that the Senate's bill did not clearly define "meeting," creating a possibility that any gathering of governors—say, over lunch—might require a detailed transcript. Moreover, the bill gave members of the public the right to file suit to prevent the closure of meetings, a proviso that, Burns claimed, "offers frightening potential for innumerable lawsuits."[22] Nor, the chairman maintained, did the right to meet privately constitute sufficient protection for the sort of sensitive information the Fed handled. He said, "The very deletion from the public transcript of any discussion . . . would at once lead to the inference that it was a problem area," starting rumors and encouraging speculation.[23] Besides, the chairman believed, "as long as we must keep a verbatim transcript of . . . meetings the threat exists that the substance of these meetings may be made public."[24] The chairman wanted the House, which now took up the Sunshine bill, to grant his agency a complete exemption from the measure.

Sponsors of the bill claimed that Burns grossly exaggerated the problems the Sunshine law would create. The central bank, they argued, would not have to explain exactly why it closed meetings, as he claimed. They also noted that the Fed had kept extensive written transcripts of OMC meetings for years without ill effects. Moreover, backers of this legislation claimed that the maintenance of transcripts—even closed ones—was the key to accountability. The knowledge that someone was taking down an official's words would act as a strong brake on chicanery. "We have taken every step to try to accommodate every reasonable problem that the board has been able to raise," Senator Chiles said. "I have to think that it boils down to the general feeling that, to be included in such a bill as this somehow casts a reflection on the Federal

Reserve System."[25] Senator Chiles had a good point, but probably more important to the Fed was its desire to preserve the veil of secrecy that had long kept critics at bay and had preserved its room to maneuver. People at the Fed also genuinely believed that the Sunshine Act's administrative requirements would be very burdensome, although in retrospect these fears seem much exaggerated.

The central bank called on its powerful network of supporters. As usual, Burns enlisted the administration to resist the inclusion of the Fed under the Sunshine bill.[26] The central bank also persuaded the members of its regional bank boards, usually prominent businessmen and professionals, to lobby on its behalf. The chairman worked successfully to line up bankers behind the Fed, giving a speech on "The Proper Limits of Openness in Government" to a group of them at the same time the House was debating the Sunshine bill. The Fed also tapped into its own extensive contacts within the lower chamber.

Though the House did not exempt the central bank from the Sunshine bill, it did give the Fed considerable privileges. Sympathetic legislators amended the measure to define "meeting" as a gathering prior to a formal vote, exempting the many discussions within the Fed that did not culminate in such a decision. Another amendment allowed the central bank to keep minutes of closed meetings, records that would be much vaguer than complete transcripts.[27]

The Sunshine Act had little influence on the way the central bank did business. The Fed could and did close all meetings that dealt with bank regulation, monetary policy, or international finance, and the minutes of these gatherings revealed few specifics. The Fed insisted that the Sunshine Act did not even apply to the OMC, which, because it included the regional bank presidents, had a special quasigovernmental status that the measures's language did not cover. The board of governors did admit the public to meetings where they discussed the regulations they issued to protect borrowers, but they had never seriously opposed admitting the public to such gatherings.

II

Debate over the proper role of the Federal Reserve deeply influenced the issue of financial regulation. In early 1976, the Congress decided to look into reports that many banks, including First National Citibank and Chase Manhattan, the nation's second and third largest, had encountered serious difficulties in recent years. Such stories naturally caused alarm, and there was concern that the regulators of these institutions, including the Fed, had been too accommodating of their charges. "We have been remiss in our surveillance over the regulators," Representative Reuss said. "There has to be a no-holds-barred GAO audit."[28] Some legislators talked of subpoenaing examiners' reports on specific banks and holding companies. Representative Benjamin Rosenthal, Democrat from New York and chairman of the Government Operations Committee, insisted, "We cannot accept anything less than the availability to view raw data."[29]

This prospect horrified Burns and everyone else at the Fed, as well as officials at the other agencies that regulated financial institutions. Banks gave auditors information in confidence, and regulators believed that to reveal it would be comparable to the IRS's publishing tax returns. They also feared that if banks thought that the information they gave to the government might be disclosed to the public, institutions would become less candid. Legislators promised to keep any such knowledge private, but Congress was notoriously leaky. As one Fed governor said, "The best way to keep a secret is not to tell."[30] Besides, Burns claimed, examiners' reports were complex technical documents that even a well-educated person could easily misinterpret. They would as likely confuse as enlighten lawmakers—though Burns did not explain why legislators could not find experts to properly explain this information to them. The Fed chairman especially feared that, by demanding information on specific institutions, Congress could bring their solvency into question. "When we cast doubt on the integrity of our individual banks," he said, "we take a risk—a great risk that could endanger a large part of our financial system."[31]

The federal banking regulators and Congress eventually worked out a reasonable compromise. Though Representative Rosenthal grumbled, "The regulators have been conditioned to secrecy. . . . And now someone has the temerity to suggest that they let the sunshine in," his committee refused his request to subpoena bank audits.[32] For their part, regulators recognized that the Congress had a right to know how they went about their business. They agreed to give the GAO a sample of examiners' reports, selected by statistical techniques and covering a span of five years, provided that the GAO kept them secret, which it did. This was the sort of agreement that many senators, including William Proxmire, seemed to have desired from the start, and it allowed the General Accounting Office to report to Congress on the process of bank regulation.[33]

Though a sensible agreement resolved this dispute, debate over the future of the Federal Reserve wrecked a major attempt at financial reform. Ever since the Depression, the United States had suffered with an exceedingly complex structure for regulating banks. Three separate agencies oversaw commercial banks: the Comptroller of the Currency, in the Treasury Department, audited banks with national charters; the Federal Reserve regulated all bank holding companies as well as those institutions that belonged to its system and held state charters; and the FDIC oversaw state banks not associated with the central bank that enjoyed deposit insurance. Savings and loans, or thrifts, which paid depositors slightly higher interest rates on savings deposits but had to limit lending primarily to home mortgages, fell under the jurisdiction of the Federal Home Loan Bank Board.

During the mid-1970s, concerns about the adequacy of this system developed. In 1974, for the first time since the early 1930s, major banks failed—the Franklin National Bank of New York and the United States National Bank of San Diego. In both cases, more effective regulation might have prevented collapse. Franklin went under because of incompetence beyond the bounds of everyday sloth and carelessness, while fraud brought down U.S. National. At the same time, many savings and loans found themselves in trouble—not because of mismanagement but because of the structure of their business. They took in short-term deposits, mainly savings accounts, and bought home mortgages with maturities of twenty-five years or more. This business did well when interest rates were stable, but when the cost of money suddenly jumped, as it had in 1973–74, thrifts found themselves in a vise. They had to pay much higher rates for short-term deposits, while their income, which was tied to long-term mortgages, remained static.

Burns contributed to the impetus for reform. In late 1974, he made a speech in which he warned that, although the banking system generally "remains strong and sound," "even viewed in the most favorable light, the present system [of divided regulatory authority] is conducive to subtle competition among regulatory authorities, sometimes to relax constraints, sometimes to delay corrective measures."[34] Apparently, events in Philadelphia led him to make this statement. There the First Pennsylvania Bank had just taken up a national charter in place of a state one, shifting itself from the Fed's jurisdiction to that of the comptroller—a move that coincided with a warning from the Fed that the bank ought to slow its breakneck expansion.[35]

Considerable discussion went on within the central bank about the proper direction of reform. Some were leery of giving one body authority over all banks, fearing that it would represent a dangerous concentration of power. Others argued the Fed should take charge of such a unified operation, while a few thought that the central bank ought to leave the field of bank regulation altogether and devote its energy to monetary policy. A majority, however, desired a more centralized banking system in which the Fed would play a larger role.[36] This attitude reflected a certain bureaucratic imperialism as well as a belief that the central bank was a more effective regulator than either the comptroller or the FDIC.[37] Burns, with the backing of most of the people in his agency, proposed to merge the office of the comptroller into the central bank, thereby giving the Fed authority over almost all large banks.[38] The chairman also suggested that the central bank get control over the reserves of all banks, regardless of whether or not they belonged to its system. Almost everyone at the Fed supported this change. As it was, member institutions had to keep their reserves on deposit with the central bank, where their money earned no interest, whereas banks outside the Fed umbrella could put reserves in instruments such as Treasury bills, which did bring in a return. The amount of money involved was significant, and consideration of it had led many small and medium-sized banks to drop their affiliation with the central bank. "Unless the erosion of membership is arrested," Burns warned, "a steadily diminishing portion of commercial bank deposits will be lodged with members and the execution of monetary policy will therefore become less and less precise." This development had political as well as economic implications. "Membership attrition," the chairman argued, "has been most acute among smaller banks—those with deposits of less than $100 million. If the exodus continues and the remaining members are only the larger banks, the Federal Reserve will then be perceived as a big banker's bank. This would almost certainly generate disenchantment with the System."[39]

In 1975, the Senate Banking Committee looked into sweeping reform. It took up a measure that would make savings and loans more like banks, allowing them to offer customers more services and to make a greater variety of loans. This proposal would also allow the Fed to set reserve rates for all banks regardless of whether they belonged to the system. Finally, it would create a completely new agency that would regulate all commercial banks, taking over the responsibilities then shared by the Fed, the comptroller, and the FDIC.

Although Burns strongly supported the first two of these reforms, he vehemently opposed the third, which would reduce the Fed's authority over banks. The creation of a new agency, he claimed, would leave bank oversight at a "standstill for some time and would result in a loss of the Fed's authority in the eyes of central bankers and financial ministers around the world."[40] But the danger extended into the long as well as the short term. "Knowing less and less about banks," the chairman warned, "we at the board would end up living in an ivory tower."[41] "Our [the Fed's] experience as a regulator," he further contended, "has convinced us that the behavior of monetary aggregates is directly affected by regulatory decisions."[42] The chairman backpedaled furiously from earlier warnings that the division of authority over banks between the Fed, the FDIC, and the comptroller created a sort of competition in laxity. "I must say," he claimed, "that when I made that speech [about regulatory reform] . . . I was in an angry mood. . . . A more balanced account would have noted that there has been a great deal of competition in excellence."[43] Burns opposed anything that would weaken his Fed, regardless of the merits of the case.

At the end of 1975, the Senate passed a complex measure that dealt primarily with thrifts, allowing them to make a wider variety of loans. It faced opposition only from small banks, which feared competition. Otherwise, the administration, leading senators, and most interest groups that followed financial regulation thought the bill a good idea. Savings and loans had formidable problems, and allowing them to diversify their portfolios seemed reasonable.[44] The more controversial aspects of the original proposal, such as the creation of a single agency to regulate banks and the centralization of all reserves within the Fed, fell by the wayside.

In the House, debate veered off in a completely different direction because Henry Reuss, the chairman of the Banking Committee, turned financial reform into an attack on the Federal Reserve. Though he had commissioned an extensive study of the changes that the government needed to make in the financial system, Reuss gave the Fed priority in any legislation. He had become convinced that the central bank was too cozy with big business and insufficiently attentive to the nation's elected authorities, and he put forward several proposals to rectify this shortcoming. The first would alter the term of the Fed chairman, making it coterminous with that of the president, so that upon taking office the chief executive could appoint his own person to lead the central bank. The second would change the status of the presidents of the Fed's twelve district banks. Reuss said of these people, "They do not necessarily represent a public viewpoint, yet they make public monetary policy, and affect the regulation of the banks to whom they owe their positions." The representative would give the White House the authority to appoint these officials. Finally, Reuss wanted to change the composition of the boards of the Fed's regional banks. "It would be hard to find, anywhere in government," Reuss said, "as white, male, upper-class and exclusive groups as the board members of these Reserve Banks." At least this part of his criticism was on target—only two of the 108 regional board members were black, and none was a woman, and a study of the members of the boards indicated that the vast majority were affiliated with large industrial companies or banks. "The study," Reuss claimed, "raises a substantial question about the Federal Reserve's oft-repeated claim to independence. . . . One might ask, independent from what? Surely not banking or big business if we are to judge from the massive interlocks revealed by this analysis of the district boards."[45] To rectify this imbalance, he proposed to expand the size of these boards from nine to twelve, with provision that the Fed should appoint people linked to labor, agriculture, and consumer groups to these new positions. The representative also revived the proposal, discarded by the Senate, for a unified banking agency, and he suggested new limits on the powers of bank holding companies.

Reuss had found a simple explanation for a complex state of affairs. Certainly, Fed officials tended to identify with the interest of business and banks, but these attitudes sprang not from specific institutional arrangements but from the nature of their jobs. People at the central bank spent their days dealing with banks and their problems, and naturally many came to appreciate the perspective of these institutions. Moreover, the Fed looked to bankers as its natural constituency, just as the Agriculture Department looked to farm groups. But this condition was common to the central banks of all capitalist countries—the details of the Fed's organization chart had little to do with it. As one student of these institutions put it, "Central banks have a long and conservative heritage. Commonly, they have been closely linked to the major financial inistutions of the day, and their organizational ethos has been one of stressing stability."[46] The presidents of the district banks, whom Reuss portrayed as agents of the business leaders of their regions, had to meet the approval of the board of governors and were often civil servants long associated with the Fed. Paul Volcker, for instance, led the powerful New York Fed after 1975. For their part, the boards of the regional banks were, to a large extent, merely convenient bodies through which the Fed could keep in touch with business people across the country. Certainly, the board of governors consulted with and listened to these groups, but there was never any question as to who was in charge. Reuss's proposals would have made the central bank more amenable to political pressure by giving the president more control over top officials, but it seems unlikely that his plan would have significantly changed the Fed's bureaucratic culture.

Irrespective of the accuracy of Reuss's insights, however, the Fed saw his proposals as a threat. Obviously, making the term of the chairman coterminous with that of the president and turning the presidents of the district banks into executive appointees would probably reduce the Fed's independence significantly. Moreover, provisions to rearrange the boards of the regional banks promised to complicate, though not cripple, the task of keeping in touch with businesspeople, who were not only political supporters but also a source of important economic intelligence. Few at the central bank would have disagreed with Burns when he described Reuss's bill as "a most awful piece of legislation."[47]

Burns argued strenuously against Reuss's reforms. He attacked plans to strip the central bank of its regulatory functions in the same terms he had used the previous fall. The chairman followed two lines of attack against proposals for reorganization. First, he asked congressmen if they really wanted to expand the president's authority over the Fed—an argument that struck a chord in light of the Watergate revelations. It had become a matter of faith among many legislators that the executive had too much power, and they shied away from anything that would increase its influence.[48] This attitude created an insuperable dilemma for those in Congress who wanted to give elected officials more power over the Fed. An unwieldy deliberative body, Congress simply could not administer monetary policy. The White House could do so, but control of the central bank would represent a huge accretion of power for the president, a step that most lawmakers opposed. The Fed did not hesitate to exploit this contradiction to the hilt. Second, Burns argued, "this bill seems to me and my colleagues on the Board to propose change for the sake of change."[49] "The business directors [of the regional Fed banks]," he claimed, "have a vital interest in a sound and growing economy, an interest shared by all business borrowers and households."[50] "What is wrong with the present system?" Burns asked Reuss. "Wherein has it failed? What is wrong with the present method of selecting bank presidents? Do we have a poor lot?"[51] The representative responded, "It has failed because you don't have publicly responsible, Presidentially appointed and senatorially confirmed officials making a branch of national economic policy, which is quite as important as fiscal policy."[52] Burns, however, saw all attempts to reform the Fed as backdoor efforts to secure a more expansive monetary policy—and indeed, Reuss did believe that a Fed more responsive to political pressure would supply credit more liberally. For Burns, the question was not, "Is the Fed democratic?" but rather, "What monetary policy should we pursue?"

Reuss's legislation met with strong resistance, to which the Fed contributed mightily. Burns enlisted the administration to fight the measure,[53] mobilized the central bank's many contacts in the financial and business world to lobby against it, and lined up the Fed's friends in the House. To defuse criticism from one quarter, the governors quietly began to appoint more minorities and women to the district boards.[54] Others waded in to defend their own interests. Large bank holding companies attacked provisions that would restrict their activities, while small banks, fearing competition, resisted expanding the powers of savings and loans.

Most of Reuss's proposals died in his own committee, where he was unable to command a majority. Provisions to expand the lending powers of thrifts and to limit the activities of bank holding companies disappeared, as did those stripping the Fed of its bank regulatory function and making the regional bank presidents executive appointees. Reuss attributed these defeats to "the strength of the banker and Federal Reserve lobby,"[55] but he himself deserves much of the blame. He handled his committee ineptly, for instance scheduling key votes when supporters would be out of town. Consumer advocate Ralph Nader said, "Reuss doesn't know how to manage his committee."[56]

The Senate disposed of the few important provisions remaining in Reuss's bill. Senator Proxmire, though himself a strong critic of the central bank, excised the provision making the Fed chairman's term coterminous with that of the president. Though eager to increase Congress's authority over the central bank, the senator did not want the chief executive to do the same.[57] Proxmire also deleted conditions on the appointment of new members to the expanded regional boards. The Senate's bill said almost nothing about the regulation of banks or the powers of thrifts, and with respect to the Fed, it merely enlarged the boards of the district banks from nine to twelve and made the appointment of the Fed chairman subject to Senate approval.[58] The Congress, however, failed to enact even this modest measure before it adjourned.

Defeated in his own branch of government, Henry Reuss tried his luck with the judiciary—a sure sign that a representative is beaten. He filed suit against the Fed, arguing that the practice of allowing the presidents of the regional banks to vote at OMC meetings was unconstitutional. The subject of these gatherings, he insisted, was a matter of public policy, but these officials did not owe their appointments to the president.[59] Nothing came of the action.

III

The struggle over the Federal Reserve's independence even touched its international dealings. For Burns, world finance in 1976 was a relatively calm area—an unaccustomed state of affairs. The dollar remained stable, and foreign pressure for a more expansive monetary policy subsided as the American economy recovered. The United States' trade balance did swing from a $9 billion surplus in 1975 to a $9 billion deficit the following year, but this development actually reassured foreigners, who looked to exports to fuel their own economic recoveries. At home, it raised little concern both because the current account remained in surplus and because most assumed that the trade deficit reflected an American economy that was growing faster than its competitors, not any basic imbalance. The major crisis of the year involved an international effort to rescue the United Kingdom from bankruptcy. Alone among the industrial democracies, Britain had tried to spend its way out of the 1973 oil shock—a policy that had created runaway inflation and a huge trade deficit that, in turn, threatened to lead to a complete collapse of the pound sterling. To prevent such a disaster, the IMF arranged a $5.2 billion loan for London on the condition that Whitehall cut spending and keep monetary growth in bounds. The Fed provided $1 billion for this fund, and the Treasury another $1 billion, but Burns played only a secondary role in the operation.[60]

Burns's major contribution to international policy in 1976 involved a practice called recycling. The increase in oil prices after 1973 had thrown the world's balance of payments into confusion, allowing the OPEC countries to pile up huge surpluses at the expense of everyone else. Though most of the industrialized democracies contrived to pay for petroleum, developing nations did not fare so well. They managed to keep afloat thanks only to loans from large Western banks—mainly American—that took in sizable deposits from Arab countries to finance this lending. The whole process, commonly referred to as "recycling," drew Burns's fire. "We ought to drop the word 'recycling' from our vocabulary," he said. "That term is not conducive to clear thought. What it means is piling debt on top of debt, and more realistically bad debt on top of good debt. I do not think the nations of the world are facing up to the problem, and all the talk about recycling is an escape in my judgment from reality."[61]

In 1976, however, Burns found himself defending the mechanism that made recycling possible. The size of deposits held by Arab governments in American banks concerned many representatives and senators, who feared that these would give Middle Eastern countries influence over bank policies that they might then use against the economic interest of the state of Israel. Several legislators, led by Senator Frank Church (D-Ida.), demanded that the Fed and private banks hand over information about how much each Arab nation had on deposit with each U.S. bank. Burns flatly refused, telling others at the Fed that he would even ignore a subpoena if Congress issued one.[62] Bankers feared that, if they revealed information about these deposits, Arabs would withdraw their money and put it in Swiss banks, and Burns had similar concerns.[63] Whatever the Fed chairman's opinion of recycling, he knew that the world could not dispense with it until there was some alternative. Nor did he wish American banks to lose lucrative business. Finally, he feared that opening the financial affairs of other governments without their consent would make them reluctant to deal with the Fed in the future.

As was usually the case with requests for information, Burns and the Congress managed to work out a compromise. Apparently, the Kuwaiti finance minister told Senator Charles Percy (R-Ill.) that his country would withdraw its deposits from American banks if the Congress made their size public, and this intelligence encouraged legislators to moderate their demands.[64] In the spring of 1976, the Fed published an aggregate of the deposits of Middle Eastern and North African oil-producing states with the six largest American banks. The total was $11.3 billion, or 5.7 percent of these institutions' total deposits.[65] Lawmakers did not find this situation particularly threatening.

IV

With respect to monetary policy, Burns remained committed to the course on which he had embarked in 1975. The recovery, he believed, would proceed without incident. "I think we'll have a good year," the chairman said. "The expansion we've had has developed some momentum."[66] But inflation was too rapid. Though consumer prices increased at only a 3.9 percent rate in the first quarter of 1976, Burns argued, "this recent improvement in price performance stems entirely from declines in the prices of food and fuels—prices that have tended to move erratically. . . . The underlying trend of costs and prices is thus still clearly upward, and inflation must remain a major consideration in formulating public policy."[67] In the long run, he estimated that prices were increasing at about 5 to 6 percent a year—a calculation that drew little criticism.

To bring inflation down, Burns planned to ratchet back monetary growth. Since the turnover of money (M1) increased an average of about 3 percent a year, and since most believed that the American economy could, over time, expand without strain at about that same pace, Burns calculated that the central bank would have to slow monetary growth to 1 to 2 percent a year if it wanted to stabilize prices. The chairman realized that if the Fed moved immediately toward this goal it would almost certainly precipitate a recession. "We should strive for [this target]," he said, "not this year, but gradually over the next few years."[68] In 1975, Burns announced that the central bank would allow currency and demand deposits (M1) to expand at between 5 and 7.5 percent. By the end of 1976, the Fed's Open Market Committee, in several steps, rolled this target back to 4.5 to 6.5 percent.[69] Though he did not admit it, the chairman's strategy called for a relatively slow recovery in which economic slack, in the form of unemployment and idle capacity, would hold down prices. But Burns also hoped that a show of determination on the Fed's part would reduce the hardship involved in reducing inflation. If the central bank convinced people that it simply would not accommodate higher prices, business and labor might rein in their demands for fear that increases would lower sales and reduce the number of jobs.

This policy met with considerable opposition. At 8 percent, unemployment was still quite high, and many thought that it merited priority rather than inflation. The arguments were the same that the Fed's critics had used in 1975. Economist James Tobin wrote, "Both unemployment and inflation involve redistributions of income and wealth, in which some citizens gain relative to others. It is hard to say that one of these redistributions is more unfair than the other." At the same time, though, he argued that joblessness represented a considerable loss to society as a whole since it involved lower total production, whereas higher prices entailed no such cost.[70] Besides, Tobin contended, "the path of inflation . . . depends on the overall state of the recovery . . . and not on the combination of policies and events that put it there."[71] In other words, with the economy's many idle resources, inflation would diminish regardless of what the central bank did. If the government really wanted to hold down prices, Tobin thought, it ought to negotiate a deal with labor unions to keep wages, and therefore costs, in line. Monetary policy and fiscal policy should concentrate on stimulating demand and recovery. Economist Walter Heller put it more simply. "This economy is still running way below par," he said. "There are just no bottlenecks, no excess demand in sight for this year through 1977." A tight monetary policy, he continued, "will slow us down long before we're reached our economic potential."[72]

Many Democrats in Congress seized upon these arguments. Representative Reuss warned that Burns's 1 percent monetary growth target was a recipe for "stagnation" and "depression."[73] The Senate Banking Committee issued a report declaring that the Fed should not raise interest rates even if the failure to do so resulted in monetary growth higher than the central bank's targets.[74] Representative Brock Adams (D-Wash.) warned, "The Federal Reserve must be made aware by Congress that we are watching them. They must not substitute their judgment."[75]

Burns responded in his usual Olympian fashion. "I don't think this country is going to have much of an economic future," he said, "unless we keep working at this problem and unwind the inflation that is still underway. And I think we had better stop fooling ourselves in talking, as some people do, about living with a rate of inflation of 5 or 6 percent. If we start thinking in those terms, we are not going to get a 5 or 6 percent rate: we are going to get a lot more. Our objective must be a zero rate of inflation."[76] Burns's reasoning followed the line that he had pursued since at least 1974. Because years of rising prices had deeply ingrained inflation into the economic structure and the popular mind, he thought that stimulus would show up mainly as higher prices rather than in greater production. More rapid price increases would, in turn, discourage investment and consumption, slowing the economy. "Inflation," he contended, "leads to imbalances in the economy and eventually brings on recession."[77] A more expansive monetary policy might increase employment over the near term, but in time it would generate higher prices and put the country back where it had started. The administration saw things the same way. "The models [on which Keynesians rely]," Alan Greenspan said, "don't—and can't—reflect this sort of thing [the affect of rising prices on consumer and business psychology]."[78] Burns conceded that his plan was not particularly appetizing but added, "Slowly undernourishing inflation and thus weakening it seems the most realistic strategy open to us."[79]

The Humphrey-Hawkins full employment bill added another dimension to the debate. This measure, introduced by Senator Humphrey and Representative Augustus F. Hawkins (D-Calif.), required that the government reduce adult joblessness to 3 percent by stimulating the economy and offering public-service employment to all comers at the "prevailing" wage—usually translated as generous union rates. The motive behind this proposal was as much political as economic. President Ford would never sign such a bill, but Democrats, especially organized labor, hoped that its very existence would draw a clear line between the two parties on economic issues during the fall campaign.

Burns objected to this measure both in concept and detail. Once again he warned that, in the current atmosphere, economic stimulus would make inflation worse, which would in turn slow the economy. No program could promise full employment unless it first stabilized prices. Burns also criticized carving a permanent unemployment goal into the statute books. "Humphrey-Hawkins," the Fed chairman said, "continues the old game of setting a target for the unemployment rate. You set one figure. I set another figure. If your figure is low, you are a friend of mankind; if mine is high, I am a servant of Wall Street. . . . I think that is not a profitable game. . . . Numbers taken out of the air without regard to history cannot be used in developing a workable scheme aimed at full employment."[80] He believed that policy should instead concentrate on conditions in the labor market, trying to reach a balance between available openings and job seekers rather than hitting any numerical target. The chairman also reiterated concerns he had expressed earlier that, by offering everyone work at wages above the minimum, a public jobs program such as that envisaged in Humphrey-Hawkins would draw workers from the private sector into the public one, pushing up wages and prices across the board.

The Fed chairman also worried that Humphrey-Hawkins would give the president unprecedented authority over the central bank. The measure stated, "If the President determined that the Board's policies are inconsistent with the achievement of the goals and policies proposed under this Act, the President shall make recommendations to

the Board . . . to insure closer conformity to the purpose of this Act."
As one internal Fed memo noted, "Clearly, this language does threaten the independence of the Federal Reserve"—for Burns, a call to war.[80] Once again, he played on congressional fears of executive power. The chairman told lawmakers that while they may "have an idealistic concept of the White House" and "think of the President at his desk surrounded by wise advisers, calling on each of them for his opinion, calling in competent, highly qualified public citizens, and then pondering these issues of monetary policy. . . . the fact of the matter is, if monetary policy . . . found its home in the White House, some fellow in the basement of the White House—he might even be called a Haldeman—would in effect be making monetary policy."[81]

As it turned out, the Democrats never united behind Humphrey-Hawkins. Many economists associated with the party expressed serious doubts about it. For instance, Charles Schultze, who had led the Bureau of the Budget under President Lyndon Johnson, warned that if the government provided jobs to all comers at the "prevailing" wage it would create an "exodus from private industry" by lower-paid workers that would drive up labor costs across the board and "make the inflation problem worse."[82] Perhaps more important, the Democratic presidential nominee, Jimmy Carter, the former governor of Georgia, was skeptical of Humphrey-Hawkins. Though he endorsed the measure to preserve party unity, he avoided the subject when campaigning. The bill probably muddied the waters more than it cleared them because it forced people like Schultze, who strongly disapproved of the policies of the administration and the Fed, to line up against their own party.

Despite criticism from the Congress and the stir over Humphrey-Hawkins, events in the first half of 1976 went well for the Fed. The economy grew at an impressive 8.5 percent rate in the first quarter and at a still-strong 4.9 percent in the second, unemployment declined from 8 to 7.5 percent, wholesale prices increased at less than 3 percent, and consumer prices increased at only 5 percent. Moreover, during the first months of the year the money supply grew relatively slowly, at less than 5 percent, and so the central bank did not feel the need to raise interest rates.

In the summer, however, conditions deteriorated. First, the money supply grew faster than the Fed desired, with both M1 and M2 at the very top of their target ranges. The central bank responded by raising the cost of money, driving the prime rate from 6.75 percent in January to 7.25 percent in June. At the same time, though, the economy ran into trouble. Consumer spending weakened and businesses, which had rebuilt their inventories over the winter, reversed course and began to cut purchases to reduce stocks. Burns's critics saw this as an indication that his cautious monetary policy was already beginning to bite. But the chairman insisted, "Temporary pauses of this kind aren't uncommon during periods of cyclical expansion." The data, he argued, "suggest that a resumption of the upward trend is already under way."[83] But the upswing was not strong. The economy grew at only 2.5 percent in the second half, and unemployment crept back up to near 8 percent.

The 1976 presidential contest complicated the outlook. Burns very much wanted Gerald Ford to win—he had developed considerable respect for the president and enjoyed an exceptionally close relationship with his administration. Prosperity would, of course, greatly help the Republican's chances. Moreover, attacks on Burns's policies were a staple of Democratic campaign rhetoric. For instance, Sargent Shriver, who had been the vice-presidential candidate in 1972 and now aimed at the top place, said, "If Arthur Burns won't reduce interest rates, then I will find some way to reduce him!"[84] Even Jimmy Carter, perhaps the most moderate candidate, spoke of the need to lower interest rates and to "coordinate" policies between the Fed and the White House. But whatever Burns's proclivities, he was still smarting from accusations that, to reelect Richard Nixon, he had allowed the money supply to grow too rapidly in 1972, touching off the inflation of 1973–74. As one business economist put it, the Fed chairman "is going to try his best not to be accused of electing another President through monetary policy."[85]

In response to the economic pause—as the summer slowdown was known—the Fed and the administration did nothing. Burns and Greenspan were convinced that it was a passing phenomenon, and both thought it unwise to alter policy because of a few months of contrary news. Nor did anyone in the administration believe that action taken during the summer would affect the economy before the election. To increase spending or cut interest rates would sacrifice consistency for no tangible gain.[86]

This policy succeeded and failed. After faltering in the summer, consumer spending picked up again, expanding as rapidly in the second half of 1976 as in the first. Companies continued to draw down inventories, but Burns and his counterparts in the administration knew that this process had to end sooner or later and that when it did, the economy would pick up. Weak monetary growth in the third quarter did lead the Fed to cut interest rates, with the prime rate declining from 7.25 percent in June to 6.25 percent in December. This move, however, represented no large change in policy, which was keyed not to the cost of money but to changes in the money supply. Over all of 1976, currency and demand deposits (M1) grew 5.7 percent, faster than in 1975 but still well within the Fed's stated target. But no rebound materialized before the election, which Gerald Ford lost by a narrow margin to Jimmy Carter. The closeness of the results make it likely that, had the economy performed better in the autumn, the outcome would have been different.

This defeat called into question everything Burns had accomplished. In most respects, 1976 went well for him. He had defeated serious attacks on the central bank and run monetary policy according to his own lights, shrugging off criticism from Democrats in Congress. The economy had also performed fairly well. Production had expanded smartly, at a 4.6 percent rate, while inflation remained under 5 percent. The country had failed to make progress only against unemployment, but this reflected in large part rapid growth in the labor force. Though the jobless rate did not decline over 1976, employment increased by 2.5 million, ending the year at an all-time high.[87] But a key ingredient to Burns's success had been strong backing from the White House, which provided him with important political and moral support. Jimmy Carter, however, had criticized Burns on the campaign trail and would have to rely on liberal Democrats in Congress—a group that had little use for the Fed chairman—to get legislation passed. Whether Burns could function under such conditions was very much in doubt.

Nevertheless, the Fed chairman was determined to carry on. His term ran until January 1978, and the accession of a new and untried chief executive made it all the more important that monetary policy remain in tested hands. "The Federal Reserve," Burns said, "has been a citadel of non-partisan economic and financial analysis and policy.

. . . If the Fed Chairman were to resign [when a new President came in], I think it would tend to introduce a political dimension into Fed operations. And I wouldn't want to be the one to do that."[88] "My personal plan," he told a reporter, "is to stay in this job. I'll thus give my friends an opportunity to cheer and my critics an opportunity to criticize."[89]

9

Changes at the Top

✦

I

Arthur Burns and President-elect Jimmy Carter viewed each other suspiciously. During the campaign, the Georgian had been quite critical of the Federal Reserve. "The monetary restrictions of the last few years did nothing but slow down the economy. It wasn't a sensible way to counteract the price rises that were occurring." The Democrat had also expressed support for proposals to allow each president, upon taking office, to appoint his own Fed chairman, as well as for procedures to "coordinate" monetary and fiscal policy—either of which, Burns believed, would seriously compromise the Fed's independence.[1] Moreover, the new president, by virtue of being a Democrat, would almost certainly rely heavily on Keynesian economists and respond to the demands of traditional Democratic interest groups such as organized labor, and neither was particularly sympathetic toward the Fed chairman. Carter had won election promising a more stimulative economic policy, and in late November he announced that he would aim to expand production by 6 percent over 1977 and to reduce unemployment from 8 to 6.5 percent.[2] To hit these targets, the new administration thought that it would probably have to increase spending or cut taxes. Burns had little enthusiasm for such measures. "I cannot stress too strongly," he said, "the importance of being cautious in launching new federal programs with potentially large budgetary impact . . . There is a clear need for fiscal discipline at the present stage of our struggle with inflation."[3] Such talk caused the new administration to fear that Burns might use monetary policy to neutralize any steps it took to stimulate the economy.

Fortunately, Burns and Carter understood that they had to live with each other. The Fed could not directly challenge a newly elected president, and Burns knew that if he wanted a third term as chairman, he would have to secure reappointment from Carter by early 1978. For its part, the administration realized that it was stuck with Burns for at least a year. At a meeting a couple of weeks after the election, Burns and Carter tried to put each other's greatest fears to rest. The Fed chairman said that he thought the president's targets for economic growth realistic and that his mind was "by no means closed" to tax reduction, although he continued, "Because I anticipate a resurgence of the economy, I see no advantage in a tax cut at the present time."[4] Carter claimed to have received a pledge of "cooperation" from Burns and added, "I understand the autonomy of the Federal Reserve System and would not like to eliminate that autonomy."[5]

Despite this show of togetherness, relations between Burns and the Carter White House were not as close as during the previous administration. He and President Ford had had similar views of the economy and great mutual trust—neither feared that the other would intentionally undercut him. No such congruence existed between the Fed chairman and the Carter administration. Treasury Secretary W. Michael Blumenthal did have lunch with Burns every week starting soon after the inauguration, but the president only initiated monthly meetings with Burns in April. Regular communications did go on between the Fed and the White House staff, and the Fed chairman attended scheduled meetings among the heads of the OMB, CEA, and Treasury.[6] Nevertheless, dealings between the Carter White House and the central bank more closely resembled those during the Nixon

administration, with each side prodding the other, occasionally
through public statements, to get what it wanted—although the Georgian never used the sort of underhanded tactics to which Nixon sometimes resorted.

Not surprisingly, the good feelings of November broke down soon
after the inauguration. Announcing, "We are in a state of stagnation
at this time," President Carter proposed a $31 billion program to
stimulate the economy, including public works projects, 750,000 public service jobs, a small permanent tax cut, and a one-time tax rebate
of $50 to every American.[7] Burns soon expressed skepticism. "As far
as I can judge," he said, "the economy is improving on its own . . . and
it is not clear to me, as of this day, that any stimulation is required."[8]
"In view of the kind of economy we have now," he added, "with built-
in inflationary pressures, we should not be concentrating on increasing spending or on lowering taxes."[9] The Fed chairman especially disliked the rebate, which he considered an unwarranted giveaway.
"People shouldn't receive gifts of money from their government," he
said.[10] But Burns restrained his criticism. He did not go out of his way
to voice his objections, which he made primarily in response to questions posed by members of Congress. Though conceding a lack of
enthusiasm for Carter's stimulus package, he added, "I think the program . . . a modest and reasonable one."[11] As Walter Heller put it,
"When Arthur barks, he also wags his tail."[12]

The administration had little interest in the nuances of Burns's
stance. One official bluntly told the Fed chairman, "This isn't the way
to get reappointed." Another said to a reporter, "We wished to hell
he'd shut up." President Carter apparently wanted to go after the Fed
chairman in public, but Secretary Blumenthal dissuaded him, realizing
that however upset the White House was, an open break with Burns
would merely draw attention to the chairman's critique.[13]

To a large extent, disagreement between Burns and the White
House hinged on a technical point that nevertheless had great practical ramifications—how to encourage investment. Although consumption and homebuilding had recovered well from the recession,
capital spending had not. "In the two-and-a-half years of the expansion," Burns noted, "real capital outlays have increased only . . . half
as much as they did, on average, over like periods in the previous five
expansions."[14] Even this improvement had not greatly augmented

the country's capacity to produce because, as one Fed memo pointed out, "The composition of business fixed investment is . . . heavily weighted towards light equipment."[15] This weakness presented great dangers. The country could not increase productivity and living standards without investing in more efficient production techniques, nor could it grow indefinitely without additional manufacturing capacity. The labor force was also expanding fast, and if business did not build new facilities, there might not be enough good jobs to go around. Finally, investment constituted a large part of total economic activity, and as long as it remained depressed, full recovery was unlikely.

Burns blamed weak investment on thin and uncertain profits. He noted, "Ours is still predominantly a profit-motivated economy in which, to a very large extent, whatever happens—or doesn't happen—depends on perceived profit opportunities."[16] But as the Fed chairman had long argued, inflation created phantom profits by understating depreciation and exaggerating gains from sales out of inventories, and companies then had to pay taxes on these illusory gains. According to Burns's calculations, American firms were earning about $40 billion less than official estimates, and the real (inflation-adjusted) return on stockholders equity was a third less than during the 1950s and 1960s.[17] Uncertainty about the future also discouraged investment. "My frequent discussions with businessmen," Burns claimed, "leave little doubt in my mind that a strong residue of caution in businessmen's thinking has carried over from the recession of 1974–75. . . . In contrast to the widely shared conviction of just a few years ago that the business cycle had been mastered, a surprising number of businessmen are now seized by concern that the world economy may have entered a downphase of some long cycle." "More troublesome still," he continued, "the specter of serious inflation continues to haunt the entire business community. The fear that inflation will not be effectively controlled is indeed a key reason for the high-risk premiums that businessmen nowadays typically assign to major investment undertakings. . . . They have learned the hard way—from the frenetic conditions of 1973–74—that inflation is totally inimical to a healthy business environment."[18] He added, "In an inflationary environment, it is far more difficult for businessmen to estimate future prices, future costs, and future profits."[19] To spur capital spending, he thought, the federal government needed to take a hard line against inflation and reduce corporate taxes.

The president and his advisers blamed weak investment on anemic demand. CEA Chairman Charles Schultze estimated that even if the American economy grew very rapidly over the next two years, it would still be operating 3 percent below its full potential by the end of 1978.[20] One memo, designed for the president's use in a press conference, stated, "I share Chairman Burns's concerns about business profitability. It is important, though, to understand factors which affect profits. Inflation has indeed been such a factor reducing after-tax profits as Chairman Burns suggests. But a principal cause has been the fact that the severe 1974–75 recession, from which we are still recovering, dealt a major blow to profits. Capacity utilization by industry—which strongly affects profits—has been increasing from its recession lows, but is still below historical norms. Profits have been recovering, but that recovery also has some distance to go. . . . A central cause of business profitability has been, and must continue to be, healthy markets for the products of American industry."[21] Economist James Tobin actually thought that the Fed's tough anti-inflation policy was retarding investment because business feared that the central bank might choke off recovery.[22]

Burns rejected this analysis. Just because the economy as a whole had capacity to spare did not mean that every industry did. A Fed report on the companies producing basic materials noted, "Relatively little capacity has been added in the past four years even though bottlenecks and shortages of materials were evident in 1973 and 1974."[23] Burns warned, "Economic analysts who insist . . . that capital spending will automatically catch fire as capacity margins diminish are, in my judgment, thinking too mechanically. Much will depend on the process by which the economy reaches more intensive utilization of resources."[24] An inflationary boom like that of 1973 would probably discourage capital spending because business leaders remembered how they had embarked on ambitious investment programs in 1973–74 only to be badly burned in the subsequent recession.

Each side had a strong case. Companies would not expand capacity unless they had a market to absorb new output. Likewise, they would not invest unless fairly sure of making an adequate profit. The debate was essentially a variation of that going on between Burns and his critics since 1975. The matter hinged on the effect of economic stimulus on prices. If, as Burns argued, the economy had a severe inflationary bias, then fiscal and monetary stimulus would encourage more rapid price increases, retarding production and capital spending. But if, as the president's advisers believed, inflation was indeed under control—albeit at the relatively high rate of 5 to 6 percent—then stimulus would spur output and investment. Each side could point to factors that favored its interpretation. Only experience would determine who was right.

In April, changing economic circumstances drew Burns and the administration closer together. As the Fed chairman had predicted, the economic pause of the second half of 1976 had given way to rapid growth in 1977, with production up at a 7.1 percent annual rate in the first quarter and at 5.8 percent in the second. Unemployment fell from 8 percent in January to 7 percent in June. At the same time, prices leapt upward at between 8 and 10 percent. Charles Schultze pointed out that this jump resulted from rapid increases in food prices, which were quite volatile, and he contended that the basic rate of inflation remained around 5 or 6 percent.[25] Nevertheless, rapid price increases and strong growth argued against economic stimulus. Accordingly, the president changed his economic policy. First, Carter dropped the $50 rebate, which he had never liked. "The idea of the rebate really grated on him," Schultze said. "It was like giving somebody something for nothing."[26] The chief executive had supported the rebate only to give the economy a quick boost, and once such action appeared unnecessary, he jettisoned it without regret. This decision cut the White House's stimulus package by one-third, to about $20 billion. The administration also began to talk vaguely about balancing the federal budget in 1981, although this plan assumed that rapid growth would generate much higher revenues.

At this time, the White House arranged the first of regular monthly meetings between Burns and Carter. The Fed chairman allowed his pedagogical instincts to run free in these get-togethers, and as one White House staffer said, "Arthur does most of the talking. The President's a good student and likes to listen."[27] Apparently, Burns's economics lectures really did interest Carter because by most accounts the two got along fairly well on a personal level.

II

After nearly eighteen months of relative quiet, international financial affairs heated up again in mid-1977, demanding more of Burns's attention than at any time since the Arab oil embargo. The American trade deficit, which had totaled about $9 billion in 1976, more than tripled over the next year to $31 billion thanks to higher oil imports, weak exports attributed to sluggish economic growth abroad, and an inflow of manufactured goods that, in retrospect, reflected the declining competitiveness of many American industries. This huge gap naturally created uncertainty, which the Carter administration inadvertently encouraged. At an international conference in June, Secretary Blumenthal tried to put pressure on the Japanese and German governments, which had huge trade surpluses, by hinting that the United States wanted the yen and deutschmark to appreciate.[28] This maneuver had unintended consequences. Currency markets, already concerned about the U.S. deficit, took the secretary's words as a signal to sell the greenback. The decline was gradual over the summer but became precipitate in the autumn. In the last three months of 1977, the dollar declined 15 percent against the Swiss franc, 10 percent against the deutschmark and the yen, and 7 to 8 percent against the British, Belgian, and Dutch currencies.[29]

During 1977 the administration refused to act to halt the decline. A Treasury memorandum stated, "We are not indifferent or unconcerned about our exchange rate and we are not looking toward a large reduction in the rate to deal with our balance of payments problem. We recognize that the strength of the dollar depends on our fundamental economic performance, and we are concentrating on fundamentals. . . . The dollar should be allowed to reflect underlying economic and financial conditions, and we intervene in the market not on the basis of the level or movement of the [exchange] rate but only to counter disorderly exchange market conditions."[30] A White House staff memo noted, "The decline in the exchange value of the dollar has occurred mainly in relation to currencies such as the Japanese yen and German mark—countries whose balance of trade is in substantial surplus. Exchange rate realignments of this kind will help produce the adjustments in trade needed for a stronger world economy."[31] The administration wanted rapid domestic growth, and if that created a large trade deficit and a fall in the dollar's value, so be it. If other countries did not want their currencies to appreciate, they should import more.

Arthur Burns opposed this laissez-faire approach. Remembering 1973, he feared that devaluation would make inflation worse. Moreover, he claimed, "continued uncertainty about the future of the dollar could produce a disorderly, unsettling flight from dollar assets. It could lead to hesitation about spending or investing decisions around the world that would be inimical to prosperity—including the expansion of our exports."[32] The Fed chairman had little patience with those who used the German and Japanese trade surpluses as an excuse for inaction. When William Proxmire argued that the United States should resist depreciation of the dollar but welcome the appreciation of the deutschmark and yen, Burns shot back, "You are playing with words. If you want those currencies to appreciate, and if they appreciate, the dollar depreciates. Now you prefer not to use that word, but you can't get away from the fact."[33] For the moment, Burns urged aggressive intervention in currency markets to defend the greenback, and he suggested that the Treasury issue bonds denominated in foreign currencies both to obtain funds for intervention and to reassure markets that Washington was serious about protecting the dollar. In the long term, he believed that the government had to maintain a hard line against inflation to keep prices in the United States level with those abroad, reduce corporate taxes to attract foreign investment and make American companies more competitive, and conserve energy to limit petroleum imports.[34] As usual, however, he did not talk of raising interest rates—the most effective way for the government to defend the dollar in the short run.

The Treasury refused even to let the Fed intervene in currency markets. It only allowed the central bank to act when exchange markets were "disorderly"—that is, showed signs of panic. Though Burns mused, "When I see the dollar depreciate against the currencies of countries whose economies are demonstrably weaker. . . . I ask myself, 'is the market orderly?' " the administration remained unmoved.[35] In 1977 the central bank spent only $800 million defending the dollar, whereas the Europeans expended $18 billion to the same end.[36]

In 1977 Burns also began to show more concern about the debts of the developing countries. The OPEC oil price increase of 1974 had saddled most third world nations with severe payments deficits, which they had covered with loans from Western—mainly American—banks. To finance this lending, these institutions took large deposits from the petroleum-producing nations, which were earning huge surpluses. This merry-go-round of debt had always worried the Fed chairman, who thought it dangerous, but he recognized that the international community had to finance third world deficits somehow. As the volume of such credits continued to rise, however, he decided that he needed to act. "A major risk," Burns said, "in all of this [lending] is that it would render the international credit structure especially vulnerable in the event the world economy were again to experience recession on the scale of the one from which we are now emerging."[37]

Mexico had already provided an example of the dangers inherent in the situation. At the end of 1976, it had told Washington that it could not pay its debts and needed help. The timing could not have been worse—new presidents were taking office in both countries. Partly at Burns's urging, the United States took a hard line, demanding that Mexico go to the IMF, which would inevitably demand an austerity program. In the end, loans from the fund, credits from the Fed through "swap" lines, and larger Mexican oil revenues rescued the situation, but there remained no regular mechanism to deal with such crises.[38]

Burns decided, "International financial affairs require a 'rule of law' to guide us through the troubled circumstances that now exist."[39] The IMF provided a structure through which to impose order, but as the Fed chairman noted, "Countries typically prefer to tap foreign credit markets to the maximum extent possible rather than borrow from the International Monetary Fund which, in aiding countries that experience significant payments disequilibrium, makes credit available only after the borrower has agreed to follow internal policies judged appropriate by the Fund. Commercial banks, as a practical matter, have neither the inclination nor the leverage to impose restrictive covenants on sovereign governments."[40] As a first step toward a more orderly system, authorities had to learn the extent of third world debt, since as one Fed memo noted, "Limited information exists on the total external indebtedness of the L[esser] D[eveloped] C[ountries]."[41] Under Burns's direction, the Fed began to improve its data on American banks' foreign loans and to negotiate with other central banks a system to determine the structure of these obligations. The Fed chairman conceded that this effort "will fill only a fraction of the information gap," but it would constitute an important first step.[42] With reliable information in hand, the international community could begin to develop hard-and-fast rules for international lending. "I believe," Burns said, "that the time may come and probably should come when at least some informal surveillance of private lending by the IMF will be the proper course."[43] Presumably, this surveillance would require debtor nations to take strong measures to remedy payments deficits.

Unfortunately, the problem of international debt rated low on American priorities. In the summer of 1977, the administration negotiated, both with the other industrial democracies and with several OPEC members, a $10 billion IMF facility to loan money to countries with oil-induced deficits. The United States' share was $1.7 billion.[44] Burns strongly supported this plan, which would reduce calls on American banks for foreign credits, give the IMF a carrot with which to encourage debtor countries to adopt strong measure to close deficits, and get the OPEC countries to take more responsibility for international finance. But the Congress refused to approve the American contribution, saying the money would go to bail out private banks.[45] Despite Burns's warnings, the problems of international finance and debt seemed remote to most Americans. Even private bankers were not particularly interested in Burns's ideas. Paul Volcker noted, "Arthur Burns once recalled that he had summoned a group of leading bankers to Washington . . . to warn them about the risk of repeating in foreign lands their most recent excesses in real estate lending [where they had suffered large losses]. What he got for his trouble was a response that they knew more about banking than he did."[46] The chairman, working with the New York Fed, did put together a system to gauge the exposure of American banks abroad, but in retrospect it did not work very well.[47] Despite a considerable investment of effort, the Fed chairman enjoyed only limited accomplishments in this realm during 1977—an unfortunate outcome in light of the subsequent gyrations of the dollar and the third world debt crisis.

III

In 1977 Henry Reuss trotted out yet another package of reforms directed at the central bank. That spring, he pried out of the Fed minutes of its regional board meetings. These, he found, contained several instances in which Fed officials encouraged board members and bankers to lobby against legislation that affected the central bank, such as the GAO audit. The representative also claimed to have discovered some examples of conflict of interest. For instance, he noted that one member of the New York Fed's board belonged to a law firm retained by Chemical Bank, which had bid unsuccessfully to purchase the assets of the failed Franklin National Bank from the FDIC. Overall, Reuss thought that the minutes revealed "a pattern of disdain for public accountability," and he soon introduced a measure to rectify the situation.[48] His newest bill would prohibit Fed employees from talking with the officers of any institution regulated by the central bank with the intent "to influence actions affecting the Federal Reserve System," eliminating what Reuss saw as improper contacts.[49] The measure also required the Fed to give Congress, in addition to its annual targets for monetary growth, projections for both interest rates and the composition of its portfolio of government securities over the next year.[50] Finally, the bill linked the Fed chairman's term with that of the president.

Burns, as usual, refused to give an inch. He had let Reuss see the minutes of the regional boards' meetings on the condition that the representative keep them private, and he thought that by publicizing them Reuss had broken his word. "Apart from a number of misrepresentations," the Fed chairman told the congressman, "nothing has come out of your committee concerning these minutes."[51] Burns pointed out that the conflict-of-interest charges were flimsy, to say the least. With respect to the New York board member with ties to Chemical Bank, he noted that Reuss could link neither the man's law firm to the bank's bid for Franklin, nor the New York Fed's board to the FDIC's review of bids. Although he sidestepped the matter of whether the central bank had lobbied against legislation that affected it, Burns insisted that the Fed had always acted properly and argued that prohibiting conversation between Fed officials and bankers on certain subjects was probably unconstitutional and certainly so vague as to cause trouble. He reiterated concerns expressed the previous year about allowing the president to appoint his own Fed chairman, warning that it would represent a dangerous increase in executive power. Burns also resisted making any estimates about either the cost of money or the composition of the central bank's portfolio in the future. The Fed keyed its policy to monetary growth and adjusted interest rates to get the desired outcome. It could not commit itself to any specific level of interest rates for the future unless it was willing to dump its money supply targets, which few desired. Moreover, projections of interest rates were notoriously inaccurate, and by making one of these "official" the Fed was more likely to confuse than clarify things. Nor could the Fed accurately predict the composition of its portfolio over time because this depended in large part on what others offered in the marketplace.[52]

Burns's arguments hit home, convincing even the administration that most of Reuss's ideas were unwise.[53] The House Banking Committee reported out a bill that did no more than align the Fed chairman's term to that of the president, and the Senate jettisoned even that, passing a measure that merely required Senate confirmation of the chairman and vice-chairman of the Federal Reserve Board.[54] Burns did not oppose this bill, which soon became law.

The low point came in August when consumer advocate Ralph Nader produced evidence that he claimed proved that Burns "was misleading the Congress on a serious matter." For years, the Fed chairman had denied that the Open Market Committee made long-term projections for interest rates. But Nader had put his hands on such estimates by the Fed's staff, and the existence of these, he said, showed that Burns had been lying. Moreover, these projections were far off the mark, suggesting to the consumer advocate that Fed policy rested on inadequate statistics.[55] The excited Nader immediately sent this information off to Henry Reuss, but it did not go much further. Transcripts of Burns's testimony showed that he had always conceded that the Fed's staff made projections of interest rates. The chairman claimed that the OMC paid little attention to these, largely because they were almost always wrong, and that as a body the OMC made no estimate of where interest rates might go in the long term. Although Reuss was no friend of the central bank, he was far too fair-minded to go after it on such dubious grounds.

The chairman's dogged defense of the Fed's independence suggests certain conclusions about the nature of that independence. Scholars have usually attributed the Fed's autonomy to a combination of two factors. Some argue that the central bank's independence is essentially a "smokescreen" devised by legislators who understand that tight money policies are often necessary but who also want to avoid the blame for the hardships they inevitably entail. Others contend that the Fed's autonomy represents a concession to politically powerful business interests leery of letting elected officials manage monetary policy.[56] Burns's experience indicates that both explanations have validity, but that institutional factors also play a large role in preserving the central bank's independence. The chairman almost always had the votes in Congress to prevent any serious encroachment on the Fed's prerogatives, which strongly suggests that lawmakers agreed, however grudgingly, with the thrust of central bank policy—even though few said as much. Likewise, bankers and business leaders rallied to the defense of the central bank whenever its position seemed in jeopardy, and their opinions carried weight with Congress and the president. Yet in neither case were these reactions automatic. The Fed and its chairman constantly lobbied representatives and senators, explaining their actions and trying to win support. They also helped mobilize business and financial groups in support of the central bank. The people at the Fed liked managing their own affairs and believed, with some justification, that they knew more about monetary policy than anyone else, and their actions were key to preserving the central bank's autonomy.

The division between the executive and legislative branches also shaped the outcome of debates over the Fed's independence. Congress, because of its diffuse structure, could not manage monetary policy, but senators and representatives feared to let the president do so lest the executive become even more powerful—witness Senator Proxmire, a consistent critic of the Fed, torpedoing plans to make the terms of the president and Fed chairman coterminous. To a degree, the central bank retained its autonomy because no one knew what else to do.

IV

The concurrence of views that developed between Arthur Burns and the administration in April did not last long. Despite momentary agreement, the Fed continued to rank inflation as the economy's chief problem, whereas the White House gave priority to unemployment.

Once conditions forced the government to choose between these two goals, relations inevitably frayed.

The central bank wanted to ratchet back monetary expansion and squeeze inflation out of the economy. Over 1977, the OMC slightly reduced its target for growth of the M1 money supply, from 4.5—6.5 percent to 4—6.5 percent, while cutting its goals for the broader M2 and M3 measures considerably more, by 1.5 to 2 percentage points.[57] When the money supply (M1) grew at an extremely rapid 20 percent annual rate in April, the central bank drove up the cost of funds, with the prime rate going from 6.25 to 6.75 percent in May.[58]

The administration criticized this action. In early June, Bert Lance, the chief of the Office of Management and Budget (OMB) and a close friend of Jimmy Carter, said that although "it isn't appropriate for me to tell the Federal Reserve how to conduct their business, . . . my concern is that banks have raised their prime rates" even though "the loan demand just isn't there." "We tried," he said, "to control inflation through interest rates previously—and it didn't work."[59]

Burns appeared unmoved. He warned that "preoccupation with maintaining low interest rates" would turn the central bank into an "engine of inflation" that would pump money into the economy whenever the demand for credit increased.[60] The Fed chairman said, "The increase of short-term interest rates that has occurred since last April has served to check what would otherwise have been an explosion of the money supply. By taking measures to check the growth of money, we have demonstrated that we remain alert to the dangers of inflation. As a consequence, long-term interest rates, which nowadays are extremely sensitive to expectations of inflation, have remained substantially stable."[61] And indeed, long-term interest rates had not increased. When monetary growth leapt forward again in July, the central bank pushed interest rates higher still, with the prime rate up another half a percentage point by September, to 7.25 percent.

Fed policy, however, could have been tougher. It halted the rapid monetary growth of April and July but did not undo it—the Fed did not push interest rates up enough to roll monetary expansion back to the central bank's target. Apparently, the OMC thought these two months were anomalies that, although troublesome, did not merit drastic action. No doubt, knowledge that the administration opposed higher interest rates also encouraged caution, especially since the chairman was up for reappointment soon. In 1975 and 1976, when he could count on President Ford's backing, Burns had responded aggressively when monetary growth overshot the mark. Without that sort of support, the chairman was more cautious. He still acted, but he required stronger evidence. Since monetary growth generally outpaced projections throughout 1977, this meant that Burns was usually behind the curve.

The Carter administration, however, saw signs that the economy was slowing and so did not view the central bank's actions as particularly moderate. In September, Charles Schultze told the president, "Maintenance of a satisfactory rate of economic growth over the rest of this year, and particularly into 1978, is by no means assured."[62] Consumer spending fell 1.5 percent in September, and the CEA chairman warned that capital spending "has not developed the momentum we expected. New orders for capital goods moved erratically during the summer and were lower, on average, than in the second quarter. Private surveys of business plans indicate a growth rate of only around 5 or 6 percent next year in plant and equipment outlays (adjusted for inflation). These lackluster signals are not consistent with the strength needed for a strong economy in 1978."[63] Unemployment had stopped declining, and GNP growth slowed somewhat in the fourth quarter of 1977, to less than a 4 percent rate. Meanwhile, inflation, to which Burns gave priority, remained under 5 percent in the second half. In such an environment, higher interest rates seemed wrongheaded. The CEA staff, seeing "no signs of acceleration in the underlying rate of inflation that would require additional monetary restraint at this time," argued, "Another turn of the monetary screw now could push up interest rates enough to shake confidence."[64] Moreover, the administration believed that gains in the velocity of money—the rate at which it changed hands—were slowing. The turnover of money had increased very rapidly in the two years since the recession, allowing modest growth in the money supply to finance a robust recovery. A slowdown in such gains, however, meant that the money supply would have to expand faster to accommodate the same level of GNP growth.[65]

Burns's criticism of many of the president's reform proposals did not help matters. Upon taking office, the chief executive had sent to Congress a whole series of complex, far-reaching measures to tackle the nation's pressing problems. These included a package of subsidies and taxes to encourage the conservation of oil and to develop alternate energy sources, higher payroll taxes to stabilize the social security system, and the elimination of many income tax deductions to make levies "fairer." Democratic constituency groups were also pushing hard for an increase in the minimum wage, higher farm price support, and national health insurance. They got fairly rapid action on the first two from the Congress, although the president, who feared the effect of such moves on prices, did persuade legislators to limit increases. Burns looked at all these initiatives with dismay. Increases in the minimum wage and social security taxes would push up the costs of labor, while higher farm price supports would make food more expensive and the federal deficit larger. The Fed chairman lamented, "The Congress recently has literally been legislating inflation."[66] He also argued that, because companies could not know the cost of reforms, the president's initiatives hurt business confidence and discouraged investment. "I strongly suspect," Burns said, "that the ability of businessmen to assimilate new policy proposals into their planning framework has now been stretched pretty far."[67]

President Carter argued that he had no choice but to act as he did. "When I'm faced," he said, "with the problem of whether to ignore the depleting reserve . . . on social security and letting the integrity of the social security system be threatened . . . or proposing bold measures to correct the social security problem . . . I, of course, propose those corrections to Congress."[68] The same considerations applied to his other initiatives. With respect to many of these matters, the president was right. Washington could not allow the social security system to become unstable, nor could it ignore the country's huge bill for imported oil—especially since the government controlled the pricing and allocation of domestically produced crude. On such matters, Burns sometimes displayed great ambivalence. For instance, he had long called for an aggressive policy to limit petroleum imports and had once said, "Oil prices should rise rather than move down, in the interest of conserving energy supplies, and in the interest of stimulating more exploration, more research."[69] But since he could not estimate the effect of higher oil prices and other conservation measures on the economy, Burns often developed doubts when confronted with specifics.

Burns did, however, have a strong case against tax reform. A centerpiece of Carter's program was the elimination of the special, lower levy on capital gains. But the Fed chairman argued, "There are many people in our country who have experienced unrealized capital gains in large part because of inflation. Such capital gains are illusory, and any tax on them would be a tax not on income, but on capital, or a capital levy."[70] For instance, if prices increased 6 percent, an investor had to earn that much just to stay even, *plus* enough to cover taxes on the 6 percent. In such circumstances, tax rates had a huge effect on incentives to invest. With 6 percent inflation and a 20 percent tax rate, an investor had to earn 7.5 percent just to break even. But if Uncle Sam demanded 50 percent of any gain, the same investor had to make a 12 percent return. Burns argued, "There are literally thousands of highly successful business firms and farming operations in our country that would never have been launched had it not been for the opportunities afforded by preferential capital-gains treatment. Even with existing capital-gains treatment, the disincentives to mobilizing and employing high-risk venture capital have become enormous. An end to preferential treatment of capital gains could spell an end to the much-shrunken venture capital market in America. If the marketplace for venture capital dried up because of unwise policy, no amount of government stimulus will restore the lost dynamism."[71]

Instead of tax reform, Burns wanted tax reduction. He gave priority to cutting corporate levies. "The need to reduce business taxes has become especially acute: first, in order to offset the impending increases in social security and energy taxes; and second, to neutralize the massive overpayment of income taxes that stems from applying standard accounting rules to our inflation-ridden economy." He frowned upon limited provisions, such as increases in the investment tax credit. "I would reduce the corporate tax rate across the board, rather than try fine tuning," Burns said. "That way you spread the benefits."[72] The Fed chairman also toyed with the idea of a cut in personal income taxes, though here he displayed more caution, calling for matching reductions in federal outlays and hoping to time cuts to coincide with an economic slowdown. "What I find missing in so much of our thinking today," Burns argued, "is the notion that there is such a thing as the middle class, that the great energies of our people are largely concentrated in that class."[73] A tax cut would spur these people to greater enterprise. Again, he desired across-the-board reductions because "in view of the limited knowledge that all of us have about the effects of taxation, spreading out the benefits is likely to achieve the best results."[74]

The Fed chairman also urged structural reforms to reduce the cost of doing business and slow inflation. His recommendations consisted of measures he had been pushing for years: a subminimum wage for teenagers to encourage companies to hire them; repeal of the Davis-Bacon act, which required contractors to pay the "prevailing wage"— high union rates—on all federal construction projects; relaxation of environmental and worker safety regulations; deregulation of transportation; and more.[75] Since most ran counter to the interests and ideas of Democratic constituency groups and lawmakers, they had little chance of becoming law, though in time the administration did end regulation of transportation.

At least superficially, however, Burns's call for tax reduction affected the administration. Concerned that the economy might be slowing, the White House reversed its economic policy yet again and began to cast about for ways to stimulate the economy.[76] It eventually decided on a $25 billion tax cut that would increase the personal deduction, liberalize the investment tax credit, cut excise taxes, and reduce individual and corporate income taxes across the board by about 2 to 3 percentage points.[77] But this proposal fell short of Burns's requirements in certain important ways: it did not match tax reductions with spending cuts, and higher-income taxpayers would enjoy only a small proportional reduction in levies, even though this group included most successful entrepreneurs and investors.[78] Nor did the administration drop its plans to raise the capital gains tax. But the package did at least tip its hat in Burns's direction, especially with respect to corporate levies.

While in the fall of 1977 the administration was developing ways to stimulate the economy, the central bank had ratcheted interest rates up another notch. During the fall, the money supply (M1) increased rapidly, at a 7.5 percent annual rate during the last quarter. This reflected not a one-month bulge, as had been the case in the spring and summer, but a consistent, across-the-board advance. The central bank responded by pushing the cost of money even higher, driving the prime rate to 7.75 percent. Moreover, for the first time that year, long-term rates increased, although not by much.[79]

The Fed's critics were outraged. Economist Walter Heller described this policy as "a poor bargain for the country." He attributed inflation to wages that were increasing 5 to 6 percent faster than productivity, creating "a self-propelled cost-price merry-go-round that is rooted in market rigidities and excess market power and hence highly resistant to aggregative policies and overall economic slack." Because wages were rigid, he argued, "the harsh discipline of weak labor and product markets, on which monetarism relies to deescalate inflation, has given us precious little relief in the past two-and-a-half years."[80] In the Senate, an unhappy William Proxmire tried to pin Burns down on the future of interest rates, but the Fed chairman refused, saying, "I don't know what is going to happen." The lawmaker lamented, "I keep trying to nail that custard pie to the wall."[81]

The administration supported this criticism—sort of. Responding to a journalist's question, a member of the press secretary's office posted a statement on interest rates, noting that the velocity of money was expanding slowly and therefore "recent rates of monetary growth have not . . . been inflationary, even though they have been above the targets set by the Federal Reserve." The notice continued, "If short-term interest rates were to increase substantially further . . . a diversion of savings flows from mortgage lending institutions could begin to occur, and this would reduce the supply of funds for housing. Long-term interest rates might also be driven up."[82]

The White House, however, quickly backed away from this announcement without actually disowning it. No one in authority had approved the statement, and the people in the administration did not want a confrontation with the Fed. "It [the statement] isn't a big deal," Schultze said. "It's nothing we haven't said before."[83] "We certainly wouldn't retract it," he added, "but it wasn't designed to add to the fray."[84] Secretary Blumenthal went further, saying that Fed policy "has been about right." He added that, if higher interest rates began to hurt the economy, "I have no doubt that he [Burns] will adjust."[85] The president said of his relationship with the Fed chairman, "There are differences of opinion expressed on long-range trends and so forth, but it's been very harmonious."[86]

Burns took a similar line. When asked about rumors of discord between himself and the administration, he said, "I pay no attention to such reports, . . . and I hope you don't." But neither did he back down. He argued that any failure by the central bank to contain monetary growth "might be interpreted as indicating that the Federal Reserve was faltering in its determination to lean against inflationary pressures. . . . No such faltering has occurred, nor is it likely to occur. . . . The resolve of the Federal Reserve to undernourish and weaken inflation remains undiminished." "Simply opening up the monetary faucets or spewing out funds from the Treasury," the chairman continued, "doesn't seem a promising course in view of the widespread concerns [about inflation] that now exist—particularly in the business and financial community."[87] The Fed and the White House disagreed on monetary policy, but neither was willing to break openly with the other.

V

In the fall of 1977, President Carter had to decide whether to reappoint Arthur Burns to a third term as chairman of the Federal Reserve Board. Although seventy-three, Burns had no plans to slow down. "I certainly would be pleased to be offered another term," he said. "I almost certainly would accept. . . . I'm not in a hurry to leave the Federal Reserve. The work we do is much too important."[88]

Burns had much support. Many in the business and financial community saw him as the only government official seriously committed to fighting inflation. Andrew Brimmer, a former Fed governor who had sharply disagreed with Burns on many occasions, said, "A decision to retain him . . . would be seen as a positive step by the business and banking communities. Not to do it would be a negative sign that would be difficult for Carter to overcome."[89] Henry Ford II argued, "From a businessman's standpoint . . . it would be unfortunate if Arthur Burns weren't reappointed."[90] Another executive said of the chairman's foes, "The pygmies have taken over and are getting rid of the last giant."[91] Had business leaders voted on the next Federal Reserve chairman, Burns would have won handily. The *Chicago Tribune* summed up the opinions of many when it argued, "Mr. Burns's policy inclinations bring needed balance to the frenzied activism of the Carter administration."[92] The Fed chairman also had much support in the Congress, including lawmakers such as Jacob Javits and Abraham

Ribicoff who were usually identified as "liberals." Many of these people were personal friends of Burns's, but they also feared inflation and
thought of the Fed chairman as a bulwark against rising prices. A
group of nine senators formally urged the president, by letter, to give
the Fed chairman another term. Javits and John Sparkman argued in
the *Wall Street Journal*, "Arthur Burns should be reappointed Chairman because he is the very embodiment of the fight for the independence of the Federal Reserve Board that is one of the firm bases for the
strength of the U.S. economy. Arthur Burns should remain as chairman because he has the confidence of the business and financial
world. He should not be replaced at a time when this confidence is
being tested, not only in our own country but around the globe"—the
last a reference to the decline of the dollar against other currencies.[93]

Burns had many enemies as well, however. Senators Proxmire,
Edward Kennedy (D-Mass.), and Humphrey, as well as Representative Reuss and House Speaker Tip O'Neill (D-Mass.), all wanted President Carter to appoint someone else. Proxmire said, "The Fed under
Arthur Burns has been the [0–21] Tampa Bay [Buccaneers football
team] of the federal government. If President Carter decides to replace
this lovable gentleman all he has to do is refer to the record. I think
the country will understand."[94] Liberal economists also wanted someone new at the Fed. Lester Thurow argued, "The basic question is, 'Do
we want a Federal Reserve System that will systematically produce
unemployment whenever troubles appear in the economy?' The Fed's
current tightening of monetary policies in the face of a 7 percent
unemployment rate are merely indications that nothing was learned at
the Fed in the unfortunate depression of 1974–75. Inflationary problems certainly exist, but they cannot be cured by raising the unemployment rate."[95] Paul Samuelson contended, "By value judgment
and temperament, Burns gives greater weight to the evil of inflation in
comparison with the evil of unemployment than does President
Carter, the Democratic majority in the two houses of Congress and
the electorate at the polls."[96] Labor leader George Meany, who genuinely loathed Burns, raged, "When [is] someone with guts going to
take a look at this man and retire him."[97] Perhaps most important, the
White House staff wanted to be rid of the Fed chairman. Charles
Schultze believed he had to go, as did Hamilton Jordan, perhaps the
most influential person around the president, and Stuart Eizenstat,

who was in charge of coordinating domestic policy. They wanted their own person running the central bank.[98] Moreover, as one member of the CEA said, "There were a lot of people on the Carter staff . . . that despised Burns—faulted him for running much too tight a monetary policy."[99] Perhaps the *New Republic* best summed up the case for replacing the Fed chairman. "The administration," it contended, "would not be able to put its ideas to a fair test with a Nixon man in charge of the Fed. Unless Burns is replaced, people will always wonder what might have been."[100] The *Los Angeles Times* echoed this line when it argued that the Fed chairman should "be somebody whose views and personality do not continually thrust him into an adversial relationship with the President."[101]

The question of Burns's future involved large issues of economic policy as much as the career of an individual. One CEA member has said that, at this time, many around the president, such as Labor Secretary Ray Marshall and Stuart Eizenstat, "were not really concerned at all about what was developing on the inflation front."[102] During 1977, the White House was casting about for ways to reduce inflation without tightening monetary or fiscal policy, looking into incomes policies and the deregulation of certain segments of the economy. But thus far, despite growing concern about prices, this thinking had not led to action. Unfortunately, Democratic leaders in the Congress had little interest in such matters—as the president later said, "All they knew about it [economics] was stimulus and Great Society programs."[103] Barry M. Bosworth, director of the Council on Wage and Price Stability, lamented, "We can't come up yet with a workable program on how you go about unwinding the present [inflationary] spiral, at least, not that has any chance of success."[104] This omission presented great dangers, as Charles Schultze realized. "We could," he warned, "for a while, deal with unemployment problems without facing up to inflation. For a year, or perhaps two, inflation might not get significantly worse. But if we are successful on the unemployment front, then by mid-1979 or 1980, the rate of inflation will begin to grow—and then it may be too late to address it."[105] Though many in the administration distrusted and disagreed with Burns, he was the only government official with a plan for fighting inflation, which everyone agreed was a serious problem.[106]

President Carter found his decision on Burns's future very difficult. He had developed a certain rapport with the Fed chairman and knew that reappointment would raise his rather anemic stock with the business community. Moreover, he feared inflation, even though he was not sure what to do about it. But all of his advisers opposed giving Burns another term, even those such as Treasury Secretary Blumenthal who had fairly good relations with the Fed. Burns was also a Republican, and even more than most residents of the Oval Office, Carter resisted giving jobs to members of the opposition.[107] Moreover, the president disliked recent developments in monetary policy, saying in early 1978, "I think the interest rates last year went up too much."[108] Finally, he found the impunity with which Burns criticized him annoying, preferring at least that the chairman keep such sentiments private.[109] He did not credit warnings that the failure to give Burns another term would fatally shake financial confidence, saying, "I don't believe anybody is indispensable . . . a President or the Chairman of the Federal Reserve Board."[110]

Arthur Burns expected reappointment. He got along fairly well with Carter personally and remembered how President Kennedy had reappointed Chairman Martin in late 1961, even though many of Kennedy's advisers thought that Martin ran too tight a monetary policy. Moreover, after eight years at the center of events, Burns had no doubt begun to think of himself as indispensable. One Fed staffer described his attitude in December, "We had to move our Christmas tree this year because of building renovations and at the [Christmas] party last week the Chairman talked about how we could look forward to our remodeled offices next year. . . . He seemed confident he would be here as chairman next year and, after he finished, he got a very long ovation."[111]

Soon after Christmas, the president summoned Burns to Washington to inform the chairman of his decision. Burns flew up from Florida, where he had been vacationing, to learn that Carter would replace him with William G. Miller, the president of Textron Corporation, a large conglomerate. Though surprised and unhappy, Burns graciously told Carter that he considered Miller a solid appointment. "Mr. President," he said, "you have chosen wisely and well." The president was equally generous, saying at a news conference a few days later, "Dr. Arthur Burns has done an outstanding job of directing the Federal Reserve System. He has symbolized the integrity of our monetary system and the independence of the Federal Reserve. . . . He has served the people of our country well."[112]

VI

Arthur Burns left the Federal Reserve as soon as possible. He could have remained a governor for another six years, but he resigned from the board to give his successor, as he said, "the fullest opportunity to establish his leadership."[113] Had he stayed, Burns would inevitably have formed a separate center of authority within the Fed, making it very difficult for Miller to take charge effectively, and Burns was not one to play the spoiler.[114] He announced that he would leave the central bank at the end of March, which would give the Senate enough time to confirm Miller.

In his last months at the Fed, Burns participated in one important initiative. In November, the decline of the dollar against other currencies had become precipitous and seemed in danger of spinning out of control. This development convinced the administration that it had to defend the greenback, and the Treasury authorized the Fed to draw on its $20 billion in swap, or credit, lines with other central banks to support the dollar in exchange markets.[115] The central bank also raised interest rates a little in January to protect the greenback—something it had done only once before during Burns's tenure and a step from which the chairman had almost inevitably shrunk.[116] When Burns left the central bank, the outcome of these operations was still unclear.

Upon his retirement in March, Arthur Burns expressed pride in the Federal Reserve's accomplishments during his tenure, although he conceded that the nation still faced serious economic problems. "I feel," he said, "a great deal of anguish about the international position of the dollar, both for the sake of this country and for the sake of the international economy. . . . We must give far more serious attention to assuring the integrity of the dollar than we have done."[117] He also lamented that "last year witnessed no progress toward a less inflationary environment"—though he did not mention the central bank's recent failure to contain M1 monetary growth, which had been a hefty 7.9 percent over 1977.[118] Nevertheless, Burns said, "I think I leave the Fed in a strong position."[119] He was, he contended, "not aware of any serious mistakes" made during his years at the Fed, though he conceded "numerous minor" ones.[120] Although Burns was departing the central bank, he claimed he was not yet ready to abandon the public stage. "Those . . . who think the time for farewell has come are mistaken," he said. "Neither a shedding of tears—nor any special rejoicing—is yet in order."[121]

10

Careers New and Old

I

Burns maintained a high profile after he left the Federal Reserve. He joined the American Enterprise Institute in Washington, where he started writing a book about inflation,[1] and he often spoke in public and testified before Congress. Burns also kept up his extensive network of contacts both in the United States and abroad, through which he wielded influence. For instance, in 1978 the leader of the Bundesbank enlisted Burns to lobby Chancellor Schmidt against a spending package that the chancellor was considering to stimulate the German economy.[2] In 1979, six of the leaders of the Group of Seven wealthiest industrial democracies consulted him before their annual summit, with only President Carter abstaining.[3] On another level, Burns became a regular at stag dinners hosted by Richard Nixon for prominent political, intellectual, and journalistic figures—occasions that helped rehabilitate the former president's reputation.[4] Once again,

Burns showed loyalty to Richard Nixon when the latter was in political exile.

In September 1979 Burns outlined his thinking about the economic problems of the industrial democracies in the Per Jacobsson lecture, an annual event sponsored by the IMF. Much of his argument was familiar. People expected too much of their governments, he said, and in trying to meet these demands authorities increased spending and spun out regulations that fired inflation and squeezed business. This not only raised prices but retarded production by deterring investment and innovation, aggravating the imbalance between what people wanted and what the economy could provide. To remedy these conditions, he thought, governments had to balance their budgets, restrict monetary growth, reduce regulation, and cut corporate taxes. But Burns had added a new twist to his case. He contended that at any time the Federal Reserve "could have restricted the money supply and created sufficient strains in financial and industrial markets to terminate inflation with little delay." Political constraints, however, made such strong action impossible. "As the Federal Reserve," Burns explained, "kept testing and probing the limits of its freedom to undernourish the inflation, it repeatedly evoked violent criticism from both the executive and Congress and therefore had to devote much of its energy to warding off legislation that could destroy any hope of ending inflation."[5] Prices kept going up not because governments lacked the means to act but because they lacked the will, and therefore the solution to inflation required changes in the way people thought.

As Burns spoke, events were providing Americans with a painful education. Inflation in the United States accelerated every year after 1977, and by early 1980 consumer prices were going up at more than a 15 percent annual rate. Observers attributed this increase to wages that grew faster than productivity, oil price hikes sparked by the Iranian revolution, the devaluation of the dollar, and government measures such as higher social security taxes, a more generous minimum wage, larger farm price supports, and more extensive worker safety and environmental regulations, all of which pushed up costs.[6] The Carter administration had underestimated the danger of inflation, an error against which Burns had warned it. As Charles Schultze later admitted, "We were always, in terms of an anti-inflation program, six months to a year behind the game."[7] For its part, the Fed did not resist the trend but allowed the money supply to expand very rapidly. By 1979, the price explosion had choked off economic growth, and productivity was actually falling.

These hardships made Burns's tough line against inflation more attractive. In the spring of 1980, the Gallup poll showed that a whopping 74 percent of Americans considered inflation the country's chief problem.[8] Even many who had previously insisted that inflation merited lower priority than unemployment began to modify their stance. They came to realize that inflation not only changed figures in ledgers but actually distorted economic activity. For instance, Arthur Okun, who had chaired the CEA under President Johnson, said at this time, "There is ample grounds for the suspicion . . . that various aspects of our chronic inflation may account for some of the puzzle of the productivity slowdown. . . . Buyers and sellers face genuine increases in their real transaction costs. Managerial effort is diverted from the promotion of productivity to the development of nonmonetary yardsticks. The search for inflation hedges may distort the composition of investment. Uncertainty shrinks the time horizon and creates an aversion to long-lived projects. . . . Research and development budgets may get squeezed."[9]

Burns did all he could to encourage this intellectual current. He accepted an offer from Henry H. Fowler, who had been President Lyndon Johnson's Treasury secretary, to chair the Committee to Fight Inflation, an organization that Fowler had put together after being inspired by Burns's Per Jacobsson lecture. This group consisted of former officials from both parties, including Michael Blumenthal (recently sacked by President Carter), George Shultz, and William Simon, and its program was essentially that laid out by Burns: tax cuts for business, spending reductions, deregulation, and tight money. Burns also made himself available to Republican candidates during the 1980 presidential election. George Bush and Senator Howard Baker (R-Tenn.) consulted with him before the primaries, and after Ronald Reagan won the nomination he put Burns in charge of a panel studying international economic questions for the campaign.[10]

Even before the 1980 presidential election, some aspects of policy were going the direction Burns desired. A year earlier, as part of a cabinet shakeup, President Carter had appointed William Miller Treasury secretary, replacing him at the Fed with Paul Volcker. Under Volcker, the central bank embarked on a course of severe monetary restraint that would last, with some starts and stops, for three years. Moreover, the Carter administration had deregulated transportation and was moving in this direction for petroleum. The president had also proposed some spending cuts, although of these Burns said they "don't amount to much. . . . We are talking about very marginal adjustments."[11] He added pessimistically, "The White House has developed a habit, recently, of changing its mind about the budget at rather short intervals. I don't know where it will stand tomorrow."[12]

One important current worried Burns—the constant drumbeat for tax reduction. In 1980, recession naturally inclined people to look for ways to stimulate production, and in the late 1970s a group of economic thinkers calling themselves "supply-siders" had suggested that Washington could, by cutting tax rates, encourage people to greater effort and enterprise. This would increase the supply of goods and services and thereby strike a blow against both recession and inflation. These ideas received enthusiastic support from the right wing of the Republican Party and formed a centerpiece of Ronald Reagan's presidential campaign. But though Burns agreed that lower taxes would be a tonic to enterprise, he thought that the government had to balance its budget first. No extra incentives to produce could counterbalance the inflationary effects of a large deficit. Speaking for the Committee to Fight Inflation, Burns said, "We're not in favor of a significant tax reduction at the present time." Though he still supported cuts in corporate levies, he thought Congress should spread these over several years, with only nominal reductions in the first two.[13]

The election of Ronald Reagan as president in November 1980 gave Burns new opportunities to push his ideas, but it also created new problems. The economist served as an adviser to the president, first as a member of the committee that forged the administration's economic plan and then as one of a group that consulted regularly with the Treasury secretary. The administration also took many of the steps that Burns had been urging: it cut domestic spending considerably, deregulated petroleum, and relaxed federal regulation of business. Some in the new administration did talk of reducing the Fed's autonomy, but Burns's stern opposition—Paul Volcker described his reaction as "apoplectic"—put an end to the matter.[14] But President Reagan refused to abandon his pledge to slash corporate and personal income taxes by 30 percent, and Burns made no secret of his opposition to such a move. "I would not cut personal income taxes at this time," he told Congress. Spending reductions "must precede or be concurrent with whatever cuts are made in corporate or personal income taxes." To say the least, this talk annoyed the administration. OMB director David Stockman responded that any strategy "based on temporizing and gradualism" would be "a recipe for failure."[15] Arthur Burns's warnings changed nothing. Congress voted in 1981 to cut income and corporate taxes 25 percent, with reductions phased in over three years, and these reductions, coupled with the severe 1981–82 recession and heavy spending on defense and middle-class entitlement programs like Medicare, created immense deficits that persisted even after recovery.

In May 1981 President Reagan appointed Arthur Burns ambassador to West Germany. The Bonn embassy was an important post for which Burns was well qualified, having considerable international experience and many friends in Germany, including Chancellor Helmut Schmidt. But the administration also knew that this position would take Burns out of the country and away from the debate on economic policy.[16] Though he must have realized that ulterior motives colored the offer, Burns also understood the importance and prestige of the Bonn job. He also thought, "Being a practicing Jew, I vaguely felt that there might be a certain moral fitness, perhaps a step toward further reconciliation, in becoming ambassador to a country that had perpetrated during the Nazi era unspeakable crimes against my coreligionists, including members of my own family."[17] After some hesitation, Burns accepted.

II

As ambassador to West Germany, Arthur Burns believed that he had a duty not only to represent the American government in Bonn but also to communicate legitimate German concerns to Washington. "I concluded," he said, "soon after coming to Bonn that my embassy must concentrate on clearing away the underbrush of emotion and faulty perception that now and then disturbed the relationship between the United States and the country to which I was accredited."[18] The seventy-seven-year-old economist quickly brought his German up to speed and, as he had in the American capital, made an immense number of friends that ran the gamut from Helmut Schmidt's successor, Helmut Kohl, to Petra Kelly, the leader of the radical Green Party.[19] He also tried to reach out to German youth, meeting regularly with groups of ten to fifteen university students in Bonn and Berlin and occasionally with larger groups.

Burns realized that Washington and Bonn did not have identical interests. "The United States," he said, "having become a world power in the last forty years, brings a global view to international affairs. German interests, on the other hand, are mainly regional. A nation located in the heart of Europe, having lost a large portion of its prewar territory to the Soviet Union and Poland, being troubled over the fate of still another portion that became a separate German state under Soviet domination, could hardly be expected to show great boldness in foreign affairs with any frequency."[20] The diplomatic atmosphere of the early 1980s sharpened these differences. During this time, the Cold War intensified, and West Germans found this development particularly worrisome. Detente between the West and Moscow in the early 1970s had allowed West Germans to reestablish contact with their brethren on the other side of the Iron Curtain and had rendered the status of West Berlin more secure. Heightening tensions threatened to undo these gains. People in the United States, on the other hand, had less invested in relations with the Soviet Union. As Burns put it, "A typical American citizen, if asked to identify how detente has affected his life, would be hard put to respond."[21]

Burns believed that the alliance between the United States and West Germany survived such divergences because it rested on a foundation deeper than self-interest. "A shared ethos is the philosophic and ethical essence of our relationship," he said. "It is the basic element that, in times of crisis and challenge, makes natural allies of the Western democracies." "This shared ethos," he continued, "is based on values that are fundamental to both of our societies and that bind them together—namely, respect for human rights, faith in democracy and devotion to the rule of law."[22] Burns saw the alliance between the United States and Germany, and indeed between all industrial democracies, as both the product and the bulwark of Western civilization.

Between 1981 and 1985, Burns had to deal with a series of prickly issues that threatened this alliance. In 1981 and 1982 the determination of the American government to prevent the construction of a natural-gas pipeline from the Soviet Union to Western Europe poisoned relations. The Europeans welcomed this new source of fuel but Washington feared that its NATO allies would become dependent on a hostile power for energy and did everything within its power to block the project, banning the export of vital technology and withholding credit. This infuriated the Europeans, who thought that they could best decide their own security interests. When the economics minister in Bonn told Burns, "The Federal Republic of Germany is a sovereign country, . . . and . . . the German government would appreciate our [the United States] finally grasping that fact," the ambassador counseled Washington to back down.[23] After George Shultz became secretary of state in 1982, he convinced the president that this policy was ineffective and hurting relations, and the administration gave in.

Soon another issue began to drive the United States and Europe apart—the deployment of American intermediate-range nuclear missiles in Germany and other NATO countries. Washington acted at the request of European governments, which wanted these weapons to counterbalance similar Soviet missiles aimed west. The deployment, however, prompted huge antinuclear and peace demonstrations in Europe, which the Soviets encouraged. Nevertheless, the allied governments, firmly supported by Washington, stood their ground and the missiles were installed.

The final and, for Burns, most painful rift developed in 1985, when President Reagan, in the course of a trip to Germany to the end of the Second World War, laid a wreath at a German cemetery in Bitburg that contained the graves of several members of the notorious Waffen-SS. The White House advance men who had planned the occasion had not realized the presence of these graves, and when it became known, many outraged Americans demanded the cancellation of the visit. Burns had never been enthusiastic about this trip, which was to commemorate the fortieth anniversary of the end of World War II. In Burns's mind, this anniversary "was a time when the spiritual need of the German people was to be by themselves. . . . It was time to recall and come to terms with the past, a time for meditation, a time for prayer, a time for rededication to democracy, tolerance, and international good will."[24] Nevertheless, Burns knew that having promised to go, the president could not back out. To do so would damage the credibility of Chancellor Helmut Kohl, a staunch American ally, and it would anger many Germans who, Burns said, "could not overlook that those buried at Bitburg were among their kith and kin."[25] The ambassador papered over the uproar as best he could, adding to Reagan's itinerary a visit to the Bergen-Belsen concentration camp, which the German government had wanted to include in the first place.[26] This reopening of the wounds of the Second World War hurt Burns, who had devoted much effort to healing them.

During his tenure as ambassador, Burns demonstrated a special concern for German youth. Largely through his meetings with small groups of students, he managed to develop a certain rapport with these people. As a teacher who participated in one of these gatherings described it, students "had come to the residence expecting to hear a long-winded lament from the representative of the mighty United States about the irresponsibility of the peace movement, or the unwarranted romanticism of German youth." Instead, they got an impassioned plea for greater understanding of their own history and of the value of Western culture. "Never forget," Burns said, "that there is so much more to your country than the memory of that one 'Herr Hitler.' No doubt, he was a God-forsaken atrocity of a man. But . . . there are Beethoven, Goethe, Schiller, Kant. Look, you can reach back to so many outstanding individuals who were Germans and on whom you can base your self-perception, one that is filled with pride."[27]

At the same time, Burns strongly defended the role that the United States played in Europe, trying to win over the often skeptical students. He took the position, "I have no difficulty understanding people who disagree with the policies of my government. . . . But understanding fails me when supposedly educated young people equate the motives or objectives of the United States vis-à-vis Europe, with those of the Soviet Union."[28] To his mind, the difference was obvious—American liberty versus Soviet tyranny. The ambassador believed that much of the suspicion young Germans exhibited toward the United States reflected an ignorance of history. "German textbooks," he said, "give little or no attention to the vast changes that have occurred in our [American] society since 1945; they even neglect the contemporary history of their own country." Burns noted that young Germans knew little of events like the Berlin airlift or the Soviet invasions of Hungary in 1956 and Czechoslovakia in 1968 to crush dissident regimes. But American schools, he thought, did little better. "The schools of both countries have served the new generation poorly by their slight of attention to the principles that inform our Western civilization."[29]

III

In the summer of 1985 Arthur Burns retired and returned to Washington. There he rejoined the American Enterprise Institute and wrote a short book on his experience as ambassador.[30] He and his wife also resumed their lively social lives and reestablished contact with their many friends.

Burns also began a new research project, a study of the changes in American banking since the 1950s. He argued that the industry had evolved beyond recognition. In the 1950s, banks were a tightly regulated group of companies, segmented both geographically and by function so as to minimize competition and to channel such rivalry as did exist into accepted and well-understood paths. But by the 1980s, banking had become a freewheeling industry characterized by fierce competition and porous boundaries between the different aspects of the business. Since both government financial regulation and the management of economic policy rested on certain assumptions about the banking system, Burns's work had considerable practical implications.

In the spring of 1987, while delivering a lecture on this subject at the University of Pittsburgh, Burns suffered a heart attack. From his hospital bed, he edited an overview of the changes in the banking system, producing *The Ongoing Revolution in American Banking*, which he intended as the first installment of a larger work.[31] This slim volume, which appeared in 1988, featured an outline of Burns's thinking as well as an extensive series of statistical tables and charts that made his case in quantitative terms.

In June 1987, almost exactly two years after leaving Bonn, Arthur Burns died of complications following heart surgery. In addition to the rabbi from his synagogue, the speakers at his memorial service included a Nobel-laureate economist, a United States senator, the secretary of state, the chairman of the Federal Reserve Board, and two former presidents of the United States.[32]

11

Conclusion

✦

I

Arthur Burns's tenure at the Federal Reserve between 1970 and 1978 straddled what is perhaps the great divide of recent American history. In the decades after the Second World War, output and productivity expanded smartly in the United States, financing higher living standards and new government programs and easing social change. In 1973, this happy state of affairs ended. That year saw runaway inflation, the final collapse of fixed exchange rates, the Arab oil embargo, and the start of the worst recession in decades. Damaging as these crises were, however, they concealed even more severe problems. As the *Wall Street Journal* noted in late 1991, "The U.S. economy since about 1973 has been suffering from a slowly debilitating disease. Growth in productivity has dropped, the competitiveness of industry has declined, the once-steady rise in living standards has faltered, and wages have stagnated."[1] The means of individual Americans and of the country as a whole no longer matched expectations, creating tremendous frustration and forcing people to abandon cherished goals. This new "era of limits," in which the growth of per capita income in the United States slowed dramatically, not only dominated the economic picture but also strongly influenced social and political developments. As chairman of the powerful central bank, Burns was at the center of events, trying to stave off disaster and devise lasting solutions.

II

When Arthur Burns went to the Fed in 1970, he did not know what the future held. Harbingers of things to come existed in the form of inflation, low productivity growth, and weak investment, but at the time Burns believed that these difficulties stemmed largely from economic rigidities—particularly the excessive power of labor unions. Modest fiscal and monetary restraint coupled with an effective incomes policy would get inflation under control, he thought, and with costs stable and the future clear, business would invest more, spurring growth and improving productivity. President Nixon's decision to impose wage-price controls in August 1971 represented a victory for these ideas.

Unfortunately, Burns had underestimated the American economy's difficulties, and his program self-destructed. The chairman gave controls priority because he considered inflexible wages and prices the country's chief economic problem. Since he feared that political support for controls would crumble if interest rates went up too much and calculated—erroneously—that the American economy had considerable untapped capacity, Burns pursued a very accommodating monetary policy designed to keep the cost of money stable. In 1972, he persuaded the OMC—against the better judgment of several members—to keep interest rates down even though that meant allowing rapid monetary growth. By early 1973, a combination of devaluation, bad harvests, and government overstimulation created shortages that forced up prices and undermined controls. Two years after President Nixon had frozen wages and prices, inflation was worse than ever. Though failure was not wholly the fault of the central bank, even

Burns admitted that the Fed had not handled the situation well, and many others, ranging from Milton Friedman to William Proxmire, considered its actions nothing short of disastrous.

By 1975, these and subsequent crises had led the Fed chairman to conclude that the U.S. economy had serious structural imbalances. The stagnation of per capita income and productivity was not, he thought, a temporary phenomenon but a permanent condition that had its roots in the political system. "The American people," Burns said, "have come to rely increasingly on government for the solution of economic and social problems. This has led during the past thirty-odd years to a rapid increase in government expenditures, to higher and persistent federal deficits, and to intricate government regulations over our business and personal lives."[2] These policies increased both the demand for goods and services and the cost of doing business, creating inflation that, in turn, conjured up phantom profits on which companies had to pay taxes, further reducing earnings. "We have experienced since the mid-sixties," Burns argued, "a depression in true corporate profits, and this has naturally been accompanied by a depressed stock market. Venture capital investment during much of this period nearly dried up."[3] Poor earnings discouraged investment and innovation, slowing economic growth and accounting, at least in part, for weak productivity gains. Greater reliance on government, Burns thought, both reflected and intensified a deterioration of the work ethic, which was not only bad in and of itself but also further damaged economic performance.

Subsequent research bore out much of this analysis. A study by the Council of Economic Advisers in 1979 concluded that environmental, health, and safety regulations had shaved 0.4 percentage points annually off productivity gains after 1973, and slower growth in the capital invested per worker had reduced these gains by another half point a year. Likewise, the proportion of GNP devoted to research and development shrank from 3 percent in 1964 to 2.2 percent in 1978, and most observers blamed this development for some of the deceleration of productivity growth.[4] Moreover, a consensus existed among economists that real profits had declined since the mid-1960s, at least in part because of the distortions created by rising prices—and historically, earnings were closely linked to research spending and investment.[5] Although these factors accounted for only about half of the slowdown in productivity growth after 1973, the approximately 1 percentage point a year they did represent could make a big difference in living standards over time.[6] Burns's arguments about the work ethic were less persuasive. Some antecdotal evidence does support his claims—for instance, Douglas Fraser, the head of the United Auto Workers, believed that younger workers were less conscientious than their elders.[7] But there was little proof that, on the average, people were not working as hard. Indeed, the percentage of the population holding jobs actually increased over the 1970s.[8]

To restore prosperity, Burns thought, the government had to subdue inflation and improve corporate earnings. He floated a lot of ideas about how to accomplish these goals but stuck fairly consistently to four of them. Washington had to balance its budget, restrain monetary growth, relax regulations wherever possible, and cut corporate taxes. Although this program would cause hardship over the near term, Burns thought that it would eventually increase investment, productivity, and living standards.

Burns's application of the monetary plank of his plan during 1974 and 1975 stirred great controversy. As the economy slid into deep recession in the fall of 1974, the central bank allowed monetary growth to slow considerably—a policy that many people, including economists Paul Samuelson and Herbert Stein, believed intensified the downturn. This outcome was not entirely by design. The Fed pumped considerable reserves into the banking system over the winter, but a sharp drop in the demand for credit neutralized this action. Still, these developments do not seem to have worried Burns much. He argued that the speculative excesses of the previous two years had made a sharp recession inevitable and that, by putting too much money into the economy, the Fed would merely lay the foundation for another wave of inflation, which would put the country right back where it had started. Once companies had worked off excess inventories and brought costs under control, he said, the economy would recover. This attitude horrified many Democratic congressmen and senators. To them, Burns was a latter-day Herbert Hoover, sacrificing jobs for outdated ideas of "monetary responsibility." In Burns's eyes, it was his critics whose thinking was obsolete. Following Keynes's teachings, they believed that recession required economic stimulus, but the chairman argued that in a world of narrow profit margins and expectations of inflation, higher demand would probably translate into higher prices. On at least some points, Burns was right. The economy did turn around more or less as he forecast, in May 1975, and the inflation rate slowed by half between 1974 and 1976.

Both Burns and his critics probably exaggerated the importance of monetary policy. The recession was almost certainly inevitable, although the Fed's actions quite likely intensified it somewhat.[9] The decline of inflation in 1975 flowed largely from the downturn in economic activity, though again the central bank's policy probably encouraged this trend. Inflation has an important—though unquantifiable—psychological component, and the Fed's firm stance no doubt reassured many about the future of prices. Considering the stubbornness of inflation during the 1970s, the emphasis on containing it was understandable and prudent.

Central bank policy during the recovery generates less disagreement—at least in retrospect. The Fed kept monetary growth modest despite dire warnings from many quarters that this might well halt the economic rebound. But production recovered well throughout the second half of 1975, while inflation dropped to around 5 to 6 percent by early 1976, bearing out Burns's predictions. Even critics of this policy such as Senator Proxmire subsequently conceded its wisdom.[10]

Nevertheless, Arthur Burns had an uneven record as an inflationfighter. Despite some fierce rhetoric, at no point during Burns's tenure did the Fed wage the sort of no-holds-barred war against inflation that it would fight between 1980 and 1982 under the chairmanship of Paul Volcker, when it put the economy through the wringer to stabilize prices. Even between 1974 and 1976, when the central bank received much criticism for its tight policy, the M1 money supply grew about 5 percent a year, and the M2 measure increased considerably faster. This path hardly constituted monetary strangulation. Moreover, in 1977 the Fed fell away from Burns's goal of monetary restraint and allowed the aggregates to shoot up again—an unfortunate development in light of the resurgence of inflation in the late 1970s. As the *New York Times* noted, "In retrospect, the performance of the Federal Reserve in controlling the money supply during Mr. Burns's tenure received mixed grades."[11]

Why, then, did the central bank face constant demands for a more expansive policy? In the 1970s, people still clung to expectations formed during the heady quarter-century after 1945, when living standards and production advanced strongly. Unfortunately, weak productivity gains and investment meant that the economy could no longer meet those expectations. But many in Washington, conditioned by a generation of Keynesian economists to think of economic policy as demand management, blamed shortcomings on insufficient demand and called for ever-larger federal deficits and more rapid monetary expansion to stimulate production. The Humphrey-Hawkins bill, for instance, was essentially a plan to expand demand as fast as possible. Some other countries actually implemented such programs, with disastrous results. Britain in 1974 and France in 1981 tried to spend their way out of recession while ignoring inflation, a course that led to skyrocketing prices and the collapse of their currencies, which in turn forced London and Paris to reverse course.

These attitudes fueled perhaps the most serious attack on the Fed's independence in its history. In early 1975, many congressmen and senators—perhaps a majority—were ready to legislate a more liberal monetary policy. Arthur Burns resisted this prospect with all the resources at his disposal. As Paul Volcker described it, "When he [Burns] sensed a congressional threat to the effective functioning of the Federal Reserve, he fought and cajoled and he negotiated with the same Congress until they eventually arrived at new arrangements for consultation, for communication, and for accountability that seemed fully congruent with the needs of the Congress and the Federal Reserve alike."[12] The *New York Times* later concluded, "Supporters and critics agreed that his [Burns's] tenacity helped defuse a major threat to the [Federal Reserve] Board's independence."[13] Sometimes the chairman overdid it, bitterly resisting proposals that posed little danger and so arousing congressional ire unnecessarily. For instance, he refused to give Congress official projections of how the Fed expected its policies to affect the economy, though after Burns left the central bank such reports became standard practice and do not seem to have impaired the Fed's autonomy—indeed, they may have forced it to think policy through more clearly. Nevertheless, Burns's skill and stubbornness allowed the central bank to emerge from the 1970s—a decade when the Congress clipped the wings of many agencies—with its independence intact.

In addition to supervising monetary policy, Arthur Burns had responsibilities in international finance, where he swam against the

current. During the early 1970s, the industrial democracies abandoned fixed exchange rates for floating ones, largely because inflation
had undermined stated "pegs" and the growth of currency markets
had made the defense of even realistic par values prohibitively expensive. Burns resisted this development as best he could, defending the
Bretton Woods system as long as possible and, once that course was
no longer realistic, intervening in currency markets to keep the dollar
stable. But international finance had low priority in Washington, and
floating exchange rates, which in theory adjusted automatically to
keep accounts in balance, had great appeal. The Fed chairman, however, distrusted currency markets. Speculators and short-term
investors, he thought, dominated trading, generating outcomes that
had no necessary correspondence to payments equilibrium. Burns
thought it unwise to leave the dollar's value to these institutions, especially since foreign trade was a large and growing segment of the
American economy. But though the Treasury often allowed the central bank to intervene in currency markets, no administration during
Burns's tenure was willing to make big sacrifices to stabilize the dollar. Most people in the White House saw little benefit to such efforts
and calculated, probably rightly, that public opinion would not stand
for them.[14]

Finally, Burns effectively performed the first duty of a Fed chairman—keeping the financial system out of the ditch. Either the Penn
Central bankruptcy in 1970 or the several crises of 1974 could have
sparked financial panics with far-reaching consequences—perhaps
even depression. In both cases the Fed, working with other responsible agencies, prevented disaster. It has not always done as well—for
instance, the Fed's actions between 1929 and 1933 considerably
intensified the Great Depression. Marriner Eccles, William McChesney Martin, Paul Volcker, and Alan Greenspan probably would have
managed in fine fashion too, but Burns nevertheless deserves credit for
his handling of these complex problems.

III

Arthur Burns's stewardship of the Federal Reserve does not lack for
critics, especially in the field of monetary policy. William Greider, in

his book *Secrets of the Temple*, a populist critique of the central bank, wrote, "If it was fair to indict the central bank for regularly yielding to inflation over a period of years, for failing to resist short-term political pressures for economic growth, then Arthur Burns was as guilty as any chairman." "His reputation as an inflation fighter," Greider sneered, "seemed to inflate right along with the value of money."[15] Similar noises came from the right. The *National Review* approvingly quoted columnist Maxwell Newton on Burns, "No man in this century did more to destroy the value of American money."[16]

Though it is hard to deny in hindsight that monetary policy should have been tighter during Burns's tenure at the Federal Reserve, particularly in 1972–73 and 1977, these critics overlook the context in which Burns operated. In the 1970s, Americans demanded the same rapid increases in living standards that they had enjoyed in the postwar decades. After 1973, however, the growth in per capita output slowed dramatically, making it impossible for the economy to provide accustomed gains. Many, taking their cue from Keynes, blamed shortcomings on inadequate demand, and throughout his years at the central bank Burns faced constant pressures for lower interest rates and more money. Even in 1977, when it is clear in retrospect that policy should have been tighter, every increase in the cost of money stirred fierce criticism. Burns's refusal to accommodate the desire for stimulus inspired dangerous attacks on the Fed's independence, but most of the time the chairman kept monetary policy in bounds, avoiding the disastrous experiences of Britain and France in 1974 and 1981, respectively. Moreover, Burns's tenacious defense of the Fed's independence meant that, when public opinion swung in favor of drastic measures to contain prices, the central bank was free to act.

Some economists have advanced a subtler critique of monetary policy under Burns. They point out that between 1970 and 1978, the money supply grew fastest during booms and slowest during downturns—exactly the opposite of what countercyclical policy is supposed to do. This argument exaggerates the capacity of the Fed to control the money supply. The demand for credit waxes and wanes with the business cycle, and the central bank cannot easily counteract these shifts. For instance, in the winter of 1974–75 the Fed put a good deal of money into the financial system, but the rapid decline in the demand for loans undid this policy. Nevertheless, this critique has merit. Burns did sometimes allow the exigencies of the moment to distract him from the big picture, particularly in 1972 and 1977, and the results were not happy.

Others, such as AFL-CIO chief George Meany, charged Burns with insensitivity toward workers and consumers. The thrust of the chairman's policies, they claimed, was to expand corporate profits at everyone else's expense. These arguments have more than a kernel of truth. Reduced to the most basic level, Burns wanted to cut consumption and increase investment by putting more money into the hands of those in charge of capital spending—namely, businessmen. His hostility toward organized labor was no secret, nor was his cautious attitude toward worker safety, environmental, and consumer protection regulations. Moreover, though he came from a working-class family, Burns had few contacts with such people during his years at the Fed.

In another sense, however, Arthur Burns had a better grasp of the problems of wage earners than his critics. Most polls taken after 1973 indicated that people considered inflation the nation's chief problem—even during the Watergate crisis and the 1974–75 recession. Even more important for the well-being of workers, real wages stopped increasing after 1973, largely because productivity stagnated. Burns advanced a program to address the issues of high inflation and weak productivity gains, whereas the sort of economic measures supported by organized labor and many liberal Democrats, such as the Humphrey-Hawkins bill, did not.

Though it has aroused less comment, Burns's stance on international questions also has its critics. Enthusiasts of floating exchange rates such as Milton Friedman and George Shultz believed his attachment to fixed parities mistaken, and even many like Paul Volcker who shared Burns's doubts about currency markets thought his defense of fixed rates both at the Camp David meeting in 1971 and in early 1973 quixotic. Twenty years of international financial instability have tempered much of the ardor for floating rates, but this second critique is undeniable. It is difficult to imagine how the American government could have rescued the dollar in August 1971 or February 1973, as Burns desired, without imposing politically unacceptable domestic sacrifices.

At the same time, Paul Volcker has faulted Burns for failing to develop a realistic policy to stabilize exchange rates. The Fed chairman wanted fixed currency parities but refused to manipulate interest rates to defend them, effectively renouncing the government's most potent weapon in this area. Burns saw domestic and international financial policy as separate and simply would not consider adjusting the former to the needs of the latter except in extreme circumstances—and then his steps were so hesitant and tentative that they had little impact.[17] Yet experience suggests that, without the backing of monetary policy, it is futile even to try to maintain fixed exchange rates. Moreover, domestic and international finance did not work at cross-purposes to the extent that Burns imagined. True, attempting to maintain fixed parities after the Arab oil embargo would almost certainly have been a disaster. But during the first half of 1973 and the second half of 1978, both domestic and international conditions called for higher interest rates. The Fed chairman, however, failed to make the link, even though he was deeply concerned about both sets of problems.

Again, though, Burns's actions appear more constructive when viewed in context. Though he never developed a realistic alternative to floating exchange rates, the Fed chairman did help make these work. The uncertainties inherent in the floating rates demanded even closer cooperation between countries because there were few hard-and-fast rules to govern policy. On top of this, the economic instability of the 1970s—the collapse of fixed exchange rates, inflation, the oil crisis, and recession—created the danger of an international free-for-all of devaluation and protectionism that would have had disastrous consequences for the world economy. That the globe avoided catastrophe owes much to the tradition of economic cooperation that had developed after the Second World War between the industrial democracies, but Burns also deserves credit. His was the strongest and most consistent voice for international financial cooperation in the American government, and at important junctures, such as the negotiation of the Smithsonian agreement in 1971, he got his way. He also enjoyed tremendous respect abroad, and his presence at the central bank reassured other governments that someone with power in Washington was sympathetic to their concerns. Paul Volcker said, "It was in no small part due to his [Burns's] personal efforts—extending well beyond any formal mandate of a Federal Reserve Chairman—that central bankers working together and with their governments helped defuse the very real international threat."[18]

Beyond the management of policy, how much influence did Burns's ideas have on events, both during and after his tenure at the central bank? Of course, no one can separate out the extent to which an individual shapes the intellectual climate and the degree to which it shapes him. Yet Burns had great prestige and a powerful office, and anyone who followed economic events in the 1970s was exposed to his thinking. Moreover, he always thought of himself as an educator and did his best to influence opinion through his many public statements. Burns also had an extraordinary range of contacts both in the United States and abroad on whom he had influence. Many who held high office in Washington during the 1980s had worked with Burns at one time or another: their numbers included Alan Greenspan, George Shultz, Paul Volcker, and a majority of Fed governors.[19] Indeed, many of these men had started or advanced in government under Burns's sponsorship. They were strong individuals who realized that Burns was not perfect, but they all admired him and conceded that he shaped their thinking. As Paul Volcker said, "We squabbled quite a lot about this and that. . . . But there was never much doubt that on the main issues he was like a great oak under which we could take intellectual and moral shelter."[20]

Burns had an important message to deliver. He argued that the American economy had deep-seated structural problems—chief among them inflation—that required extensive reform. This attitude was new. Most people took the prosperity of the postwar era for granted, and the chairman's argument that the good times had gone and would return only when the country changed its ways ran very much against the grain. Burns also advanced a straightforward program to remedy the situation: budget cuts, tight money, deregulation, and reductions in corporate levies. At first glance these proposals seem like a throwback to the laissez-faire policies of conservative Republicans like Robert Taft in the 1930s and 1940s.[21] But Burns was not and had never been an advocate of laissez-faire. He supported measures to even out the business cycle and combat monopoly, and though skeptical of the welfare state, he strongly favored initiatives like worker training that promised to expand economic opportunity. But Burns attributed the stagnation of productivity and living standards to the perverse incentives created by misguided government policies and the inflation they caused. By containing prices, reducing corporate levies, and easing regulation, he thought that Washington could lower the cost of doing business, which would in turn encourage badly needed investment and innovation.

Burns was pushing a radical change in the way people thought about economics. Ever since the Great Depression and the onset of Keynesian intellectual hegemony, the majority of economists and government officials, both Republicans and Democrats, had thought of economic policy in terms of demand management. American productivity was boundless, and the problem was how to make use of it. Moreover, Keynesian theory concerned itself chiefly with finance and government policy, not the actual structure of the economy. Indeed, Keynes had developed his ideas in part to avoid having to address difficult problems of economic organization, which he was doubtful of resolving.[22] These attitudes even affected critics of Keynesian economics. Monetarists devoted most of their efforts to schemes to keep demand on an even keel by regulating the money supply. John Kenneth Galbraith, coming at the subject from the left, wanted to redirect resources from the private to the public sector. These economists all had ideas about what determined the output of goods and services, but such matters were not central to professional discourse because the regular growth of economic capacity in the United States rendered them less than pressing. Politicians and interested members of the public, who rarely had the time to absorb the nuances of economic theory, devoted even less thought to the issues of supply.

Burns, however, had his intellectual roots in the Progressive era, and Keynes did not define his outlook. He recognized quite early that the economic problems of the 1970s reflected not insufficient demand but problems in the production and distribution of goods and services. Though critics of Burns like Paul Samuelson and James Tobin were, in important respects, better economists than he, they were too enmeshed in their intellectual tradition to recognize quickly what was going on. They assumed that the problems of the mid-1970s reflected one-time events such as the oil embargo, the devaluation of the dollar, and mismanagement of government policy. The proper application of Keynesian techniques, along with a period of calm, would restore things to "normal." Though not an unreasonable assumption, it was wrong. The country's capacity to produce was not increasing at its historical rate, and Keynesian theory had little to say about this problem.

Whatever the flaws of Burns's thinking, he recognized this situation and addressed it.

Burns stood in the vanguard of an intellectual change that had great ramifications outside the academic world. By the 1980s, almost everyone had come to agree that stable prosperity would require thoroughgoing reform. Moreover, the focus of political debate shifted from questions of consumption to those of output. People on the right, like Burns or Martin Feldstein, argued that the growth of per capita output had fallen off because government was hampering business. Washington taxed, spent, and regulated too much, impairing efficiency and output, and the federal government should get out of the way and let companies do their job. On the left, people like Robert Reich held that the economy was suffering because the private sector simply was not up to dealing with the growing complexities of economic life. They urged Washington to step in directly and take a greater hand in managing business. Neo-Keynesians like Alan Blinder revised Keynes's thinking, bringing to it a greater sensitivity to issues of supply. Politicians drew on these ideas, reshaping both policy and public discourse about the economy.

Burns deserves some credit for creating this new atmosphere. Of course, in the 1970s a lot of people were trying to figure out the economic crisis, but the Fed chairman was prominent, forceful, and generally ahead of the curve in his thinking. Martin Anderson, one of Ronald Reagan's chief advisers during his first term of office and a friend of Burns's, insisted, "The first person who introduced me to the essence of supply-side economic policy was Arthur F. Burns."[23]

The economic reforms of the late 1970s and early 1980s, most of which Burns supported, yielded mixed results. Between 1980 and 1982, the nation suffered through a terrible recession—far worse than that of 1974–75—but starting in 1983, inflation stabilized at a relatively low level, the economy embarked on a sustained expansion, and productivity grew a little faster.[24] Had Washington followed Burns's advice and balanced its budget, the country might have done better still, since continuing deficits absorbed a huge portion of the nation's capital. On the other hand, it may be that the large deficits, by stimulating demand, provided the impetus for recovery. In any event, a speculative boom in real estate, the stock market, and corporate buyouts set the stage in the late 1980s for another recession. More important, since recessions inevitably punctuate all expansions, the basic problem remained unsolved—real income during the 1980s remained stagnant and in many cases fell. It is easy to blame government policy for this failing, and indeed Washington must shoulder much of the onus for conditions. Yet it seems that the country's economic problems went beyond government mismanagement. The decline of the international competitiveness of many American industries and the extensive corporate restructuring of the 1980s and early 1990s strongly suggested that a return to the stable prosperity of the 1950s and 1960s required a thorough reorganization of the private sector—a process over which Washington could probably have only limited influence.

These problems should not, however, obscure the progress made during the 1980s. Whatever the vicissitudes—and they were legion— the decade after 1982 was an improvement, economically, on the preceding one. The nation brought the scourge of inflation under control, which was not only a good thing in and of itself but which also allowed the country to address its other problems. High and accelerating inflation made it difficult for firms to answer such basic questions as, "What prices should we charge?" "What exactly are our costs?" "Just how large are our profits?" and "Are we more or less efficient than our competitors?" By reducing price increases to a relatively low and stable pace, enterprises large and small could accurately take stock of their position. Moreover, the shift of public debate from questions of demand to those of output allowed the nation to come to grips with its long-term economic difficulties, most of which originated from that quarter.

IV

Our judgments of the past depend on the questions we ask of it. The American economy performed poorly after 1973, and that poses the question, "What went wrong?" From this point, the historian looking at Burns naturally goes into his mistakes—and he made many, some of them considerable. In the early 1970s, his analysis of the nation's difficulties, which centered on economic rigidities, led him to push a program that combined controls with monetary expansion—a mix that proved disastrous. The prescription he assembled in the middle of the decade, which emphasized combating inflation with tight money and budgets and helping business by cutting regulation and taxes, had greater utility, but Burns allowed the Fed to deviate from his plan in 1977, when it permitted rapid monetary growth.

But the Fed chairman operated in a very difficult context. At this time the American economy—and those of the other industrial democracies—had structural problems whose solution went beyond fiscal and monetary tinkering. Government had to rework the way it approached economic policy. But popular opinion, however upset with immediate problems, would not tolerate the type of drastic measures that might bring improvement, and indeed, much support existed for massive stimulus—a course that experience suggests would have made things worse. At the same time domestic and international financial instability raised the specter of a general collapse that could have led to depression.

In this light, another question comes to mind—"Why were things not worse?" Here Arthur Burns's leadership deserves some credit. He resisted massive monetary stimulation at considerable political risk. He tenaciously defended the independence of the one government agency, the Federal Reserve, whose raison d'être was the preservation of the dollar's value. He consistently urged international cooperation in an atmosphere that often encouraged nations to turn in on themselves. Finally, he did his best to open Americans' eyes to the severity of the difficulties they faced and to build a constituency for substantial reform. These were vital contributions that required great confidence and courage—two qualities everyone agreed Arthur Burns had in abundance.

APPENDIX 1

Financial Statistics

	M1 Growth Rate[1]	M2 Growth Rate[2]	Fed Funds Rate[3]	3-Month Treasuries[4]	Long-term Treasuries[5]
1969					
1st Quarter	5.9%	5.9%	6.58%	6.09%	5.88%
2nd Quarter	3.9%	4.0%	8.33%	6.19%	5.92%
3rd Quarter	1.7%	(1.1%)	8.98%	7.01%	6.14%
4th Quarter	2.1%	1.5%	8.94%	7.35%	6.53%
annual	3.5%	2.6%			
1970					
Q 1	5.7%	3.2%	8.57%	7.21%	6.56%
Q 2	5.9%	8.4%	7.88%	6.67%	6.82%
Q 3	8.4%	12.7%	6.70%	6.33%	6.65%
Q 4	3.8%	8.5%	5.57%	5.35%	6.27%
annual	6.1%	8.4%			
1971					
Q 1	8.3%	16.7%	3.86%	3.84%	5.82%
Q 2	10.6%	12.6%	4.56%	4.24%	5.88%
Q 3	4.0%	5.8%	5.48%	5.00%	5.75%
Q 4	1.7%	8.1%	4.75%	4.23%	5.51%
annual	6.3%	11.2%			
1972					
Q 1	7.4%	11.8%	3.54%	3.44%	6.04%
Q 2	7.9%	10.1%	4.30%	3.77%	6.08%
Q 3	8.3%	10.7%	4.74%	4.22%	6.00%
Q 4	9.1%	10.4%	5.14%	4.86%	5.92%
annual	8.4%	10.6%			
1973					
Q 1	8.2%	9.6%	6.54%	5.70%	6.86%
Q 2	5.6%	7.9%	7.82%	6.60%	6.97%

Q 3	5.2%	7.7%	10.56%	8.32%	7.39%
Q 4	5.1%	9.0%	10.00%	7.50%	7.26%
annual	6.2%	8.8%			
1974					
Q 1	7.2%	10.2%	9.32%	7.62%	7.55%
Q 2	4.8%	7.1%	11.25%	8.15%	8.09%
Q 3	3.6%	6.1%	12.09%	8.19%	8.49%
Q 4	4.2%	6.5%	9.35%	7.36%	8.09%
annual	5.0%	7.7%			
1975					
Q 1	2.3%	6.2%	6.30%	5.75%	7.86%
Q 2	6.2%	9.8%	5.42%	5.39%	8.21%
Q 3	6.1%	9.6%	6.16%	6.33%	8.41%
Q 4	2.7%	6.7%	5.41%	5.63%	8.28%
annual	4.4%	8.3%			
1976					
Q 1	4.6%	10.6%	4.83%	4.92%	8.00%
Q 2	6.9%	10.0%	5.19%	5.16%	8.01%
Q 3	3.7%	8.6%	5.28%	5.15%	7.90%
Q 4	7.2%	12.6%	4.88%	4.67%	7.54%
annual	5.7%	10.9%			
1977					
Q 1	6.9%	10.9%	4.66%	4.63%	7.62%
Q 2	8.1%	9.0%	5.16%	4.84%	7.68%
Q 3	8.1%	9.9%	5.82%	5.50%	7.60%
Q 4	7.5%	8.2%	6.51%	6.11%	7.78%
annual	7.9%	9.8%			

SOURCES: Federal Reserve Board, *Annual Statistical Digest, 1971–1975* (Washington, D.C.: Board of Governors of the Federal Reserve System, 1976), pp. 121, 126; *Annual Statistical Digest, 1972–1976* (Washington, D.C.: Board of Governors of the Federal Reserve System, 1977), p. 2; *Annual Statistical Digest, 1973–1977* (Washington, D.C.: Board of Governors of the Federal Reserve System, 1978), p. 2; *Federal Reserve Bulletin* 56 (January 1970):A33–34; *Federal Reserve Bulletin* 57 (January 1971):A33–44; *Federal Reserve Bulletin* 58 (January 1972):A36; Edward R. Fry, Darwin Beck, and Mary W. Weaver, "Revision of Money Stock Measures and Member Bank Reserves and Deposits," *Federal Reserve Bulletin* 60 (December 1974):822.

1. M1 consists of currency plus demand deposits. The numbers indicate the annual rate of growth.
2. M2 consists of M1 plus all time deposits under $100,000. The numbers indicate the annual rate of growth.

3. This is the rate that banks charge each other for funds on deposit with the Federal Reserve. Since the Fed can quickly change this rate by buying or selling securities in the open market, the central bank exercises tremendous control over it. This rate is important because banks must have reserves, in the form of money on deposit with the Fed, against deposits. Therefore, the Fed funds rate is, in a sense, the cost to banks of expanding deposits and loans.
4. Market rate.
5. This is an index of the market price of Treasury securities with a maturity of ten years or more.

APPENDIX 2

Domestic Economic Statistics

	GNP Growth[1]	CPI Increase[2]	WPI Increase[3]	Unemployment Rate[4]
1969				
1st Quarter	2.7%	5.5%	4.3%	3.3%
2nd Quarter	1.6%	6.6%	5.7%	3.5%
3rd Quarter	2.0%	5.4%	3.2%	3.6%
4th Quarter	(1.4%)	5.8%	5.2%	3.6%
annual	1.2%	5.8%	4.6%	
1970				
Q 1	(3.0%)	6.8%	4.1%	4.2%
Q 2	0.7%	6.0%	2.0%	4.8%
Q 3	1.2%	4.4%	3.1%	5.2%
Q 4	(4.1%)	5.4%	1.8%	5.9%
annual	(1.3%)	5.7%	2.8%	
1971				
Q 1	8.8%	3.8%	3.7%	5.9%
Q 2	2.9%	4.1%	4.9%	6.0%
Q 3	3.5%	3.9%	3.6%	6.0%
Q 4	6.5%	2.3%	1.5%	6.0%
annual	5.5%	3.6%	3.5%	
1972				
Q 1	4.7%	3.3%	4.6%	5.8%
Q 2	9.2%	2.5%	4.9%	5.7%
Q 3	5.7%	4.4%	7.2%	5.5%
Q 4	7.8%	3.4%	9.4%	5.3%
annual	7.0%	3.4%	6.5%	
1973				
Q 1	8.5%	8.6%	21.1%	5.0%
Q 2	0.2%	7.4%	23.4%	4.9%

Q 3	2.6%	10.3%	13.2%	4.8%
Q 4	1.4%	9.0%	15.5%	4.7%
annual	3.2%	8.8%	18.3%	
1974				
Q 1	(3.9%)	14.2%	24.5%	5.2%
Q 2	(3.7%)	10.3%	12.2%	5.1%
Q 3	(2.3%)	14.2%	35.2%	5.5%
Q 4	(7.7%)	10.1%	13.4%	6.6%
annual	(4.4%)	12.2%	21.3%	
1975				
Q 1	(10.0%)	6.0%	(6.3%)	8.4%
Q 2	6.3%	7.1%	7.2%	8.9%
Q 3	10.9%	7.3%	11.1%	8.4%
Q 4	3.0%	7.6%	5.6%	8.4%
annual	2.5%	7.0%	4.4%	
1976				
Q 1	8.5%	3.9%	(0.5)%	7.6%
Q 2	4.9%	6.1%	6.3%	7.5%
Q 3	3.8%	5.3%	0.7%	7.9%
Q 4	1.2%	4.2%	7.2%	7.9%
annual	4.6%	4.9%	3.4%	
1977				
Q 1	7.1%	10.0%	8.8%	7.5%
Q 2	5.8%	8.1%	8.4%	7.1%
Q 3	5.6%	4.2%	1.8%	6.9%
Q 4	3.2%	4.6%	7.7%	6.6%
annual	5.5%	6.7%	6.7%	

SOURCES: W. John Layng and Toshiko Nakayama, "The Anatomy of Price Change in 1970," *Monthly Labor Review* 94 (February 1971):38–41; Toshiko Nakayama, "Price Changes in 1971: Rate of Inflation Slows Down," *Monthly Labor Review* 95 (February 1972):40–47; Toshiko Nakayama et al., "Price Changes in 1973—an Analysis," *Monthly Labor Review* 97 (February 1974):15–25; Toshiko Nakayama, "Price Changes in 1974—an Analysis," *Monthly Labor Review* 98 (February 1975):15–24; Toshiko Nakayama, "Price Changes in 1975—an Analysis," *Monthly Labor Review* 99 (February 1976):21–30; Toshiko Nakayama et al., "Price Changes in 1977—an Analysis," *Monthly Labor Review* 101 (February 1978):3–11; *Survey of Current Business* 50 (February 1970):S-13; 51 (February 1971):S-13; 52 (January 1972):S-1, S-13; 53 (January 1973):S-13; 54 (January 1974):S-1, S-13; 55 (February 1975):S-13; 56 (January 1976):S-1, S-13; 57 (February 1977):S-13; 58 (January 1978):S-1, S-13; 58 (December 1978):S-1, S-13.

1. Rate is annual growth.

2. This measures the change in the consumer price index at an annual rate. Figures are seasonally adjusted.

3. This measures the change in the wholesale price index at an annual rate. Figures are seasonally adjusted.

4. This measures the ratio of those looking for employment against the total workforce.

APPENDIX 3

Exchange Rates[1]

	Deutsch- mark	Japanese Yen	Swiss Franc	French Franc	British Pound
1969					
1st Quarter	24.913	.27938	23.184	20.185	239.00
2nd Quarter	24.994	.27899	23.143	20.123	238.97
3rd Quarter	25.107	.27842	23.230	18.914	238.66
4th Quarter	27.011	.27938	23.183	17.929	239.46
1970					
Q 1	27.154	.27953	23.212	18.026	240.36
Q 2	27.503	.27884	23.205	18.098	240.25
Q 3	27.537	.27892	23.234	18.114	238.79
Q 4	27.504	.27954	23.114	18.110	238.94
1971					
Q 1	27.543	.27957	23.249	18.123	241.41
Q 2	28.045	.27977	23.975	18.104	241.84
Q 3	29.266	.28559	24.785	18.126	244.08
Q 4	30.221	.30623	25.292	18.239	250.35
1972					
Q 1	31.297	.32600	25.852	19.605	259.74
Q 2	31.494	.32956	26.048	19.911	259.72
Q 3	31.445	.33210	26.471	19.984	244.53
Q 4	31.220	.33213	26.401	19.801	236.34
1973					
Q 1	33.370	.35789	29.077	20.950	241.87
Q 2	36.626	.37753	31.691	22.591	253.01
Q 3	41.762	.37724	34.077	23.881	247.72
Q 4	39.274	.36393	31.958	22.721	237.79

1974					
Q 1	36.861	.34460	31.237	20.278	227.98
Q 2	39.944	.35729	33.594	20.496	239.75
Q 3	38.317	.33631	33.540	20.909	235.06
Q 4	39.741	.33339	36.451	21.541	232.92
1975					
Q 1	42.798	.34132	40.098	23.362	239.20
Q 2	42.455	.34205	39.672	24.477	232.38
Q 3	39.172	.33549	37.503	22.958	212.74
Q 4	38.500	.32948	37.736	22.602	202.24
1976					
Q 1	38.841	.33086	38.770	22.116	199.92
Q 2	39.078	.33434	40.073	21.264	180.61
Q 3	39.516	.34383	40.325	20.372	176.50
Q 4	41.524	.34052	40.886	20.056	165.14
1977					
Q 1	41.729	.35044	39.668	20.089	171.34
Q 2	42.322	.36346	39.815	20.188	171.89
Q 3	43.343	.37580	41.708	20.445	173.51
Q 4	45.012	.40542	45.861	20.677	181.45

Sources: *Federal Reserve Bulletin* 56 (January 1970):A-89; 57 (January 1971):A-89; 58 (January 1972):A-91; 59 (January 1973):A-93; 60 (January 1974):A-91; 61 (January 1975):A-77; 62 (January 1976):A-75; 62 (July 1976):A-75; 63 (January 1977):A-68; 63 (July 1977):A-68; 64 (January 1978):A-68.

1. Numbers indicate the number of cents needed to purchase one unit of the currency in question.

APPENDIX 4

The Prime Rate[1]

Date of Change	Prime Rate
Dec. 18, 1968	6.75%
Jan. 7, 1969	7%
March 17, 1969	7.5%
June 9, 1969	8.5%
March 25, 1970	8%
Sept, 21, 1970	7.5%
Nov. 12, 1970	7.25%
Nov. 23, 1970	7%
Dec. 22, 1970	6.5%
Jan. 6, 1971	6.25–6.5%
Jan. 15, 1971	6.25%
Jan. 18, 1971	6%
Feb. 16, 1971	5.75%
March 11, 1971	5.25%–5.5%
March 19, 1971	5.25%
April 23, 1971	5.25%–5.5%
May 11, 1971	5.5%
July 7, 1971	6%
Oct. 20, 1971	5.75%
Nov. 4, 1971	5.5%
Dec. 31, 1971	5.25%
Jan 24, 1972	5%
Jan 31, 1972	4.75%
April 5, 1972	5%
June 26, 1972	5.25%
Aug. 29, 1972	5.5%
Oct. 4, 1972	5.75%
Dec. 27, 1972	6%
Feb. 27, 1973	6.25%
March 26, 1973	6.5%

April 18, 1973	6.75%
May 7, 1973	7%
May 25, 1973	7.25%
June 8, 1973	7.5%
June 25, 1973	7.75%
July 3, 1973	8%
July 9, 1973	8.25%
July 18, 1973	8.5%
July 30, 1973	8.75%
Aug. 6, 1973	9%
Aug. 13, 1973	9.25%
Aug. 22, 1973	9.5%
Aug. 28, 1973	9.75%
Sept. 18, 1973	10%
Oct. 24, 1973	9.75%
Jan. 29, 1974	9.5%
Feb. 11, 1974	9.25%
Feb. 19, 1974	9%
Feb. 25, 1974	8.75%
March 22, 1974	9%
March 29, 1974	9.25%
April 3, 1974	9.5%
April 5, 1974	9.75%
April 11, 1974	10%
April 19, 1974	10.25%
April 25, 1974	10.5%
May 2, 1974	10.75%
May 6, 1974	11%
May 10, 1974	11.25%
May 17, 1974	11.5%
June 26, 1974	11.75%
July 5, 1974	12%
Oct. 7, 1974	11.75%
Oct. 21, 1974	11.5%
Oct. 28, 1974	11.25%
Nov. 4, 1974	11%
Nov. 14, 1974	10.75%
Nov. 25, 1974	10.5%
Jan. 9, 1975	10.25%
Jan. 15, 1975	10%
Jan. 20, 1975	9.75%
Jan. 28, 1975	9.5%
Feb. 3, 1975	9.25%
Feb. 10, 1975	9%
Feb. 18, 1975	8.75%

Feb. 24, 1975	8.5%
March 5, 1975	8.25%
March 10, 1975	8%
March 18, 1975	7.75%
March 24, 1975	7.5%
May 20, 1975	7.25%
June 9, 1975	7%
July 18, 1975	7.25%
Aug. 12, 1975	7.75%
Sept. 15, 1975	8%
Oct. 27, 1975	7.75%
Nov. 5, 1975	7.5%
Dec. 2, 1975	7.25%
Jan. 12, 1976	7%
Jan. 21, 1976	6.75%
June 1, 1976	7%
June 7, 1976	7.25%
Aug. 2, 1976	7%
Oct. 4, 1976	6.75%
Nov. 1, 1976	6.5%
Dec. 13, 1976	6.25%
May 13, 1977	6.5%
May 31, 1977	6.75%
Aug. 22, 1977	7%
Sept. 16, 1977	7.25%
Oct. 7, 1977	7.5%
Oct. 24, 1977	7.75%

SOURCES: *Federal Reserve Bulletin* 58 (January 1972):A-34; Federal Reserve Board, *Annual Statistical Digest, 1972–1976* (Washington, D.C.: Board of Governors of the Federal Reserve System, 1977), p. 101; *Annual Statistical Digest, 1973–1977* (Washington, D.C.: Board of Governors of the Federal Reserve System, 1978), p. 89.

1. The rate that banks charge their most creditworthy cusomters.

APPENDIX 5

Federal Spending[1]

Year[2]	Federal Outlays	Federal Surplus (Deficit)[4]	Surplus (Deficit) as % of GNP[5]	Spending as % of GNP[3]
1969	$184.5	$3.2	.35%	20.4%
1970	$196.6	($2.8)	.29%	20.5%
1971	$211.4	($23.0)	2.25%	20.7%
1972	$231.9	($23.2)	2.09%	20.9%
1973	$246.5	($14.3)	1.15%	19.9%
1974	$268.4	($3.5)	.26%	19.8%
1975	$324.6	($43.6)	3.02%	22.5%
1976[6]	$366.4	($66.4)	4.10%	22.6%
1977	$402.7	($45.0)	2.44%	21.8%
1978	$450.8	($48.8)	2.37%	21.9%

SOURCES: U.S. Bureau of the Census, *Statistical Abstract of the United States, 1976*, 97th ed. (Washington, D.C.: U.S. Department of Commerce, 1976), p. 229; *Statistical Abstract of the United States: 1980*, 101st ed. (Washington, D.C.: U.S. Department of Commerce, 1980), p. 258.

1. Figures are billions of dollars.

2. These are fiscal years. From 1969 through 1976, these ran from July of the previous year through June of the year in question. For example, fiscal 1969 ran from July 1, 1968 through June 30, 1969. Starting in 1977, the fiscal year ran from October of the previous year through September of the year in question. For instance, fiscal 1977 ran from October 1, 1976 through September 30, 1977.

3. The ratio between all government spending and the total production of goods and services.

4. The difference between receipts and expenditures.

5. The ratio betrween the government's surplus (deficit) and the total production of goods and services.

6. During the transition quarter, when the fiscal year was shifted back, the federal government ran a deficit of $13 billion.

APPENDIX 6

International Accounts

	Trade Balance[1]	Current Account[2]
1969		
1st Quarter	($39)	$92
2nd Quarter	$225	$17
3rd Quarter	$565	$338
4th Quarter	$852	$342
annual	$1603	$789
1970		
Q 1	$1289	$504
Q 2	$751	$292
Q 3	$704	$192
Q 4	$142	($166)
annual	$2886	$822
1971		
Q 1	$269	$400
Q 2	($1012)	($810)
Q 3	($472)	($855)
Q 4	($1494)	($1529)
annual	($2709)	($2794)
1972		
Q 1	($1698)	($2798)
Q 2	($1600)	($2645)
Q 3	($1534)	($2216)
Q 4	($1494)	($2144)
annual	($3126)	($9803)
1973		
Q 1	($943)	($17)

Q 2	$248	$643
Q 3	$712	$2782
Q 4	$1381	$3475
annual	$1398	$6883
1974		
Q 1	($147)	$716
Q 2	($1484)	$281
Q 3	($2333)	$30
Q 4	($1379)	$689
annual	($5343)	$1716
1975		
Q 1	$1457	$3167
Q 2	$3285	$4608
Q 3	$2079	$4608
Q 4	$2226	$5388
annual	$9047	$18,443
1976		
Q 1	($1351)	$1703
Q 2	($1583)	$2141
Q 3	($2816)	$319
Q 4	($3603)	$176
annual	($9353)	$4339
1977		
Q 1	($7018)	($2749)
Q 2	($6612)	($2670)
Q 3	($7250)	($2868)
Q 4	($10,170)	($6934)
annual	($31,050)	($15,221)

SOURCES: *Federal Reserve Bulletin* 56 (January 1970):A-72, A-73; 57 (January 1971):A-72; 58 (January 1972):A-72, A-73; 59 (January 1973):A-74, A-75; Federal Reserve Board of Governors, *Annual Statistical Digest, 1972–1976* (Washington, D.C.: Board of Governors of the Federal Reserve System, 1977), pp. 200–202; *Annual Statistical Digest, 1973–1977* (Washington, D.C.: Board of Governors of the Federal Reserve System, 1978), p. 234.

1. The difference between exports and imports, in millions of dollars.
2. The sum of the trade balance, money spent by tourists (both Americans abroad and foreigners in the United States), the balance on services, government spending, and interest and dividends (both paid to Americans on foreign securities and to foreigners by American companies and borrowers), in millions of dollars.

Notes

Preface

1. *Wall Street Journal,* March 5, 1975, pp. 1, 27; *New York Times,* June 2, 1977, pp. D-1, D-13; Ronald W. Reagan et al., *In Memoriam: Arthur F. Burns, 1904–1987,* pp. 19, 23.

2. John Maynard Keynes, *The General Theory of Employment, Interest, and Money,* p. 383.

1. The Chairman

1. His birthplace is now in Ukraine.

2. Interview with Helen Burns, Aug. 30, 1990.

3. Milton Friedman, *In Memoriam,* p. 11; Rebecca Strand Johnson, "Arthur Burns," in Larry Schweikart, ed., *Encyclopedia of American Business and Biography: Banking and Finance, 1913–1989.*

4. Peter M. Turkoff and William B. Scott, *New School: A History of the New School of Social Research* (New York: Free Press, 1986), p. xii.

5. Wesley Clair Mitchell, *Business Cycles.*

6. Guy Alchon, *The Invisible Hand of Planning: Capitalism, Social Science, and the State in the 1920s,* p. 106.

7. Mark Perlman, "Foreword," in Arthur Burns, *The Ongoing Revolution in American Banking*, p. xvi.

8. Geoffrey H. Moore, "Arthur F. Burns," in *International Encyclopedia of the Social Sciences*, vol. 18, p. 85.

9. Ibid.

10. Helen Burns interview.

11. Arthur F. Burns, *Production Trends in the United States since 1870*.

12. Moore, "Arthur F. Burns," p. 82.

13. Ron Chernow, "In Praise of Patience: Being the True-Life Saga of a Young Writer Nearly Killed with Kindness, Only to Be Saved by a Savage Dose of Truth," p. 32.

14. *Business Week*, July 22, 1961, p. 62.

15. Friedman, *In Memoriam*, p. 7. At Columbia, Friedman was Mitchell's student, but he had both studied as an undergraduate at Rutgers and done much of his work at the NBER under Burns's direction.

16. Ibid.

17. Wesley Clair Mitchell and Arthur F. Burns, *Measuring Business Cycles*.

18. Ibid., p. viii.

19. Tjalling C. Koopmans, "Measurement without Theory," p. 161.

20. Arthur F. Burns, *The Business Cycle in a Changing World*, p. 42.

21. Ibid., pp. 1–53; this chapter, "The Nature and Causes of Business Cycles," sets forth Burns's thinking about the business cycle.

22. Though a decline in the business cycle usually involves a recession, such is not invariably the case. Technically speaking, a recession involves a drop in economic output over two consecutive quarters, and some downturns in the business cycle do not witness such a decline. For instance, many students of the business cycle argue that it turned down in 1966–67 and 1985–86, but in neither case was the drop substantial enough to register as a recession.

23. Although the United States has experienced literally dozens of recessions, it has by most accounts seen only four depressions: 1837–43, 1873–79, 1893–97, and 1929–40.

24. Economists had always added a caveat that allowed them to explain economic downturns within this framework. Although in an economy that produced $1 billion worth of goods the population would have an income of $1 billion, people might not want to buy exactly what was produced. Any mismatch between what people wanted to purchase and what was available accounted for the ups and downs of the economy. Such mismatches, however, would not last long because the normal workings of the market would clear them up.

25. The formula to determine the multiplier is to divide one by the ratio of savings to income. If consumers save 10 percent of their income, this ratio is 0.1, and so the multiplier is ten. Under these conditions, a deficit of $10 million would increase the level of economic activity by $100 million. It would also increase the level of savings by $10 million, enough to finance the original deficit. Even the staunchest Keynesian would concede, however, that there

would be "leakage"—that is, some of the increase in income would go to pay higher prices or to purchase imports, limiting the effect of the multiplier.

26. This description oversimplified the complexities of Keynes's thought, but it does reflect the ideas that most early Keynesians took from their master.

27. Paul Volcker, *In Memoriam*, p. 15.

28. Arthur F. Burns, "Keynesian Economics Once Again," in *The Frontiers of Economic Knowledge*, p. 228.

29. Burns, "The Nature and Causes of Business Cycles," in *Business Cycle*, p. 45; "Economic Research and Keynesian Thinking of Our Times," in *Frontiers of Economic Knowledge*, pp. 3–25; "Keynesian Economics Once Again," in *Frontiers of Economic Knowledge*, pp. 207–235.

30. Milton Friedman and Anna Schwartz, *A Monetary History of the United States, 1867–1960*.

31. Interview with Philip Jackson, July 20, 1990. Almost everyone interviewed spoke of the gracious nature of Dr. and Mrs. Burns and of their social skills.

32. Milton Viorst, "The Burns Kind of Liberal Conservative," *New York Times Magazine*, Nov. 9, 1969, p. 31.

33. Edward S. Flash, Jr., *Economic Advice and Presidential Leadership: The Council of Economic Advisers*, pp. 101–102; Erwin C. Hargrove and Samuel A. Morley, eds., *The President and the Council of Economic Advisers: Interviews with CEA Chairmen*, pp. 99–100. Eisenhower had been president of Columbia University during the late 1940s, but he had not met Burns while there, except in receiving lines.

34. Helen Burns interview; Hargrove and Morley, eds., *The President and the CEA*, p. 100.

35. Sherman Adams, *Firsthand Report: The Story of the Eisenhower Administration*, p. 156.

36. At this time, the federal government's fiscal year ran from July of the previous year through June of the year in question. For example, fiscal 1953 ran from July 1, 1952 to June 30, 1953.

37. Hargrove and Morley, eds., *The President and the CEA*, pp. 90–92; Thursday, Oct. 1, 1953 entry, Whitman Files, Whitman Diaries, Box 1, Aug.-Oct. 1953, Dwight D. Eisenhower Library, Abilene, Kan.

38. Hargrove and Morley, eds., *The President and the CEA*, pp. 92–94; Robert J. Donovan, *Eisenhower: The Inside Story*, pp. 209–221; Dwight D. Eisenhower, *Mandate for Change 1953–1956*, pp. 304–307; Robert M. Collins, *The Business Response to Keynes, 1929–1964*, pp. 152–158.

39. Donovan, *Eisenhower*, p. 221.

40. Eisenhower, *Mandate for Change*, pp. 501–502; Flash, *Economic Advice*, pp. 118–138, 172.

41. Hargrove and Morley, eds., *The President and the CEA*, pp. 104–105.

42. Sherman, *Firsthand Report*, p. 156.

43. Viorst, "Burns Kind of Liberal Conservative," p. 128.

44. Stephen E. Ambrose, *Nixon: The Education of a Politician, 1913–1962*, pp. 561–562.

45. Technically, since Mutual Life Insurance was a mutual company owned by its policyholders, Burns was a trustee, not a director. As a practical matter, though, they are the same thing.

46. Ron Chernow, *The House of Morgan: An American Banking Dynasty and the Rise of Modern Finance*, p. 539.

47. Helen Burns interview.

48. Burns, "The New Environment for Monetary Policy," in *Business Cycle*, p. 151.

49. Burns, "Wages and Prices by Formula," in *Business Cycle*, p. 251.

50. Burns, "The Perils of Inflation," in *Business Cycle*, p. 296.

51. Stephen E. Ambrose, *Eisenhower: The President*, p. 460; Dwight D. Eisenhower, *Waging Peace, 1956–61*, pp. 309–310.

52. Richard M. Nixon, *Six Crises*, pp. 366–367.

53. For instance, Mrs. Burns indicates that the Nixons never came over for dinner, even though they and the Burnses both lived in Manhattan for several years in the 1960s.

54. Viorst, "Burns Kind of Liberal Conservative," pp. 130–131. Burns's replacement was John R. Meyer, a professor of economics at Harvard.

55. Nicolas Spulber, *Managing the American Economy from Roosevelt to Reagan*, p. 60.

56. They referred to this phenomenon as the Phillips Curve, after economist A. W. Phillips, who published a study that demonstrated an inverse correlation between the rate of increase in wages and the unemployment level.

57. James Tobin, *The New Economics One Decade Older*, p. 101.

58. James Tobin and Murray Weidenbaum, *Two Revolutions in Economic Policy: The First Economic Reports of Presidents Kennedy and Reagan*, p. 27.

59. U.S. Bureau of the Census, *Statistical Abstract of the United States, 1987* (Washington, D.C.: U.S. Government Printing Office, 1986), p. 463. For figures on economic growth and unemployment in the 1960s, see Herbert Stein, *Presidential Economics: The Making of Economic Policy from Roosevelt to Reagan and Beyond*, pp. 397–398.

60. Arthur Burns, "Examining the New 'Stagnation' Theory," *Morgan Guarantee Survey*, May 1961, Box 196, U.S. Economy, 1961—Debate—Arthur Burns vs. the CEA (3), Burns Papers, Eisenhower Library.

61. Burns, "The Quest for Full Employment and Economic Stability, 1960–66," in *Business Cycle*, pp. 270–271.

62. Hargrove and Morley, eds., *The President and the CEA*, pp. 121–122.

63. Burns, "Wages and Prices by Formula," in *Business Cycle*, pp. 232–253.

64. U.S. Congress, Joint Economic Committee, *January 1963 Economic Report of the President*, 1963, p. 495.

65. Burns, "The Perils of Inflation," in *Business Cycle*, pp. 293–295; "Evaluations of the Advice of Academic Consultants," Box A-10, Federal

Reserve System (1), Arthur F. Burns Papers, Gerald R. Ford Library, Ann Arbor, Mich. The Burns papers at the Eisenhower Library contain his papers prior to 1969, while those at the Ford Library document from 1969 to 1978.

66. In 1966 the money supply, measured as currency plus demand deposits (M1), equaled 22.84 percent of total production. For 1967 this figure was 22.45 percent, and for 1968, 21.97 percent. Stein, *Presidential Economics*, p. 397.

67. U.S. Congress, *January 1963 Economic Report*, p. 513.

68. Arthur F. Burns to Edwin G. Nourse, Jan. 30, 1970, Box A-9, Economy, General, Burns Papers.

69. *Atlanta Constitution*, Dec. 18, 1977, p. 6.

2. White House Prelude

1. Arthur F. Burns, "Recommendations for Early Actions or Consideration: A Report to the President-elect," Jan. 18, 1969, in the author's possession.

2. James A. Reichley, *Conservatives in an Age of Change: The Nixon and Ford Administrations*, p. 73.

3. Andrew Brimmer, "Politics and Monetary Policy: The Federal Reserve and the Nixon White House," p. 6. By law, a member of the Federal Reserve Board can serve only one fourteen-year term, prior to which he or she can serve the remainder of an unfilled term. Martin had served five years of an unfilled term and a fourteen-year term of his own, which expired in January 1970.

4. Rowland Evans and Robert Novak, *Nixon in the White House: The Frustration of Power*, p. 14; Reichley, *Conservatives in an Age of Change*, pp. 68–70, 77; transcript of interview with Burns on "The President's Men," Oct. 23, 1969, Box A-12, Interviews—AFB (2), Burns Papers.

5. Reichley, *Conservatives in an Age of Change*, pp. 76–77.

6. *New York Times*, Jan. 25, 1969, p. 14.

7. Interview with Herbert Stein, Dec. 3, 1990.

8. Evans and Novak, *Nixon in the White House*, p. 43.

9. Robert B. Semple, Jr., "Nixon's Inner Circle Meets," *New York Times Magazine*, Apr. 3, 1969, p. 45.

10. Burns, "Recommendations for Early Action," p. 90.

11. Ibid., pp. 54–58, 70–81, 90–92.

12. Memo for the President from Arthur Burns, Mar. 17, 1969, White House Special Files (WHSF), President's Handwriting, Mar. 16 through 31, 1969, President's Office File, Box 1, Nixon Papers Project, Alexandria, Va.

13. Martin Anderson, *Revolution: The Reagan Legacy*, p. 144.

14. Interview with John D. Ehrlichman, Feb. 19, 1991.

15. Dan Rather and Gary Paul Gates, *The Palace Guard*, p. 64.

16. William Safire, *Before the Fall: An Inside View of the Pre-Watergate White House*, pp. 10, 281; *Washington Post*, May 31, 1971, p. E1; memo for Burns from Dwight L. Chapin, Apr. 15, 1969, Box A-33, White House Staff Memoranda, Apr. 1–21, 1969, Burns Papers.

17. Rather and Gates, *The Palace Guard*, p. 65.

18. Ibid., p. 67; Reichley, *Conservatives in an Age of Change*, pp. 131–143; Evans and Novak, *Nixon in the White House*, pp. 44–45.

19. *Time*, Oct. 24, 1969, p. 90.

20. Burns interview with Louis Cassels of UPI, May 1969, Box A-12, Interviews—AFB (2), Burns Papers.

21. Memorandum for the President, July 31, 1968, Box A-28, Treasury (5), Burns Papers; memo to K. R. Cole, Jr. from Paul McCracken, Feb. 14, 1969, Box 19, Memos to the White House, Feb. 1969, Paul McCracken Papers, Bentley Library, University of Michigan, Ann Arbor.

22. Reichley, *Conservatives in an Age of Change*, p. 76. The Family Assistance Plan failed to become law, defeated in Congress by an unusual coalition of conservatives who disliked the idea of universal benefits and liberals who thought the program too stingy. Nixon also deserves some of the blame for this defeat because he did not push the program nearly as hard as he might have. Domestic policy was not his great interest, and as time went by he seemed to develop second thoughts about the whole idea of guaranteed income.

23. Evans and Novak, *Nixon in the White House*, pp. 37–43, 194–200, 217–223; *New York Times*, Nov. 5, 1969, p. 28.

24. Henry Kissinger, *Years of Upheaval*, p. 81.

25. John Ehrlichman, *Witness to Power: The Nixon Years*, p. 241.

26. Report of the Task Force on Inflation, [April 1969], Box A-29, Treasury (15), Burns Papers.

27. Ibid.

28. Ehrlichman, *Witness to Power*, p. 254.

29. Evans and Novak, *Nixon in the White House*, pp. 177–187.

30. The measure used is M1, which represents currency and demand deposits. Unless noted otherwise, all subsequent references to the "money supply" refer to M1.

31. U.S. Congress, Senate, Committee on Banking and Currency, *Nomination of Arthur F. Burns*, pp. 10–11.

32. Richard Nixon, *Public Papers of the President of the United States, Richard Nixon, 1969*, pp. 97–102.

33. *New York Times*, Apr. 15, 1969, p. 28.

34. Stein, *Presidential Economics*, pp. 147–151.

35. *New York Times*, May 25, 1969, III, pp. 1, 9.

36. Ibid., May 28, 1969, pp. 59, 61.

37. A good general history of the international monetary system after World War II is Robert Solomon, *The International Monetary System, 1945–1976: An Insider's View*.

38. The flow of money between countries is usually divided into two accounts. First is the current account, which includes trade in goods and services, spending by tourists (both citizens traveling abroad and foreigners visiting), and interest and dividends (both earned by citizens on foreign securities

and paid to foreigners on assets they own). Second is the capital account, which keeps track of investment that crosses a country's borders. These investments can be long-term (such as the Toyota Motor Co. building a plant in Kentucky), or short-term (an American depositing money in a German bank because interest rates are higher there than in the United States). The sum of these two accounts is the balance of payments.

39. At this time Americans could not legally own gold, and the center of the world's gold market was in London.

40. Certain transactions with the International Monetary Fund, such as a part of each country's quota, which provided the IMF's capital, had to be paid in gold.

41. Other countries pegged their currencies to a dollar valued at $35 to an ounce of gold, and if Washington raised that official price to, say, $38.50 (10 percent), the value of the greenback vis-à-vis other currencies would decline by 10 percent.

42. Burns to Dwight D. Eisenhower, Feb. 2, 1968, Burns Papers, Box 15, Eisenhower, Dwight D. (1), Eisenhower Library; Joanne Gowa, *Closing the Gold Window: Domestic Politics and the End of Bretton Woods*, pp. 137–141; Burns, "The Perils of Inflation," in *Business Cycle*, pp. 300–302.

43. Paul A. Volcker and Toyoo Gyohten, *Changing Fortunes: The World's Money and the Threat to American Leadership*, pp. 65–66. Volcker and Gyohten wrote their parts of this book separately, and subsequent references to it in footnotes will use only the name of the author who wrote the information cited.

44. The Allies created the IMF after World War II. An international bank, it lent money to countries with balance-of-payments deficits, set rules to govern international finance, and approved any changes in the official values of currencies.

45. Gowa, *Closing the Gold Window*, pp. 131–137.

46. Ibid., pp. 137–141; Burns, "The Perils of Inflation," in *Business Cycle*, pp. 300–302.

47. Interview with Robert Solomon, Dec. 6, 1990.

48. Hargrove and Morley, eds., *The President and the CEA*, p. 366.

49. Gowa, *Closing the Gold Window*, pp. 141–146.

50. Nixon, *Public Papers 1969*, pp. 265–267.

51. Construction workers, as a rule, supported Nixon's policy toward the Vietnam War, which had met with substantial opposition from Democrats. Workers displayed this support in a muscular way when, in 1969, they clashed with anti-war demonstrators in New York City, making short work of the protesters.

52. Memo from Burns, July 12, 1969, White House Central Files (WHCF), Business-Economics (BE) 5–3, Box 61, Inflation-Money Scarcity, Jan.–Aug. 1969, Nixon Project; Burns gave the president seven different memos on reforming the construction industry, all dated Oct. 14, 1969, Box A-7, Construction, Cabinet Committee (1), Burns Papers; Evans and Novak, *Nixon in*

the White House, pp. 187–194; Nixon, *Public Papers 1969*, pp. 706–707; *New York Times*, Sept. 5, 1969, p. 23.

53. Nixon, *Public Papers 1969*, pp. 812–814.

54. Transcript of "The President's Men," Oct. 23, 1969; minutes of the meeting of the Cabinet Committee on Economic Policy, Dec. 18, 1969, Box A-4, Cabinet Committee on Economic Policy, Burns Papers.

55. Sept. 11, 1969, JDE Notes of Meetings with the President 1969 [3 of 4], Box 3, John D. Ehrlichman Files, Nixon Project.

56. *New York Times*, Nov. 11, 1969, pp. 61, 72; Nov. 12, 1969, p. 46.

57. U.S. Congress, Joint Economic Committee, *The 1970 Economic Report of the President*, p. 26.

58. Senate Committee on Banking and Currency, *Nomination of Burns*, p. 16.

59. *New York Times*, Dec. 30, 1969, p. 32.

60. Joint Economic Committee, *1970 Economic Report*, p. 1.

61. Stein, *Presidential Economics*, pp. 148–154.

62. Dec. 19, 1969, JDE Notes on Meetings with the President 1969 [4 of 4], Box 3, Ehrlichman Files; memo for the President from Ehrlichman, Dec. 9, 1969, WHCF, Finance (FI), Box 1, EX FI, Jan. 1969–May 1970, Nixon Project; memo for the President from George Shultz, Oct. 7, 1969, WHCF, BE 5-3, Box 62, Inflation-Money Scarcity, Sept.–Dec. 18, 1969, Nixon Project; memo for the President from Paul McCracken, Oct. 28, 1969, WHCF, BE 5-3, Box 62, Inflation-Money Scarcity, Sept.–Dec. 18, 1969, Nixon Project; memo for the President from Paul McCracken, Nov. 15, 1969, Box 19, Memos to the White House, Nov. 1969, McCracken Papers.

63. *Business Week*, Oct. 25, 1969, pp. 102–106.

64. Richard Nixon, *The Public Papers of the President of the United States, Richard Nixon, 1970*, pp. 44–46.

65. Oct. 23, 1969, JDE Notes of Meetings with the President [3 of 4]. Box 3, Ehrlichman Files.

3. Managing the System

1. The regional banks are located in Boston, New York, Philadelphia, Cleveland, Chicago, Richmond, Atlanta, Dallas, St. Louis, Kansas City, Minneapolis, and San Francisco. Each has branch offices in every major city in its jurisdiction.

2. The federal government has three separate agencies that regulate commercial banks. The Comptroller of the Currency, which is part of the Treasury Department, oversees all banks with national charters. The Federal Reserve audits institutions that have state charters and belong to it, as well as bank-holding companies. The Federal Deposit Insurance Corporation examines all state institutions that belong to the FDIC and are not Fed members.

3. These include making loans and arranging check clearing and electronic funds transfers.

4. The president of the New York Fed always has a vote, while the four remaining votes rotate among the other presidents.

5. Hobart Rowen, "Keeping Secrets at the Fed," p. 54. This implied criticism of Martin was not really fair. Burns's predecessor had indeed led, but his tactics were subtle and low-key.

6. Interview with Andrew Brimmer, June 1, 1992.

7. *Wall Street Journal*, July 30, 1976, pp. 1, 23.

8. Interview with Lyle Gramley, Dec. 7, 1990.

9. Ibid.

10. Ibid.

11. Ibid.

12. Jackson interview.

13. Interview with Stephen Axilrod, June 8, 1992.

14. Brimmer interview.

15. Axilrod interview.

16. Robert Holland and Charles Partee.

17. *Business Week*, Mar. 1, 1969, pp. 25–26.

18. Ibid., Jan. 30, 1971, p. 39.

19. Interview with Robert Holland, July 20, 1990.

20. Ibid.

21. Ibid.

22. Volcker, *In Memoriam*, p. 12.

23. *Wall Street Journal*, Feb. 27, 1970, p. 21.

24. Holland interview.

25. Interview with Joseph Coyne, Dec. 7, 1990.

26. Rowen, "Keeping Secrets at the Fed," p. 54.

27. Ibid. Senator William Proxmire (D-Wis.) had proposed a measure under which the Fed would set different reserve requirements depending on the disposition of a bank's assets. The idea was that if a bank gave more "desirable" credits, such as home mortgage loans, it would face lower reserve requirements, which would reduce the cost of making such loans. Although Brimmer was not happy with the draft of the bill, he thought the general concept sound. The other members of the board, including Burns, disliked the idea of regulating credit flows and doubted that any such regulation would be successful. The bill never got out of committee.

28. JDE Notes of Meetings with the President, Nov. 20, 1970, Box 4, 7/1/70–12/31/70, Ehrlichman Files.

29. *Washington Post*, Feb. 26, 1976, p. A-3; Apr. 18, 1975, p. A-2.

30. Jackson interview.

31. Chernow, *The House of Morgan*, p. 555.

32. Jackson interview.

33. Ibid.

34. Gramley interview.

35. Ibid.

36. Jackson interview.

37. Interview with Henry Reuss, Dec. 6, 1990.

38. Helen Burns interview.

39. Interview with J. William Stanton, June 5, 1992.

40. Gramley interview.

41. Stein interview.

42. Donald F. Kettl, *Leadership at the Fed*, p. 140.

43. Arthur F. Burns, *The Anguish of Central Banking*, pp. 15–16.

4. Stagflation

1. *Federal Reserve Bulletin* 56 (Apr. 1970):339–340. This action also represented an important concession to monetarists. For the first time, the Fed gave higher priority to measures of the money supply than to conditions in money markets.

2. John T. Wooley, *Monetary Politics: The Federal Reserve and the Politics of Monetary Policy*, pp. 196–197.

3. Memo to the President from Peter Flanigan, Apr. 24, 1970, WHCF, FG 131, Box 1, Beginning–6/30/70, Nixon Project.

4. Mar. 16, 1970, JDE Notes of Meetings with the President, Box 3, 1/1/70–6/30/70 [3 of 5], Ehrlichman Files.

5. *New York Times*, Aug. 16, 1970, p. 45.

6. Ibid., July 26, 1970, sec. IV, pp. 2–3.

7. U.S. Congress, Joint Economic Committee, *The 1971 Economic Report of the President*, pp. 251–258, 267–276; memo from Murray Wernick and Joseph Zeisel to Mr. Partee, Apr. 16, 1970, Box B-59, Incomes Policy, 1970, Burns Papers.

8. Nov. 17, 1970, JDE Notes of Meetings with the President, Box 4, 7/1/70–12/31/70 [5 of 8], Ehrlichman Files.

9. Tobin, *The New Economics*, pp. 95–96.

10. Fred Hirsch and John H. Goldthorp, eds., *The Political Economy of Inflation*; Leon Lindberg and Charles S. Maier, eds., *The Political Economy of Inflation and Economic Stagnation: Theoretical Approaches and International Case Studies*. Most of the essays in these collections support the view that inflation is a monetary phenomenon, though often one driven by deeper social maladjustments. The most succinct statement of this idea is J. S. Flemming, "The Economic Explanation of Inflation," in Hirsch and Goldthorp, eds., *The Political Economy of Inflation*, pp. 13–36.

11. *New York Times*, May 19, 1970, pp. 1, 57.

12. Ibid., Aug. 16, 1970, p. 45.

13. Milton Friedman to Arthur Burns, May 18, 1970, Box K-12, Milton Friedman (4), Burns Papers. Realizing that he had overreacted, Friedman wrote Burns a rather touching apology a week and a half later. Milton Friedman to Arthur Burns, May 29, 1970.

14. Clarification re Burns May 18, 1970 speech, May 1970, Box B-59, Incomes Policy, 1970, Burns Papers; memo from Peter M. Flanigan to Nixon,

May 20, 1970, WHCF, BE 5-3, Box 62, Inflation-Money Scarcity, May–Sept. 1970, Nixon Project.

15. Nixon, *Public Papers 1970*, p. 509.

16. *Wall Street Journal*, July 24, 1970, p. 3; memo from Herbert Stein, Mar. 11, 1971, Box B-23, CEA Jan.–Mar. 1971, Burns Papers.

17. Stein, *Presidential Economics*, pp. 159–162.

18. These were popularly known as the "back office problems." At times, paperwork ran days or even weeks behind, and trading hours on the stock exchange had to be cut radically for months to allow companies to catch up. Brokerage firms overcame these bottlenecks by investing heavily in computers, but to cover this expense they needed a good deal of business, whereas popular interest in securities declined sharply with the 1970 crash.

19. For examples of how Burns was kept abreast of events, see John D. Staffels to Chairman Burns, June 12, 1970, Sept. 28, 1970, and Sept. 10, 1970, Box B-96, Securities Investor Protection Act of 1970 (2), Burns Papers.

20. *Wall Street Journal*, Aug. 25, 1970, p. 21; *Federal Reserve Bulletin 56* (Aug. 1970):628–633.

21. Ever since the 1930s, the federal government had set caps on the interest rates banks could pay customers. Although designed to protect banks' profit margins and keep interest rates low for borrowers, non-banking institutions had, by the late 1960s and early 1970s, devised mechanisms to circumvent these caps, draining commercial banks of funds.

22. *New York Times*, June 20, 1971, sec. III, pp. 1, 4; *Federal Reserve Bulletin 56* (Oct. 1970):758–763.

23. *New York Times*, June 20, 1971, sec. III, pp. 1, 4; Lawrence Malkin, "A Practical Politician at the Fed," pp. 148–151.

24. *New York Times*, Sept. 24, 1970, p. 40.

25. U.S. Congress, Joint Economic Committee, *1970 Midyear Review of the Economy*, p. 521.

26. *Wall Street Journal*, Nov. 30, 1970, p. 12.

27. Memo for the President from McCracken, June 13, 1970, Box 19, White House memos, June 1970, McCracken Papers.

28. *Wall Street Journal*, Nov. 30, 1970, p. 12. The revision of economic figures is common and often involves rather large changes. The numbers on the money supply presented in Appendix 1 are figures that were revised in 1974.

29. *New York Times*, Sept. 7, 1970, p. 16.

30. JDE Notes of Meetings with the President, Nov. 19, 1970, Box 4, 7/1/70–12/31/70 [6 of 8], Ehrlichman Files.

31. Ibid., Nov. 17, 1970, Box 4, 7/1/70–12/31/70 [5 of 8], Ehrlichman Files.

32. Ibid., Nov. 16, 1970, Box 4, 7/1/70–12/31/70 [6 of 8], Ehrlichman Files.

33. As is stood then, state governments controlled offshore oil drilling, and they were restricting production there to keep prices high. Nixon transferred

control of these offshore fields to the federal government, which removed the restrictions on production.

34. *New York Times*, Dec. 9, 1970, pp. 93, 105; Nixon, *Public Papers 1970*, pp. 1088-1095.

35. Arthur F. Burns, "The Basis for Lasting Prosperity," in *Reflections of an Economic Policymaker: Speeches and Congressional Statements, 1969–78*, pp. 103–116.

36. Joint Economic Committee, *1971 Economic Report*, p. 249.

37. U.S. Congress, Senate, Committee on Banking, Housing, and Urban Affairs, *Selective Credit Policies and Wage-Price Stabilization*, p. 30.

38. Joint Economic Committee, *1971 Economic Report*, pp. 251–258, 255.

39. Ibid., p. 265.

40. *Congressional Register* 177 (1971):13232.

41. Reichley, *Conservatives in an Age of Change*, pp. 271–272.

42. Jack Rasmus, "The Political Economy of Wage-Price Controls in the U.S., 1971–74," pp. 36–49.

43. *New York Times*, Feb. 24, 1971, p. 23.

44. Troika Meeting, Feb. 23, 1971, memo for the President's File, WHCF, FI, Box 1, Jan.–Apr. 1971, Nixon Project; memo for Paul McCracken from Herbert Stein, Feb. 8, 1971, WHCF, FI, Box 1, Jan.–Apr. 1971, Nixon Project; *Wall Street Journal*, Feb. 10, 1971, p. 8.

45. Memo from John S. Ripley to Board of Governors, Feb. 9, 1972, Box B-76, Joint Economic Committee, Burns Papers.

46. Hobart Rowen, "One Thing About Nixon's Policy—It Certainly Isn't Secret," *Washington Post*, Mar. 7, 1971, p. G1; "Critique of 'A Formal Model of the Economy for the Office of Management and Budget' by Arthur Laffer and R. David Ranson," [4/71], Box B-85, OMB, Apr. 1–26, 1971, Burns Papers.

47. Arthur F. Burns to Richard Nixon, Feb. 20, 1971, WHCF, FG 131, Box 1, 1/1/71–12/31/71, Nixon Project.

48. Wooley, *Monetary Politics*, pp. 157–158.

49. Papers of the Federal Reserve System, Part 2: Minutes of the Federal Open Market Committee, 1923–1975, reel 26, Feb. 1971, p. 87.

50. Draft of memo from R[obert] S[olomon], Oct. 21, 1970, Box B-33, Exchange Rates, Feb.–Oct. 1970, Burns Papers.

51. Ibid.

52. Banks borrowed in the Eurodollar market. This came into being in the early 1960s when the first American capital controls cut foreign borrowers off from U.S. money markets. American balance-of-payments deficits had left many abroad holding large amounts of dollars, and bankers in Europe (often Americans stationed there) brought these two groups together. They would sell bonds from those foreigners who wanted to borrow dollars to those abroad with large greenbacks holdings. Eventually, even American firms started borrowing in this market.

53. Robert F. Gemmill to Robert Solomon, Oct. 14, 1970, Box B-33, Eurodollars, Feb.–Oct. 1970, Burns Papers; C. A. Coombs to Chairman Burns, May 21, 1970, Box B-34, Eurodollars, Apr. 1971–Sept. 1973, Burns Papers. Banks must hold reserves against all liabilities, and they do not earn interest on these reserves. If a certain type of liability has a lower reserve requirement, it costs a bank less to maintain. The Export-Import Bank is a government-owned corporation that makes loans to foreign countries and companies buying American goods.

54. Nov. 11, 1970, JDE Notes of Meetings with the President, Box 4, 7/1/70–12/31/70 [5 of 8], Ehrlichman Files.

55. Ehrlichman, *Witness to Power*, p. 256; Dec. 15, 1970, JDE Notes of Meetings with the President, Box 4, 7/1/70–12/31/70 [7 of 8], Ehrlichman Files.

56. FOMC Minutes, Apr. 6, 1971, reel 26.

57. Solomon, *International Monetary System*, pp. 179–180.

58. *Wall Street Journal*, May 7, 1971, p. 19.

59. Memo for the President from McCracken, June 2, 1971, Box 20, White House Memos, June 1971, McCracken Papers.

60. Memo for the President from Herbert Stein, May 10, 1971, WHCF, FI 9, Box 55, EX FI 9, Jan.–June 1971, Nixon Project.

61. *New York Times*, May 11, 1971, p. 64.

62. Alfred Hayes to Arthur Burns, Mar. 23, 1971, Box B-4, BIS Meeting, Basel, Apr. 1971 (1), Burns Papers. The New York Fed was always the strongest defender of fixed exchange rates among those involved in the management of international financial policy.

63. Arthur Burns to John Connally, May 19, 1971, Box B-2, Balance of Payments (4), Burns Papers. This is a copy of a letter sent to the president.

64. The federal government would not actually make loans itself but rather guaranteed that it would repay loans made by others if the company was unable to do so.

65. Summary of Attachments, [June 21, 1971], Box B-78, Lockheed, June 6–10, 1971, Burns Papers.

66. U.S. Congress, Senate, Committee on Banking, Housing, and Urban Affairs, *Emergency Loan Guarantee Legislation*, pp. 579–598. Of course, whether either the Penn Central or Lockheed was "creditworthy" is debatable.

67. Arthur Burns to George Shultz, Dec. 18, 1970, Box B-85, Office of Management and Budget, 1970–Mar. 1971, Burns Papers.

68. *Wall Street Journal*, June 17, 1971, p. 9; July 21, 1971, p. 30.

69. Scott Mouw, "Passing the Buck: Congress and the 1971 Lockheed Loan Guarantee."

70. Ibid.

71. William Simon to Wright Patman and John Sparkman, [June 1974], Box B-30, Emergency Loan Guarantee Board, 1974, Burns Papers.

72. Memo from Mrs. Smelker, Mar. 10, 1971, Box B-90, Wages and Prices (1), Burns Papers.

73. *New York Times*, May 24, 1971, p. 30; July 25, 1971, sec. IV, p. 4.

74. Memo for the President from McCracken, Aug. 9, 1971, Box 20, White House Memos, Aug. 1971, McCracken Papers; Solomon, *International Monetary System*, pp. 187–196; memo for the President from Stein, June 5, 1971, Box 20, White House Memos, June 1971, McCracken Papers; memo to the President from McCracken, July 12, 1971, Box 20, White House Memos, July 1971, McCracken Papers.

75. Joint Economic Committee, *1971 Economic Report*, p. 242; U.S. Congress, Subcommittee on Foreign Economic Policy to the Joint Economic Committee, *A Foreign Economic Policy for the 1970s*, p. 1406.

76. Arthur Burns, "The Economy in Mid-1971," in *Reflections*, pp. 119–128.

77. *Des Moines Register*, July 6, 1971, p. 4.

78. *Baltimore Sun*, Aug. 5, 1971, p. A-14.

79. *Congressional Record* 117 (1971):26943–26944, 30208.

80. Memo from Peter Flanigan to Richard Nixon, June 28, 1971, WHCF, EX BE 5–3, Box 62, Inflation-Money Scarcity, Oct. 1970–71, Nixon Project.

81. Safire, *Before the Fall*, p. 491.

82. *New York Times*, Apr. 6, 1971, pp. 53, 57.

83. Ehrlichman interview.

84. William Safire to H. R. Haldeman, Aug. 3, 1971, WHSF, Haldeman Files, Box 84, William Safire, Aug. 1971, Nixon Project.

85. Pierre A. Rinfret to Connally, Aug. 3, 1971, WHSF, BE 5, Box 3, National Economy, Nixon Project; memo from Flanigan to Nixon, Aug. 3, 1971, WHSF, FG 131, Box 24, Federal Reserve System, Nixon Project; *New York Times*, July 11, 1977, pp. 29, 30.

86. Memo from Safire to Haldeman, Aug. 5, 1971, WHSF, Haldeman Files, Box 84, William Safire, Aug. 1971, Nixon Project; Safire, *Before the Fall*, pp. 491–495; Richard Nixon, *Public Papers of the President, Richard Nixon, 1971*, pp. 855–861.

87. Memo from Richard W. McCaren, Feb. 19, 1971, Box B-23, CEA Jan.–Mar. 1971, Burns Papers.

88. Memo from Herbert Stein, Mar. 11, 1971, Box B-23, CEA Jan.–Mar. 1971, Burns Papers.

89. Reichley, *Conservatives in an Age of Change*, pp. 221–223.

90. Washington would use the Fed's "swap," or credit, line with the Bank of England to cover London's dollar holdings. The central bank would borrow sterling and used these to purchase the Bank of England's dollars at the pegged rate of $2.40. This action would guarantee the British that they would not lose money in the event of a devaluation of the dollar. The Fed had many swap lines with different countries, although the British one was the largest.

91. Nixon, *Public Papers 1971*, p. 888.

92. Safire, *Before the Fall*, pp. 513–514.

93. Volcker, *Changing Fortunes*, p. xiv.

94. Aug. 14, 1971, JDE Notes of Meetings with the President, Box 5, 8/3/71–12/31/71 [1 of 5], Ehrlichman Files.

95. Safire, *Before the Fall*, p. 519.

96. Ibid.

97. Ibid.

98. Hargrove and Morley, eds., *The President and the CEA*, p. 377.

99. *Wall Street Journal*, May 7, 1970, p. 4; Nov. 6, 1970, p. 3; *New York Times*, May 26, 1970, pp. 1, 52.

100. James Daniel, "He Manages the Nation's Money Supply," pp. 68–72.

5. New Arrangements

1. Memo for the President from Charles W. Colson, Aug. 31, 1971, WHSF, Presidential Office File, Box 13, President's Handwriting, Aug. 16 through 31, 1971, Nixon Project.

2. Though the COLC had important responsibilities as long as controls lasted, its staff soon came to dominate the organization, and the council itself became a secondary body.

3. Memo for Richard Nixon re Labor Group, Sept. 10, 1971, WHCF, EX BE 3, Box 8, Economic Controls, Sept. 10–12, 1971 and Sept. 13–14, 1971, Nixon Project; memo for Richard Nixon re Business Group, Sept. 13, 1971, WHCF, EX BE 3, Box 8, Economic Controls, Sept. 10–12, 1971 and Sept. 13–14, 1971, Nixon Project.

4. *Time*, Feb. 21, 1972, p. 22.

5. *New York Times*, Aug. 16, 1971, pp. 1, 14.

6. Arnold R. Weber, *In Pursuit of Price Stability: The Wage-Price Freeze of 1971*, pp. 99–100, 105.

7. List of Membership in Committee on Interest and Dividends, Burns Papers, Box B-14, Committee on Interest and Dividends, Oct. 1–10, 1971.

8. Interview with Dewey Daane, Dec. 29, 1987.

9. Minutes of CID, Jan. 19, 1972 meeting, p. 3, Box B-15, Committee on Interest and Dividends, Jan. 1972, Burns Papers.

10. "Press Release on Nixon's Economic Moves," Aug. 16, 1971, Box 469A, "Release Calling for a Rollback of Interest Rates," Patman Papers, Lyndon Johnson Library, Austin, Tex.

11. *Wall Street Journal*, Nov. 5, 1971, p. 2; minutes of meeting between CID and bankers, Feb. 9, 1972, Burns Papers, Box B-15, Committee on Interest and Dividends, Feb. 1972.

12. U.S. Congress, Senate, Committee on Banking, Housing, and Urban Affairs, *Economic Stabilization Legislation*, pp. 455–461.

13. Daane interview.

14. Kettl, *Leadership at the Fed*, pp. 127–130.

15. U.S. Congress, Subcommittee on Priorities and Economy in Government of the Joint Economic Committee, *Housing Subsidies and Housing Policies*, p. 356.

16. "Simple Arithmetic of Wages and Prices in 1971–72," Box B-90, Prices and Wages (1), Burns Papers.

17. Minutes of Nov. 2, 1971 CID Meeting, Box B-15, Committee on Interest and Dividends, Nov. 1971 (2), Burns Papers.

18. *Wall Street Journal*, Nov. 3, 1971, p. 3.

19. This policy did not require a reduction in the real wages of workers but merely that increases be kept below those of productivity plus inflation.

20. Senate Committee on Banking, Housing, and Urban Affairs, *Economic Stabilization Legislation*, p. 463.

21. Robert F. Lanzillotti, Mary T. Hamilton, and R. Blaine Roberts, *Phase II in Review: The Price Commission Experience*, p. 18.

22. Arnold R. Weber and Daniel J. B. Mitchell, *The Pay Board's Progress: Wage Controls in Phase II*, pp. 149–152, 163–168; *Wall Street Journal*, Nov. 18, 1971, p. 2; Nov. 19, 1971, p. 2; Nov. 26, 1971, p. 7; and Dec. 13, 1971, p. 14. The issues involved in these contracts were extremely complex and, in some cases, unique to the industries in question. For instance, the United Mine Workers agreement involved provisions to bail out the union's Welfare and Retirement Fund, while the railroad contract dealt with the complex thicket of work rules that employers wanted to pare.

23. Ehrlichman, *Witness to Power*, p. 256; U.S. Congress, Joint Economic Committee, *The 1972 Economic Report to the President*, pp. 119–124.

24. Evans and Novak, *Nixon in the White House*, pp. 428–429.

25. JDE Notes of Meetings with the President, Feb. 13, 1972, Box 6, 1/4/72–8/4/72 [1 of 6], Ehrlichman Files.

26. U.S. Congress, Joint Economic Committee, *The 1972 Midyear Review of the Economy*, p. 124.

27. FOMC minutes, Oct. 19, 1971, reel 27.

28. Memos for the President from McCracken, Oct. 19 and Oct. 27, 1971, Box 20, Memos to the White House, Oct. 1971, McCracken Papers. The decline he refers to was in the week-to-week figures.

29. Memo for the President from Herbert Stein, Dec. 29, 1971, Box B-23, CEA, 1972, Burns Papers.

30. Memo for the President from George Shultz, Dec. 18, 1971, WHSF, President's Office Files, Box 15, President's Handwriting, Dec. 16–31, 1971, Nixon Project.

31. Milton Friedman to Arthur Burns, Dec. 13, 1971, Box K-12, Friedman, Milton (2), Burns Papers.

32. *New York Times*, Jan. 3, 1972, pp. 41, 45.

33. *Congressional Record* 118 (1972):13141.

34. Memo to the President from Peter M. Flanigan, Oct. 26, 1971, WHCF, FG 131, Box 1, 1/1/70–[12/31/71], Nixon Project; JDE Notes of Meetings with the President, Dec. 20, 1971, Box 6, 8/3/71–12/31/71 [5 of 5], Ehrlichman Files.

35. The deficit turned out to be about $25 billion, partially because of robust economic growth during the first half of 1972.

36. Arthur Burns to George Shultz, Feb. 4, 1972, Box B-85, OMB 1972–73, Burns Papers; Reichley, *Conservatives in an Age of Change*, pp. 26–27. These purchases included a two-year supply of toilet paper.

37. Ehrlichman interview.

38. Schedule Proposal from Fred Malek, Mar. 31, 1971, WHCF, FG 131, Box 1 [1/1/72–12/31/72], Nixon Project; Schedule Proposal from Fred Malek, Mar. 3, 1972, memo from Malek for Arthur Burns, Oct. 25, 1971, Haldeman Files, Box 86, Fred Malek, Oct. 1971, Nixon Project.

39. U.S. Congress, Senate, Committee on Banking, Housing, and Urban Affairs, *Par Value Modification Act-1972*, p. 125.

40. U.S. Congress, House, Committee on Banking and Currency, *To Provide for a Modification in the Par Value of the Dollar*, p. 59.

41. JDE Notes of Meetings with the President, Oct. 25, 1971, Box 5, 8/3/71–12/31/71 [3 of 5], Ehrlichman Files.

42. Since a nation with a deficit would be transferring more money abroad than it was receiving, its currency would be in surplus on world markets, and the working of supply and demand would push its value down. The situation for surplus countries would work exactly in reverse.

43. The question of how much damage exchange-rate uncertainty did to business confidence is very difficult to ascertain, since confidence is impossible to quantify, and its sources are difficult to define. It seems fairly certain that floating rates were a drag on the economy, but not a serious one. Whether a longer period of floating would have done more damage or instead allowed people to adjust to the new order is impossible to know.

44. Solomon, *International Monetary System*, p. 196.

45. Arthur Burns to Richard Nixon, Oct. 14, 1971, WHSF, Haldeman Files, Box 85, John M. Huntsman, Oct. 1971, Nixon Project.

46. Memo to the President from McCracken, Nov. 10, 1971, Box 20, Memo to the White House, Nov. 1971, McCracken Papers.

47. Leonard Silk, "Dollars and Diplomacy," *New York Times*, Dec. 27, 1971, p. 27.

48. *New York Times*, Sept. 24, 1971, p. 18.

49. The Group of Ten consisted of Belgium, Britain, Canada, France, Italy, Japan, the Netherlands, Sweden, Switzerland, the United States, and West Germany. These eleven countries could style themselves the Group of Ten because the Swiss, following their tradition of neutrality, insisted that they were merely observers, not actually members. In practice, there was little difference.

50. Never, after 1971, did the market price of gold drop to the official price. The increase to $38 an ounce cut the gap but did not completely fill it.

51. These numbers are the sum of the increase in the price of gold and further changes in the parities by other countries. For instance, the 7.5 percent Italian revaluation consisted of the increase of the gold price by 8.57 percent minus a devaluation of the lira against that new parity by 1 percent. The 13.6 percent German revaluation involved the 8.57 percent increase in the price of gold plus a further 5 percent revaluation of the deutschmark.

52. Solomon, *International Monetary System*, pp. 207–209. The Canadians had floated their currency throughout most of the 1950s, and had resumed doing so in 1970. They were far more comfortable with this approach than the other industrial democracies.

53. Interview with Edward Bernstein, Southern Oral History Program, Southern History Collection, Wilson Library, University of North Carolina, Chapel Hilil, p. 159.

54. Nixon, *Public Papers 1971*, pp. 1195–1196.

55. Helen B. Junz to R. Solomon, Dec. 23, 1971, Box B-34, Exchange Rates, 1971–75, Burns Papers.

56. Weber and Mitchell, *The Pay Board's Progress*, pp. 175–195.

57. Frank Fitzsimmons of the Teamsters did not walk off, largely because he had already committed his union to Nixon's reelection. He and one business member belonged to the new Pay Board, which otherwise consisted of the five public members of the old board.

58. *Wall Street Journal*, Jan. 29, 1973, p. 5.

59. Helen Tice to Chairman Burns, Nov. 17, 1972, Box B-90, Profits, Burns Papers.

60. Joint Economic Committee, *1972 Midyear Review of the Economy*, pp. 119–123.

61. Joint Economic Committee, *1972 Economic Report of the President*, pp. 192–194.

62. Ibid.

63. U.S. Congress, Subcommittee on Priorities and Economy in Government of the Joint Economic Committee, *Housing Subsidies and Housing Policies*, pp. 341–342.

64. JDE Notes of Meetings with the President, Sept. 7, 1972, Box 6, 9/7/72–12/13/72 [2 of 9], Ehrlichman Files.

65. Joint Economic Committee, *1972 Economic Report of the President*, pp. 191–193.

66. Arthur Burns to Richard Nixon, June 22, 1972, WHSF, President's Office Files, Box 17, President's Handwriting, June 16–30, Nixon Project.

67. Notes on Basel Meeting—Mar. 12, 1972, Dewey Daane Papers, Vanderbilt University, Nashville, Tenn.

68. Solomon, *International Monetary Systems*, p. 217.

69. Economists refer to this phenomenon as the "J-curve," because the trade balance deteriorates some before improving, forming a curve that looks like the letter *J*.

70. The international community agreed to authorize SDRs in the mid-1960s when it seemed likely that the United States would return to a payments surplus. Since up until that point U.S. deficits had supplied increases in world reserves, something to replace the greenback had to be devised since American surpluses would reduce the number of dollars available.

71. Burns, "Essentials of International Monetary Reform," in *Reflections*, pp. 448–454.

72. FOMC Minutes, July 18, 1972, second meeting, p. 2, reel 28.

73. *Congressional Record* 118 (1972):17235.

74. Hobart Rowen, "Burns, the Catalyst," *Washington Post*, May 25, 1972, p. A-23.

75. Solomon, *International Monetary System*, pp. 223–224.

76. Ibid., p. 224.

77. JDE Notes of Meetings with the President, Sept. 7, 1972, Box 6, 8/7/72–12/13/72/ [2 of 9], Ehrlichman Files.

78. Interview with Edwin Truman, June 3, 1992.

79. Ibid.; interview with Ralph Bryant, June 3, 1992.

80. Memo from Arthur F. Burns, "A Note on Price Policy," June 24, 1972, WHCF, EX BE 3, Box 14, Economic Controls, June–July 1972, Nixon Project.

81. White House Press Release, June 19, 1972, Richard Nixon to Arthur Burns, June 30, 1972, WHCF, EX BE 3, Box 14, Economic Controls, June–July 1972, Nixon Project.

82. "Options for 1973 Dividend Restraint Program," Box B-15, Committee on Interest and Dividends, May–Aug. 1972, Burns Papers; minutes of June 15, 1972 CID meeting, Box B-15, Committee on Interest and Dividends, May–Aug. 1972, Burns Papers.

83. *Wall Street Journal*, June 7, 1972, p. 5; Aug. 15, 1972, p. 3; Nov. 10, 1972, p. 2.

84. *Federal Reserve Bulletin* 59 (May 1973):347.

85. Burns, "The Problem of Inflation," in *Reflections*, pp. 144–145.

86. Ibid., p. 146.

87. *Washington Post*, Oct. 13, 1972, pp. A-1, A-24.

88. Gramley interview.

89. Burns, "The Problem of Inflation," p. 152. Later, the chairman denounced such reasoning, having firsthand experience about how it could mislead policymakers.

90. *Washington Post*, Oct. 13, 1972, pp. A-1, A-24.

91. Robert Samuelson, "Why Price Controls Stopped Working," pp. 19–30.

92. Stanford Rose, "The Agony of the Federal Reserve," pp. 90–93, 180–190.

93. Arthur Burns to Hedley Donovan, July 5, 1974, Box B-50, *Fortune* article on Federal Reserve (1), Burns Papers; Andrew F. Brimmer to Hedley Donovan, July 10, 1974, Box B-50, *Fortune* article on Federal Reserve (1), Burns Papers.

94. Hargrove and Morley, eds., *The President and the CEA*, p. 396.

95. Memo for Henry Reuss, June 13, 1972, Box 319, JEC-92d Congress, Reuss Papers, Fromkin Collection, University of Wisconsin, Milwaukee; *New York Times*, Nov. 11, 1972, sec. III, p. 17.

96. *New York Times*, Nov. 12, 1972, pp. 57, 60.

97. JDE Notes of Meetings with the President, Aug. 7, 1972, Box 6, 1/4/72–8/4/72 [5 of 6], Ehrlichman Files.

98. Memo from Herbert Stein to the President, Dec. 7, 1972, WHCF, EX FI, Finance [9 of 14, Oct.–Dec. 1972], Nixon Project.

99. Milton Friedman, "The Fed on the Spot," *Newsweek*, Oct. 16, 1972, p. 98.

100. Burns, "The Problem of Inflation," p. 145.

6. The Great Crash

1. The legal authority for controls rested on a blanket authorization by the Congress that allowed the president to regulate wages and prices more or less as he wished, but which lasted for only one year.

2. Memo to Richard Nixon from George Shultz, Dec. 5, 1972, WHCF, EX BE 3, Box 14, Economic Controls, Oct.–Dec. 21, 1972, Nixon Project.

3. The freeze was Phase I. The controls imposed after the freeze expired were Phase II.

4. Memo for Richard Nixon from George Shultz, Jan. 8, 1973, WHCF, EX BE 3, Box 14, Economic Controls, Jan. 1973, Nixon Project.

5. U.S. Congress, Joint Economic Committee, *Wage and Price Control: Evaluation of a Year's Experience.*

6. *New York Times*, Jan. 12, 1973, p. 13.

7. Ibid., Jan. 13, 1973, p. 10.

8. Richard Nixon to Arthur Burns, Feb. 14, 1973, WHCF, EX BE 5–3, Box 62, Inflation-Money Scarcity, 1972–74, Nixon Project.

9. *Wall Street Journal*, Feb. 15, 1973, p. 31.

10. FOMC Minutes, Jan. 16, 1973, reel 29.

11. U.S. Balance-of-Payments Problem: Recent Developments and Prospects, Feb. 5, 1973, Box B-2, Balance of Payments (4), Burns Papers.

12. FOMC Minutes, Jan. 16, 1973, reel 29.

13. Solomon, *International Monetary System*, pp. 229–230.

14. Ibid., pp. 229–231.

15. *New York Times*, Feb. 12, 1973, pp. 45, 56.

16. "International Economic Issues," Mar. 5, 1971, Box 318, Subcommittee on International Finance, 92d Cong., Reuss Papers.

17. U.S. Congress, Joint Economic Committee, *The 1973 Economic Report of the President*, pp. 411–415.

18. U.S. Congress, House, Subcommittee on International Finance of the Committee on Banking and Currency, *To Amend the Par Value Modification Act of 1972*, pp. 114–118.

19. Notes on Conversation between Governor Daane and Dr. Zijlstra, Mar. 1, 1973, Daane Papers.

20. This meant that the central banks ceased intervening in markets, and trading was at a minimum as market participants waited to see what would happen.

21. Solomon, *International Monetary System*, pp. 231–234; *New York Times*, Mar. 20, 1973, pp. 1, 56.

22. Stein interview.

23. Volcker, *Changing Fortunes*, pp. 103–104.

24. Ibid., p. 113.

25. Arthur Burns to George Shultz, July 9, 1973, Treasury Dept. Jan.–July 1973; George Shultz to Arthur Burns, Aug. 8, 1973, Treasury Dept. Aug.–Dec. 1973, Box B-101, Burns Papers.

26. U.S. Bureau of the Census, *Statistical Abstract of the United States: 1977*, 98th ed. (Washington, D.C.: U.S. Department of Commerce, 1977), p. 471.

27. U.S. Congress, Joint Economic Committee, *The 1973 Midyear Review of the Economy*, pp. 228–231.

28. J. Charles Partee to Chairman Burns, July 31, 1974, Box B-60, Inflation, Burns Papers.

29. *Wall Street Journal*, Jan. 25, 1974, p. 8.

30. U.S. Congress, Senate, Committee on Housing, Banking, and Urban Affairs, *Economic Stabilization Legislation—1973*, pp. 591–592.

31. Notes of BIS Governors' meeting on Sunday afternoon, Jan. 7, 1973, Daane Papers.

32. Since banks needed to keep cash on deposit at the Fed in a fixed proportion to their deposits, the cost of such funds was very important to the ability of the banking system to extend credit.

33. *New York Times*, Feb. 12, 1973, pp. 39, 40.

34. Senate Committee on Housing, Banking, and Urban Affairs, *Economic Stabilization Legislation—1973*, p. 593.

35. CID press release, Feb. 23, 1973, and enclosed letter from David C. Melnicoff to William B. Eagleson, Jr., President, Girard Bank, Philadelphia, Box B-15, Committee on Interest and Dividends, Jan.–Mar. 1973, Burns Papers.

36. *Wall Street Journal*, Mar. 23, 1973, p. 3; *New York Times*, Mar. 25, 1973, sec. III, pp. 1, 4; Mar. 27, 1973, pp. 63, 72; U.S. Congress, House, Committee on Banking and Currency, *The Credit Crunch and Reform of Financial Institutions*, p. 368.

37. Joint Economic Committee, *1973 Midyear Review of the Economy*, pp. 261–263.

38. *New York Times*, Mar. 26, 1973, p. 49; *Congressional Record* 119 (1972):3718.

39. Joint Economic Committee, *1973 Economic Report to the President*, p. 429.

40. JDE Notes of Meetings with the President, Apr. 18, 1973, Box 7, Jan. 4–May 2, 1973 [6 of 6], Ehrlichman Files.

41. Ibid.; *New York Times*, Sept. 17, 1973, pp. 49, 52.

42. George Shultz to Wright Patman, Mar. 28, 1973, WHCF, FI 2, Box 9, EX FI 2, 1973–July 1974, Nixon Project.

43. *Congressional Record* 119 (1973):8454.

44. *New York Times*, Apr. 28, 1974, sec. III, p. 24.

45. Richard Nixon, *Public Papers of the Presidents of the United States, Richard Nixon, 1973*, pp. 234–238, 341.

46. *New York Times*, Mar. 11, 1973, p. 32.

47. Arthur Burns to Richard Nixon, June 1, 1973, WHSF, Box 3, [CF] BE 5, National Economy 10/1/71–[6/10/74], [1972–74], Nixon Project.

48. JDE Notes of Meetings with the President, Apr. 18, 1973, Box 7, Jan. 4–May 2, 1973 [6 of 6], Ehrlichman Files.

49. Nixon, *Public Papers 1973*, p. 341; *Wall Street Journal*, May 3, 1973, p. 3.

50. Arthur Burns to Richard Nixon, June 1, 1973, WHSF, Box 3, [CF] BE 5, National Economy 10/1/71–[6/10/74], [1971–74], Nixon Project. Burns's proposal for a horsepower tax contains one important oversight that was uncharacteristic. He assumed that two engines with the same horsepower got the same gas mileage, which is not always the case.

51. *New York Times*, June 5, 1973, p. 11; June 8, 1973, p. 51.

52. Stein, *Presidential Economics*, p. 186.

53. Nixon, *Public Papers 1973*, pp. 584–587.

54. *New York Times*, July 15, 1973, sec. III, p. 8.

55. *Wall Street Journal*, Aug. 13, 1973, pp. 1, 12.

56. Memo from Herbert Stein to Richard M. Nixon, Oct. 12, 1973, WHSF, BE 5 Box 3, National Economy, 10/1/71–[6/10/74], Nixon Project.

57. U.S. Congress, Senate, Subcommittee on Production and Stabilization of the Committee on Banking, Housing, and Urban Affairs, *Oversight on Economic Stabilization*, pp. 683–685.

58. *New York Times*, June 22, 1973, pp. 1, 47.

59. *Wall Street Journal*, Dec. 11, 1973, p. 2.

60. Ibid., July 19, 1973, pp. 1, 18.

61. U.S. Bureau of the Census, *Statistical Abstract of the United States: 1976*, 97th ed. (Washington, D.C.: U.S. Department of Commerce, 1976), p. 737.

62. *New York Times*, Aug. 17, 1973, p. 44; Oct. 18, 1973, p. 76.

63. George Shultz to Ronald Reagan, Oct. 18, 1973, WHCF, FI 2, Box 9, EX FI 2, 1973–July 1974, Nixon Project.

64. *New York Times*, Sept. 14, 1973, pp. 1, 16; *Wall Street Journal*, Sept. 17, 1973, p. 2; *Washington Post*, Sept. 14, 1973, p. A-22; Sept. 15, 1973, pp. A-1, A-10; Sept. 19, 1973, p. A-27.

65. Solomon, *International Monetary System*, pp. 277–279.

66. U.S. Congress, House, Subcommittee on International Finance of the Banking and Currency Committee, *International Monetary Reform*, pp. 41–47.

67. Daniel Yergin, *The Prize: The Epic Quest for Oil, Money, and Power* (New York: Touchstone, 1991), p. 615.

68. Memo for the President from Herbert Stein, Dec. 5, 1973, WHSF, Subject Files, Confidential Files, Box 27, [CF] FI-Finance [1971–74], Nixon Project.

69. *New York Times*, Feb. 17, 1974, sec. III, pp. 1, 4.

70. House Subcommittee on International Finance, *International Monetary Reform*, p. 28.

71. The North Sea oil fields had not yet come on line.

72. Charles J. Siegman, "Redeeming Official Liabilities with Gold Revaluation Profits," May 17, 1974, Box B-52, Gold, May 1974, Burns Papers.

73. *Washington Post*, Nov. 14, 1973, pp. A-1, A-16; transcript of Arthur Burns Press Conference, Nov. 13, 1973, Box B-52, Gold-BIS Meeting, Nov. 1973, Burns Papers.

74. Communiqué, Washington Energy Conference, Feb. 13, 1974, Box B-32, Energy: Washington Energy Conference, Feb. 1974 (6), Burns Papers; *New York Times*, Jan. 19, 1974, pp. 1, 45. The participants were Belgium, Britain, Canada, Denmark, France, Ireland, Italy, Japan, Luxembourg, the Netherlands, Norway, the United States, and West Germany.

75. Solomon, *International Monetary System*, p. 305.

76. The Germans loaned the Italian government $2 billion, with the Italian gold stock as security.

77. *Wall Street Journal*, Feb. 4, 1974, p. 21; Arthur Burns to William Simon, July 16, 1974, Box B-102, Treasury Dept., July–Aug. 1974, Burns Papers.

78. *Wall Street Journal*, Jan. 30, 1974, p. 3.

79. Ibid., June 6, 1974, p. 10; Solomon, *International Monetary System*, pp. 339–340.

80. IMF Press Release, June 13, 1974, Box 66, International Monetary Fund, 1974, Burns Papers.

81. House Subcommittee on International Finance, *International Monetary Reform*, pp. 6–7.

82. Ibid., p. 7.

83. *New York Times*, Feb. 4, 1975, pp. 43, 49.

84. *Wall Street Journal*, Apr. 5, 1974, p. 3.

85. U.S. Congress, House, Subcommittee on Domestic Finance of the Committee on Banking and Currency, *Congressional Oversight of the Federal Reserve System*, p. 11.

86. *Washington Post*, July 17, 1974, p. C-15.

87. Interview with Wright Patman, I, Aug. 11, 1972, Lyndon Johnson Library, pp. 37– 38.

88. *Washington Post*, July 17, 1974, pp. E-1, E-2.

89. *Business Week*, May 1, 1974, p. 34.

90. *New York Times*, Oct. 26, 1973, p. 42. The *Times* came out specifically for Patman's GAO audit of the Fed.

91. *Wall Street Journal*, Aug. 8, 1975, p. 1.

92. U.S. Congress, House, Committee on Banking and Currency, *Federal Reserve Policy and Inflation and High Interest Rates*, p. 291.

93. Burns, "Objectives of the Federal Reserve System," in *Reflections*, p. 346.

94. "Financial Institutions: Reform and Public Interest," [Aug. 1973], Box 317, Committee on Banking and Currency, 93d Cong., Reuss Papers.

95. Nicholas von Hoffman, "Thanks Zeus, . . . er, Dr. Burns," *Washington Post*, May 5, 1975, pp. B-1, B-12.

96. *Washington Post*, Feb. 19, 1974, pp. D-8, D-11.

97. U.S. Congress, Senate, Committee on Banking, Housing, and Urban Affairs, *Federal Reserve Reform and Audit*, pp. 23–24.

98. Kettl, *Leadership at the Fed*, p. 156.

99. Summary of Reserve Bank Conference Call, 11:30 A.M., Feb. 6, 1974, Box B-51, GAO Audit, Jan.–Apr. 1974, Burns Papers.

100. Kettl, *Leadership at the Fed*, p. 156; see folder on GAO Audit, Box 51, Burns Papers, for just how broad Burns's list of contacts was.

101. Stanton interview.

102. Memo from Bob Weitraub to Reuss, [10/18/73], Box 339, Banking and Currency, Reuss Papers.

103. U.S. Congress, House, Subcommittee on Domestic Monetary Policy of the Committee on Banking, Finance, and Urban Affairs, *Maintaining and Making Public Minutes at Federal Reserve Meetings*, p. 58.

104. Milton Friedman, "The Inflationary Fed," *Newsweek*, Aug. 27, 1973, p. 74.

105. *Congressional Record* 119 (1973):36533–36534.

106. *Washington Post*, Apr. 23, 1974, pp. A-1, A-4; House Committee on Banking and Currency, *Federal Reserve Policy and Inflation and High Interest Rates*, pp. 263–264.

107. Lindley H. Clark, Jr., "Speaking of Business," *Wall Street Journal*, Jan. 7, 1974, p. 10; Feb. 11, 1974, p. 10. Final figures showed growth in the money supply at a little above 5 percent for this period.

108. Wade Greene, "Economists in Recession," *New York Times Magazine*, May 12, 1974, p. 19.

109. Memo for Secretary Kissinger from A. Kenis Cliff, Apr. 23, 1974, WHCF, FG 131, Box 1, 1/1/73–[7/31/74], Nixon Project.

110. Subcommittee on Production and Stabilization, *Oversight on Economic Stabilization*, pp. 672–675.

111. U.S. Congress, Subcommittee on International Finance of the Joint Economic Committee, *How Well Are Fluctuation Exchange Rates Working?*, pp. 176–179.

112. *Wall Street Journal*, Feb. 7, 1974, pp. 1, 34; Jan. 31, 1974, p. 2; Apr. 1, 1974, p. 6; Feb. 25, 1974, p. 7; *New York Times*, Nov. 1, 1973, pp. 1, 48; Nov. 5, 1973, p. 2; Feb. 7, 1974, pp. 1, 34; memo from Herbert Stein to Richard M. Nixon, WHCF EX BE 3, Box 17, Economic Controls, Feb.–Apr. 1974, Nixon Project.

113. Joint Economic Committee, *1973 Midyear Review of the Economy*, p. 231; Subcommittee on Production and Stabilization, *Oversight on Economic Stabilization*, pp. 668–672.

114. U.S. Congress, Senate, Committee on the Budget, *The Federal Budget and Inflation*, p. 238.

115. U.S. Congress, Joint Economic Committee, *The 1974 Economic Report of the President*, p. 746.

116. For example, economic growth in Japan averaged over 9 percent a year in the 1950s and 10 percent in the 1960s. After 1973, it slowed to less than 5 percent. In the United States, worker productivity increased at an average of 3 percent a year after 1945, but after 1973 the gain slowed to about 1 percent.

117. Otto Eckstein, *The Great Recession*, pp. 72–89.

118. Burns, "The Menace of Inflation," in *Reflections*, p. 161.

119. House Committee on Banking and Currency, *Federal Reserve Policy and Inflation and High Interest Rates*, pp. 258, 263.

120. Burns, "The Menace of Inflation," p. 161.

121. Ibid., pp. 162–163.

122. *Business Week*, May 5, 1974, p. 3.

123. *Wall Street Journal*, Apr. 1974, p. 3.

124. Ibid., Apr. 23, 1974, p. 3.

125. Burns, "Key Issues of Monetary Policy," in *Reflections*, p. 179.

126. Memo for the President's file from Herbert Stein, July 2, 1974, WHSF, Subject File, Confidential Files, FI, Box 27, FI [1971–74], Nixon Project.

127. *Washington Post*, Apr. 21, 1974, p. K-2; Hobart Rowen, "Arthur Burns: In a Tight Money Squeeze," *Washington Post*, Aug. 8, 1974, p. A-23; Walter W. Heller, "The Untimely Flight from Controls," *Wall Street Journal*, Feb. 15, 1974, p. 14; *Business Week*, June 15, 1974, p. 79.

128. *New York Times*, Sept. 1, 1974, pp. 1, 29.

129. Ibid., July 13, 1974, p. 30.

130. Ibid., Apr. 1, 1974, p. 50.

131. *Los Angeles Times*, Feb. 28, 1974, sec. II, p. 6.

132. *Des Moines Register*, June 26, 1974, p. 6.

133. Burns, "The Problem of Inflation," p. 148.

134. Burns, "The Current Recession in Perspective," in *Reflections*, pp. 210–211.

7. Under Siege

1. Robert M. Fisher to Chairman Burns, Oct. 9, 1974, Box B-91, Real Estate Investment Trusts, Burns Papers.

2. Committee on Bank Regulatory and Supervisory Policy to the Board of Governors, Jan. 28, 1975, Box B-14, Committee on Bank Regulatory Supervision, Jan.–Feb. 1975, Burns Papers; U.S. Congress, House, Committee on Banking, Currency, and Housing, *To Lower Interest Rates*, pp. 280–281.

3. A. S. Nissen to Mr. Debs, July 15, 1974, Box B-89, President Nixon, meetings with, July 11–Aug. 20, 1974, Burns Papers.

4. Jackson interview.

5. Emanuel Melichar to Mr. Fisher, June 5, 1974, Box B-13, Cattle Industry Loans, June–July 1974, Burns Papers.

6. "Pan Am Problem: Federal Options," Sept. 1974, and "Long Range Policy Issues Which Must be Considered in Reaching a Decision on Pan Am," [Sept. 1974], Box B-87, Pan American, Burns Papers; Brent Scowcroft and William Seidman to the President, Feb. 14, 1975, President's Handwriting File, Box 6, Civil Aviation—Pan Am, Ford Library.

7. William Simon to Arthur Burns, Sept. 5, 1974, Box B-102, Treasury Dept., Sept.–Oct. 15, 1974, Burns Papers; Frank G. Zarb to the President, May 12, 1975, SHCF, BE 4–11, Box 10, 8/9/74–1/20/77, Ford Library.

8. New York Times, June 15, 1974, pp. 39–43.

9. "Pan Am Problem: Federal Options," and "Long Range Policy Issues Which Must be Considered in Reaching a Decision on Pan Am," [Sept. 1974], Box B-87, Pan American, Burns Papers; Brent Scowcroft and William Seidman to the President, Feb. 14, 1975, President's Handwriting File, Box 6, Civil Aviation—Pan Am, Ford Library.

10. William Simon to Arthur Burns, Sept. 5, 1974, Box B-102, Treasury Dept., Sept.–Oct. 15, 1974, Burns Papers; Frank G. Zarb to the President, May 12, 1975, SHCF, BE 4–11, Box 10, 8/9/74–1/20/77, Ford Library.

11. Brimmer interview.

12. House Committee on Banking, Currency, and Housing, To Lower Interest Rates, p. 216.

13. Ibid., pp. 212–214; Wall Street Journal, Sept. 27, 1974, p. 4. Franklin had a national charter and so fell under the regulatory jurisdiction of the comptroller.

14. Wall Street Journal, Feb. 10, 1975, p. 13.

15. New York Times, Feb. 15, 1976, sec. IV, p. 4.

16. Division of Research and Statistics to the Board of Governors, June 14, 1974, Box B-29, Emergency Lending Plans (9), Burns Papers.

17. Jackson interview.

18. New York Times, Jan. 22, 1976, pp. 1, 61.

19. Wall Street Journal, Sept. 27, 1990, pp. A-1, A-12.

20. New York Times, Aug. 11, 1974, sec. III, p. 2.

21. Safire, Before the Fall, p. 524.

22. Richard Nixon, Public Papers of the Presidents of the United States, Richard Nixon, 1974, p. 609.

23. Stein interview.

24. U.S. Congress, Senate, Committee on the Budget, The Federal Budget and Inflation, pp. 225, 229.

25. Hargrove and Morley, eds., The President and the CEA, p. 415.

26. Wall Street Journal, Aug. 23, 1974, p. 1.

27. Reichley, Conservatives in an Age of Change, pp. 383–384.

28. Kettl, Leadership at the Fed, p. 132.

29. Hargrove and Morley, eds., The President and the CEA, p. 429.

30. Kettl, Leadership at the Fed, p. 135.

31. Hargrove and Morley, eds., The President and the CEA, p. 429.

32. Arthur F. Burns, "Ford and the Federal Reserve," in Kenneth W.

Thompson, ed., *The Ford Presidency; Twenty-Two Intimate Perspectives of Gerald R. Ford*, p. 136.

33. *Washington Post*, July 15, 1975, p. D-7.

34. *New York Times*, Sept. 24, 1976, p. D-6.

35. The new governors were Philip Coldwell, president of the Dallas Federal Reserve Bank; Philip Jackson, a mortgage banker from Alabama; Charles Partee, a Fed economist; Stephen Gardner, undersecretary of the Treasury and former head of the Girard Bank in Philadelphia; and David Lilly, head of the Toro Corporation.

36. *New York Times*, Sept. 6, 1974, pp. 1, 16; *Wall Street Journal*, Sept. 6, 1974, p. 3.

37. Stein, *Presidential Economics*, p. 213.

38. FOMC Minutes, Sept. 20, 1974, Oct. 10, 1974, and Dec. 16–17, 1974, reel 31.

39. *New York Times*, Feb. 26, 1975, pp. 53, 57.

40. Hargrove and Morley, eds., *The President and the CEA*, p. 445.

41. U.S. Congress, Joint Economic Committee, *Financial and Capacity Needs*, p. 196.

42. FOMC Minutes, Nov. 19, 1974, reel 31, p. 46.

43. Walter W. Heller, "Now, Now Mr. Economist, Don't Be Afraid," *New York Times*, June 30, 1975, p. 29; *New York Times*, June 5, 1975, p. 53; *Business Week*, Apr. 2, 1975, pp. 105–106.

44. *Newsweek*, Mar. 10, 1975, pp. 60–62.

45. Burns, "The Current Recession in Perspective," pp. 208, 210.

46. U.S. Congress, Joint Economic Committee, *The 1975 Economic Report of the President*, p. 434.

47. U.S. Congress, House, Ways and Means Committee, *The President's Authority to Adjust Imports of Petroleum: Public Debt Ceiling Increase; and Emergency Tax Proposals*, p. 261.

48. FOMC Minutes, Sept. 10, 1974, reel 31, p. 76.

49. To see the influence of inflation on long-term interest rates, one only need compare the cost of money in 1970 and 1976. Three-month Treasury bills were paying substantially more in 1970 than in 1976, but Treasury bonds with maturities of ten years or greater paid about a percentage point more in 1976 than in 1970. The best explanation for this difference is higher expectations of inflation, which led investors to seek compensation for the devaluation of their dollars over time.

50. *New York Times*, Feb. 14, 1975, p. 53.

51. U.S. Congress, Senate, Committee on Banking, Housing, and Urban Affairs, *Monetary Policy Oversight*, pp. 53–55.

52. *Chicago Tribune*, May 11, 1975, sec. II, p. 1.

53. Burns, "Monetary Targets and Credit Allocation," p. 368.

54. *Atlanta Constitution*, Feb. 15, 1975, p. A-4; Mar. 9, 1975, p. A-4; *Denver Post*, Feb. 28, 1975, p. 22; *Gallup Opinion Index* 118 (Apr. 1975):2. Sixty percent of respondents to the Gallup survey considered "the

high cost of living" the nation's chief problem. Twenty percent chose unemployment.

55. House Committee on Banking, Currency, and Housing, *To Lower Interest Rates*, p. 199.

56. Clayton Fritchey, "Reforming the Federal Reserve," *Washington Post*, Oct. 18, 1975, p. A-23.

57. Senate Committee on Banking, Housing, and Urban Affairs, *Monetary Policy Oversight*, pp. 47–48.

58. Draft of H.R. 212, Box 335, Credit Allocation—1975, Reuss Papers.

59. Burns, "Monetary Targets and Credit Allocation," pp. 367, 371; Reuss interview.

60. Ibid., pp. 368–374.

61. *Washington Post*, Feb. 22, 1975, p. A-4.

62. Memo from William Proxmire to Members, Senate Committee on Banking, Housing, and Urban Affairs, Mar. 10, 1975, Box B-17, Concurrent Resolution on Monetary Policy, 1975, Burns Papers. Hearings would take place twice a year before each committee, staggered so that the chairman testified each quarter.

63. Senate Committee on Banking, Housing, and Urban Affairs, *Monetary Policy Oversight*, pp. 45–47.

64. This was a congressional resolution, not a law, and so did not need the president's signature.

65. In the 1970s, economists tended to emphasize M1, but during the 1980s M2 began to receive greater weight.

66. Memo from the staff for the Federal Open Market Committee, Apr. 10, 1975, B-17, Concurrent Resolution on Monetary Policy, 1975, Burns Papers.

67. U.S. Congress, Joint Economic Committee, *Midyear Review of the Economic Situation and Outlook—1975*, p. 146.

68. *Washington Post*, Apr. 25, 1975, p. D-10.

69. *New York Times*, Aug. 28, 1975, p. 52.

70. Conversation with James Galbraith, Apr. 16, 1993.

71. Memo from Bob Auerback to Paul Nelson, Sept. 23, 1977, House Banking Committee Files, 95th Full Committee Files, Staff Memos, 1977–78. This particular memo, which dealt with Burns's reappointment, ostensibly described the qualities desired in a new chairman, but it might more aptly be titled, "What We Do Not Like About Arthur Burns."

72. U.S. Congress, Senate, Committee on Banking, Housing, and Urban Affairs, *First Meeting on the Conduct of Monetary Policy*, p. 178.

73. Press Release, Aug. 27, 1975, Box 340, Targets Debates, Reuss Papers.

74. *New York Times*, Aug. 28, 1975, p. 52.

75. Joint Economic Committee, *1975 Economic Report of the President*, p. 484.

76. "Economic Policy Review," Mar. 24, 1975, Box 57, EPB: CIEC, Full Board Meeting, Seidman Files, Ford Library.

77. Senate Committee on Banking, Housing, and Urban Affairs, *First Meeting on the Conduct of Monetary Policy*, pp. 176–178.

78. U.S. Congress, Senate, Committee on the Budget, *Second Concurrent Resolution on the Budget—Fiscal Year 1976*, p. 139.

79. *New York Times*, May 2, 1975, pp. 1, 44; *Wall Street Journal*, May 2, 1975, p. 3.

80. Memo for the President from Alan Greenspan, May 2, 1975, Box B-20, Finance—Finance and Monetary Conditions Report (3), President's Handwriting File, Ford Library.

81. *New York Times*, June 5, 1975, p. 53.

82. Albert Ando, Lawrence R. Klein, R. A. Gordon, Franco Modigliani, Paul A. Samuelson, and James Tobin, To the Editor, *New York Times*, Feb. 26, 1975, p. 38.

83. House Ways and Means Committee, *President's Authority to Adjust Imports of Petroleum*, p. 852.

84. Arthur Burns to Gerald R. Ford, Mar. 28, 1975, Box 20, Finance—Taxation (3), Presidential Handwriting File, Ford Library.

85. Eckstein, *The Great Recession*, pp. 130–132.

86. *Business Week*, Aug. 11, 1975, p. 15.

87. Ibid., p. 16.

88. *New York Times*, July 14, 1975, pp. 37, 39.

89. Fritchey, "Reforming the Federal Reserve," p. A-23.

90. Gerald R. Ford, *Public Papers of the President, Gerald R. Ford, 1975*, vol. I, p. 555.

91. *New York Times*, July 14, 1975, pp. 37, 39.

92. House Committee on the Budget, *Second Concurrent Resolution on the Budget—Fiscal Year 1976*, p. 154.

93. U.S. Congress, House, Committee on Banking, Currency, and Housing, *Federal Reserve Consultations on the Conduct of Monetary Policy*, p. 94.

94. *Business Week*, Oct. 27, 1975, pp. 26–28.

95. U.S. Congress, House, Committee on Appropriations, *The Federal Budget for 1977*, p. 181.

96. U.S. Congress, Senate, Committee on Banking, Housing, and Urban Affairs, *Third Meeting on the Conduct of Monetary Policy*, p. 2.

97. Stanton interview.

98. Wooley, *Monetary Politics*, p. 148.

99. Jan Brenneman to Chairman Burns, Nov. 10, 1977, Box B-19, Congressional Liaison Memos, Nov. 1977, Burns Papers.

100. Memo from Bob Auerback to Paul Nelson, Sept. 23, 1977, House Banking Committee Files, 95th Full Committee Files, Staff Memos, 1977–78.

101. Ken G[uenther] to Chairman [Burns], Oct. 7, 1975, Box B-84, New York City Financial Difficulties, Oct.–Dec. 1975, Burns Papers.

102. House Committee on the Budget, *Second Concurrent Resolution on the Budget—Fiscal 1976*, pp. 140–141.

103. Burns, "The Real Issues of Inflation and Unemployment," in *Reflections*, p. 218.

104. *Midyear Review of the Economic Situation and Outlook—1975*, p. 141.

105. Burns, "Immediate and Long-Range Problems," in *Reflections*, p. 194.

106. Burns, "The Real Issues of Inflation and Unemployment," p. 219.

107. Burns, "Immediate and Long-Range Problems," pp. 193–194. Bureau of Labor Statistics data suggested that there was indeed an increase in absenteeism in the early 1970s that it could not account for, though the jump was not as large as Burns implied with this statement. Diane Sower to Joseph S. Zeisel, Jan. 23, 1975, Box B-77, Labor-General, Burns Papers.

108. Sometimes government regulations actually imposed inefficiency. Trucks, for instance, were often required to carry cargos only one way, forcing them to return empty and so wasting fuel and the time of the driver and vehicle.

109. Burns, "The Real Issues of Inflation and Unemployment," pp. 219–220.

110. Burns, "Immediate and Long-Range Problems," p. 193.

111. Ibid., pp. 195–196; House Ways and Means Committee, *President's Authority to Adjust Imports of Petroleum*, p. 871.

112. Greene, "Economists in Recession," p. 19.

113. Burns, "Immediate and Long-Range Problems," p. 193.

114. *Wall Street Journal*, Sept. 25, 1975, p. 3.

115. Ibid. Burns would pay for his plan, in part, by reducing unemployment insurance to thirteen weeks. It usually lasts twenty-six weeks, but because of the recession, Congress had extended the limit to sixty-five weeks. There was at the time a study of Massachusetts that suggested that high unemployment benefits were discouraging people from seeking new employment. James Annable to Chairman Burns, Feb. 20, 1976, Box B-113, Unemployment, Jan.–July 1976, Burns Papers. Studies available to the administration suggested that the extension of unemployment insurance to sixty-five weeks raised the jobless rate by as much as 1 percent. Paul W. MacAvoy and Barry Chiswick to William Seidman, Box 109, Unemployment-General (3), Seidman Files, Ford Library. Needless to say, the whole question generated much controversy.

116. U.S. Congress, Senate, Committee on Banking, Housing, and Urban Affairs, *Second Meeting on the Conduct of Monetary Policy*, p. 30.

117. Ibid.

118. *Washington Post*, Oct. 4, 1975, p. A-3.

119. House Committee on the Budget, *Second Concurrent Resolution on the Budget—Fiscal 1976*, pp. 158–159.

120. Hobart Rowen, "Economic Impact: Burns of the Fed," *Washington Post*, Oct. 5, 1975, p. A-15.

121. Ando, Klein, Gordon, Modigliani, Samuelson, and Tobin, To the Editor, *New York Times*, Feb. 26, 1975, p. 38. The full-employment budget sur-

plus measures what the budget surplus or deficit would be if the economy was at full employment. While a useful idea, the problem with it rests in the actual level of full employment, which is very difficult to determine at best.

122. Ralph W. Smith to Ted Truman, July 27, 1977, Box B-64, International Finance—General, May–July 1977, Burns Papers.

123. *Washington Post*, Feb. 4, 1975, p. D-6. The term "disorderly markets" is a code word signifying that governments mean to prop up a given currency. This is because the IMF's rules on such intervention ban such actions except when markets are "disorderly."

124. Solomon, *International Monetary System*, pp. 341–342; Ralph W. Smith to Ted Truman, July 27, 1977, Box B-64, International Finance—General, May–July 1977, Burns Papers.

125. Communiqué of the Ministerial Meeting of the Group of Ten, Jan. 14, 1975, Box B-55, G-10, Interim Committee Meetings, Washington, Jan. 14–16, 1975, Burns Papers; "Proposal for a New Financing Agreement," Dec. 3, 1974, Box B-53, Group of Ten Deputies, 1974–75, Burns Papers.

126. International Economic Outlook [5/20/75], Box 72, International Economic Policy Review, 1975 (1), Seidman Files.

127. Since the official price of gold was $42.22 an ounce, and the market price was in the vicinity of $150, governments could only sell gold, not buy it.

128. Current holding constituted the level of the ceiling.

129. Memo for the President from William Simon, Aug. 28, 1975, WHCF BE 5, Box 19, BE 5, 8/1/75–8/31/75, Ford Library.

130. U.S. Congress, House, Subcommittee on International Finance of the Committee on Banking and Currency, *To Delay Until July 1, 1975, the Date for Removing Restrictions on Private Ownership of Gold*, pp. 78–81. Burns's fear did not come to pass.

131. Memo for the President from Arthur Burns, Aug. 28, 1975, WHCF, BE 5, Box 19, BE 5, 8/1/75–8/31/75, Ford Library.

132. Memo for the President from William Simon, Aug. 28, 1975, WHCF BE 5, Box 19, BE 5, 8/1/75–8/31/75, Ford Library.

133. IMF Press Release, Aug. 31, 1975, Box B-71, IMF-IBRD Meeting, Washington, Sept. 1–5, 1975 (3), Burns Papers.

134. Gyohten, *Changing Fortunes*, pp. 126–127.

135. Attending the meeting were Britain, France, Italy, Japan, the United States, and West Germany. At the next summit, Canada joined the group.

136. In part, the European recovery came later because the recession there had started later, but it was also more sluggish, especially in the United Kingdom and Italy.

137. Memo of Conversation, Meeting of Economic Policy Board, Aug. 9, 1975, WHCF FG 6–30, Box 69, FG 6–30, 6/1/75–8/31/75, Ford Library.

138. Ibid.

139. "Economic Recovery and Cooperation: Fundamental Issues," [11/75], Presidential Handwriting File, Box 49, Trips-Foreign-Economic Summit-1975 (1), Ford Papers.

140. Ibid.; Memo of Conversation, Meeting of Economic Policy Board, Aug. 9, 1975, WHCF FG 6–30, Box 69, FG 6–30, 6/1/75–8/31/75, Ford Library.

141. Ibid.

142. *New York Times*, Oct. 5, 1975, p. 53.

143. "Economic Recovery and Cooperation: Fundamental Issues," [11/75], Presidential Handwriting File, Box 49, Trips-Foreign-Economic Summit-1975 (1), Ford Papers.

144. Memo from William Simon to the President, [8/29/75], Presidential Handwriting File, Box 5, Business and Economics, National Economy, 6/75–8/75, Ford Library.

145. *New York Times*, July 30, 1975, p. 38.

146. Gerald R. Ford, *A Time to Heal*, p. 316.

147. U.S. Congress, Joint Economic Committee, *New York City's Economic Crisis*, p. 142.

148. Ibid., p. 149.

149. U.S. Congress, House, Subcommittee on Economic Stabilization of the Committee on Banking, Currency, and Housing, *Debt Financing Problems of State and Local Government: The New York City Case*, pp. 1656–1657.

150. Ralph W. Smith to John E. Reynolds, Nov. 10, 1975, Box B-84, NYC Financial Difficulties, Oct.–Dec. 1975, Burns Papers. The U.S. system of federalism is poorly understood abroad, and apparently many foreigners thought that financial instability in the nation's largest city reflected similar problems at the federal level.

151. *New York Times*, Jan. 11, 1976, pp. 1, 42.

152. Ibid., Oct. 5, 1975, p. 53.

153. Ibid., Oct. 3, 1975, pp. 1, 14.

154. *Debt Financing and the Problems of State and Local Governments*, pp. 1655, 1661.

155. *Wall Street Journal*, Nov. 12, 1975, p. 4.

156. *Second Meeting on the Conduct of Monetary Policy*, p. 17.

157. Minutes of the EPB Executive Committee Meeting, Nov. 14, 1975, CEA Records, DNA-RG 459, Box 59, EPB-Nov. 1975, Ford Library.

8. Monetary Caesar

1. *Forbes*, July 1, 1976; *New York Times*, Apr. 30, 1976, p. D-2.

2. *Wall Street Journal*, May 2, 1977, p. 1.

3. Throughout 1975 and 1976, the Gallup poll indicated that the public considered the "high cost of living" the nation's chief problem—even during the depth of the recession. *Gallup Opinion Index* 118 (Apr. 1975):2; 122 (Aug. 1975):19; 125 (Nov./Dec. 1975):93; 127 (Feb. 1976):3; 131 (June 1976):29; 137 (Dec. 1976):29.

4. Hobart Rowen, "The Coming Problem of Inflation," *Washington Post*, May 13, 1976, p. A-23.

5. Nicholas von Hoffman, "Secrets at the Fed," p. 48.

6. *Wall Street Journal*, Jan. 12, 1976, pp. 1, 11.

7. Burns, "The Independence of the Federal Reserve System," in *Reflections*, p. 382.

8. Ibid., p. 383. The Occupation authorities had modeled the postwar German Bundesbank on the Fed.

9. Burns, "The Importance of an Independent Central Bank," in *Reflections*, p. 421.

10. Kettl, *Leadership at the Fed*, pp. 153, 159. The FOIA allows the public to view records for which no compelling reason for privacy exists.

11. Ibid.

12. Burns, "The Proper Limit of Openness in Government," in *Reflections*, pp. 392–393.

13. U.S. Congress, House, Committee on Banking, Currency, and Housing, *Federal Reserve Consultations on the Conduct of Monetary Policy*, pp. 16–19; Kettl, *Leadership at the Fed*, p. 153.

14. Burns, "The Proper Limits of Openness in Government," p. 394.

15. U.S. Congress, House, Subcommittee of the Committee on Government Operations, *Government in the Sunshine*, p. 148.

16. Arthur Burns to Abraham Ribicoff, June 17, 1975, Box B-53, Government in the Sunshine, June 1975, Burns Papers.

17. Burns, "The Proper Limits of Openness in Government," pp. 394–395.

18. House Subcommittee of the Committee on Government Operations, *Government in the Sunshine*, pp. 133–135.

19. Arthur Burns to Abraham Ribicoff, June 17, 1975, Box B-53, Government in the Sunshine, June 1975, Burns Papers.

20. Burns, "The Proper Limits of Openness in Government," p. 394.

21. Don Winn to Chairman Burns, May 21, 1975, B-52, Government in the Sunshine, May 1975, Burns Papers.

22. Burns, "The Proper Limits of Openness in Government," p. 394.

23. *New York Times*, Dec. 14, 1975, sec. III, p. 15.

24. Burns, "The Proper Limits of Openness in Government," p. 394.

25. *New York Times*, Dec. 14, 1975, sec. III, p. 15.

26. L. William Seidman to Arthur Burns, Dec. 12, 1975, WHCF FG 131, 4/1/75–12/31/75, Ford Library.

27. Ken Guenther to Arthur Burns, July 29, 1976; [July 30, 1976]; July 30, 1976; [Aug. 1976]; Aug. 2, 1976; Aug. 5, 1976; Box B-53, Government in the Sunshine, June–Aug. 1976, Burns Papers.

28. *Washington Post*, Feb. 9, 1976, p. A-3.

29. Ibid.

30. Ibid.

31. *New York Times*, Jan. 22, 1976, p. 59.

32. Ibid., Mar. 26, 1976, pp. 47, 55; *Washington Post*, Feb. 9, 1976, p. A-3.

33. Federal Reserve Press Release, May 6, 1976, Box B-51, GAO Audit, Jan.–May 1976, Burns Papers.

34. *Wall Street Journal*, Oct. 22, 1974, p. 3.

35. Ibid., Apr. 26, 1976, pp. 1, 17. The Fed's advice was sound. First Pennsylvania failed in 1980, and the FDIC had to put $325 million into the bank to save it.

36. Memo from Paul Metzger to Chase, Doyle et al., Aug. 14, 1974, Box B-7, Bank Regulatory Reform, Aug.–Sept. 1974, Burns Papers.

37. Other regulatory agencies might not agree with the Fed's assessment of their relative efficiency.

38. *Wall Street Journal*, Dec. 18, 1975, p. 15.

39. Burns, "Vital Issues of Banking Legislation," in *Reflections*, pp. 229–236. Large banks with operations spread out over a considerable area and serving customers with sizable deposits really needed the services that the Fed could provide, such as money transfers and discount window borrowing. Smaller institutions had less call for these.

40. *New York Times*, Mar. 19, 1976, p. 56.

41. U.S. Congress, House, Subcommittee on Financial Institutions Supervision, Regulations, and Insurance of the Committee on Banking, Currency, and Housing, *The Financial Reform Act of 1976*, p. 890.

42. Memo from the Chairman, FRB, to the Chairman, CEA, Mar. 8, 1976, Council of Economic Advisers Records, Box 9, Federal Reserve Board—General, Ford Library.

43. U.S. Congress, Senate, Committee on Banking, Housing, and Urban Affairs, *First Meeting on the Conditions of the Banking System* p. 124.

44. With the benefit of hindsight, the wisdom of this reform is less clear. Savings and loans got the power to make a wider variety of loans in the early 1980s, and few capitalized effectively on the new opportunities. Most made atrocious investments that accounted for the savings-and-loan debacle of the late 1980s.

45. Henry Reuss, "A Private Club for Public Policy," pp. 370–372; *Washington Post*, Aug. 15, 1976, pp. A-1, A-18.

46. John T. Woolley, "Central Banks and Inflation," in Lindberg and Maier, *The Politics of Inflation and Economic Stagnation*, p. 319.

47. Arthur Burns to Gerald Ford, Mar. 18, 1976, WHCF, FG 131, 1/1/76–1/20/77, Ford Library.

48. "Legislation Bearing on the Fed's Independence," [c.10/77], Box B-51, GAO Audit, July–Oct. 1977, Burns Papers.

49. U.S. Congress, House, Committee on Banking, Currency, and Housing, *To Promote the Independence and Responsibility of the Federal Reserve System*, p. 24.

50. *Washington Post*, Aug. 31, 1976, p. C-9.

51. House Subcommittee on Financial Institutions Supervision, Regulations, and Insurance, *The Financial Reform Act of 1976*, p. 944.

52. Ibid.

53. Chairman of the FRB to Chairman of the CEA, Mar. 8, 1976, Box B-24, CEA 1975–76, Burns Papers; William Simon to Henry Reuss [Mar. 1976], Box B-102, Treasury Department, Jan.–June 1976, Burns Papers.

54. Reuss interview. By the time left the Fed, Reuss believes that the composition of the regional boards was showing signs of significant change.

55. *Wall Street Journal*, Apr. 28, 1976, p. 14.

56. *Forbes*, July 1, 1976, pp. 57–58.

57. "Legislation Bearing on the Fed's Independence," [c.10/77], Box B-51, GAO Audit, July–Oct. 1977, Burns Papers.

58. Ken Guenther to Board of Governors, July 30, 1976, Box B-43, Federal Reserve Reform Act (1), Burns Papers; *Wall Street Journal*, Aug. 2, 1976, p. 2. Prior to this time, Fed governors had to get Senate approval, but the president selected one of these governors as chairman without having to go through the upper house.

59. *New York Times*, June 22, 1976, p. 51.

60. *Federal Reserve Bulletin* 62 (July 1976):581–591. The British rescue served as a prototype for many of the operations mounted to save Third World debtors in the 1980s.

61. Joint Economic Committee, *Financial and Capacity Needs*, p. 211.

62. Jackson interview.

63. *Washington Post*, Apr. 4, 1976, pp. A-1, A-18; Chernow, *The House of Morgan*, p. 609.

64. *Washington Post*, Apr. 4, 1976, pp. A-1, A-18.

65. *Wall Street Journal*, Mar. 12, 1976, p. 14.

66. Ibid., Jan. 19, 1976, p. 3.

67. *New York Times*, May 4, 1976, pp. 55, 59.

68. Ibid., May 11, 1976, p. 48.

69. Ibid., Nov. 5, 1975, pp. 63, 69; *Federal Reserve Bulletin* 62 (Dec. 1976):1019–1034. The targets for M2 and M3 came down as well, although not as much. In early 1975 the targets for M2 and M3 were 8.5 to 10.5 percent and 9 to 12 percent, respectively. By the end of 1976 these were 7.5 to 10 percent for M2 and 9 to 11.5 percent for M3.

70. James Tobin, "Monetary Policy, Inflation, and Unemployment," in *Essays in Economics: Theory and Policy*, pp. 30–31.

71. Ibid., p. 19.

72. *New York Times*, May 26, 1976, p. 53.

73. Ibid., May 12, 1976, p. 59.

74. Ibid., June 13, 1976, sec. III, p. 15.

75. Ibid., May 21, 1976, p. D-8.

76. House Committee on Banking, Currency, and Housing, *Federal Reserve Consultations on the Conduct of Monetary Policy*, p. 25.

77. U.S. Congress, House, Committee on Banking, Finance, and Urban Affairs, *Conduct of Monetary Policy*, p. 95.

78. *New York Times*, Feb. 7, 1976, sec. III, p. 15.

79. Burns, "The Importance of an Independent Central Bank," p. 418.

80. "Legislation Bearing on the Fed's Independence," [c.10/77], Box B-51, GAO Audit, July–Oct. 1977, Burns Papers.

81. U.S. Congress, Joint Economic Committee, *The Thirtieth Anniversary*

of the Employment Act of 1946—A National Conference on Full Employment, p. 205.

82. Reichley, Conservatives in an Age of Change, p. 398.

83. Wall Street Journal, July 1, 1976, p. 3.

84. Ibid., Jan. 12, 1976, pp. 1, 11.

85. New York Times, Dec. 11, 1975, p. 79.

86. Reichley, Conservatives in an Age of Change, pp. 402–403.

87. Census, Statistical Abstract of the U.S.: 1977, p. 388.

88. Washington Post, Dec. 24, 1975, pp. C-4, C-5.

89. Newsweek, June 7, 1976, p. 67.

9. Changes at the Top

1. Carter on Monetary Policy, [Sept. 1976], Staff Secretary Special Files, First Debate: Carter on Economic Issues, Ford Library.

2. New York Times, Nov. 24, 1976, pp. 1, 14.

3. Wall Street Journal, Nov. 12, 1976, p. 3.

4. New York Times, Nov. 19, 1976, pp. C-1, D-11.

5. Ibid., Nov. 16, 1976, pp. 1, 32–33.

6. W. M. Blumenthal to Burns, Dec. 22, 1976, Box 103, Treasury Dept., Dec. 1976, Burns Papers; Hargrove and Morley, eds., The President and the CEA, pp. 482–483; interview with Stuart Eizenstat, July 16, 1993.

7. Jimmy Carter, Public Papers of the Presidents of the United States: Jimmy Carter, 1977, pp. 47–55, 201.

8. Wall Street Journal, Feb. 4, 1977, p. 3.

9. U.S. Congress, Senate, Committee on the Budget, First Concurrent Resolution on the Budget—Fiscal Year 1978, p. 214.

10. Wall Street Journal, Feb. 4, 1977, p. 3.

11. House Committee on Banking, Finance, and Urban Affairs, Conduct of Monetary Policy, p. 119.

12. Wall Street Journal, Dec. 16, 1977, pp. 1, 22.

13. Ibid., July 7, 1977, pp. 1, 17.

14. Burns, "The Need for Better Profits," in Reflections, p. 42.

15. Larry Slifman to Milton Hudson, Nov. 22, 1977, Box B-12, Capital Spending (2), Burns Papers.

16. Burns, "The Need for Better Profits," p. 41. Burns estimated that the return after inflation on stockholders' equity in the 1950s and 1960s was 5.5 percent, compared with 3.5 percent after 1970.

17. Ibid., pp. 41–46. Burns calculated that profit margins, adjusted for inflation, were about 5.5 percent in the 1950s and 1960s, compared to 3.5 percent in the 1970s. For a fuller examination of Burns's thoughts on the effect of inflation on profits, see chapter 7.

18. Ibid., p. 46.

19. House Committee on Banking, Finance, and Urban Affairs, Conduct of Monetary Policy, p. 127.

20. Memo for Vice-President Mondale from Charlie Schultze, Jan. 19, 1977, Eizenstat Files, Box 144, Anti-Inflation [6], Carter Library.

21. Memo from Stu Eizenstat to the President, Oct. 27, 1977, Eizenstat Files, Box 261, Press Conferences, 8/77–10/77, Carter Library.

22. Leonard Silk, "Fed vs. White House; Uneasy Peace So Far," *New York Times*, Feb. 7, 1977, p. 35.

23. Dana Johnson to Milton Hudson, Nov. 17, 1977, Box B-12, Capital Spending (2), Burns Papers. The industries reported on were primary metals; stone, clay, and glass; textiles; paper; chemicals; and petroleum.

24. Burns, "The Need for Better Profits," p. 47.

25. President from Charlie Schultze, May 20, 1977, WHCF, Box FG-76, FG 6.3, 1/20/77–5/31/77, Carter Library.

26. Hargrove and Morley, eds., *The President and the CEA*, p. 478.

27. *Wall Street Journal*, July 7, 1977, pp. 1, 17.

28. *New York Times*, June 15, 1977, p. 29.

29. Blumenthal to the President, c.Dec. 20, 1977, Anthony M. Solomon Collection, Chronological File, 12/77, Carter Library.

30. Memo for the President from Michael Blumenthal, Aug. 9, 1977, Solomon Papers, Box 2, 8/1/77–8/15/77, Carter Library.

31. Memo for the President from Stu Eizenstat, Nov. 29, 1977, Eizenstat Files, Box 261, Press Conference, 10/77–12/77, Carter Library.

32. Burns, "Some Parting Thoughts," in *Reflections*, p. 257.

33. U.S. Congress, Senate, Committee on Banking, Housing, and Urban Affairs, *First Meeting on the Conduct of Monetary Policy (1977)*, pp. 49–50; *New Republic*, Dec. 3, 1977, pp. 8–9.

34. Burns, "Some Parting Thoughts," pp. 257–259; Truman interview. If Washington had significant liabilities in foreign currencies, it would presumably be more reluctant to see the dollar depreciate, since this would increase the size, in dollars, of these liabilities. The Carter administration eventually issued foreign currency bonds after Burns left the Fed.

35. *Wall Street Journal*, Aug. 1, 1977, p. 12.

36. Anthony M. Solomon to Arthur Burns, Dec. 28, 1977, Anthony M. Solomon Collection, Chronological File, 12/77, Carter Library; *New York Times*, Dec. 10, 1977, pp. 31, 33. Since IMF rules permit intervention in currency markets only when they are "disorderly," the word was stretched to cover a variety of meanings. The Carter administration considered a "disorderly" market one that showed signs of panic, whereas Burns and most officials in the other industrialized democracies defined a disorderly market as one whose outcome did not, they thought, reflect underlying economic realities.

37. Burns, "The Need for Order in International Finance," in *Reflections*, p. 459.

38. Truman interview.

39. Burns, "The Need for Order in International Finance," p. 463.

40. Ibid., p. 459.

41. Henry S. Terrell, "U.S. Bank Lending to Less Developed Countries," Nov. 9, 1976, Box B-64, International Finance-General, Nov. 1976, Burns Papers.

42. Burns, "The Need for Order in International Finance," p. 460.

43. U.S. Congress, Joint Economic Committee, *The 1977 Economic Report of the President*, pp. 415–418.

44. Memo for the President from Michael Blumenthal, Aug. 9, 1977, Solomon Papers, Box 2, 8/1/77–8/15/77, Carter Library.

45. Henry Reuss and Stephen Neal to Jimmy Carter, Feb. 3, 1978, WHCF, Box IT-4, IT 44, 1/20/77–1/20/81, Carter Library.

46. Volcker, *Changing Fortunes*, p. 195.

47. Ibid., pp. 196–197.

48. *Wall Street Journal*, May 25, 1977, p. 34.

49. U.S. Congress, House, Committee on Banking, Finance, and Urban Affairs, *Federal Reserve Reform Act of 1977*, p. 60.

50. The Fed conducts monetary policy chiefly by buying and selling government obligations in financial markets.

51. House Subcommittee on Domestic Monetary Policy, *Maintaining and Making Public Minutes at Federal Reserve Meetings*, p. 68.

52. Ibid.

53. W. Michael Blumenthal to Henry Reuss, July 26, 1977, Box B-103, Treasury Department, July–Aug. 1977, Burns Papers. As one might expect, Blumenthal endorsed only linking the term of the Fed chairman to that of the president because this would increase the White House's hold over the central bank.

54. *New York Times*, July 29, 1977, sec. IV, p. 7; Nov. 17, 1977, p. 22.

55. Ralph Nader to Henry Reuss, Aug. 5, 1977, House Banking Committee Files, PL 95–109 to PL 95–229, HR 7646, Federal Reserve Reform Act, Correspondence.

56. Wooley, "Central Banks and Inflation," pp. 334–340.

57. *Federal Reserve Bulletin* 64 (1978):290–305. The target for M2 went from 8.5–10.5 percent to 6.5–9 percent, and for M3 from 9–11.5 percent to 7.5–10 percent.

58. Ibid., 63 (1977):655–665.

59. *Wall Street Journal*, June 2, 1977, p. 3.

60. Ibid., Aug. 15, 1977, p. 20.

61. Burns, "The Need for Better Profits," p. 50.

62. Memo for the President from Charlie Schultze, Sept. 28, 1977, Charles L. Schultze Papers, Brookings Institution Library, Washington, D.C.

63. Memo for the President from Charlie Schultze, Oct. 12, 1977, WHCF, Box BE-12, BE 4, 10/1/77–10/31/77, Carter Library; Memo for the President from Charlie Schultze, Presidential Diaries, Box PD-19, Backup Material, 11/10/77, Carter Library.

64. Memo for the President from Lyle E. Gramley, Aug. 11, 1977, Eizenstat Files, Box 150, Banking, International, Carter Library.

65. Memo for the President from Charlie Schultze, Sept. 28, 1977, Charles L. Schultze Papers, Brookings Institution Library.

66. House Subcommittee on Domestic Monetary Policy, *Maintaining and Making Public Minutes at Federal Reserve Meetings*, pp. 28–29.

67. Burns, "The Need for Better Profits," p. 47.

68. Carter, *Public Papers 1977*, pp. 909–910.

69. U.S. Congress, House, Committee on Appropriations, *The Federal Budget for 1975*, p. 303.

70. House Committee on Banking, Finance, and Urban Affairs, *Conduct of Monetary Policy*, pp. 129–130.

71. Arthur Burns to Jimmy Carter, Sept. 19, 1977, Eizenstat Files, Box 288, Tax Reform, (9/77) [1], Carter Library.

72. *New York Times*, Aug. 2, 1977, p. 41.

73. U.S. Congress, House, Committee on the Budget, *Fiscal Year 1978 Budget*, p. 122.

74. Ibid., p. 132.

75. Memo for the President from Arthur F. Burns, Mar. 31, 1977, Eizenstat Files, Box 144, Anti-Inflation [7], Carter Library.

76. These became almost an annual ritual in the Carter administration. Every spring it would begin to worry about inflation and introduce a new anti-inflation package centering on fiscal restraint, and every fall it would begin to fear recession and devise a more stimulative policy.

77. Jimmy Carter, *Public Papers of the Presidents of the United States, Jimmy Carter, 1978*, pp. 158–176.

78. Cutting tax rates by 2 percentage points meant a 14 percent reduction in levies for someone in the lowest tax bracket, which was 14 percent, but only a 2.8 percent reduction to someone in the highest bracket, which was 70 percent.

79. The jump was about 0.2 percentage points from the year's low.

80. Walter Heller, "Monetary Policy at the Crossroads," *Wall Street Journal*, Oct. 14, 1977, p. 24.

81. Senate Committee on Banking, Housing, and Urban Affairs, *First Meeting on the Conduct of Monetary Policy (1977)*, pp. 31–40; *Wall Street Journal*, Nov. 10, 1977, p. 3.

82. Notice to the Press, Oct. 20, 1977, Box 117, White House, 1977, Burns Papers.

83. *Wall Street Journal*, Oct. 21, 1977, p. 2.

84. *Washington Post*, Oct. 23, 1977, p. F-3.

85. Ibid., Nov. 12, 1977, p. A-2.

86. Carter, *Public Papers 1977*, p. 2011.

87. *Wall Street Journal*, Nov. 10, 1977, p. 3.

88. Ibid., Nov. 30, 1977, p. 4.

89. Hobart Rowen, "Burns and the Fed: President's Options," *Washington Post*, June 26, 1977, pp. 11, 12.

90. *Wall Street Journal*, Dec. 16, 1977, pp. 1, 22.

91. Rowland Evans and Robert Novak, "Burns: On the Way Out?" *Washington Post*, Sept. 22, 1977, p. A-21.

92. *Chicago Tribune*, Nov. 3, 1977, sec. III, p. 2.

93. Edward W. Brooke, Charles McC. Mathias, Jr., Howard H. Baker, Jr., John Tower, Abraham Ribicoff, Clifford P. Case, John Sparkman, Jennings Randolph, and Russell Long to Jimmy Carter, Oct. 25, 1977, Name File, Arthur F. Burns, Federal Reserve Board (B), Carter Library; John Sparkman and Jacob K. Javits, To the Editor, *Wall Street Journal*, Dec. 22, 1977, p. 8.

94. *Washington Post*, Nov. 5, 1977, p. A-5. The Tampa Bay Buccaneers were in the midst of the worst losing streak in National Football League history.

95. Lester C. Thurow, "Carter, the Fed, and 'Confidence,' " *The Nation* 225 (Sept. 3, 1977):166–168.

96. Paul Samuelson, "Reappoint Burns?" *Newsweek*, Nov. 21, 1977, p. 81.

97. Ibid.

98. Eizenstat interview.

99. Gramley interview.

100. *New Republic*, Dec. 3, 1977, pp. 8–9.

101. *Los Angeles Times*, Dec. 7, 1977, sec. II, p. 6.

102. Gramley interview.

103. Erwin C. Hargrove, *Jimmy Carter as President: Leadership and the Politics of the Public Good*, p. 93.

104. *Washington Post*, Nov. 1, 1977, pp. D-7, D-8.

105. Memo for Mike Blumenthal from Charlie Schultze, Nov. 9, 1977, Eizenstat Files, Box 144, Anti-Inflation (5), Carter Library.

106. Hobart Rowen, "Carter Faces Dilemma Over Arthur Burns," *Washington Post*, Dec. 25, 1977, pp. E-1, E-3.

107. Brimmer interview.

108. Carter, *Public Papers 1978*, pp. 354–355.

109. Ibid. Asked how William G. Miller, who he appointed as Fed chairman, represented an improvement on his predecessor, Carter said, "I think that Miller will be much more inclined to at least consult with me and the Congress, perhaps, than Chairman Burns."

110. Carter, *Public Papers 1977*, p. 2058.

111. *New York Times*, Dec. 30, 1977, pp. A-1, D-1, D-3.

112. Carter, *Public Papers 1977*, pp. 2183–2185.

113. *New York Times*, Jan. 14, 1978, pp. 27, 29. All of the governors served fourteen-year terms, and the chairman was appointed from among them for a four-year term. Carter could choose a new chairman from outside the board because the term of one governor, David Lilly, ended in January 1978.

114. When President Harry S. Truman did not reappoint Marriner Eccles in 1948, Eccles stayed on the board, wrecking the policies of his successor, with whom he strongly disagreed.

115. *Business Week*, Jan. 16, 1978, pp. 28–29.

116. *Federal Reserve Bulletin* 64 (1978):195–210. The previous example was in 1971.

117. *New York Times*, Mar. 29, 1978, pp. D-1, D-10.

118. Burns, "Some Parting Thoughts," p. 255.

119. *New York Times*, Mar. 29, 1978, pp. D-1, D-10.
120. Ibid., Feb. 1, 1978, p. D-8.
121. Burns, "Some Parting Thoughts," p. 254.

10. Careers New and Old

1. He never completed the book on inflation.
2. John B. Goodman, *Monetary Sovereignty: The Politics of Central Banking in Western Europe*, p. 83.
3. Jackson interview.
4. Stephen E. Ambrose, *Nixon: Ruin and Recovery, 1973–1990*, p. 539.
5. Burns, *The Anguish of Central Banking*, pp. 15–16.
6. Hargrove and Morley, eds., *The President and the CEA*, p. 461.
7. Ibid., p. 479.
8. *Gallup Opinion Index*, Apr.–May 1980, p. 25. This was during the Iranian hostage crisis.
9. Arthur Okun, "Postwar Macroeconomics: The Evolution of Events and Ideas," in Martin Feldstein, ed., *The American Economy in Transition*, p. 168.
10. *New York Times*, Nov. 18, 1979, pp. D-1, D-15; Sept. 20, 1980, p. D-2.
11. Ibid., Mar. 28, 1980, p. D-2.
12. Arthur F. Burns et al., *Can We Avert Disaster?*, p. 4.
13. *New York Times*, June 29, 1980, p. D-2.
14. Volcker, *Changing Fortunes*, p. 174.
15. *New York Times*, Jan. 22, 1981, pp. D-1, D-10.
16. Jackson interview.
17. Arthur Burns, *The United States and Germany: A Vital Partnership*, pp. xi–xii.
18. Ibid., p. 2.
19. Hans N. Tuch, "Arthur Burns and the Successor Generation: Introduction and Appreciation," in Han N. Tuch, ed., *Arthur Burns and the Successor Generation: Selected Writings of and About Arthur Burns*, p. 2.
20. Burns, *United States and Germany*, p. 5.
21. Ibid., p. 6.
22. Arthur Burns, "How America Looks at Europe," in Tuch, ed., *Arthur Burns and the Successor Generation*, p. 17.
23. Ibid., p. 8.
24. Ibid., p. 13.
25. Ibid., p. 14.
26. Stephan-Goetz Richter, "Arthur Burns and the Germans," in Tuch, ed., *Arthur Burns and the Successor Generation*, pp. 50–52.
27. Ibid., p. 46.
28. Burns, "How America Looks at Europe," pp. 17–18.
29. Burns, *United States and Germany*, p. 48.
30. Ibid.
31. Arthur Burns, *The Ongoing Revolution in American Banking*.
32. These were, in order, Milton Friedman, Pete V. Domenici, George Shultz, Paul Volcker, Gerald Ford, and Richard Nixon.

11. Conclusion

1. *Wall Street Journal*, Dec. 2, 1991, p. 1.

2. Arthur Burns, "Concluding Comments," in Feldstein, ed., *The American Economy in Transition*, p. 676.

3. Ibid.

4. Edwin Mansfield, "Technology and Productivity in the United States," in Feldstein, ed., *The American Economy in Transition*, pp. 564–568.

5. Richard E. Caves, "The Structure of Industry," in Feldstein, ed., *The American Economy in Transition*, pp. 539–544.

6. In the postwar period, productivity grew about 3 percent a year, whereas after 1973 the increase was less than 1 percent.

7. David Halberstam, *The Reckoning*, pp. 489–491.

8. Richard B. Freeman, "The Evolution of the American Labor Market, 1948–80," in Feldstein, ed., *The American Economy in Transition*, p. 353.

9. R. A. Gordon, "Postwar Macroeconomics: The Evolution of Events and Ideas," in Feldstein, ed., *The American Economy in Transition*, p. 156.

10. See chapter 7.

11. *New York Times*, June 27, 1987, pp. 1, 13.

12. Volcker, *In Memoriam*, pp. 17–18.

13. *New York Times*, June 27, 1987, pp. 1, 13.

14. As Burns left the Fed, the Carter administration was preparing to abandon its laissez-faire stance toward the dollar, and in 1978 it and the other industrial democracies would spend billions propping up the greenback.

15. William Greider, *Secrets of the Temple: How the Federal Reserve Runs the Country*, pp. 341–342.

16. *National Review*, July 31, 1987, p. 18.

17. The only times Burns did this were in the late spring of 1971 and early in 1978. In neither case did the action do much good.

18. Volcker, *In Memoriam*, p. 16.

19. This was the case until 1985. The board included Paul Volcker; Henry Wallich and Charles Partee, who owed their appointments to Burns's intervention with Presidents Nixon and Ford, respectively; and Lyle Gramley, who had been Burns's speechwriter at the central bank.

20. Volcker, *In Memoriam*, p. 16.

21. Actually, Taft's views on economics were more subtle than this characterization suggests, but the many people who looked to him for leadership *were* supporters of a rather primitive laissez-faire doctrine.

22. Robert Skidelsky, *John Maynard Keynes: Vol. 2, The Economist as Saviour, 1920–1937*, pp. 229–231, 257–269.

23. Anderson, *Revolution*, p. 143.

24. Between 1973 and 1982, productivity growth averaged less than 1 percent a year. After 1982 the average was a little over 1 percent.

Bibliography

Primary Sources

Bentley Library, University of Michigan, Ann Arbor.
   Paul McCracken Papers
Gerald R. Ford Presidential Library, Ann Arbor, Michigan
   Arthur F. Burns Papers
   James E. Connor File
   Records of the Council of Economic Advisers
   President's Handwriting File
   Seidman Files
   Staff Secretary Special Files
   White House Central Files
House Banking Committee Files, Washington, D.C.
Jimmy Carter Presidential Library, Atlanta, Georgia
   Name File
   Stuart Eizenstat Files
   Presidential Diaries

Anthony M. Solomon Collection
White House Central Files
Dwight D. Eisenhower Presidential Library, Abilene, Kansas
Arthur F. Burns Papers
Whitman Files, Dwight D. Eisenhower Diaries
Whitman Files, Whitman Diaries
Papers of the Federal Reserve System. Part 2: Minutes of the Federal
Open Market Committee, 1923–75, Frederick, Maryland: University
Publications of America.
Fromkin Memorial Collection, University of Wisconsin. Milwaukee.
Henry Reuss Papers
Lyndon B. Johnson Presidential Library, Austin, Texas
Wright Patman Papers
Richard M. Nixon Presidential Papers Project, Alexandria, Virginia
John D. Ehrlichman Files
H. R. Haldeman Files
Paul McCracken Files
White House Central Files
White House Special Files
Vanderbilt University Special Collections, Nashville, Tennessee
J. Dewey Daane Papers
W. S. Hoole Special Collections, University of Alabama, Tuscaloosa
John Sparkman Papers

INTERVIEWS

Conducted by the author:
Stephen Axilrod
Andrew Brimmer
Ralph Bryant
Helen Burns
Joe Coyne
J. Dewey Daane
John Ehrlichman
Stuart Eizenstat
Lyle Gramley
Robert Holland
Philip Jackson
Henry Reuss
Robert Solomon
J. William Stanton
Herbert Stein
Edwin Truman

Conducted by the Oral History Collection, Lyndon B. Johnson Presidential Library, Austin, Texas:
Wright Patman

Conducted by the Southern Oral History Program, Southern History
Collection, Wilson Library, University of North Carolina, Chapel Hill:
Edward Bernstein

PERIODICALS

Federal Reserve Bulletin
New York Times
Wall Street Journal
Washington Post

PRINTED SOURCES

Adams, Sherman. *Firsthand Report: The Story of the Eisenhower Adminis-
tration.* New York: Harper and Brothers, 1961.
Burns, Arthur F. *The Anguish of Central Banking.* Washington, D.C.: Inter-
national Monetary Fund, 1979.
——. *The Business Cycle in a Changing World.* New York: Columbia Univer-
sity Press, 1969.
——. et al. *Can We Avert Disaster?* Washington, D.C.: American Enterprise
Institute, 1980.
——. *The Frontiers of Economic Knowledge.* Princeton: Princeton University
Press, 1954.
——. *The Ongoing Revolution in American Banking.* Washington, D.C.:
American Enterprise Institute for Public Policy Research, 1988.
——. *Production Trends in the United States since 1870.* New York: Bureau
of Economic Research, 1934.
——. *Reflections of an Economic Policymaker: Speeches and Congressional
Statements, 1969–1978.* Washington, D.C.: American Enterprise Institute
for Policy Research, 1978.
——. *The United States and Germany: A Vital Partnership.* New York: Coun-
cil on Foreign Relations, 1986.
——, ed. *Wesley Clair Mitchell: The Economic Scientist.* New York: Nation-
al Bureau of Economic Research, 1951.
Carter, Jimmy. *Public Papers of the Presidents of the United States: Jimmy
Carter, 1977.* Vol. I. Washington, D.C.: U.S. Government Printing Office,
1977.
——. *Public Papers of the Presidents of the United States: Jimmy Carter,
1977.* Vol. II. Washington, D.C.: U.S. Government Printing Office, 1978.
——. *Public Papers of the Presidents of the United States: Jimmy Carter,
1978.* Vol. I. Washington, D.C.: U.S. Government Printing Office, 1979.
——. *Public Papers of the Presidents of the United States: Jimmy Carter,
1978.* Vol. II. Washington, D.C.: U.S. Government Printing Office, 1979.
Ehrlichman, John. *Witness to Power: The Nixon Years.* New York: Simon
and Schuster, 1982.
Eisenhower, Dwight D. *Mandate for Change, 1953–56.* Garden City, N.Y.:
Doubleday, 1963.

——. *Waging Peace: 1956–61*. Garden City, N.Y.: Doubleday, 1965.

Ford, Gerald R. *Public Papers of the Presidents of the United States, Gerald R. Ford, 1974*. Washington, D.C.: U.S. Government Printing Office, 1975.

——. *Public Papers of the Presidents of the United States, Gerald R. Ford, 1975*. Vol. I. Washington, D.C.: U.S. Government Printing Office, 1977.

——. *Public Papers of the Presidents of the United States, Gerald R. Ford, 1975*. Vol. II. Washington, D.C.: U.S. Government Printing Office, 1977.

——. *Public Papers of the Presidents of the United States, Gerald R. Ford, 1976*. Vol. I. Washington, D.C.: U.S. Government Printing Office, 1979.

——. *Public Papers of the Presidents of the United States, Gerald R. Ford, 1976*. Vol. II. Washington, D.C.: U.S. Government Printing Office, 1979.

——. *Public Papers of the Presidents of the United States, Gerald R. Ford, 1976*. Vol. III. Washington, D.C.: U.S. Government Printing Office, 1979.

——. *A Time to Heal*. New York: Harper and Row, 1979.

Hargrove, Erwin C., and Samuel A. Morley, eds. *The President and the Council of Economic Advisers: Interviews with CEA Chairmen*. Boulder and London: Westview Press, 1984.

Kissinger, Henry. *White House Years*. Boston: Little, Brown, 1979.

——. *Years of Upheaval*. Boston: Little, Brown, 1982.

Mitchell, Wesley Clair. *Business Cycles*. Berkeley: University of California Press, 1913.

——, and Arthur F. Burns. *Measuring Business Cycles*. New York: Columbia University Press, 1946.

Nixon, Richard M. *Public Papers of the Presidents of the United States, Richard Nixon, 1969*. Washington, D.C.: U.S. Government Printing Office, 1971.

——. *Public Papers of the Presidents of the United States, Richard Nixon, 1970*. Washington, D.C.: U.S. Government Printing Office, 1971.

——. *Public Papers of the Presidents of the United States, Richard Nixon, 1971*. Washington, D.C.: U.S. Government Printing Office, 1972.

——. *Public Papers of the Presidents of the United States, Richard Nixon, 1972*. Washington, D.C.: U.S. Government Printing Office, 1974.

——. *Public Papers of the Presidents of the United States, Richard Nixon, 1973*. Washington, D.C.: U.S. Government Printing Office, 1975.

——. *Public Papers of the Presidents of the United States, Richard Nixon, 1974*. Washington, D.C.: U.S. Government Printing Office, 1975.

——. *RN: The Memoirs of Richard Nixon*. New York: Grosset and Dunlap, 1978.

——. *Six Crises*. New York: Warner Books, 1962.

Reagan, Ronald, et al. *In Memoriam, Arthur F. Burns, 1904–1987*. Washington, D.C.: Board of Governors of the Federal Reserve System, 1987.

GOVERNMENT REPORTS AND CONGRESSIONAL HEARINGS

Council of Economic Advisers. *Economic Report of the President, 1969*. Washington, D.C.: U.S. Government Printing Office, 1969.

United States Congress, House, Committee on Appropriations. *The Federal Budget for 1975*. 93d Congress, 2d sess., 1974.

——. *The Federal Budget for 1977*. 94th Congress, 2d sess., 1976.
United States Congress, House, Committee on Banking and Currency. *The Credit Crunch and Reform of Financial Institutions*. 93d Congress, 1st sess., 1973.
——. *Economic Stabilization*. 92d Congress, 1st sess., 1971.
——. *Economic Stabilization—1973*. 93d Congress, 1st sess., 1973.
——. *Emergency Home Finance*. 91st Congress, 2d sess., 1970.
——. *Federal Reserve Policy and Inflation and High Interest Rates*. 93d Congress, 2d sess., 1974.
——. *To Authorize Emergency Loan Guarantees to Major Business Enterprises*. 92d Congress, 1st sess., 1971.
——. *To Provide for a Modification of the Par Value of the Dollar*. 92d Congress, 2d sess., 1972.
United States Congress, House, Committee on Banking, Currency, and Housing. *Federal Reserve Consultations on the Conduct of Monetary Policy (Fourth Quarter 1975 to Fourth Quarter 1976)*. 94th Congress, 2d sess., 1976.
——. *Federal Reserve Consultations on the Conduct of Monetary Policy (Second Quarter 1976 to Second Quarter 1977)*. 94th Congress. 2nd session, 1976.
——. *To Lower Interest Rates*. 94th Congress, 1st sess., 1975.
——. *To Promote the Independence and Responsibility of the Federal Reserve System*. 94th Congress, 2d sess., 1976.
United States Congress, House, Committee on Banking, Finance, and Urban Affairs. *Conduct of Monetary Policy* (February 1977). 95th Congress, 1st sess., 1977.
——. *Conduct of Monetary Policy* (July 1977). 95th Congress, 1st sess., 1977.
——. *Federal Reserve Reform Act of 1977*. 95th Congress, 1st sess., 1977.
United States Congress, House, Committee on the Budget. *Review of the Economy and the 1975 Budget*. 93d Congress, 2d sess., 1974.
——. *Fiscal Year 1978 Budget*. 95th Congress, 1st sess., 1977.
United States Congress, House, Ways and Means Committee. *President's Authority to Adjust Imports of Petroleum; Public Debt Ceiling Increase; and Emergency Tax Proposals*. 94th Congress. 1st sess., 1975.
United States Congress, House, Subcommittee of the Committee on Government Operations. *Government in the Sunshine*. 94th Congress, 1st sess., 1975.
United States Congress, House, Subcommittee on Domestic Finance of the Committee on Banking and Currency. *Congressional Oversight of the Federal Reserve System*. 92d Congress, 1st sess., 1971.
United States Congress, House, Subcommittee on Domestic Monetary Policy of the Committee on Banking, Currency, and Housing. *An Act to Lower Interest Rates and Allocate Credit*. 94th Congress, 1st sess., 1975.
United States Congress, House, Subcommittee on Domestic Monetary Policy of the Committee on Banking, Finance, and Urban Affairs. *Federal Reserve Act Amendments of 1977*. 95th Congress, 1st sess., 1977.

——. *Maintaining and Making Public Minutes of Federal Reserve Meetings.* 95th Congress, 1st sess., 1977.

United States Congress, House, Subcommittee on Economic Stabilization of the Committee on Banking, Currency, and Housing. *Debt Financing Problems of State and Local Government: The New York City Case.* 94th Congress, 1st sess., 1975.

United States Congress, House, Subcommittee on Financial Institutions Supervision, Regulation, and Insurance of the Committee on Banking, Currency, and Housing. *Financial Institutions and the Nation's Economy (FINE) "Discussion Principles."* 94th Congress, 1st and 2d sess., 1975–76.

——. *The Financial Reform Act of 1976.* 94th Congress, 2d sess., 1976.

United States Congress, House, Subcommittee on International Finance of the Committee on Banking and Currency. *International Monetary Reform.* 93d Congress, 1st sess., 1973.

——. *International Monetary Reform.* 93d Congress, 2d sess., 1974.

——. *To Amend the Par Value Modification Act of 1972.* 93d Congress, 1st sess., 1973.

——. *To Delay Until July 1, 1975, the Date for Removing Restrictions on Private Ownership of Gold.* 93d Congress, 2d sess., 1974.

United States Congress, Joint Economic Committee. *The 1970 Economic Report of the President.* 91st Congress, 2d sess., 1970.

——. *The 1970 Midyear Review of the State of the Economy.* 91st Congress, 2d sess., 1970.

——. *The 1971 Economic Report of the President.* 92d Congress, 1st sess., 1971.

——. *The 1971 Midyear Review of the Economy.* 92d Congress, 1st sess., 1971.

——. *The 1972 Economic Report of the President.* 92d Congress, 2d sess., 1972.

——. *The 1972 Midyear Review of the Economy.* 92d Congress, 2d sess., 1972.

——. *The 1973 Economic Report of the President.* 93d Congress, 1st sess., 1973.

——. *The 1973 Midyear Review of the Economy.* 93d Congress, 1st sess., 1973.

——. *The 1974 Economic Report of the President.* 93d Congress, 2d sess., 1974.

——. *The 1975 Economic Report of the President.* 94th Congress, 1st sess., 1975.

——. *The 1976 Economic Report of the President.* 94th Congress, 2d sess., 1976.

——. *The 1977 Economic Report of the President.* 95th Congress, 1st sess., 1977.

——. *Examination of the Economic Situation and Outlook*, 93d Congress. 2d sess., 1974.

——. *Financial and Capacity Needs.* 93d Congress, 2d sess., 1974.

——. *January 1963 Economic Report of the President.* 88th Congress, 1st sess., 1963.

——. *Kissinger-Simon Proposals for Financing Oil Imports.* 93d Congress, 2d sess., 1974.

——. *Midyear Review of the Economic Situation and Outlook.* 94th Congress, 1st sess., 1975.

——. *Midyear Review of the Economic Situation and Outlook.* 94th Congress, 2d sess., 1976.

——. *New York City's Economic Crisis.* 94th Congress, 1st sess., 1975.

——. *President Ford's Economic Proposals.* 93d Congress, 2d sess., 1974.

——. *Thirtieth Anniversary of the Employment Act of 1946—A National Conference on Full Employment.* 94th Congress, 2d sess., 1976.

——. *Wage and Price Control: Evaluations of a Year's Experience.* 92d Congress, 2d sess., 1972.

United States Congress, Joint Study Committee on Budget Control, *Improving Congressional Budget Control.* 93d Congress, 1st sess., 1973.

United States Congress, Senate, Committee on Agriculture and Forestry. *Russian Grain Sale.* 94th Congress, 1st sess., 1975.

United States Congress, Senate, Committee on Banking and Currency. *Nomination of Arthur F. Burns.* 91st Congress, 1st sess., 1969.

——. *One-Bank Holding Company Legislation of 1970.* 91st Congress, 2d sess., 1970.

——. *State of the National Economy.* 91st Congress, 2d sess., 1970.

United States Congress, Senate, Committee on Banking, Housing, and Urban Affairs. *Amend the Par Value Modification Act.* 93d Congress, 1st sess., 1973.

——. *Economic Stabilization Legislation.* 92d Congress, 1st sess., 1971.

——. *Economic Stabilization Legislation—1973.* 93d Congress, 1st sess., 1973.

——. *Emergency Loan Guarantee Legislation.* 92d Congress, 1st sess., 1971.

——. *Federal Reserve Reform and Audit.* 94th Congress, 1st sess., 1975.

——. *First Meeting on the Condition of the Banking System.* 95th Congress, 1st sess., 1977.

——. *First Meeting on the Conduct of Monetary Policy.* 94th Congress, 1st sess., 1975.

——. *First Meeting on the Conduct of Monetary Policy.* 95th Congress, 1st sess., 1977.

——. *Fourth Meeting on the Conduct of Monetary Policy.* 94th Congress, 2d sess., 1976.

——. *Monetary Policy Oversight.* 94th Congress, 1st sess., 1975.

——. *Par Value Modification Act—1972.* 92d Congress, 2d sess., 1972.

——. *Second Meeting on the Conduct of Monetary Policy.* 94th Congress, 1st sess., 1975.

——. *Selective Credit Policies and Wage-Price Stabilization.* 92d Congress, 1st sess., 1971.

———. *State of the National Economy—1971.* 92d Congress, 1st sess., 1971.

———. *Third Meeting on the Conduct of Monetary Policy.* 94th Congress, 2d sess., 1976.

United States Congress, Senate, Committee on the Budget. *The 1976 First Concurrent Resolution on the Budget.* 94th Congress, 1st sess., 1975.

———. *The Federal Budget and Inflation.* 93d Congress, 2d sess., 1974.

———. *The First Concurrent Resolution on the Budget—Fiscal Year 1977.* 94th Congress, 2d sess., 1976.

———. *The First Concurrent Resolution on the Budget—Fiscal Year 1978.* 95th Congress, 1st sess., 1977.

———. *Second Concurrent Resolution on the Budget—Fiscal Year 1976.* 94th Congress, 1st sess., 1975.

United States Congress, Senate, Subcommittee on Financial Institutions of the Committee on Banking, Housing, and Urban Affairs. *NOW Accounts, Federal Reserve Membership, and Related Issues.* 95th Congress, 1st sess., 1977.

United States Congress, Senate, Subcommittee on Production and Stabilization of the Committee on Banking, Housing, and Urban Affairs. *Oversight on Economic Stabilization.* 93d Congress, 2d sess., 1974.

United States Congress, Subcommittee on Foreign Economic Policy of the Joint Economic Committee. *A Foreign Economic Policy for the 1970s.* 92d Congress, 1st sess., 1971.

United States Congres,. Subcommittee on International Economics of the Joint Economic Committee. *How Well Are Fluctuating Exchange Rates Working?* 93d Congress, 1st sess., 1973.

United States Congress, Subcommittee on International Exchange and Payments of the Joint Economic Committee. *Gold and the Central Bank Swap Network.* 92d Congress, 2d sess., 1972.

United States Congress, Subcommittee on Priorities and Economy in Government of the Joint Economic Committee. *Housing Subsidies and Housing Policies.* 92d Congress, 2d sess., 1972.

Secondary Sources

BOOKS

Alchon, Guy. *The Invisible Hand of Planning: Capitalism, Social Science, and the State in the 1920s.* Princeton: Princeton University Press, 1985.

Ambrose, Stephen E. *Eisenhower: The President.* New York: Simon and Schuster, 1984.

———. *Nixon: The Education of a Politician, 1913–1962.* New York: Simon and Schuster, 1987.

———. *Nixon: Ruin and Recovery, 1973–1990.* New York: Simon and Schuster, 1991.

———. *Nixon: The Triumph of a Politician, 1962–72.* New York: Simon and Schuster, 1989.

Anderson, Martin. *Revolution: The Reagan Legacy*, rev. ed. Stanford: Hoover Institue Press, 1990.

Blinder, Alan S. *Economic Policy and the Great Stagflation*. New York: Academic Press, 1979.

Campagna, Anthony S. *U.S. National Economic Policy, 1917–1985*. New York: Praeger, 1987.

Chernow, Ron. *The House of Morgan: An American Banking Dynasty and the Rise of Modern Finance*. New York: Atlantic Monthly Press, 1990.

Collins, Robert M. *The Business Response to Keynes, 1929–1964*. New York: Columbia University Press, 1981.

Donovan, Robert J. *Eisenhower: The Inside Story*. New York: Harper and Brothers, 1956.

Eckstein, Otto. *The Great Recession*. New York: North-Holland Publishing, 1978.

Evans, Rowland, and Robert Novak. *Nixon in the White House: The Frustration of Power*. New York: Random House, 1971.

Feldstein, Martin, ed. *The American Economy in Transition*. Chicago: University of Chicago Press, 1980.

Flash, Edward S., Jr. *Economic Advice and Presidential Leadership: The Council of Economic Advisers*. New York: Columbia University Press, 1965.

Friedman, Leon, and William F. Levantrosser, eds. *Richard M. Nixon: Politician, President, Administrator*. New York: Greenwood Press, 1991.

Friedman, Milton, and Anna Schwartz. *A Monetary History of the United States, 1867–1960*. Princeton: Princeton University Press, 1963.

Goodman, John B. *Monetary Sovereignty: The Politics of Central Banking in Western Europe*. Ithaca: Cornell University Press, 1992.

Gowa, Joanne. *Closing the Gold Window: Domestic Politics and the End of Bretton Woods*. Ithaca: Cornell University Press, 1983.

Greider, William. *Secrets of the Temple: How the Federal Reserve Runs the Country*. New York: Simon and Schuster, 1987.

Halberstam, David. *The Reckoning*. New York: Avon, 1986.

Hargrove, Erwin C. *Jimmy Carter as President: Leadership and the Politics of the Public Good*. Baton Rouge: Louisiana State University Press, 1988.

Havrilesky, Thomas. *The Pressures on American Monetary Policy*. Boston: Kluwer Academic, 1992.

Hirsch, Fred, and John H. Goldthorp, eds. *The Political Economy of Inflation*. Cambridge, Mass.: Harvard University Press, 1978.

Katz, Bernard S. *Biographical Dictionary of the Board of Governors of the Federal Reserve*. New York: Greenwood Press, 1992.

Kettl, Donald F. *Leadership at the Fed*. New Haven: Yale University Press, 1986.

Keynes, John Maynard. *The General Theory of Employment, Interest, and Money*. New York: Harcourt, Brace, Jovanovich, 1964.

Lanzillotti, Robert F., Mary T. Hamilton, and R. Blaine Roberts. *Phase II in*

Review: The Price Commission Experience. Washington, D.C.: Brookings Institute, 1975.

Lindberg, Leon, and Charles S. Maier, eds. *The Political Economy of Inflation and Economic Stagnation: Theoretical Approaches and International Case Studies*. Washington, D.C.: Brookings Institute, 1985.

Maisel, Sherman J. *Managing the Dollar*. New York: W. W. Norton, 1973.

Matusow, Allen J. *The Unraveling of America: A History of Liberalism in the 1960s*. New York: Harper and Row, 1984.

Rather, Dan, and Gary Paul Gates. *The Palace Guard*. New York: Harper and Row, 1974.

Reichley, James A. *Conservatives in an Age of Change: The Nixon and Ford Administrations*. Washington, D.C.: Brookings Institute, 1981.

Rockoff, Hugh. *Drastic Measures: A History of Wage and Price Controls in the United States*. Cambridge: Cambridge University Press, 1984.

Rutkoff, Peter M., and William B. Scott. *New School: A History of the New School of Social Research*. New York: Free Press, 1986.

Safire, William. *Before the Fall: An Inside View of the Pre-Watergate White House*. New York: Belmont Tower, 1975.

Skidelsdy, Robert. *John Maynard Keynes: Vol. 2, The Economist and Savior, 1920–1937*. London: Macmillan, 1992.

Solomon, Robert. *The International Monetary System, 1945–81: An Insider's View*. New York: Harper and Row, 1982.

Sprague, Irvine H. *Bailout: An Insider's Account of Bank Failures and Rescues*. New York: Basic Books, 1986.

Spulber, Nicolas. *Managing the American Economy from Roosevelt to Reagan*. Bloomington and Indianapolis: Indiana University Press, 1989.

Stein, Herbert. *Presidential Economics: The Making of Economic Policy from Roosevelt to Reagan and Beyond*. New York: Simon and Schuster, 1985.

Thompson, Kenneth W., ed. *The Ford Presidency*. Lanham, Md.: University Press of America, 1988.

Tobin, James. *Essays in Economics: Theory and Policy*. Cambridge, Mass.: MIT Press, 1982.

——. *The New Economics One Decade Older*. Princeton: Princeton University Press, 1972.

—–, and Murray Weidenbaum. *Two Revolutions in Economic Policy: The First Economic Reports of Presidents Kennedy and Reagan*. Cambridge, Mass.: MIT Press, 1988.

Tuch, Hans N., ed. *Arthur Burns and the Successor Generation: Selected Writings of and about Arthur Burns*. Lanham: University Press of America, 1988.

Volcker, Paul A., and Toyoo Gyohten. *Changing Fortunes: The World's Money and the Threat to American Leadership*. New York: Times Books, 1992.

Weber, Arnold R. *In Pursuit of Price Stability: The Wage-Price Freeze of 1971*. Washington, D.C.: Brookings Institute, 1973.

--, and Daniel J. B. Mitchell. *The Pay Board's Progress: Wage Controls in Phase II*. Washington, D.C.: Brookings Institute, 1978.

Williamson, John. *The Failure of World Monetary Reform, 1970–74*. New York: New York University Press, 1977.

Wooley, John T. *Monetary Politics: The Federal Reserve and the Politics of Monetary Policy*. Cambridge: Cambridge University Press, 1984.

UNPUBLISHED MANUSCRIPTS

Brimmer, Andrew. "Politics and Monetary Policy: The Federal Reserve and the Nixon White House." Paper presented at the 10th meeting of the Eastern Economic Association, New York, March 16, 1984.

Cordell, Lawrence R. "The Invisible Handshake: An Investigation of the Monetary Policy Process, 1966 to 1982." Ph.D. dissertation, University of North Carolina, 1989.

Mouw, Scott. "Passing the Buck: Congress and the 1971 Lockheed Loan Guarantee." Masters thesis, University of North Carolina, 1987.

Rasmus, Jack. "The Political Economy of Wage-price Controls in the U.S., 1971–74." Ph.D. dissertation, University of Toronto, 1977.

ARTICLES

Alter, Jonathan. "Defrocking the Fed." *Washington Monthly* 14 (1982): 12–21.

Auerback, Robert D. "Politics and the Federal Reserve." *Contemporary Policy Issues* 3 (1985):43–48.

Beck, Nathaniel. "Domestic Political Sources of American Monetary Policy, 1955–82." *Journal of Politics* 46 (1984):786–817.

——. "Elections and the Fed: Is There a Political Monetary Cycle?" *American Journal of Political Science* 31 (1987):194–216.

——. "Presidential Influence on the Federal Reserve in the 1970s." *American Journal of Political Science* 26 (1982):415–445.

Blinder, Alan S., and Stephen M. Goldfeld. "New Measures of Fiscal and Monetary Policy, 1958–73." *American Economic Review* 66 (1976):780–796.

Burns, Arthur F. "The Problem of Inflation." *Social Science* 48 (1973):67–74.

Camu, Louis. "An Atmosphere of Unease: IMF 1971." *Atlantic Community Quarterly* 9 (1971–72):421–425.

Chernow, Ron. "In Praise of Patience: Being the True-Life Saga of a Young Writer Nearly Killed with Kindness, Only to Be Saved by a Savage Dose of Truth." *In Search of A Voice: The National Book Week Lectures*. Washington, D.C.: Library of Congress, 1991.

Daniel, James. "He Manages of the Nation's Money Supply." *Reader's Digest* 100 (January 1972):68–72.

deVries, Tom. "The Future Role of the Dollar." *Atlantic Community Quarterly* 10 (1972):11–20.

Diebold, William, Jr. "The Economic System at Stake." *Foreign Affairs* 51 (1972):167–180.

Duboff, Richard. "Trade War Exercises." *Canada Dimension* 9 (1973):37–40.

Gowa, Joanne. "State Power, State Policy: Explaining the Decision to Close the Gold Window." *Politics and Society* 13 (1984):91–117.

Harrison, William B. "Annals of a Crusade: Wright Patman and the Federal Reserve System." *American Journal of Economics and Sociology* 40 (1981):317–320.

Hawley, Ellis W. "Challenges to the Mixed Economy: The State and Private Enterprise." In Robert H. Bremner, Gary W. Reichard, and Richard J. Hopkins, eds., *American Choices: Social Dilemmas and Public Policy since 1960*, pp. 159–186. Columbus: Ohio State University Press, 1986.

Hoffman, Nicholas von. "Secrets at the Fed." *The Progressive* 40 (January 1976):48.

International Encyclopedia of the Social Sciences. S.v. "Arthur Burns." by Geoffrey H. Moore.

Kane, Edward J. "All for the Best: The Federal Reserve Board's 60th Annual Report." *American Economic Review* 64 (1974):835–850.

——. "New Congressional Restraints and Federal Reserve Independence." *Challenge* 18 (1975):37–44.

——. "Politics and Fed Policymaking: The More Things Change, The More They Remain the Same." *Journal of Monetary Economics* 6 (1980):199–211.

Kessel, Reuben A. "The 1972 Report of the President's Council of Economic Advisors: Inflation and Controls." *American Economic Review* 62 (1974):527–532.

Koopmans, Tjalling C. "Measurement Without Theory." *Review of Economic Statistics* 29 (1947):161–172.

Lombra, Raymond and Michael Moran. "Policy Advice and Policymaking at the Federal Reserve." *Carnegie-Rochester Conference Series on Public Policy* 13 (1980):9–68.

Malkin, Lawrence. "A Practical Politician at the Fed." *Fortune* (May 1971):148–151.

Malmgren, Harold B. "The New Posture in U.S. Trade Policy." *World Today* 27 (1971):503–510.

Mintz, Morton, ". . . Why They're Still Needed." *Washington Monthly* 6 (1974):19–37.

Mitchell, Daniel J. B. "Phase II Wage Controls." *Industrial and Labor Relations Review* 6 (1974):19–37.

——, and Arnold R. Weber. "Wages and the Pay Board." *American Economic Review* 64 (1974):88–92.

——. "Further Reflections on Wage Controls." *Industrial and Labor Relations Review* 31 (1978):149–160.

Pierce, James L. "The Political Economy of Arthur Burns." *Journal of Finance* 34 (1979):485–496.

Poole, William. "Burnsian Monetary Policy: Eight Years of Progress?" *Journal of Finance* 34 (1979):473–484.

Reuss, Henry. "A Private Club for Public Policy." *The Nation* (October 16, 1976):370–372.

Rose, Stanford. "The Agony of the Federal Reserve." *Fortune* (July 1974):90–93, 180–190.

Rowen, Hobart. "Keeping Secrets at the Fed." *Columbia Journalism Review* 14 (July/August 1975): 51–54.

Samuelson, Robert. "Why Price Controls Stopped Working." *Washington Monthly* 6 (May 1974):19–30.

Schweikart, Larry, ed. *Encyclopedia of American Business and Biography: Banking and Finance.* S.v. "Arthur F. Burns." by Rebecca Strand Johnson.

Shultz, George P. and Kenneth W. Dam. "Reflections of Wage and Price Controls." *Industrial and Labor Relations Review* 30 (1977):139–151.

Skaggs, Neil T. "The Federal Reserve System and Congressional Demand for Information." *Social Science Quarterly* 64 (1983):566–581.

Thurow, Lester C. "Carter, the Fed, and 'Confidence.' " *The Nation* (September 3, 1977):166–168.

Weber, Arnold R. "1971 Wage-Price Freeze and Incomes Policy." *Monthly Labor Review* 95 (1972):18–21.

——. "A Wage-Price Freeze as an Instrument of Incomes Policy: or the Blizzard of '71." *American Economic Review* 62 (1972):251–257.

——. "Making Wage Controls Work." *Public Interest* 30 (1973):28–40.

Index

✦

CONTEMPORARY AMERICAN HISTORY SERIES

William E. Leuchtenberg, *General Editor*

Lawrence S. Wittner, *Rebels Against War: The American Peace Movement, 1941–1960*
1969

David R. B. Ross, *Preparing for Ulysses: Politics and Veterans During World War II*
1969

John Lewis Gaddis, *The United States and the Origins of the Cold War, 1941–1947*
1972

George C. Herring, Jr., *Aid to Russia, 1941–1946: Strategy, Diplomacy, the Origins of the Cold War* 1973

Alonzo L. Hamby, *Beyond the New Deal: Harry S. Truman and American Liberalism*
1973

Richard M. Fried, *Men Against McCarthy* 1976

Steven F. Lawson, *Black Ballots: Voting Rights in the South, 1944–1969* 1976

Carl M. Brauer, *John F. Kennedy and the Second Reconstruction* 1977

Maeva Marcus, *Truman and the Steel Seizure Case: The Limits of Presidential Power*
1977

Morton Sosna, *In Search of the Silent South: Southern Liberals and the Race Issue*
1977

Robert M. Collins, *The Business Response to Keynes, 1929–1964* 1981

Robert M. Hathaway, *Ambiguous Partnership: Britain and America, 1944–1947* 1981

Leonard Dinnerstein, *America and the Survivors of the Holocaust* 1982

Lawrence Wittner, *American Intervention in Greece, 1943–1949* 1982

Nancy Bernkopf Tucker, *Patterns in the Dust; Chinese-American Relations and the Recognition Controversy, 1940–1950* 1983

Catherine A. Barnes, *Journey from Jim Crow: The Desegration of Southern Transit* 1983

Steven F. Lawson *In Pursuit of Power: Southern Blacks and Electoral Politics, 1965–1982* 1985

David R. Colburn, *Racial Change and Community Crisis: St. Augustine, Florida, 1877–1980* 1985

Henry Williams Brands, *Cold Warriors: Eisenhower's Generation and the Making of American Foreign Policy* 1988

Marc S. Gallicchio, *The Cold War Begins in Asia: American East Asian Policy and the Fall of the Japanese Empire* 1988

Melanie Billings-Yun, *Decision Against War: Eisenhower and Dien Bien Phu* 1988

Walter L. Hixson, *George F. Kennan: Cold War Iconoclast* 1989

Mitchell G. Hall, *Because of Their Faith: CALCAV and Religious Opposition to the Vietnam War* 1990

Robert D. Schulzinger, *Henry Kissinger: Doctor of Diplomacy* 1990

Henry Williams Brands, *Spector of Neutralism: The United States and the Emergence of the Third World, 1947–1960* 1990

David Anderson, *Trapped by Success: The Eisenhower Administration and Vietnam*
1990

Steven M. Gillon, *The Democrats' Dilemma: Walter F. Mondale and the Liberal Legacy* 1992